Design of Technology-Enhanced Learning

Integrating Research and Practice

CW01498033

Design of Technology-Enhanced Learning

Integrating Research and Practice

By

Matt Bower
Department of Educational Studies,
Macquarie University, Sydney, Australia

United Kingdom – North America – Japan – India – Malaysia – China

Emerald Publishing Limited
Howard House, Wagon Lane, Bingley BD16 1WA, UK

First edition 2017

Copyright © 2017 Emerald Publishing Limited

Reprints and permissions service
Contact: permissions@emeraldinsight.com

British Library Cataloguing in Publication Data
A catalogue record for this book is available from the British Library

ISBN: 978-1-78714-183-4 (Print)
ISBN: 978-1-78714-182-7 (Online)
ISBN: 978-1-78714-911-3 (Epub)
ISBN: 978-1-83867-920-0 (Paperback)

Printed and bound by CPI Group (UK) Ltd, Croydon, CR0 4YY

ISOQAR certified
Management System,
awarded to Emerald
for adherence to
Environmental
standard
ISO 14001:2004.

ISOQAR
REGISTERED
Certificate Number 1985
ISO 14001

INVESTOR IN PEOPLE

Contents

*To my wife, who cared not one iota about what I was writing,
but generously and kindly made it possible for me to write it.*

To my boys, Dan and Zac, who are the apple of my eye.

*To educators and researchers everywhere who put their heart
into what they do.*

Preface

Technology is changing everything in our world, including education. People have the ability to access information and communicate anytime and almost anyplace through a range of increasingly powerful and easy to use apps. In education, technology enables students and teachers to rapidly collect data, represent knowledge, share perspectives, digitally construct, and collaborate from almost any location. However, too often the use of technology for learning is presented as a panacea that will solve all educational ills. The reality is that simply using contemporary technologies in education does not guarantee a successful lesson, and in fact, using technology poorly can render a learning experience confusing and meaningless.

As technologies change, it is crucial that educators (school teachers, academics, pre-service teachers, and educational designers) respond in a principled fashion based upon a deep understanding of pedagogical issues, rather than haphazardly based on intuitive or superficial reasoning. Maintaining a focus on pedagogical issues means that educators can avoid being distracted by the novelty of new technologies and concentrate upon how each technology is influencing interaction and learning. Accordingly, in order to develop an accurate and confident command of technology-enhanced learning issues, educators need to understand the research of the field. Similarly, if learning technology researchers want to have far-reaching positive impact, their work needs to penetrate beyond the surface technological features through the underlying learning and teaching issues at stake. Understanding the key issues and research across technologies enables researchers to accurately position their work and demonstrate how it is making a contribution to the field overall.

As a teacher educator and educational researcher specializing in the technology area, I frequently lamented that the technology-enhanced learning literature was disorganized and disparate for educators who wanted to utilize it. This was a problem because most educators simply do not have time to find and distil learning technology research relating to their area of focus. Why wasn't there a single resource that synthesized the key learning technology literature in a way that educators could immediately apply? At the same time, educational technology researchers are incredibly time-poor, and while they have immense expertise in their specific sub-areas, the breadth of the technology-enhanced learning literature means that it can be difficult to acquire an accurate sense of the empirical research as a whole. This is particularly true when it comes to understanding research relationships between different technological platforms from an educational design and practice perspective.

This book directly responds to these maladies by drawing technology-enhanced learning research and practice closer together. It does this by synthesizing the general and empirical learning technology literature to clearly identify the key educational potentials, issues, and design considerations relating to technology-enhanced learning. By examining this synthesis of research findings, educators can immediately adopt an evidence-based approach in their designs, and researchers can instantly position their work within the broad context of technology-enhanced learning field.

ABOUT THIS BOOK

This book has been designed to enable readers to construct an integrated understanding of the key issues surrounding technology-enhanced learning design. Chapter 1 considers the broader context of designing for learning using technology, including its key drivers at school and university levels. Without an understanding of the broader context, it is impossible for educators and researchers to reliably situate their work in a way that responds to social needs. An understanding of the broader socio-political context can also provide motivation for the use of technology in learning. However, the importance of adopting a critical approach to the design of technology-enhanced learning is emphasized.

Chapter 2 briefly introduces the Technology Pedagogy And Content Knowledge (TPACK) framework as a tool for structuring educator thinking. Technology, pedagogy, and content are indeed essential aspects of technology-enhanced learning design, and a focusing on these elements has undoubtedly led to the popularity of the TPACK model. However, the chapter also poses critical reflections on the TPACK framework in terms of its ability to support learning design practice.

In order to establish a solid conceptual foundation for analyzing technology-enhanced learning, Chapters 3–5 provide a general overview of pedagogy, technology, and content, respectively. Educators and researchers need to have an overarching understand how pedagogy operates on different levels, and the different types of pedagogies at each level, if they are to effectively analyze and utilize different types of technology in education (Chapter 3). Similarly, both educators and researchers need to have general frameworks for thinking about technology selection and utilization, which is why the concept of affordances and multimedia learning effects are interrogated in Chapter 4. The content that we teach and assess may be represented and shared in different ways using technology, and these issues are explored in Chapter 5.

Chapter 6 builds on previous chapters to unpack design thinking — what it involves and why it can be hard to learn. Importantly, teaching is positioned as a design science. Design is the nexus of scientific and artistic thinking, whereby novel and intrinsically valuable solutions emerge based on integrative knowledge. Seeing teaching as a design science helps educators and researchers to maintain a focus on understanding the elements that are most important to the design of effective learning tasks and the processes that help educators to optimize their designs. The field of Learning Design is also introduced, including the various ways it can support educators' design work.

Chapters 7–10 provide comprehensive overviews of educational research relating to Web 2.0, social networking, mobile learning and virtual worlds, respectively. These open, freely available, and relatively easy-to-use technologies have been deliberately chosen for analysis because they are contemporary, have been widely used in education, provide considerable design flexibilities, and have an extensive research base relating to their use. They are also quite different, which means they are interesting to compare and contrast from an educational and research perspective. The benefits, constraints, and design findings for each technology are distilled from the literature, and use cases ('vignettes') are also detailed to offer a clear understanding of issues surrounding learning technology utilization. Research relating to higher education and schools has been integrated on the basis that there is valuable knowledge that can be transferred between each area, though examples have been separated according to educational level so that readers can choose to focus on either university or school use cases if they wish.

It is important to note that the Web 2.0, social networking, mobile learning, and virtual worlds chapters were composed using a systematic methodology. First, search terms appropriate to each technology were used to scour educational research databases so as to source relevant literature. Papers were selected for inclusion based on the extent to which they constituted high-quality empirical research relating to the design and utilization of technology for learning purposes. A 'snowballing' approach was used, whereby relevant references from within selected papers were also considered for inclusion in the review. The benefits, issues, and design implications of all selected papers were then distilled and organized into themes for each technology. This systematic approach was adopted for each technology so that educators and researchers could have confidence that the emergent findings encapsulated the key issues surround technology-enhanced learning design.

Conducting a comprehensive and systematic analysis of Web 2.0, social networking, mobile learning, and virtual worlds also served as the basis for abstracting patterns and principles of technology-enhanced learning design in Chapter 11. By comparing and contrasting the benefits, limitations, and design implications of different technologies it is possible to detect patterns that hold across technologies, but also the nuanced differences of the technologies in application. Then in Chapter 12 future directions of the learning technology field are considered, in terms of the impact of technology trends, the critical role of the teacher, and the need for integrating technology-enhanced learning research and practice.

FOR WHOM IS THIS BOOK USEFUL?

By integrating technology-enhanced learning research and practice, this book is designed to be useful for practicing educators, pre-service teachers, postgraduate education students, and learning technology researchers.

Practicing Educators

Practicing educators (academics, school teachers, as well as educational designers) are often looking to extend beyond the anecdotal 'folk pedagogy' that pervades some institutions, and to understand how the research evidence can inform the approaches they would like to adopt. They also often want to know the technological options available to them, and are looking for great design ideas. This book addresses these needs.

Pre-Service Teachers

If our teachers of the future are to be of the highest caliber, they need to adopt a scholarly approach to their study and practice. This book very definitely shifts the focus of pre-service teacher education from a 'how-to' operational emphasis on technological skills to a more research-driven approach. As well, instead of referring pre-service teachers to research papers that often contain methodological and theoretical discussions that are not directly relevant, and that provide no explicit connection to one another, this book presents an integrated narrative that is immediately applicable to teachers in training.

Postgraduate Education and Higher Degree Research Students

Students completing postgraduate studies and higher degree research in education often desire a concentrated overview of the literature relating to technology-enhanced learning design, which explains how principles from general educational theory have been applied within the learning technology field, and also the empirical findings as they relate to the use of different technological environments. This book satisfies these requirements for them.

Learning Technology Researchers

Learning technology researchers often want to quickly identify the benefits, issues, and design findings that relate to a particular technology or technologies, and this book provides them with an immediate reference. For instance, a researcher interested in motivation or community building or digital skills or peer feedback can quickly identify the key effects for Web 2.0, social networking, mobile learning, and virtual worlds, with links back to the underlying literature. Systematically abstracting themes across technologies in this book also constitutes new knowledge for the technology-enhanced learning field, enabling researchers to acquire a more accurate sense of the literature and better situate their work. The range of practice considerations outlined in the book may also assist researchers to better respond to the real issues confronting educators and hence optimize the impact of their technology-enhanced learning research.

FORWARD REMARKS

There is often a lamentable divide between academic research and coal-face teacher practice, as though either research alone or field-based expertise hold the crucible of pedagogical wisdom when it comes to educational technology utilization. The approach adopted by this book is that research and practice are mutually informing, inextricably valuable to each other, and need to be synergistically applied in order to achieve the best educational results. In order for the technology-enhanced learning field to make greatest progress researchers and practitioners need to be working more closely together, and indeed position themselves as both educators and researchers.

We are in an exciting time in history, challenged by both increasingly rapid changes in technology and mounting pressure to prepare students for an unknown future. By offering an evidence-based and integrated portrayal of how technologies affect learning, this book is designed to provide a common foundation for educators and researchers to confidentially respond to contemporary technological and pedagogical challenges together. I hope you enjoy the book and find it useful, and I welcome your comments and feedback.

Acknowledgments

There are several people and organizations that deserve thanks for their help in making this book a reality. Extensive thanks goes to Professor John Hedberg for his wise feedback on drafts of this book and his kind-hearted mentorship over many years. Dr Michael Stevenson also deserves immense thanks for his detailed and insightful advice on the manuscript – it is a privilege to work with such a talented educator and rising-star researcher. Thank you also to Karen Woo, who generously provided ideas and suggestions on early versions of this book.

Throughout my career, there have been several eminent learning technology experts who have serendipitously conspired to support me, without thought for personal recompense. These include, but are not limited to, Professor Diana Laurillard, Professor Peter Goodyear, Emeritus Professor Tom Reeves, Professor Peter Albion, Professor Barney Dalgarno, Professor Gregor Kennedy, Professor Lori Lockyer, Professor James Dalziel, and of course, Professor John Hedberg. Enormous thanks to each of you for your generous guidance over the years, and more broadly for the positive contribution that you have made to the field of technology-enhanced learning.

Thanks also to Macquarie University for kindly providing me with a six-month sabbatical to write this book. And finally, thank you to the team at Emerald Publishing, who have the open-mindedness to support the books that academics want to write, and the experience to bring them to fruition.

Foreword

In this book, Matt has successfully coalesce the processes, design ideas, and recent research into a coherent framework that can provide guidance to teachers and academics who seek to maximize the impact of the wonderful technologies and tools we have in modern education. Matt explores the influencing theories and links their contributions to a range of research topics. He seeks not to fall into formulaic approaches or algorithms of the earlier learning sciences, but rather to clearly explore the nuances of design options. When exploring the range of technologies that can be interwoven in modern learning design, he investigates recent technologies that have had successful research studies around them to ensure that the discussion is well argued with evidence and exemplars of effective practice.

The discussion is carefully situated in contexts that employ interesting mixes of technology, pedagogy, and well-chosen theoretical ideas. The discussion links new ideas that underpin recent clever innovative exemplars. Great learning designers will use the ideas in this book to generate learning activities that are innovative and award winning. Activities that effectively employ the attributes of technologies, links to theories of their best design and how they support learning in different curriculum contexts.

John G Hedberg
Sydney, 2017

1 Technology Integration as an Educational Imperative

ABSTRACT

This chapter lays contextual foundations for the study and application of technology-enhanced learning design. Key drivers for the integration of technology into learning are identified, including the intrinsic desire to improve learning outcomes, the development of student digital learning skills, curriculum and syllabus specifications, professional requirements, providing greater access to learning, and catering to student dispositions. The need for a critical approach is established, for instance, by avoiding misconceptions such as 'digital natives' and 'technological determinism.' A 'scholarship of teaching' perspective that uses research evidence as a basis for technology-enhanced learning design is selected as the means for further inquiry.

Integrating Technology as a Tantalizing Challenge

Educators worldwide are faced with a tantalizing problem. With the rapid and widespread advances in technology, how on earth should we design tasks and environments in order to optimize interaction and learning? This book addresses this question by examining research relating to the educational uses of technology, so that we can develop an evidence-based understanding of how different design considerations may influence learning activity and outcomes.

This book is written from the perspective that teachers need to position themselves as designers of their courses and classes (Laurillard, 2012). Instead of focusing upon the use of pre-packaged digital content that requires little teacher thinking or student contribution, we will be considering how teachers and students can use technology to effectively design, create, and share. Using preexisting digital modules is relatively straightforward, whereas the design and implementation of effective technology-enhanced learning tasks is the wicked and intractable conundrum of our field.

Like great art or science, we will not assume that any mechanical prescriptions can tell us how to design. Rather, distilling the relevant research evidence relating to technology-enhanced learning design enables us to construct an understanding of what has gone before, allowing design to occur from a research-informed and principled basis. This is not to promote a form of 'technological determinism' (Oliver, 2011; Selwyn, 2010), where we assume that certain designs will lead to fixed outcomes. Unlike the hard sciences, education is inextricably influenced by the context in which it operates. However, applying a 'scholarship of teaching' approach (Kreber & Kanuka, 2013; Trigwell, Martin, Benjamin, & Prosser, 2000) where we engage with and in the research of the field enables us to discern patterns and ideas that can guide our practice.

Before thinking about how to best integrate technology into learning and teaching, it is important to first consider the broader sociopolitical context surrounding the use of technology for educational purposes and what we are trying to achieve. There are several key drivers for integrating technology into our courses, including the intrinsic desire to improve learning outcomes, the development of student digital learning skills, curriculum and syllabus specifications, professional requirements, enabling access to learning, and catering to student dispositions. These will be addressed in turn below.

Key Drivers for Integrating Technology

USING TECHNOLOGY TO IMPROVE LEARNING OUTCOMES

Ideally, educators would decide to integrate technology into their lessons and courses based on an intrinsic desire to improve learning outcomes and the student experience. Notwithstanding the limitations of using technology for educational purposes, which will be discussed throughout this book, practitioners, researchers, and organizations propose a number of arguments for utilizing technology in teaching. Digital technologies can facilitate personalized learning, for instance, where the learner can decide to choose a certain learning pathway (OECD, 2016b). They can enable collaborative learning whereby knowledge construction results from interaction and negotiation (OECD, 2016b). Digital technologies can also be used by teachers to collect data that enables them to take advantage of learning analytics in their classes (OECD, 2016b).

Newhouse (2015) provides several other compelling ways in which technology may be able to enhance learning. Technology can be used to investigate real world phenomena through the collection of data and representation of knowledge, thus facilitating higher-level problem-solving and thinking skills. By making students more active participants in their learning (through manipulating, observing, and constructing) and supporting efficient execution of lower level tasks (such as computation), technology can promote more productive and engaged learning. Technology can also facilitate more authentic forms of assessment, and cater to students with special needs through assistive technologies (Newhouse, 2015).

Adding to these, Oblinger (2012) points out that technology can enable students and classes to connect with industry experts, broadening out the boundaries of the learning community. Simulations and gamification can be used to provide students with experiential learning, for instance, whereby nursing students practice procedures or business students trade stocks. As well as providing intelligent feedback on progress, technology can offer feed-forward advice about what to learn next. Technology can also provide students with peer-to-peer support through social networking systems (Oblinger, 2012). Thus, there are several compelling practice-based reasons that educators may choose to integrate technology into their lessons.

DEVELOPMENT OF STUDENTS' DIGITAL LEARNING SKILLS

Almost all aspects of our world are being transformed by digitization (Vuorikari, Punie, Gomez, & Van Den Brande, 2016). Increasing use of Information and Communication Technologies (ICTs) in the workplace is raising the demand for people with skills to use technology for professional purposes (OECD,

2016a). Consequently, digital competence — the confident and critical use of technology — is vital for participation in today's society and economy (Ferrari, 2013; Vuorikari et al., 2016). Yet, data from the European Commission Digital Economy and Society Index found that almost half (45%) of the European Union population aged from 16 to 74 had insufficient digital skills to adequately participate in the economy (Vuorikari et al., 2016). Over 40% of workers who use technology every day do not have the requisite skills to sufficiently operate office productivity software (OECD, 2016c). Accordingly, countries around the world are taking active measures to promote and develop digital literacies (OECD, 2016b).

There are numerous organizations and initiatives that advocate the learning skills that individuals and society require for a successful future. The International Society for Technology in Education (ISTE) is the peak global body concerned with the integration of technology into learning and teaching. The ISTE Standards for Students (ISTE, 2016) outlines a set of seven capabilities students need in order to learn effectively and live productively in an increasingly global and digital world (pp. 1–2):

1. *Empowered learner* — students leverage technology to take an active role in choosing, achieving, and demonstrating competency in their learning goals, informed by the learning sciences.
2. *Digital citizen* — students recognize the rights, responsibilities, and opportunities of living, learning, and working in an interconnected digital world, and they act and model in ways that are safe, legal, and ethical.
3. *Knowledge constructor* — students critically curate a variety of resources using digital tools to construct knowledge, produce creative artifacts, and make meaningful learning experiences for themselves and others.
4. *Innovative designer* — students use a variety of technologies within a design process to identify and solve problems by creating new, useful, or imaginative solution.
5. *Computational thinker* — students develop and employ strategies for understanding and solving problems in ways that leverage the power of technological methods to develop and test solutions.
6. *Creative communicator* — students communicate clearly and express themselves creatively for a variety of purposes using

the platforms, tools, styles, formats, and digital media appropriate to their goals.

7. *Global collaborator* – students use digital tools to broaden their perspectives and enrich their learning by collaborating with others and working effectively in teams locally and globally.

The capabilities, which are now in their third iteration, provide a compelling and aspirational vision for what we might aim to achieve through the integration of technology into education.

Alternately, and intended for those in and beyond the field of Education, the updated European Commission's Digital Competence Framework for Citizens (DigiComp 2.0) identifies five technological competence areas that people require to participate in contemporary society: (1) information and data literacy, (2) communication and collaboration skills, (3) digital content creation, (4) safety, and (5) problem solving (Vuorikari et al., 2016). These dimensions are deconstructed into 21 subcomponent descriptors that can be used for technological skills assessment, development, and tracking purposes (see https://ec.europa.eu/jrc/en/digcomp/digital-competence-framework for further details).

The well-established Partnership for 21st Century Skills (P21 – a coalition of business people, education leaders, and policymakers) proposes another model of contemporary learning capabilities for students (see Figure 1.1). The framework builds upon the more traditional 'reading, writing and arithmetic' (3Rs) view of core learning capabilities, by advocating the value of other crucial learning outcomes such as life and career skills, information media and technology skills, as well as learning and innovation skills (critical thinking, communication, collaboration, and creativity). See http://www.p21.org/about-us/p21-framework for further information about the learning outcomes and associated resources. Thus, digital literacies feature explicitly through the development of information media and technology skills, but also implicitly as means by which students may develop critical thinking, communication, collaboration, and creative competencies. The C21 Canadians for 21st Century Learning & Innovation 'Shifting Minds' framework (http://c21canada.org) constitutes a commensurate initiative. Taken together, we can see across the frameworks a general trend toward empowering learners with constructive, creative, collaborative, and socially oriented problem-solving capabilities using technology.

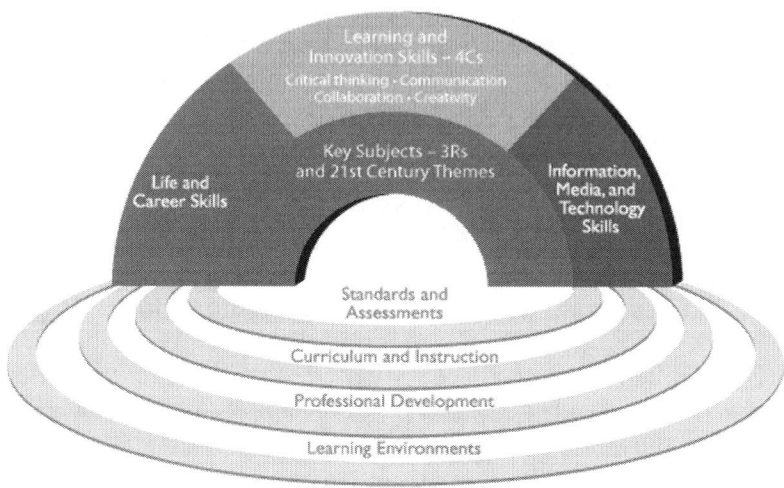

Figure 1.1. Framework for 21st Century Learning Proposed by the P21 Initiative. *Source:* Courtesy of the Partnership for 21st Century Learning, http://p21.org

EVOLVING CURRICULA AND POLICY DOCUMENTS

Countries and educational jurisdictions around the world are recognizing the importance of learning technologies and digital capabilities, and increasingly incorporating technology-related outcomes into their curricula and policy documents. For instance, at the school level, the new Australian Curriculum released by the Australian Curriculum Assessment and Reporting Authority (ACARA) has ICT capability as one of its seven general capabilities that are viewed as essential to help students live and work successfully in the 21st century (see http://www.australiancurriculum.edu.au/GeneralCapabilities/Pdf/ICT for further details). While educational standards and outcomes in the United States are controlled by individual states, the recently developed US Common Core State Standards have increased the amount of technology that is incorporated into the curriculum (see http://www.corestandards.org). In the United Kingdom, school students are required to study Information and Communication Technologies in all years, though schools can follow the designated programs of study or develop their own ICT curricula (see https://www.gov.uk/national-curriculum/overview for more information and further links). In Singapore, the fourth Masterplan for ICT in Education (http://ictconnection.moe.edu.sg/masterplan-4/overview) and the Singapore National ICT Masterplan set a vision for ICT integration in schools.

In Higher Education, the British Educational Communications and Technology Agency (BECTA) *Next Generation Learning* report emphasized the importance of having a technologically capable workforce for national prosperity (BECTA, 2010). The Australian Government's *Transforming Australia's Higher Education System* vision statement argued the need for graduates to have acquired contemporary learning capabilities that enable them to rapidly adapt to meet future challenges (Department of Education Employment and Workplace Relations, 2009). Such mandates from governments serve to position technology integration as an indisputable imperative.

PROFESSIONAL REQUIREMENTS FOR EDUCATORS

Just as professional bodies and organizations release guidelines for the use of technology by students, they often specify requirements for technology integration by teachers. For instance, the ISTE 2017 Standards for Educators recommend that teachers adopt the following roles to effectively catalyze learning and become empowered professionals (ISTE, 2017):

1. *Learner* – Educators continually improve their practice by learning from and with others and exploring proven and promising practices that leverage technology to improve student learning
2. *Leader* – Educators seek out opportunities for leadership to support student empowerment and success and to improve teaching and learning
3. *Citizen* – Educators inspire students to positively contribute to and responsibly participate in the digital world
4. *Collaborator* – Educators dedicate time to collaborate with both colleagues and students to improve practice, discover and share resources and ideas, and solve problems
5. *Designer* – Educators design authentic, learner-driven activities and environments that recognize and accommodate learner variability

6. *Facilitator* – Educators facilitate learning with technology to support student achievement of the 2016 ISTE Standards for Students
7. *Analyst* – Educators understand and use data to drive their instruction and support students in achieving their learning goals.

These provide an aspirational set of pedagogical benchmarks against which educators can evaluate their educational technology practices. For further elaboration of the ISTE Standards for Educators and the indicators for their accomplishment, see http://iste.org/standardsforeducators.

In addition to the ISTE standards, the United Nations Educational Scientific and Cultural Organization (UNESCO) sets out an ICT Competency Framework for Teachers (see Figure 1.2). The framework incorporates dimensions of (i) understanding ICT in education, (ii) curriculum and assessment, (iii) pedagogy, (iv) ICT, (v) organization and administration, and (vi) teacher professional learning (UNESCO, 2011). Each dimension encompasses three levels of possible accomplishment – technology literacy, knowledge deepening, and knowledge creation. For descriptions of each dimension, definitions of teacher learning objectives, and methods to develop and evidence accomplishment, see http://www.unesco.org/new/en/unesco/themes/icts/teacher-education/unesco-ict-competency-framework-for-teachers.

Sometimes governments define standards that teachers should meet with respect to technology integration. For instance, the Australian Professional Standards for Teachers (APST) outlined by the Australian Institute for Teaching and School Leadership (AITSL) specifies that graduate teachers should be able to:

• Implement teaching strategies for using ICT to expand curriculum learning opportunities for students (Standard 2.6)
• Demonstrate knowledge of a range of resources, including ICT, that engage students in their learning (Standard 3.4)
• Demonstrate an understanding of the relevant issues and the strategies available to support the safe, responsible and ethical use of ICT in learning and teaching (Standard 4.5).

For the full schedule of Australian Professional Teaching Standards along with illustrations of each visit http://aitsl.edu.au/australian-professional-standards-for-teachers/standards/list. The need for Australian educators to be able to effectively integrate

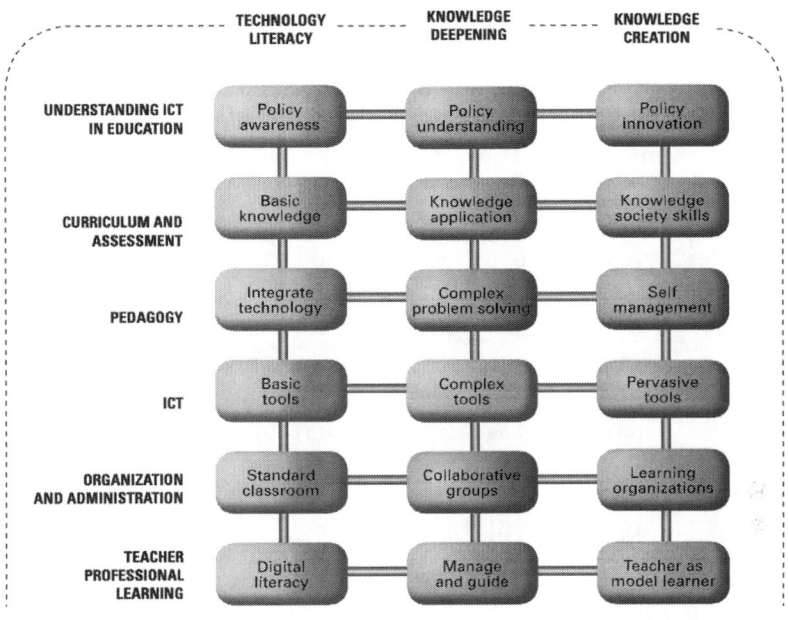

Figure 1.2.   UNESCO ICT Competency Framework for Teachers (UNESCO, 2011, p. 13).

technology into the classroom is also reflected in relevant state-based professional teaching standards. It is obviously important for teachers everywhere to understand and meet the professional requirements stipulated by their governing jurisdiction.

Thus, there are several professional and advisory bodies at international, national and district levels that collectively emphasize the importance of teachers having the knowledge, skills, and attitudes to lead the integration of technology into learning and teaching.

ACCESS TO LEARNING

Offering students flexible and convenient access to learning is seen as another key driver for the use of technology in learning, with online technologies enabling students to continue their work out of the classroom, anytime, anywhere, and collaboratively (Beetham & Sharpe, 2013; Oblinger, 2012; OECD, 2012, 2016b). For instance, students can have access to virtual science laboratories, providing them with greater access to equipment than could be afforded by a single educational institution

(OECD, 2016b). Using collaborative technologies such as video-conferencing, web-conferencing, and virtual worlds, they can interact with one another and their teachers in real-time to ask questions, discuss issues, and undertake group work activities (Bower, Kenney, Dalgarno, Lee, & Kennedy, 2014).

The efficiency with which educational institutions can disseminate resources and experiences also provides a major systemic impetus for using technology in education (BECTA, 2010). Just because students access materials and interact online, it does not necessarily mean learning experiences need be compromised. One US Department of Education survey indicated that online and blended learning outperformed conventional and face-to-face learning in terms of cost, reach, and results (Means, Toyama, Murphy, Bakia, & Jones, 2009). Importantly, providing online access to learning can also strengthen inclusion, equality, and citizenship across society (BECTA, 2010).

CATERING TO TODAY'S LEARNERS

The large majority of young people in developed nations are highly connected. For instance, they often use the Internet at home multiple times each day and spending hours on digital activities such as consuming digital content and social interaction (OECD, 2012). As an example of connectedness, approximately 94% of undergraduate students in the United States own two or more Internet-capable devices (Brooks, 2016). Approximately half of all high school students in the United States are using mobile apps and emailing their teachers with questions from home (Project Tomorrow, 2015). As a consequence, educators often argue that technology can motivate students by making learning more relevant and familiar (Howell, 2012; Sharp, 2009).

There is qualified evidence to support the claim that learners are motivated by technology-enhanced approaches. As part of the SpeakUp 2015 survey the majority of principals agreed that using more digital approaches in learning serves to increase student engagement (Project Tomorrow, 2016). In addition, a stratified random sample of 10,000 US university students found that:

- Students generally had a strongly positive orientation toward technology, with an increasing trend noted.
- About 75% of students felt that technology enriched their learning experience.

- The large majority of students preferred some form of blended mode of online learning over entirely face-to-face classes (Brooks, 2016).

It should be noted that other findings question the proposition that using technology per se increases motivation, and suggest that students are wary and discerning users of technology for learning (OECD, 2012). Beyond a novelty effect, caution should be exerted not to overly attribute motivation to technology itself – the design of the learning task can render a technology-based lesson entirely demotivating. Yet, the desire to catering to the 'digital expectancy' of students, parents, teachers, and governments is an impetus that drives teachers to integrate technology into their teaching (Howell, 2012).

Beyond Digital Natives and Technological Determinism – Toward the Critical Use of Technology in Education

We have established that there are several motivations for integrating technology into learning and teaching, including the potential to improve student learning outcomes, develop student digital learning skills, improve access to learning (as a matter of social justice as well as convenience), as well as curricula and professional requirements and the possibility of enhancing student motivation. However, this should not result in a headlong and thoughtless dive into using technology for educational purposes. Instead, we need to adopt a critical perspective in order to avoid the pitfalls of using technology for learning and fully capitalize on the opportunities. Without a critical approach toward the use of technology, it is easy for educators to fall into some of the 'mythical' misconceptions about its use (Johnson, 2015). Two such misconceptions relate to the existence of 'digital natives' and the idea of 'technological determinism.'

Conventional folklore espouses that older people cannot use technology for learning and teaching as well as younger generations who have grown up surrounded by technology. For instance, in his contentious article "Digital Natives, Digital Immigrants," Marc Prensky (2001) argued that one of the failings of contemporary education is that today's students who are comfortable and savvy with technology (so-called 'digital natives') are being taught by generations of people for whom technology is unfamiliar and unnatural ('digital immigrants').

It is important to note that while there is little doubt that technology is a fundamental part of many students' lives, it is misleading to propose that all young learners fit into the stereotype of digital natives or 'new millennium learners' (OECD, 2012). Digital divides exist between the students' profiles and preferences, so supporting diversity of practices is what matters most for the purposes of improving teaching and learning (OECD, 2012). As well, many so-called 'digital natives' who may have high levels of technological proficiency may not be careful or discerning Internet users (Bennett, Maton, & Kervin, 2008; Kennedy, Judd, Churchward, Gray, & Krause, 2008; Miller & Bartlett, 2012). According to one study, 31% of 12–15-year-olds felt that if a search engine lists the results, then the content must be truthful (Ofcom, 2011). A UK survey of 509 teachers indicated that they believed their students had at best variable digital fluencies (Miller & Bartlett, 2012). That is to say, we should not assume that because students are young (or teachers are older), it is not possible for students to be taught how to be effective users of technology for learning purposes.

Another misconception that is easy to adopt is the idea that use of particular technologies will have a predetermined learning impact (so-called 'technological determinism'). Learners, in their environments, have a degree of agency, and ultimately decide how they will use technology (Oliver, 2011). For instance, there is an important difference between students merely collecting the most readily available information online, and performing the cognitive work of evaluating and synthesizing that information into new knowledge (American Psychological Association, 2009). Thus, we need to move beyond 'technological determinism' whereby learning technologies are seen to have fixed effects, to a more nuanced perspective of technology as but one element in a complex and broad learning ecosystem (Oliver, 2011; Selwyn, 2010). To authentically and critically examine the use of technology in educational settings, we need to take into account the social, political, economic, cultural, and historical contexts at the individual, institutional, and societal levels of analysis (Selwyn, 2010).

Technology is not a simple panacea for education (Roblyer & Doering, 2013). The use and impact of technology in education is modest compared to other fields (Lim, Zhao, Tondeur, Chai, &

Tsai, 2013), with only moderate overall effect sizes observed (Tamim, Bernard, Borokhovski, Abrami, & Schmid, 2011). Merely providing schools with technology is unlikely to in and of itself have much effect because outcomes depend on how the technology is used (Cuban, 2009). There is no doubt that technology can be used to enable new forms of interaction and representation that were not previously possible. However, the extent to which technology improves learning depends on many factors, including how the learning tasks and environment are designed within the broader context of their operation. Examining how research findings relating to the use of technology for learning can be used to enhance our design thinking is the focus of this book.

Next Steps

The intrinsic desire to improve learning outcomes, the importance of developing students' digital learning skills, curriculum and syllabus specifications, professional objectives, offering improved access to learning, and catering to our students mean that technology integration is no longer an option for teachers – it is an imperative. But accepting that it is essential to integrate technology into at least some parts of our courses does nothing toward addressing our initial challenge of 'how' to best integrate technology.

We have established that we need to adopt a critical approach in order to avoid the pitfalls of overly simplistic thinking, such as students already know how to learn using technology and particular designs will lead to certain outcomes. It is also argued that a 'scholarship of teaching' approach that draws upon research evidence is the most effective basis for technology-enhanced learning design because it utilizes what is known rather than naïve anticipations. Thus, the rest of this book will focus on the critical examination of research literature relating to the design of technology-enhanced learning.

In Chapter 2, we will look at the Technology Pedagogy And Content Knowledge (TPACK) model as a foundational way to conceptualize teaching with technology, and the research findings relating to its application. Chapter 3 will then focus upon the 'pedagogy' dimension by providing an overview of different pedagogical approaches and how they may be instantiated using technology. Chapter 4 lays conceptual foundations for the use of technologies by considering their fundamental potentials (or 'affordances') and the research surrounding the use of different modalities in combination (multimedia learning effects). Chapter 5 considers how we can generally conceptualize the digital representation of content for learning and assessment purposes, with reference to examples from practice. The last of the so-called 'conceptual foundation' chapters is Chapter 6 on design, which focuses on research and development emanating from the fields of learning design and design thinking.

In order to develop a grounded understanding of the concepts at stake, the next four chapters then provide comprehensive reviews of empirical educational research relating to Web 2.0 technologies (Chapter 7), social networking (Chapter 8), mobile learning (Chapter 9), and virtual worlds (Chapter 10). Each of these chapters distills benefits, constraints, epitomes, and recommendations from the research literature. Examining quite different technologies enables us to understand which phenomena appear to relate to particular technologies, as well as abstract general themes that seem to run across the different design platforms. The outcome of synthesizing findings from the four technology chapters and relating it to the literature more generally is the focus of Chapter 11. Finally, Chapter 12 concludes our journey by considering future directions and setting a vision for practice.

So if you are ready, turn the page and let's begin!

References

American Psychological Association. (2009). How technology changes everything (and nothing) in psychology. 2008 annual report of the APA policy and planning board. *American Psychologist*, 64, 454–463.

BECTA. (2010). Next generation learning – The implementation plan for 2010-2013.

Beetham, H., & Sharpe, R. (2013). An introduction to rethinking pedagogy. In H. Beetham & R. Sharpe (Eds.), *Rethinking pedagogy for a digital age – Designing for 21st century learning* (pp. 1–15). New York, NY: Routledge.

Bennett, S., Maton, K., & Kervin, L. (2008). The 'digital natives' debate: A critical review of the evidence. *British Journal of Educational Technology*, 39(5), 775–786.

Bower, M., Kenney, J., Dalgarno, B., Lee, M. J., & Kennedy, G. E. (2014). Patterns and principles for blended synchronous learning: Engaging remote and face-to-face learners in rich-media real-time collaborative activities. *Australasian Journal of Educational Technology*, 30(3), 261–272.

Brooks, C. (2016). *ECAR study of students and information technology*. Louisville, CO: ECAR.

Cuban, L. (2009). *Oversold and underused*. Cambridge, MA: Harvard University Press.

Department of Education Employment and Workplace Relations. (2009). *Transforming Australia's Higher Education System*.

Ferrari, A. (2013). *DIGCOMP: A framework for developing and understanding digital competence in Europe*. Publications Office of the European Union.

Howell, J. (2012). *Teaching with ICT: Digital pedagogies for collaboration & creativity*. Sydney: Oxford University Press.

ISTE. (2017). *ISTE standards for educators*. Retrieved from http://iste.org/standardsforeducators

ISTE. (2016). *2016 ISTE Standards for students*. Retrieved from http://www.iste.org/standards/standards/for-students-2016

Johnson, N. F. (2015). Digital natives and other myths. In M. Henderson & G. Romeo (Eds.), *Teaching and digital technologies: Big issues and critical questions* (pp. 11–21). Sydney: Cambridge.

Kennedy, G. E., Judd, T. S., Churchward, A., Gray, K., & Krause, K.-L. (2008). First year students' experiences with technology: Are they really digital natives. *Australasian Journal of Educational Technology*, 24(1), 108–122.

Kreber, C., & Kanuka, H. (2013). The scholarship of teaching and learning and the online classroom. *Canadian Journal of University Continuing Education*, 32(2), 109–131.

Laurillard, D. (2012). *Teaching as a design science – Building pedagogical patterns for learning and technology*. New York, NY: Routledge.

Lim, C. P., Zhao, Y., Tondeur, J., Chai, C. S., & Tsai, C.-C. (2013). Bridging the gap: Technology trends and use of technology in schools. *Educational Technology & Society*, 16(2), 59–68.

Means, B., Toyama, Y., Murphy, R., Bakia, M., & Jones, K. (2009). *Evaluation of evidence-based practices in online learning: A meta-analysis and review of online learning studies*. US Department of Education.

Miller, C., & Bartlett, J. (2012). 'Digital fluency': Towards young people's critical use of the internet. *Journal of Information Literacy*, 6(2), 35–55.

Newhouse, C. P. (2015). When does technology improve learning?. In M. Henderson & G. Romeo (Eds.), *Teaching and digital technologies: Big issues and critical questions* (pp. 195–213). Sydney: Cambridge.

Oblinger, D. (2012). IT as a game changer. *EDUCAUSE Review* (May/June), 11–24. Retrieved from https://net.educause.edu/ir/library/pdf/ERM1230.pdf

OECD. (2012). *Connected minds: Technology and today's learners*. Retrieved from http://www.oecd-ilibrary.org/education/connected-minds_9789264111011-en

OECD. (2016a). *New skills for the digital economy – Measuring the demand and supply of ICT skills at work*. Retrieved from http://www.oecd-ilibrary.org/science-and-technology/new-skills-for-the-digital-economy_5jlwnkm2fc9x-en

OECD. (2016b). *Skills for a digital world*. Retrieved from http://www.oecd-ilibrary.org/science-and-technology/skills-for-a-digital-world_5jlwz83z3wnw-en

OECD. (2016c). *Survey of Adult Skills (PIAAC)*. Retrieved from http://www.oecd.org/skills/piaac/. Accessed on 25 January, 2017.

Ofcom. (2011). *UK children's media literacy*. Retrieved from https://www.ofcom.org.uk/research-and-data/media-literacy-research/children/ukchildrensml11

Oliver, M. (2011). Technological determinism in educational technology research: Some alternative ways of thinking about the relationship between learning and technology. *Journal of Computer Assisted Learning, 27*(5), 373–384.

Prensky, M. (2001). Digital natives, digital immigrants. *On the horizon, 9*(5), 1–6.

Project Tomorrow. (2015). *Digital learning 24/7 – Understanding technology-enhanced learning in the lives of today's students*. Retrieved from http://www.tomorrow.org/speakup/SU14DigitalLearning24-7_StudentReport.html

Project Tomorrow. (2016). *From print to pixel – The role of videos, games, animations and simulations within K-12 education*. Retrieved from: http://www.tomorrow.org/speakup/SU15AnnualReport.html

Roblyer, M. D., & Doering, A. H. (2013). *Integrating educational technology into teaching*. Upper Saddle River, NJ: Pearson.

Selwyn, N. (2010). Looking beyond learning: Notes towards the critical study of educational technology. *Journal of Computer Assisted Learning, 26*(1), 65–73.

Sharp, V. F. (2009). *Computer education for teachers*. Hoboken, NJ: Wiley.

Tamim, R. M., Bernard, R. M., Borokhovski, E., Abrami, P. C., & Schmid, R. F. (2011). What forty years of research says about the impact of technology on learning a second-order meta-analysis and validation study. *Review of Educational research, 81*(1), 4–28.

Trigwell, K., Martin, E., Benjamin, J., & Prosser, M. (2000). Scholarship of teaching: A model. *Higher Education Research & Development, 19*(2), 155–168.

UNESCO. (2011). *UNESCO ICT competency framework for teachers*. Paris: United Nations Educational. Retrieved from http://www.unesco.org/new/en/unesco/themes/icts/teacher-education/unesco-ict-competency-framework-for-teachers/

Vuorikari, R., Punie, Y., Gomez, S. C., & Van Den Brande, G. (2016). *DigComp 2.0: The digital competence framework for citizens. Update Phase 1: The Conceptual Reference Model*. Institute for Prospective Technological Studies, Joint Research Centre.

CHAPTER

2

The Technology Pedagogy and Content Knowledge (TPACK) Framework and Its Implications

ABSTRACT

This chapter introduces the Technology Pedagogy and Content Knowledge (TPACK) model as it relates to technology-enhanced learning design. The key features of the framework are unpacked, along with a brief examination of what TPACK looks like in practice. Approaches to developing TPACK capacity are considered, with learning-by-design emerging as the most promising technique. Issues relating to TPACK are also critically discussed, including those relating to measurement and the capacity of the framework to support educational design practice.

Introduction to the Technology Pedagogy And Content Knowledge (TPACK) Framework

In the 1980s, Shulman (1986) defined Pedagogy Content Knowledge as pedagogical[1] knowledge for a particular content area, including useful forms of conceptual representation, the most impactful techniques of explanation, common areas of student misconception, and understanding of what makes a topic difficult to learn. The TPACK framework is an extension upon Schulman's work that emphasizes the importance of teachers having technological understanding in today's educational milieu (Mishra & Koehler, 2006).

The TPACK framework asserts that technological, pedagogical, and content knowledge are not necessarily mutually exclusive, and in fact that an integrated understanding of technology, pedagogy, and content underpins effective teacher practice (Mishra & Koehler, 2006). The elements of the TPACK framework are shown in Figure 2.1.

The TPACK elements have been defined as follows:

1. Technology knowledge (TK): Knowledge about technologies including the Internet, video software, interactive whiteboards, and mobile technologies, but also non-digital technologies such as pencil and paper.
2. Pedagogical knowledge (PK): Knowledge of teaching methods and processes such as how to design lessons, manage classes, evaluate student learning, and so on.
3. Content knowledge (CK): Knowledge about the domain-specific subject matter being learned or taught, such as geometry, creative writing techniques, cyclones, or the fall of the Roman empire.
4. Pedagogical content knowledge (PCK): Subject-specific pedagogical knowledge addressing effective ways of teaching within the discipline or topic area, for instance, how to

---

[1]The term 'pedagogy' can be simply considered to mean 'teaching approach,' so that pedagogical knowledge is knowledge of teaching approaches. The various types and meanings of 'pedagogy' will be explored in more detail in the next chapter.

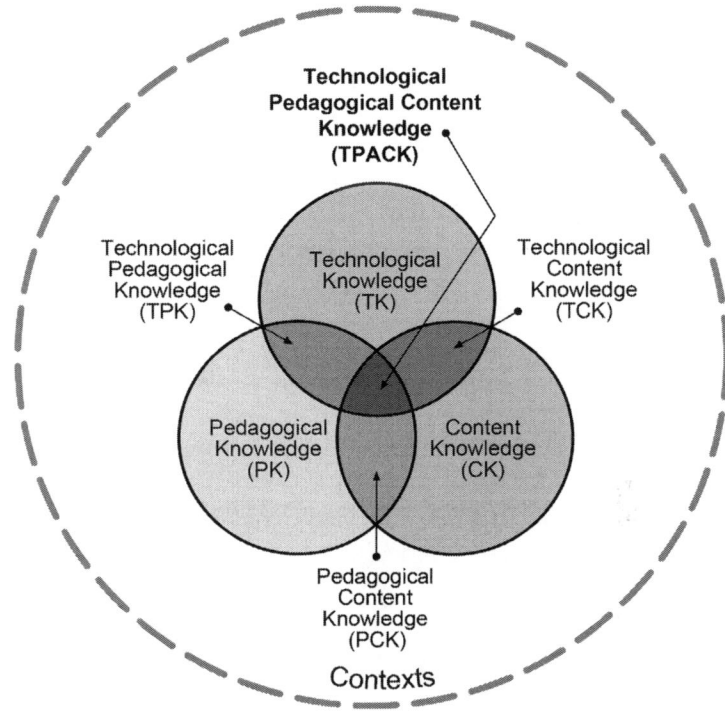

Figure 2.1.   The TPACK Framework. *Image source*: http://tpack.org. Reproduced by permission of the publisher, © 2012 by tpack.org

effectively teach geometry, creative writing, cyclones, or the fall of the Roman empire.

5. Technological content knowledge (TCK): Understanding how technology can be used to effectively represent content within the learning domain or topic area, for instance, how to use technology to represent molecular reactions, analyze literature, interpret datasets, or simulate historical events.

6. Technological pedagogical knowledge (TPK): Knowing how technologies can be used for educational purposes, for instance, facilitating collaboration or exchange of ideas.

7. Technological pedagogical and content knowledge (TPACK): The synergistic understanding of how technology can be used for pedagogical purposes to help students learn the content area, for instance, by having students upload and peer-evaluate their photosynthesis diagrams so students can learn how plants turn carbon dioxide to oxygen (see Koehler & Mishra, 2009; Mishra & Koehler, 2006; Schmidt et al., 2009).

Angeli and Valanides (2009) emphasize that overall TPACK capacity is not merely the sum of the individual knowledge components, as it requires an understanding of how the different dimensions work together.

Context is another important aspect of the TPACK framework, but one that is often overlooked (Rosenberg & Koehler, 2015). Contextual elements include grade level being taught, student background, and the availability of technologies (Mishra & Koehler, 2006). Some researchers call for a broad conception of what is meant by context to include macro-level elements (social, political, technological, and economic), meso-level elements (institutional and community), and micro-level elements (within-class conditions and mind-sets) as they relate to both students and teachers (Koh, Chai, Benjamin, & Hong, 2015; Porras-Hernández & Salinas-Amescua, 2013).

Note that the TPACK framework makes no commitments about what defines best practice in technology enabled learning, as this is neither objective nor constant. Educational researchers observe a consensus in the field that:

> TPACK is not static or fixed, but a dynamic and flexible body of knowledge influenced by both rapid changes in technology and the bidirectional relationship between knowledge and practice. (Mouza, Karchmer-Klein, Nandakumar, Yilmaz Ozden, & Hu, 2014, p. 208)

In essence, TPACK is about the synergistic integration of technology, pedagogy, and content, in context, for the purposes of learning design (Angeli & Valanides, 2009). It highlights the interconnected nature of key dimensions of technology-enhanced learning, and in doing so provides a useful means for analyzing and self-reflecting upon teacher knowledge and practice.

What Does TPACK Look Like in Practice?

While many people have engaged extensively in the theory of TPACK, relative fewer have been willing to volunteer examples of what TPACK might look like in practice. Four places to find examples include:

- TPACK Cases: http://tpackcases.org
- Practitioner's Guide to Technology Pedagogy and Content Knowledge: http://publish.wm.edu/book/1

- The Teaching Teachers for the Future website: http://www.ttf.edu.au
- University of Michigan EDT514 website: http://edt514tpack.wikispaces.com

For instance, in one example provided in the Practitioner's Guide to Technology Pedagogy and Content Knowledge (Hofer et al., 2015), a social studies teacher designed a module of work that used several web-based content creation tools so that high school students could complete project work on globalization. In order to achieve this, the teacher demonstrated the following knowledge types:

- CK: Detailed knowledge of globalization as the events and processes by which economic, social, cultural, and political systems have become more interdependent and integrated.
- PK: Knowledge of how to structure lessons and support students to successfully conduct a project-based learning unit.
- TK: Knowledge of specific tools that students were to use to conduct the project, including the Glogster multimedia poster tool (http://edu.glogster.com), the Smore newsletter tool (http://smore.com), the PhotoPeach slideshow tool (http://photopeach.com), and the Weebly web-authoring tool (http://weebly.com).
- TPK: Knowledge of how to effectively help students learn the features of the various technologies.
- CPK: Understanding of how to help students authentically engage with globalization content, processes, and concepts.
- CTK: Knowledge of how globalization content could be accessed, organized, and represented using technology.
- TPACK: Knowing how to design a cohesive unit that enables students to learn about globalization using technology, using technology to model globalization research processes, and knowing how to assess the students' use of technology to represent their understanding of globalization.
- Contextual knowledge: Knowledge of the curriculum documents and standards, student access to computers, prevailing sociopolitical impetuses to cultivate 21st-century learning skills, understanding the sociopolitical issues surrounding public sharing of student content, and knowledge of student prior learning.

The work produced by students in the class can be found at http://centennialcampussocialstudies.weebly.com. An example of one student's work is shown in Figure 2.2.

Figure 2.2.   Example of a Student's Globalization Project Created Using Weebly.

This is just one example for illustrative purposes, but of course there are an enormous variety of ways that TPACK can manifest. Throughout this book, we will be reflecting on the TPACK embedded in different tasks and lessons based on the different technologies, pedagogies, and content being utilized. The official TPACK website at http://tpack.org also has a range of excellent resources relating to TPACK, for those who are interested.

How Do Teachers Best Develop TPACK Capacity?

The majority of evidence relating to the development of TPACK capacity derives from studies of pre-service teachers (Wu, 2013). For instance, based on a review of research, Tondeur et al. (2012)

identify several elements that support pre-service teachers to develop their technology-enhanced learning design capabilities, including helping them to align theory and practice, modeling by experts, encouraging reflection on attitudes, collaboration with peers, scaffolding authentic technology experiences, and providing continuous feedback. Results from the Preparing Tomorrow's Teachers to Teach with Technology (PT3) project found that mentorship of pre-service teachers, providing them with technology-rich field experiences, designing technology-rich resources for teachers to learn from and use, and co-designing with teachers were all strategies that teacher educators could use to improve various components of TPACK understanding (Polly, Mims, Shepherd, & Inan, 2010).

Mouza et al. (2014) found that an integrative approach to improving TPACK capacity through instructional design opportunities, authentic in-field experiences, explicit reflection tasks, a theory into practice focus, and the use of role models was able to significantly improve TPACK capability across all areas. Angeli and Valanides (2009) found mapping exercises whereby technologies are selected with affordances to meet the representational, pedagogical, and learner needs that significantly improved TPACK abilities. Trainee and practicing teachers indicate that using TPACK-based rubrics and instruments is also helpful to support their evolving technology-enhanced learning design practices (Bower, 2012; Koh, Chai, & Lim, 2017).

However, beyond these approaches, the overarching consensus among teacher education researchers is that the best way for educators to develop their TPACK capabilities is by engaging in *sustained collaborative design processes* (Baran & Uygun, 2016; Koh et al., 2017; Mishra, Koehler, Zellner, & Kereluik, 2012; Norton & Hathaway, 2012; Voogt, Fisser, Tondeur, & van Braak, 2016). Mishra and Koehler (2006) advocated a learning-by-design approach in their seminal work outlining the TPACK framework. They proposed that the contextualized and sustained inquiry that can emerge from authentic design tasks helps teachers develop the deep understanding required for complex real-world practice. This includes having teachers define, design, and refine solutions for educational contexts whereby they are primarily responsible for selecting and learning the educational technologies that they use. Examples include making videos, redesigning educational websites, and collaboratively designing online courses (Mishra & Koehler, 2006). They explain mechanisms that underpin the effectiveness of collaboratively 'learning by design':

> Because their explorations of technology are tied to their attempts to solve educational problems, we argue that, teachers using this method learn 'how to learn' about technology and 'how to think' about educational technology. In contrast to a standard workshop approach that puts teachers in the role of passive consumers of technology, the learning technology by design approach puts teachers in a more active role as designers of technology. Most importantly, our approach provides opportunities for teachers to encounter the rich connections between technology, content, and pedagogy. (Koehler, Mishra, & Yahya, 2007, p. 744)

In their analysis of a small group of colleagues who undertook a learning-by-design course, Koehler et al. (2007) showed how the teachers' emphases shifted from technology-oriented discourse early in the course, to more pedagogy-oriented conversations in the middle of the course, to finally involving some technology pedagogy and content focus in the late stages of the course. However, different patterns were observed in other groups, leading the research team to conjecture that 'learning technology by design' enabled TPACK understanding to evolve, but did not guarantee it (depending on contextual and interpersonal factors, among others).

Since then there have been several attempts to develop instructional design models that support the development of educator TPACK capacity through design processes. These include TPACK-COPR that used a cycle of comprehension, observation, practice, and reflection (Jang & Chen, 2010); TPACK-IDDIRR with phases of introducing, demonstrating, developing, implementing, reflecting, and revising (Lee & Kim, 2014); and TPACK-DBL that included design-based learning elements of brainstorming, designing, engaging with theory, investigating tools, examining examples, collaborating, applying designs, and reflecting (Baran & Uygun, 2016). These frameworks are helpful to identify the sorts of design processes that may underpin TPACK development, and qualitative evidence across these studies appears to generally support the notion that sustained and structured design opportunities improve TPACK capability. Design-based approaches have also been recognized and advocated by other ICT educational researchers as the most promising way to develop TPACK abilities (Chai, Ling Koh, Tsai, & Lee Wee Tan, 2011b; Douglas & Keengwe, 2014).

Measuring TPACK?

Dozens of researchers have attempted to develop survey instruments to measure TPACK abilities (for instance, Archambault & Crippen, 2009; Chai, Koh, & Tsai, 2011a; Harris, Grandgenett, & Hofer, 2010; Pamuk, Ergun, Cakir, Yilmaz, & Ayas, 2015; Sahin, 2011; Schmidt et al., 2009; Shinas, Yilmaz-Ozden, Mouza, Karchmer-Klein, & Glutting, 2013; Yurdakul et al., 2012). In fact, as early as 2011, over 100 instruments had been developed (Koehler, Shin, & Mishra, 2011). Of these, the 47-item Teachers' Knowledge of Teaching and Technology (TKTT) instrument developed by Mishra, Koehler, and colleagues (Schmidt et al., 2009) is the foundational and most frequently used instrument for measuring TPACK (Young, Young, & Hamilton, 2013).

However, concerns have been raised about attempting to measure TPACK. There are questions over whether the different components of the model can be clearly distinguished (Archambault & Barnett, 2010; Brantley-Dias & Ertmer, 2013; Graham, 2011; Shinas et al., 2013; Zelkowski, Gleason, Cox, & Bismarck, 2013). For instance, in one study, high correlations were observed between content knowledge and pedagogical knowledge, as well as all of the technological components (TK, TCK, TPK, TPACK), with the ambiguity between categories also established using think-aloud analysis of survey respondents (Archambault & Crippen, 2009). In another study of 596 online educators, only three distinct factors emerged: PCK, TCK, and TK (Archambault & Barnett, 2010). Other researchers have experienced similar problems distinguishing between TPACK elements (Koh, Chai, & Tsai, 2010; Lee & Tsai, 2010). While some studies have been able to distinguish between all of the TPACK elements (Chai et al., 2011a; Koh, Woo, & Lim, 2013), overall results are far from conclusive.

One way in which TPACK instruments may be useful is to compare the relative effectiveness of various methods of developing TPACK capacity. For instance, Young et al. (2013) were able to compare the positive effect of eight teacher education courses that used the (TKTT) TPACK self-evaluation instrument developed by Schmidt et al. (2009) to assess the pre- and post-TPACK abilities of pre-service teachers. While the analysis did find that pre-service teacher self-ratings of TPACK capabilities did generally improve throughout the duration of courses, the three studies with the largest effect sizes (Abbitt, 2011; Baran, Chuang, & Thompson, 2011; Nordin, Morrow, & Davis, 2011) provide little or no detail of the sorts of learning activities that students completed in order to achieve their gains. In this and any other meta-analyses that may be conducted, it is also challenging to calibrate for contextual differences between studies, such as the attributes of the participants, the duration of the course, and the quality of the teacher educators involved (Young et al., 2013).

Other concerns include whether or not measurement initiatives that have appropriately considered validity evidence have been called into question (Cavanagh & Koehler, 2013). Also, the majority of approaches involve participant self-reporting of ability, which may not be a reliable measure of actual ability (Archambault & Crippen, 2009; Douglas & Keengwe, 2014; Harris et al., 2010). In responses, some studies have attempted to examine artifacts designed by teachers (Harris et al., 2010; Koh, 2013), but as Koh points out, without any associated teacher interviews there is no capacity to clarify learners' underlying thinking and it is therefore difficult to confidently establish TPACK understanding from designed products.

Promising work has been performed by Graham, Borup, and Smith (2012) who qualitatively examined the reasons that pre-service teachers provided for their technology integration decisions. These were found to relate to TK (important technological knowledge to possess), TPK (technology supporting implementation of a general pedagogical approach or being appropriate for the general characteristics of the learner), and TPACK (technology facilitating subject-specific pedagogical method, transforming a discipline-based representation to facilitate learning, or being appropriate for the content knowledge of the learner). Their analysis of design rationales showed that their design-oriented curriculum led to a 159% increase in Technology Pedagogy Content oriented rationales for technology selection decisions (Graham et al., 2012). While this approach provides important insights into TPACK development, it is more subjective and labor intensive than self-reporting techniques.

So it can be seen that measuring TPACK involves a range of complex issues surrounding reliability, validity, comparability, and feasibility. This has led to calls for the TPACK model to be used as a guiding framework for conceptualization rather than a framework for measurement (Archambault & Barnett, 2010; Graham, 2011). Given the subjectivity of assessment in education generally, Angeli and Valanides (2009) point out that an approach involving self-assessment, peer assessment, and expert assessment may produce the most reliable and fruitful insights in terms of measuring TPACK capacity.

Limitations of the TPACK Framework in Supporting Practice

While the TPACK framework has undoubtedly advanced technology-enhanced learning design research and practice, some limitations should be noted. While the TPACK model does identify domains to consider when utilizing ICT for educative purposes, it is also a pedagogically neutral model (Harris et al., 2010). For instance, it makes no commitments about which types of technologies and pedagogies might be more or less suitable for a particular content area. So TPACK helps to identify some of the 'what,' but none of the 'how.' This has resulted in some researchers examining the extent to which capabilities relating to particular pedagogical orientations can be developed within a broader TPACK framework (Chai et al., 2011b; Koh, 2013; Koh, Chai, & Tsai, 2014).

The TPACK model emphasizes that disciplinarity is a critical aspect of teacher understanding, but in order to be broadly applicable it provides no specificity about what constitutes TPACK understanding in different disciplines (Brantley-Dias & Ertmer, 2013). For this reason there have been attempts to conduct studies within particular subject areas (Doering, Koseoglu, Scharber, Henrickson, & Lanegran, 2014; Graham et al., 2009; Guzey & Roehrig, 2009; Habowski & Mouza, 2014) and develop domain-specific TPACK measurement instruments (Baser, Kopcha, & Ozden, 2016; Jang & Tsai, 2013; Zelkowski et al., 2013).

As well, consideration of context is crucial because of its critical influence upon what can be designed and learning outcomes (Koh et al., 2015; Porras-Hernández & Salinas-Amescua, 2013). Yet once again, in its (understandable) attempt to be generally applicable, the TPACK framework does not provide any comprehensive unpacking of what contextual elements might be and how they influence design and learning. This has underpinned efforts to define what context might be and mean at macro, meso, and micro levels (Koh et al., 2015; Porras-Hernández & Salinas-Amescua, 2013).

There is also nothing to say that because teachers have TPACK they will be willing to use this knowledge to affect meaningful student outcomes (Brantley-Dias & Ertmer, 2013). This concern has underpinned some efforts to examine what it means for teachers to apply TPACK in practice (Yeh, Hsu, Wu, Hwang, & Lin, 2013). Mishra, Koehler, and colleagues (Schmidt et al., 2009) themselves describe TPACK as "a useful frame for describing and understanding the goals for technology use" (p. 123). To this extent, the TPACK model is often utilized in practice as more of an organizing and descriptive framework, valuable for helping teachers to identify the aspects of practice they need to consider, but not how to best educate using technology in their discipline areas and contexts.

Concluding Remarks about TPACK

The TPACK framework is undoubtedly a useful tool to inform technology-enhanced learning design. It is also a model that has ignited extensive popular attention — both from researchers and practitioners — perhaps because of the neat way that it draws our attention to the interrelated nature of technology, pedagogy, and content. The general consensus is that the best way to develop TPACK capacity is through sustained and guided design processes. However, we need to be aware of the limitations surrounding TPACK, including its agnostic approach regarding the use of technology, pedagogy, and content in context, as well as limitations surrounding reliability, validity, comparability, and feasibility of TPACK measurement.

We should also take care to apply TPACK critically. One question worth asking is whether we should view TPACK as a theoretical framework or a conceptual one. Because the TPACK framework does not define any mechanisms underpinning relationships or how they are developed, the stance taken in this book is that the TPACK framework is a useful *conceptual* tool for organizing and analyzing educational technology thinking, but not a theory of learning. A broader question we need to ask ourselves is whether we should be aiming to develop and measure TPACK, or whether a more holistic view should be adopted. If, as a field we aim to develop TPACK capabilities per se, we are striving to achieve a framework. This may obscure our view and distract us from what is really important. Ideally we should be striving to design transformative learning environments for students, and focus upon educators cultivating the knowledge, skills, and attitudes that underpin that pursuit.

TPACK undoubtedly identifies valuable dimensions of teacher understanding that constitute foundations for technology-enhanced learning design. Accordingly, we will be examining critical issues surrounding pedagogy, technology, and content in Chapter 3, Chapter 4, and Chapter 5, respectively. However, once these foundations have been set, we will move quite quickly onto *how* we should design effective learning tasks using technology, based on research evidence from the field, in order to develop a holistic, robust, and nuanced understanding of technology-enhanced learning design issues and practice.

References

Abbitt, J. T. (2011). An investigation of the relationship between self-efficacy beliefs about technology integration and technological pedagogical content knowledge (TPACK) among preservice teachers. *Journal of Digital Learning in Teacher Education, 27*(4), 134–143.

Angeli, C., & Valanides, N. (2009). Epistemological and methodological issues for the conceptualization, development, and assessment of ICT-TPCK: Advances in technological pedagogical content knowledge (TPCK). *Computers & Education, 52*(1), 154–168.

Archambault, L. M., & Barnett, J. H. (2010). Revisiting technological pedagogical content knowledge: Exploring the TPACK framework. *Computers & Education, 55*(4), 1656–1662.

Archambault, L. M., & Crippen, K. (2009). Examining TPACK among K-12 online distance educators in the United States. *Contemporary Issues in Technology and Teacher Education, 9*(1), 71–88.

Baran, E., Chuang, H.-H., & Thompson, A. (2011). TPACK: An emerging research and development tool for teacher educators. *Turkish Online Journal of Educational Technology-TOJET, 10*(4), 370–377.

Baran, E., & Uygun, E. (2016). Putting technological, pedagogical, and content knowledge (TPACK) in action: An integrated TPACK-design-based learning (DBL) approach. *Australasian Journal of Educational Technology, 32*(2), 2.

Baser, D., Kopcha, T. J., & Ozden, M. Y. (2016). Developing a technological pedagogical content knowledge (TPACK) assessment for preservice teachers learning to teach English as a foreign language. *Computer Assisted Language Learning, 29*(4), 749–764.

Bower, M. (2012). A framework for developing pre-service teachers' Web 2.0 learning design capabilities. In D. Polly, C. Mims, & K. A. Persichitte (Eds.),

Developing technology-rich teacher education programs: Key issues (pp. 58–76). Hershey, PA: IGI Global.

Brantley-Dias, L., & Ertmer, P. A. (2013). Goldilocks and TPACK: Is the construct 'just right'?. *Journal of Research on Technology in Education, 46*(2), 103–128.

Cavanagh, R. F., & Koehler, M. J. (2013). A turn toward specifying validity criteria in the measurement of technological pedagogical content knowledge (TPACK). *Journal of Research on Technology in Education, 46*(2), 129–148.

Chai, C. S., Koh, J. H. L., & Tsai, C.-C. (2011a). Exploring the factor structure of the constructs of technological, pedagogical, content knowledge (TPACK).

Chai, C. S., Ling Koh, J. H., Tsai, C.-C., & Lee Wee Tan, L. (2011b). Modeling primary school pre-service teachers' Technological Pedagogical Content Knowledge (TPACK) for meaningful learning with information and communication technology (ICT). *Computers & Education, 57*(1), 1184–1193.

Doering, A., Koseoglu, S., Scharber, C., Henrickson, J., & Lanegran, D. (2014). Technology integration in K–12 geography education using TPACK as a conceptual model. *Journal of Geography, 113*(6), 223–237.

Douglas, A., & Keengwe, J. (2014). Using technology pedagogical content knowledge development to enhance learning outcomes. Paper presented at the Society for Information Technology & Teacher Education International Conference.

Graham, C. R. (2011). Theoretical considerations for understanding technological pedagogical content knowledge (TPACK). *Computers & Education, 57*(3), 1953–1960.

Graham, C. R., Borup, J., & Smith, N. B. (2012). Using TPACK as a framework to understand teacher candidates' technology integration decisions. *Journal of Computer Assisted Learning, 28*(6), 530–546.

Graham, C. R., Burgoyne, N., Cantrell, P., Smith, L., St Clair, L., & Harris, R. (2009). Measuring the TPACK confidence of inservice science teachers. *TechTrends, 53*(5), 70–79.

Guzey, S. S., & Roehrig, G. H. (2009). Teaching science with technology: Case studies of science teachers' development of technology, pedagogy, and content knowledge. *Contemporary Issues in Technology and Teacher Education, 9*(1), 25–45.

Habowski, T., & Mouza, C. (2014). Pre-service teachers' development of technological pedagogical content knowledge (TPACK) in the context of a Secondary Science Teacher Education program. *Journal of Technology and Teacher Education, 22*(4), 471–495.

Harris, J., Grandgenett, N., & Hofer, M. (2010). Testing a TPACK-based technology integration assessment rubric. Paper presented at the Society for Information Technology & Teacher Education International Conference.

Hofer, M. J., Bell, L., Bull, G. L., Barry III, R. Q., Cohen, J. D., Garcia, N., … Kim, R. (2015). *Practitioner's guide to technology, pedagogy, and content knowledge (TPACK): Rich media cases of teacher knowledge.* Association for the Advancement of Computing in Education.

Jang, S.-J., & Chen, K.-C. (2010). From PCK to TPACK: Developing a transformative model for pre-service science teachers. *Journal of Science Education and Technology, 19*(6), 553–564.

Jang, S.-J., & Tsai, M.-F. (2013). Exploring the TPACK of Taiwanese secondary school science teachers using a new contextualized TPACK model. *Australasian Journal of Educational Technology, 29*(4), 566–580.

Koehler, M. J., & Mishra, P. (2009). What is technological pedagogical content knowledge (TPACK)?. *Contemporary Issues in Technology and Teacher Education, 9*(1), 60–70.

Koehler, M. J., Mishra, P., & Yahya, K. (2007). Tracing the development of teacher knowledge in a design seminar: Integrating content, pedagogy and technology. *Computers & Education, 49*(3), 740–762.

Koehler, M. J., Shin, T. S., & Mishra, P. (2011). How do we measure TPACK? Let me count the ways. *Educational technology, teacher knowledge, and classroom impact: A research handbook on frameworks and approaches* (pp. 16–31).

Koh, J. H. L. (2013). A rubric for assessing teachers' lesson activities with respect to TPACK for meaningful learning with ICT. *Australasian Journal of Educational Technology, 29*(6), 887–900.

Koh, J. H. L., Chai, C. S., Benjamin, W., & Hong, H.-Y. (2015). Technological pedagogical content knowledge (TPACK) and design thinking: A framework to support ICT lesson design for 21st century learning. *The Asia-Pacific Education Researcher, 24*(3), 535–543.

Koh, J. L., Chai, C. S., & Lim, W. Y. (2017). Teacher professional development for TPACK-21CL. *Journal of Educational Computing Research, 55*(2), 172–196.

Koh, J. H. L., Chai, C. S., & Tsai, C.-C. (2010). Examining the technological pedagogical content knowledge of Singapore pre-service teachers with a large-scale survey. *Journal of Computer Assisted Learning, 26*(6), 563–573.

Koh, J. H. L., Chai, C. S., & Tsai, C.-C. (2014). Demographic factors, TPACK constructs, and teachers' perceptions of constructivist-oriented TPACK. *Educational Technology & Society, 17*(1), 185–196.

Koh, J. H. L., Woo, H.-L., & Lim, W.-Y. (2013). Understanding the relationship between Singapore preservice teachers' ICT course experiences and technological pedagogical content knowledge (TPACK) through ICT course evaluation. *Educational Assessment, Evaluation and Accountability, 25*(4), 321–339.

Lee, C.-J., & Kim, C. (2014). An implementation study of a TPACK-based instructional design model in a technology integration course. *Educational Technology Research and Development, 62*(4), 437–460.

Lee, M.-H., & Tsai, C.-C. (2010). Exploring teachers' perceived self efficacy and technological pedagogical content knowledge with respect to educational use of the World Wide Web. *Instructional Science, 38*(1), 1–21.

Mishra, P., & Koehler, M. J. (2006). Technological pedagogical content knowledge: A framework for teacher knowledge. *Teachers College Record, 108*(6), 1017–1054.

Mishra, P., Koehler, M. J., Zellner, A., & Kereluik, K. (2012). Thematic considerations in integrating TPACK in a graduate program. *Developing technology-rich teacher education programs: Key issues*, 1–12.

Mouza, C., Karchmer-Klein, R., Nandakumar, R., Yilmaz Ozden, S., & Hu, L. (2014). Investigating the impact of an integrated approach to the development of preservice teachers' technological pedagogical content knowledge (TPACK). *Computers & Education*, *71*, 206–221.

Nordin, H., Morrow, D., & Davis, N. (2011). Pre-service teachers' experience with ICT integration in secondary schools: A case study of one New Zealand context. Paper presented at the Society for Information Technology & Teacher Education International Conference.

Norton, P., & Hathaway, D. (2012). Lessons from the ITS program: Five design strategies on which to build technology-rich teacher education. In D. Polly, C. Mims, & K. A. Persichitte (Eds.), *Developing technology-rich teacher education programs: Key issues* (pp. 13–27). Hershey, PA: IGI Global.

Pamuk, S., Ergun, M., Cakir, R., Yilmaz, H. B., & Ayas, C. (2015). Exploring relationships among TPACK components and development of the TPACK instrument. *Education and Information Technologies*, *20*(2), 241–263.

Polly, D., Mims, C., Shepherd, C. E., & Inan, F. (2010). Evidence of impact: Transforming teacher education with preparing tomorrow's teachers to teach with technology (PT3) grants. *Teaching and Teacher Education*, *26*(4), 863–870.

Porras-Hernández, L. H., & Salinas-Amescua, B. (2013). Strengthening TPACK: A broader notion of context and the use of teacher's narratives to reveal knowledge construction. *Journal of Educational Computing Research*, *48*(2), 223–244.

Rosenberg, J. M., & Koehler, M. J. (2015). Context and technological pedagogical content knowledge (TPACK): A systematic review. *Journal of Research on Technology in Education*, *47*(3), 186–210.

Sahin, I. (2011). Development of survey of technological pedagogical and content knowledge (TPACK). *Turkish Online Journal of Educational Technology-TOJET*, *10*(1), 97–105.

Schmidt, D. A., Baran, E., Thompson, A. D., Mishra, P., Koehler, M. J., & Shin, T. S. (2009). Technological pedagogical content knowledge (TPACK): The development and validation of an assessment instrument for preservice teachers. *Journal of Research on Technology in Education*, *42*(2), 123–149.

Shinas, V. H., Yilmaz-Ozden, S., Mouza, C., Karchmer-Klein, R., & Glutting, J. J. (2013). Examining domains of technological pedagogical content knowledge using factor analysis. *Journal of Research on Technology in Education*, *45*(4), 339–360.

Shulman, L. S. (1986). Those who understand: Knowledge growth in teaching. *Educational Researcher*, *15*, 4–14.

Tondeur, J., van Braak, J., Sang, G., Voogt, J., Fisser, P., & Ottenbreit-Leftwich, A. (2012). Preparing pre-service teachers to integrate technology in education: A synthesis of qualitative evidence. *Computers & Education*, *59*(1), 134–144.

Voogt, J., Fisser, P., Tondeur, J., & van Braak, J. (2016). Using theoretical perspectives in developing understanding of TPACK. *Handbook of Technological Pedagogical Content Knowledge (TPACK) for Educators* (p. 33), New York, NY: Routledge.

Wu, Y.-T. (2013). Research trends in technological pedagogical content knowledge (TPACK) research: A review of empirical studies published in selected journals from 2002 to 2011. *British Journal of Educational Technology, 44*(3), E73–E76.

Yeh, Y.-F., Hsu, Y.-S., Wu, H.-K., Hwang, F.-K., & Lin, T.-C. (2013). Developing and validating technological pedagogical content knowledge-practical (TPACK-practical) through the Delphi survey technique. *British Journal of Educational Technology, 45*(4), 707–722.

Young, J. R., Young, J. L., & Hamilton, C. (2013). The use of confidence intervals as a meta-analytic lens to summarize the effects of teacher education technology courses on preservice teacher TPACK. *Journal of Research on Technology in Education, 46*(2), 149–172.

Yurdakul, I. K., Odabasi, H. F., Kilicer, K., Coklar, A. N., Birinci, G., & Kurt, A. A. (2012). The development, validity and reliability of TPACK-deep: A technological pedagogical content knowledge scale. *Computers & Education, 58*(3), 964–977.

Zelkowski, J., Gleason, J., Cox, D. C., & Bismarck, S. (2013). Developing and validating a reliable TPACK instrument for secondary mathematics preservice teachers. *Journal of Research on Technology in Education, 46*(2), 173–206.

3 Pedagogy and Technology-Enhanced Learning

ABSTRACT

This chapter critically examines the implications of different pedagogical perspectives, approaches, and strategies for the design and implementation of technology-enhanced learning. The key tenets of different pedagogical perspectives are unpacked, including behaviorism, cognitivism, constructivism, socio-constructivism, and connectivism, with reference to how technology can be used to instantiate them. A range of different pedagogical approaches, including collaborative learning, problem-based learning, inquiry-based learning, constructionist learning, design-based learning, and games-based learning are discussed in relation to the use of technology and the previously identified pedagogical perspectives. Pedagogical strategies at a more instantaneous level are also considered, as are the goals of technology-enhanced learning in terms of promoting authentic and meaningful learning. The critical role of the teacher when applying pedagogies using technology, as well as associated issues, are discussed throughout.

Pedagogy and Its Various Meanings

When the term 'pedagogy' is literally translated from its Greek origins (*paidagōgeō*) it means "to lead the child," though contemporary use of the term no longer carries exclusive connotations to children (Beetham & Sharpe, 2013). It has been defined variously as "the method and practice of teaching" (*Oxford Dictionary*) and "the art, science or profession of teaching" (*Merriam Webster Dictionary*). Thus, we can see that the term "pedagogy" can have various connotations, from instrumentalist to creative to scientific, but in all cases it refers to teaching practice.

Pedagogy can operate at different levels (Goodyear, 2005). Pedagogy can relate to broad epistemological perspectives relating to how knowledge is acquired, to approaches that are used to structure learning tasks or modules, or to instantaneous classroom teaching strategies. For example, one might assert that "I adopt constructivist pedagogies in all of my classes" (indicates broad teaching perspective regarding how knowledge is effectively generated), or that "I used problem-based learning tasks for students to understand the laws of motion" (teaching approach) or "I deconstructed the process into distinct steps in order for students to understand how to complete it" (a teaching strategy used for a particular learning activity).

There is often contention as to whether each of the broad pedagogical positions constitutes 'theory' of how learning occurs or an overarching teaching paradigm, thus the word 'perspective' will be used to refer to each (even though some of them such as behaviorism, cognitivism, and social constructivism are quite deeply theorized). It should also be noted that the boundaries between the perspectives are often blurred. Placing these issues aside and focusing on core characteristics, the descriptions below aim to provide a brief overview of the most renowned pedagogical perspectives.

Pedagogical Perspectives

BEHAVIORISM

Behaviorism is based on the idea that learning is an observable change in behavior that is brought about by learner responses to stimulus from the environment. A stimulus might be a prompt from a teacher (such as 'what is the capital of France?') and the learner provides their response in word, symbol, or action (for instance, by writing 'Paris'). Behaviorists assert that when a stimulus-response pair is reinforced by rewarding positive behavior (for instance, through affirmation) and providing negative reinforcement (such as corrections) in the absence of the desired behavior, the learner is conditioned to produce the appropriate response.

Behaviorism is founded on the work of B. F. Skinner who in the 1930s reasoned that since there was no way to observe internal thinking processes (at the time), teaching should focus solely on external behaviors. In a series of experiments, Skinner was able to teach animals to perform elaborate sequences of operations by providing appropriate feedback, and proposed that human learning could be optimized by applying the same principles. See Skinner (1974) for an overview of behaviorism.

Three assumptions underpin behaviorism:

1. A focus on observable behavior rather than the internal thought processes that occur
2. The environment shapes behavior and thus determines what is learnt
3. Timing of instructional events and practice are central to explaining learning processes. (McLeod, 2003)

From a behaviorist perspective, instruction should take the form of stimulus (teacher questions) and responses (student answers), with immediate feedback to reinforce desired responses. Thus the teacher's role becomes one of determining what is to be learnt, presenting appropriate stimulus for students to encourage certain behaviors, and then reinforcing appropriate behaviors (through rewards or negative reinforcers for incorrect responses).

One strength of behaviorism is that it maintains a clear focus on achieving precisely defined learning outcomes (McLeod, 2003). However, it also places students in a role of passive recipients of learning where they are externally motivated by stimuli and consequences in order to learn (McLeod, 2003). It takes no account of learners' inner thinking processes (Hung, 2001).

Behaviorism is often associated with a transmission-based model of education (Richardson, 1996), where students are considered empty vessels and teachers pour information into them. Influential scholars have recently reignited the 'direct instruction' mantle by claiming that less structured approaches to learning result in inferior learning outcomes for any given task (Kirschner, Sweller, & Clark, 2006). Other educators criticize this claim arguing that a longer term view needs to be adopted that focuses on developing students' underlying ability to learn more independently (for instance, see Kuhn, 2007).

Typical behavioral uses of technology include the use of multiple choice questions and flashcards. For instance, Quizlet (http://quizlet.com) enables teachers to make their own quizzes in a variety of forms such as flashcards, guessing games, races, as well as standard quizzes, using a behaviorist approach to providing feedback in order to promote learning (see Figure 3.1).

From the behaviorist perspective, technology becomes a means for the teacher to provide the to-be-learnt content and offer somewhat automated assessment. This can be useful to help students remember key facts and demonstrate their understanding, but learning is teacher-directed and the extent to which students can engage in authentic, constructive, or creative thinking is limited. However, using the same quizzing engines students could be asked to create questions for their own practice or for that of their peers, thus shifting from a behaviorist pedagogy to learning that involves higher levels of production and creativity. Accordingly, pedagogy is by no means a fixed, inherent attribute of a learning technology but rather depends on how the technology is used within the learning context.

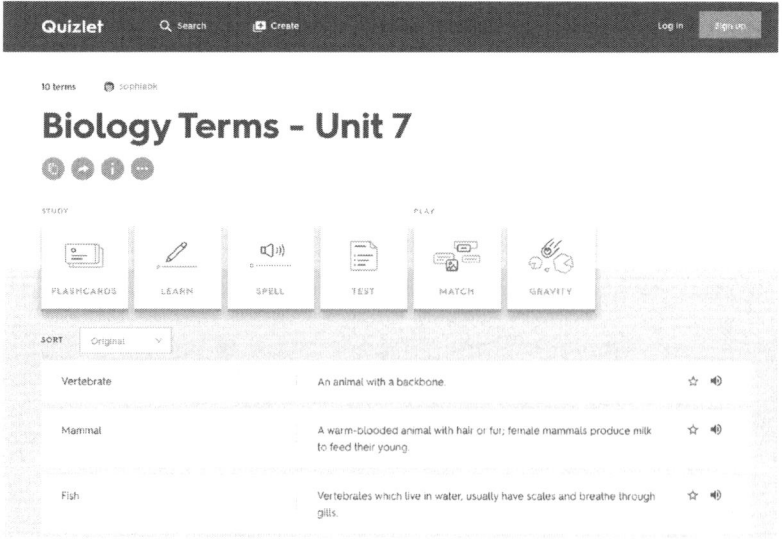

Figure 3.1. The Quizlet Website Enabling Teachers (or Students) to Create Behaviorist Quizzes in a Variety of Formats.

COGNITIVISM

According to cognitivism, learning is an *internal* mental process of forming and reorganizing knowledge structures (or 'schema') to form understanding (McLeod, 2003). The cognitivist perspective is based upon what we know about how cognition occurs, including how elements such as sensory perception, executive control, working memory, and long term memory work together when we learn (Cooper, 1993). Cognitivists adopt an 'information processing' view of learning, whereby understanding occurs by receiving, storing, and retrieving information (McLeod, 2003).

Cognitivism arose as a result of a growing understanding of how learning was influenced by the way brains function, including cognitive load, processing of multimedia, and the like (Mayer, 2005). Historically cognitive research has resulted in many findings that are directly relevant to instruction. For instance, information generally only stays in working memory for around 30 seconds and will be lost if not used or committed to long term memory (Peterson & Peterson, 1959). Others have shown that only a small number of items can be stored in working memory at any one time, usually around seven (Miller, 1956). Consequently, cognitivism has allowed educators to utilize an understanding of how the brain works when designing lessons and instruction.

While the exact cognitive processes underpinning learning are dependent on the individual and learning task at hand, neuroscientists and cognitive psychologists have identified the following key processes:

1. *Attention* – auditory stimuli (for example, verbal instructions) and visual stimuli (for instance, images or text) are used to engage learners' vigilance network (Byrnes, 2001)
2. *Selection* – learners select pertinent elements from the vast amounts of sensory information being processed by the brain and holds them in working memory for further processing (Sylwester, 1995)
3. *Retrieval* – students retrieve relevant records from permanent (long term) memory to assist in the interpretation of the sensory information they have received (Byrnes, 2001)
4. *Comprehension* – the external information (words, images, sounds) is processed using the schema retrieved from permanent memory to create a 'situational model' (Seidenberg & McClelland, 1989)

5. *Synthesis* – assimilation of new information within the existing declarative, procedural, and conceptual knowledge structures to form efficient, context-sensitive schema (Byrnes, 2001)
6. *Memorization* – storing details of the learning episode in long term memory, which will include both foreground and background elements of the experience (Sylwester, 1995)
7. *Abstraction* – transformation of the episodic aspects of the experience into semantic and conceptual forms, the context free nature of which supports transfer to future problem-solving scenarios (Sylwester, 1995).

This complex trail of brain activity has informed several instructional models within education, such as Gagné's Conditions of Learning framework (Gagné, 1985) and subsequent refinements (Clark & Lyons, 2004; Clark, 2003). With the emergence of cognitivism, the process of 'metacognition' (understanding of one's own thinking) became another important way to improve learning performance (Yilmaz, 2011).

Thus, from a cognitivist perspective, the role of the teacher is to provide instructional 'episodes' that support the different cognitive processes required for learning. As part of this, educators are responsible for considering the prior learning, characteristics, and needs of the learner, and how these may impact on the cognitive processing of information (McLeod, 2003). Cognitivism constitutes an advance on behaviorism by relating learning more to the learner and their existing cognitive structures rather than presenting information that may be somewhat unlinked to their prior understanding (McLeod, 2003). Cognitivism also takes advantage of what is known about how the mind works. However, a cognitivist approach still maintains a narrow focus on specific outcomes of learning (McLeod, 2003) and struggles to address learning of more complex knowledge forms such as tacit knowledge or argumentative knowledge. Cognitivism does not generally account for social aspects of learning – how people learn from and with one another.

From a technological point of view, applying a cognitivist approach means designing and using technology in a way that accounts for the information processing capabilities of the mind. For instance, Figure 3.2 shows how a web-conferencing environment can be redesigned to align with cognitivist principles in order to better account for how people select and process

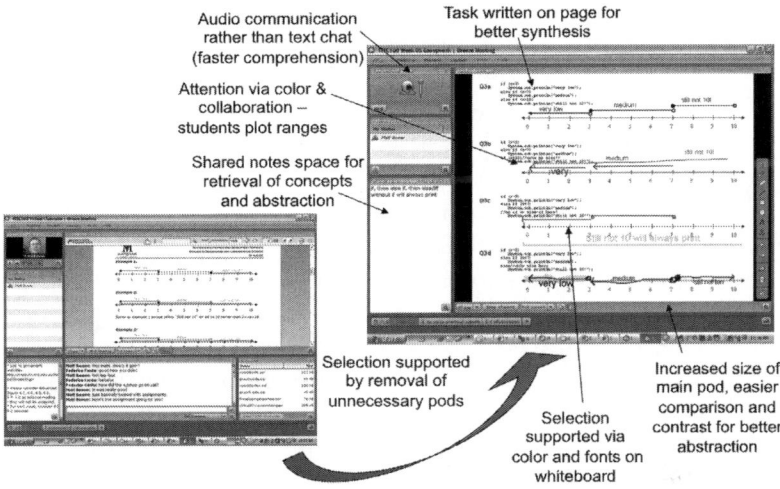

Figure 3.2.   Cognitivist Redesign of a Web-Conferencing Task.

information. The redesign aimed to promote improved attention through the use of color, selection through simplification of the interface, retrieval through a notes area, audio communication for faster comprehension, co-location of related information for synthesis, and easier comparison of related tasks for better abstraction (for elaboration see Bower, 2008). It can be seen how this sort of cognitivist design of technology-enhanced learning focuses on more instantaneous aspects of the learning episode rather than higher level issues relating to student-directed or communal learning.

Many of the principles that underpin the designing of learning tasks from a cognitivist perspective are drawn from multimedia learning principles. These are covered in some detail in the next chapter. Advances in medical imaging (for instance MRI scanning) allow increasingly more accurate observation and modeling of thinking processes, which in turn means that there are potentially many significant advances in cognitivist learning theory on the horizon.

CONSTRUCTIVISM

The fundamental principle of constructivism is that individuals actively construct understanding based on experience. Rooted in the work of Jean Piaget, constructivists assert that learning occurs through the processes of assimilation (interpreting phenomenon in terms of existing knowledge structures) and accommodation (modification of cognitive structures in order to make sense of the environment) (Piaget, 1970).

The constructivist perspective values circumstances where learners realize aspects of their mental models are inconsistent or incomplete (which Piaget referred to as a state of 'disequilibrium'), because this can provide the impetus for reconciling their misconceptions ('equilibration'). This is the process of shifting from attempting to assimilate information into existing mental models, to mental reorganization in order to accommodate new knowledge.

Constructivism can refer to a set of epistemological ('nature of knowledge') beliefs about where reality lies, a set of psychological beliefs about learning and cognition, and/or a set of educational beliefs about how to support learning (Kanselaar, 2002). Philosophically, whereas objectivist perspectives of behaviorism and cognitivism see reality as external to the knower, constructivism (particularly 'radical constructivism') views reality as personally created by the knower via their experiences (Jonassen, 1991).

Constructivism shares commonalities with cognitivism insofar as cognitive structures (schema, mental models) are used to enable the individual to go beyond the provided information, and the learner's prior knowledge is used as a starting point for designing learning tasks (McLeod, 2003). The key difference is that constructivist learning encourages processes of scientific inquiry such as selecting information, proposing hypotheses, testing, making decisions, and generalization as critical for deep learning to occur (Bruner, 1990).

Thus, from the constructivist perspective, the role of the teacher is to create the conditions for students to discover principles for themselves (Bruner, 1990). Rather than explaining everything that students should know, the teacher's role is to engage in learning conversations (for instance, 'Socratic dialog') that encourage students to fill in the gaps and go beyond the information that has been given (Caulatta, 2015). Constructivist teaching fosters learning by challenging misconceptions, encouraging student questions, and seeking their elaboration (Gilakjani, Lai-Mei, & Ismail, 2013).

By presenting knowledge from a variety of perspectives and engaging students in more active knowledge construction, constructivists propose that students can learn more deeply than when they are passive recipients of information. However, the more open-ended nature of constructivist learning relies to a large extent on the intrinsic motivation of learners (Jonassen, 1991). Also, the more open-ended nature of constructivism is intrinsically less objective than cognitivism and behaviorism, meaning that it can sometimes be more difficult to measure the extent to which learning has occurred (McLeod, 2003).

Technology often facilitates constructivist learning by providing simulations or 'virtual manipulables.' For instance, the projectile motion applet (available from http://galileoandeinstein. physics.virginia.edu/more_stuff/Applets/Projectile/projectile.html) enables learners to track the path of projected objects with different initial velocity, angle, and mass (see Figure 3.3). This can give rise to experimentation where students try to determine the angle that produces the maximum range and the impact of mass on distance travelled. Rather than being told the answers, students can perform inquiry processes to construct an understanding for themselves. When used in this way, the technology constitutes a 'mindtool' that encourages students to think deeply about phenomena and helps them to establish interrelationships (Jonassen, Howland, Marra, & Crismond, 2008).

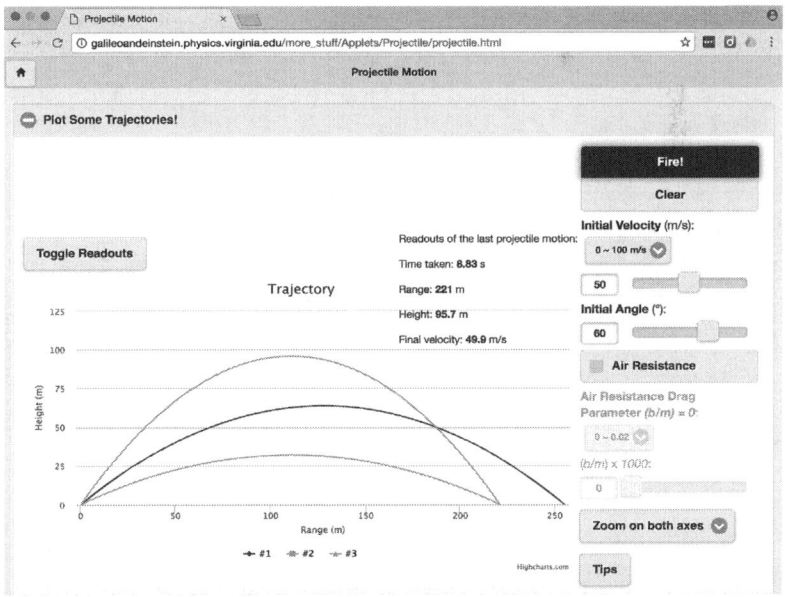

Figure 3.3. A Projectile Motion Applet from the University of Virginia That Promotes Constructivist Learning through Experimentation.

However, it is easy to imagine that without sufficient motivation or direction, students may not fully engage with the technology or have the skills to undertake fruitful inquiry. Thus, the teacher plays a critical role in generating interest and purpose, as well as monitoring and supporting constructive learning processes (for instance, in this case, helping students to isolate variables of change in order to establish causation and effects).

SOCIAL CONSTRUCTIVISM

Social constructivism extends upon classic constructivism by emphasizing the critical importance of cultural and social elements in learning. From the social constructivist perspective, knowledge is seen as a socially constructed phenomenon, and the interpretation of knowledge depends on the cultural context in which the knowledge was formed (Hung, 2001). Social constructivist learning is viewed as a social product arising through conversation, discussion, and negotiation between learners, their peers, and teachers (Woo & Reeves, 2007). Whether social constructivism is a separate learning paradigm to constructivism or a subordinate one is in many ways a moot question, and perhaps also an esoteric one. The term 'cognitive constructivism' is often used to clearly distinguish the classical Piagetian ideas of constructivism from the more interpersonally oriented social constructivist (or 'socio-cultural') perspective (Mayes & De Freitas, 2013).

At the heart of social constructivism is the concept of the 'Zone of Proximal Development' (Vygotsky, 1978). The Zone of Proximal Development is what a person does not yet know but is able to learn through interaction with a more knowledgeable peer or teacher. This aspect of social constructivism highlights the critical influence of the social context on learning, as opposed to behaviorism, cognitivism, and classic constructivism, which do not account for the role of other people in learning to the same degree.

Another core concept of social constructivism is the idea of 'scaffolding' – cognitive support provided by the teacher or constructed learning environment. The idea of 'scaffolding' is to provide a high level of support at the initial (more difficult) phases of learning and gradually remove that support as the learner grows in competence. Support can include cues, heuristics, hints, examples, and so on. It is, however, important to adopt a 'fading' approach to scaffolding over time so that students do not become reliant on the assistance being provided (Teles, 1994).

From a socio-constructivist perspective, meaning can be constructed through a range of interpersonal activities, such as "defining the task, generating ideas, sharing resources and perspectives, negotiating, synthesizing individual thoughts with those of others, completing the tasks, and refining them on the basis of further sharing of insights and critiques" (Woo & Reeves, 2007, pp. 20–21). Thus, the role of the teacher from a social constructivist perspective is to not only be part of the learner's social learning environment by responding to questions and providing intellectual guidance, but also to structure activities so that students have the opportunity to learn from and with one another. This can be accomplished by helping students to publish their work, provide constructive feedback to each another, and collaboratively reflect on what they have learnt (Woo & Reeves, 2007). From a social constructivist perspective, teachers value the learners as active co-constructors of meaning, establishing relationships with their students based on the idea of guidance rather than instruction (Adams, 2006). The teacher is also responsible for the enculturation of learners into the societal ways of thinking within different discipline areas (Woo & Reeves, 2007).

There are a number of ways technology can be used to facilitate social constructivist learning. One of the greatest examples of social constructivism in action is Wikipedia. People from all around the world combine their knowledge to produce an online encyclopedia that is far more comprehensive than any similar resource that has been produced commercially (see Figure 3.4). One often unnoticed aspect of Wikipedia is that it includes a discussion or 'talk' page where people can negotiate meaning using discussion, thus the technology mediates both the conceptual representation and the associated dialogue.

Similar social constructivist learning can take place in the classroom and other learning contexts as students use wikis to facilitate collaborative writing in schools (for instance, see Li, Chu, & Ki, 2014) and group work processes in university courses (for example, Guo & Stevens, 2011). As other examples, students can use blogs to document and collaboratively develop their illustration skills (Garcia, Elbeltagi, Brown, & Dungay, 2015), and communally share and cultivate their critical reasoning abilities (Tan, Ladyshewsky, & Gardner, 2010). Social networking can be used to facilitate discussions, offer question and answer

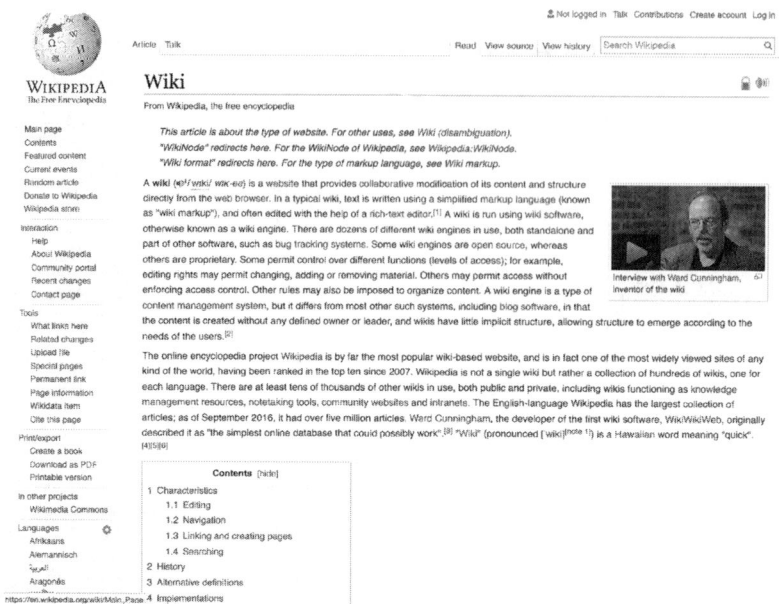

Figure 3.4. Wikipedia, an Example of Social Constructivism in Practice.

opportunities, and share resources (Buzzetto-More, 2012). The combination of an immersive environment and opportunities for collaboration make virtual worlds particularly appropriate for application of social constructivist pedagogies (Girvan & Savage, 2010). In each case, the technology provides a means of communication and production, but it is the teacher who helps to establish goals, scaffold learning processes, provide feedback, and stimulate learning conversations. Issues surrounding the use of wikis, blogs, social networking, and virtual worlds to support social constructivist learning will be discussed in Chapters 7–10.

CONNECTIVISM

In 2005, George Siemens proposed that traditional learning theories did not adequately account for the digitally networked world that we now live in, including the access to vast amounts of knowledge, the hyper-complexity of information, the nonlinear way in which learning occurs, and the distributed nature of learning between people and machines (Siemens, 2005). In response, he put forward a new epistemology of learning, 'connectivism,' based upon the following principles:

- learning and knowledge rests in diversity of opinions
- learning is a process of connecting specialized nodes or information sources
- learning may reside in nonhuman appliances
- capacity to know more is more critical than what is currently known
- nurturing and maintaining connections is needed to facilitate continual learning
- ability to see connections between fields, ideas, and concepts is a core skill
- currency (accurate, up-to-date knowledge) is the intent of all connectivist learning activities
- decision-making is itself a learning process. (verbatim from Siemens, 2005, p. 4)

Thus, according to connectivism, learning knowledge is a networked phenomenon, and in order to be effective, it is proposed that learning networks need to be decentralized, distributed, disintermediated, disaggregated, dis-integrated, democratic, dynamic, and desegregated (Downes, 2006).

From a connectivist perspective, learning can occur in an organic or 'rhizomatic' way (Cormier, 2008). For instance, in the now-infamous 'Connectivism and Connective Knowledge' Massive Open Online Course (MOOC) run by Stephen Downes and George Siemens in 2008 (CCK08), learning was spread across a network of wikis, blogs, forums, social networks, aggregators, social bookmarking systems, and other Web 2.0 sites, most of which was initiated and developed by learners and took place outside the official course website (Downes, 2008). Figure 3.5 shows a map of how knowledge was developed in the CCK08 MOOC.

It should be noted that while there has been considerable publicity about MOOCs and their potential to revolutionize education, not all MOOCs are so organic and connectivist in nature. The distinction is drawn between more traditional MOOCs or 'xMOOC's which are more structured, teacher driven, mastery oriented, and formally assessed, and connectivist MOOCs or 'cMOOC's which are more organic, student driven, divergently productive, and alternatively assessed (Siemens, 2012).

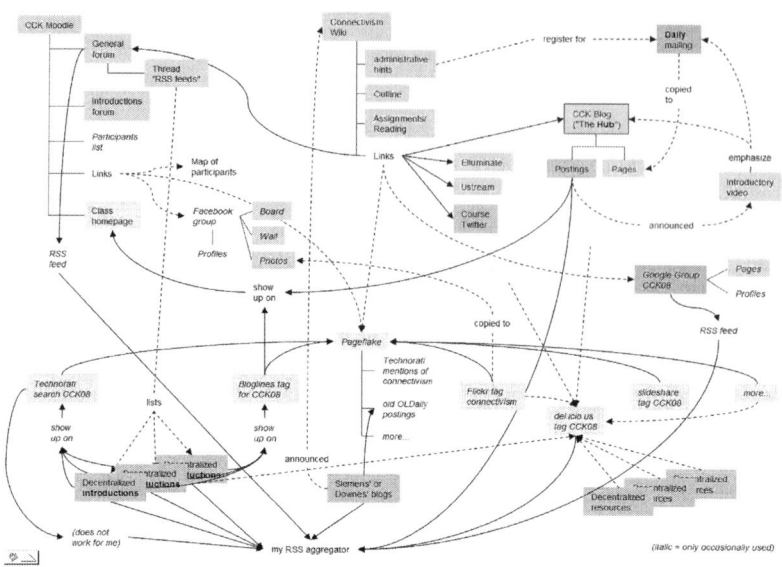

Figure 3.5. Map of How Knowledge Was Developed in the CCK08 MOOC, Courtesy of Matthias Melcher CC-BY-SA (https://www.flickr.com/photos/37794987@N00/2843707657).

Many educators are reluctant to acknowledge connectivism as a new educational 'theory.' For instance, Kop and Hill (2008) contend that while a connectivist view is useful to develop pedagogies within a milieu of rapidly evolving networked technologies, it does not constitute a new learning theory as distinct from ones that have preceded it. In line with claims about the nature of theory proposed by P. Miller (1993), Kop and Hill (2008) argue that a theory should either be validated by empirical research or describe changes in relationships within one or more areas of behavior, and connectivism does not satisfactorily fulfill these criteria. Bell (2010) sees connectivism more as a phenomenon that can be a useful referent for analyzing some technology-enhanced learning settings.

Proponents of connectivism argue that a connectivist view more closely aligns with how people learn in today's networked world. Connectivist pedagogies are seen to help people develop the digital and critical literacies that are required to survive and thrive in a world where almost everyone publishes information on the World Wide Web (Downes, 2006; Siemens, 2005).

Educators should also be mindful of pedagogical issues that stem from learning and teaching using a connectivist paradigm.

Developing students' sense of presence, their self-directed learning techniques and their critical literacies to process the unstructured information can all be challenges to learning (Kop, 2011). While many students in connectivist learning environments may be actively engaged, others may prefer to lurk or be frustrated by the less structured approach to learning (Milligan, Littlejohn, & Margaryan, 2013). The degree of participation and contribution in connectivist learning environments may be influenced by students' underlying confidence, experience, and motivation (Milligan et al., 2013).

From the connectivist perspective, the teacher's role becomes one of setting goals, motivating learners, communicating requirements, facilitating connection, and helping to organize people and information, often using technology. It may be necessary for teachers to monitor and counteract passive participation by providing active guidance and encouragement, if appropriate for the circumstances. This may involve supporting stages of awareness and receptivity, connection forming and selection filtering, contribution and involvement, and reflection and metacognition (Pettenati & Cigognini, 2007). Addressing critical literacies including evaluation of sources and safe use of the Internet becomes an imperative because in connectivist learning environments learners are necessarily engaging with the outside world.

Despite the various criticisms and issues, there is no doubt that connectivism has struck a chord with many contemporary educators by explaining the change in learning context brought about by digital technologies, and thus it is likely to grow in terms of prevalence and investigation.

Other Pedagogical Approaches

While behaviorism, cognitivism, constructivism, socio-constructivism, and connectivism constitute broad epistemological positions on how learning and knowledge formation occurs in technology-enhanced environments, there are many other learning theories and pedagogical approaches at the educator's disposal (some of which fall within the previously discussed perspectives). Collaborative learning, problem-based learning, inquiry-based learning, constructionist learning, design-based learning, and games-based learning as they relate to technology are briefly outlined below in order to provide a grounding for future discussions and analysis.

COLLABORATIVE LEARNING

Collaborative learning describes a situation in which certain types of interpersonal interactions are expected to lead to learning (Dillenbourg, 1999). The role of the teacher becomes one of setting up initial conditions such as the number and constituency of groups, to specify the learning scenario and roles, to encourage productive interaction through rules and tools, and to monitor and regulate interactions (Dillenbourg, 1999). Computer supported collaborative learning (CSCL) is where technology is used to facilitate collaborative learning, and has become a major area of study in its own right (Naidu & Järvelä, 2006). Collaborative learning can be facilitated using discussion forums, web-conferencing systems, virtual worlds, and potentially any other technology that enables multi-user access and contribution. However, the extent to which learning occurs is very much dependent on the ability of the teacher to establish and manage an effective learning environment (Naidu & Järvelä, 2006). Collaborative learning is by definition social constructivist in nature.

PROBLEM-BASED LEARNING

Problem-based learning approaches use open ended, authentic, and substantial problems to drive learning (Savery, 2006). They incorporate explicit teaching and assessment of generic and metacognitive skills in order to help students abstract their understanding. Learning activities center around collaborative learning in groups, thus aligning very much with the social constructivist perspective. For example, students may be presented with an authentic problem (for instance, creating a supermarket checkout queue simulator) that is used both as a driving force to develop metacognitive skills (for instance, reflection upon steps taken to solve the problem and delegation of time) and for the subject of group work (externalizing knowledge, developing collaborative skills) (see Kay et al., 2000). In contemporary educational settings the role of technology often becomes one of structuring and facilitating collaboration, as well as modeling phenomena and providing a means to conduct research.

INQUIRY-BASED LEARNING

Inquiry-based learning focuses on students asking questions and pursuing lines of investigation to form an understanding of concepts and principles (Edelson, Gordin, & Pea, 1999).

Inquiry-based learning is similar to problem-based learning insofar as it is student-centered rather than teacher-directed, and both approaches have elements of inquiry and problem solving in them. However inquiry-based learning is underpinned by scientific processes such as observation of phenomena, formulation and testing of hypotheses, and generalization of results (Savery, 2006), whereas problem-based learning addresses more interdisciplinary and ill-structured problems. For instance, a student may form an understanding of gravity using an inquiry-based learning approach by using a stop-watch to measure the displacement of different falling objects. Technology can be used to facilitate inquiry learning by helping to capture data, simulate phenomena, analyze data, and present findings (Edelson et al., 1999).

CONSTRUCTIONIST LEARNING

Constructionism is based on the idea that students learn best when they produce an artifact. It emphasizes that there is not necessarily a 'right' answer, and through productive learning experiences along somewhat individualized lines of investigation people can construct their understanding in a way that accords with their intellectual style (Papert & Harel, 1991). The construction should relate to a personally meaningful product in order to achieve maximal educational benefit (Willis & Tucker, 2001). Technology is often the medium for the productive experience, for instance, by creating robots or writing computer programs. The more self-directed and potentially less structured nature of constructionist learning environments can lead to widely varying student engagement and achievement, especially in younger learners who may lack motivation (Bruckman, Edwards, Elliott, & Jensen, 2013). The role of the teacher becomes one of setting up a learning environment where inventive processes are valued, as well as supporting learners who may not be comfortable with more open-ended learning contexts. Constructionism aligns with broadly constructivist views of learning.

DESIGN-BASED LEARNING

Design-based learning shares a great deal in common with constructionist learning, but tends to focus more on scaffolding design processes and broadens out the idea of what might be developed (for instance, the aim might be to create a social solution rather than build a physical one). Some studies have reported improved student learning outcomes and an increased desire to pursue careers in the domain of practice as a result of design-based learning approaches (Apedoe, Reynolds, Ellefson, & Schunn, 2008; Doppelt, Mehalik, Schunn, Silk, & Krysinski, 2008; Zahn, Pea, Hesse, & Rosen, 2010). There are several mechanisms that are espoused to underpin the positive effects of design-based learning, including drawing on students' prior knowledge, promotion of intellectual quality (through discussing, problem solving, theorizing, and drawing conclusions), and achieving deeper understanding through increased student agency (van Haren, 2010). Technology can be used to facilitate reflection, discussion, and creation of artifacts (by, for instance, using multimedia design tools). In order to facilitate successful 'learning by design' teachers need to have deep knowledge of the topic area, the capacity to foster a collaborative production-house learning environment, and the ability to facilitate a shift in student learning from experiential to more conceptual and analytic forms (Neville, 2010).

GAMES-BASED LEARNING

Games provide motivation for students to learn by doing (Squire, 2006). Digital and networking technologies mean that games can be both distributed and intensely social (Squire, 2006). Noneducational games such as *SimCity* can be used for educational purposes, or content can be reconceptualized as challenges, goals, and practices in a game context (Squire, 2006). Good games encourage students to create and encourage interaction, production, risk taking, customization, agency, incremental development, challenge, practice, lateral thinking, reflection, collaboration, and context-sensitive as well as lateral thinking (Gee, 2005). Apart from the plethora of commercial mathematics, English, and other discipline-specific games, 'serious games' designed to help students develop authentic life skills can also enhance students' 21st-century digital literacies (Ott, Popescu, Stănescu, & de Freitas, 2013). The role of the teacher becomes one of helping students to identify beneficial games, create links to topics of study, develop cyber-safe gaming practices, and generally create an environment that encourages productive use of digital games. Games-based learning can be behaviorist, cognitivist, constructivist, social constructivist, or connectivist in nature, depending on the design of the tasks. Placing students in the role of designers of games is a way to foster their creativity

(Prensky, 2008), and there are a number of three-dimensional simulated environments such as *Second Life*, *Open Sim*, *Minecraft*, and *Kodu* that can be used to facilitate this.

Summary of Pedagogical Perspectives and Approaches

Analyzing the pedagogical perspectives and approaches above reveals the following key dimensions of variation:

1. View of learning − external (Ext) or internal (Int)
2. Definer of the task − student (Stu) or teacher (Tea)
3. Structure of problem − ill-defined (Ill) or well-defined (Well)
4. Director of activity − student (Stu) or teacher (Tea)
5. Degree of interpersonal interaction − individual (Ind) or social (Soc)
6. Extent to which a product is output − none (None) or product (Prod).

In reality, the attributes of the pedagogies are not binary, but rather fall on a spectrum along each dimension. Table 3.1 summarizes the attributes of the different pedagogical perspectives and approaches for each of the six dimensions.

The description of the pedagogies is presented in accordance with (Conole, Dyke, Oliver, & Seale, 2004) but using different dimensions and pedagogies. The ratings are, by necessity, coarse generalizations and there may be quite a variety of possibilities along each polarity for each pedagogy, depending on how the teacher and students engage in the task. It is important to note that the pedagogical perspectives and approaches cannot be neatly reduced to the attributes above, and educators should understand the nuances of each in order to apply them appropriately. However, a broad understanding the attributes of the pedagogies as outlined in Table 3.1 is useful in terms of technology-enhanced learning, because it may relate to the sort of technology that is suitable. For instance, if the task structure is well-defined, then technologies that provide more structure may be preferable. If the activity is to be completed socially rather than individually, then technologies with communication capabilities will most likely be required. If students are to produce a final product, then a technology that enables creative output will often be needed.

Table 3.1.   Attributes of Different Pedagogical Perspectives and Approaches.

	Learning seen as: Ext – Int	Task definer: Stu – Tea	Problem structure: Ill – Well	Activity director: Stu – Tea	Interpersonal interaction: Ind – Soc	Product output: None – Prod
Behaviorism	X----------	----------X	----------X	--------X--	--X--------	-X---------
Cognitivism	---------X-	---------X-	---------X-	--------X--	--X--------	--X--------
Constructivism	--------X--	--------X--	--------X--	----X------	----X------	----X------
Social constructivism	-----X-----	--------X--	-------X---	----X------	---------X-	-----X-----
Connectivism	-X---------	--X--------	--X--------	--X--------	---------X--	-----X-----
Collaborative learning	-----X-----	--------X--	-------X---	---X-------	---------X-	-----X-----
Problem-based learning	------X----	--------X--	-------X---	---X-------	---------X-	---X-------
Inquiry-based learning	-------X---	---X-------	--X--------	--X--------	-------X---	--X--------
Constructionist learning	-------X---	------X----	--X--------	--X--------	-------X---	----------X
Design-based learning	-------X---	------X----	--X--------	--X--------	-------X---	----------X
Games based learning	--------X--	---------X-	---------X-	--X--------	----X-----	-X---------

Pedagogical Strategies to Promote Learning

All of the aforementioned pedagogical perspectives and approaches can be used to help orient and structure learning modules and tasks. Yet at a micro-level there are a variety of pedagogy-in-action strategies that teachers can and should adopt in order to support student learning. These cannot be generally prescribed in advance because they are necessarily contingent on the learning context, which includes fixed factors (for instance, the curriculum, available resources) but also variable factors such as student prerequisite knowledge, motivation, expectations, as well as unforeseen environmental factors.

Based on a comprehensive review of educational research, Laurillard (2012) argues that in order to facilitate successful learning, teachers need to (a) align goals, activities, and assessment, (b) monitor alternative conceptions, (c) scaffold theory-based practice, (d) foster conceptual knowledge development, and (e) encourage metacognition. Approaches for effectively achieving each of these teaching principles are outlined in Table 3.2.

There are hundreds of other specific and often more behaviorally oriented strategies available that educators can employ

Table 3.2.   Strategies for Effective Teaching.

Principles	Guidelines for Teacher's Roles and Actions
Align goals, activities, assessment	• Draw on learners' experiences to align their goals with the teacher's • Use assessments that tap understanding, not facts or isolated skills • Test deep conceptual understanding rather than surface knowledge
Monitor alternative conceptions	• Actively inquire into students' thinking • Ask about internal relations within the structure • Recognize students' preconceptions that make the topic challenging • Draw out the preconceptions that may not be predictable • Use formative assessment to make students' thinking visible to themselves, their peers, and their teacher
Scaffold theory-based practice	• Simplify the task, so that the learner can manage components of the process and recognize when a fit with task requirements is achieved • Provide feedback and modeling that can guide modification of actions and the concepts that generated them • Design exercises within the learner's zone of proximal development • Design exercises that provide the meaningful intrinsic feedback that learners are able to interpret and use to revise their actions • Create tasks and conditions that reveal student thinking • Give learners the means to build an external representation of their knowledge to share with others
Foster conceptual knowledge development	• Use examples to help students discern the concept in focus from the similarities and contrasts between instances • Analyze the architecture of variation that reveals conceptual structure • Develop a "discursive microworld" for conceptual learning • Work with preconceptions so students challenge and replace them
Encourage metacognition	• Encourage students to practice and discuss metacognitive strategies • Model the use of metacognitive strategies • Encourage students to practice and discuss these strategies • Engage students in grading their own and their peers' performance • Encourage group discussion of both content and learning processes • Show students have different conceptualizations • Compare descriptions and highlight differences and inconsistencies

Source: From Laurillard (2012, p. 79).

when using technology to facilitate learning. As our focus is on design and it is not possible to write about the specific details of every different context, the list presented in Table 3.2 serves as an empirically grounded and comprehensive set of pedagogical strategies to act as a reference point for technology-enhanced learning design throughout this book.

Reflecting on the Aims of Pedagogy

Several different pedagogical perspectives, approaches, and strategies have been outlined above, but a higher-level question for educators to ask themselves is, 'what type of learning would I like my students to achieve?' Answering this question may influence the pedagogies and technologies we use. Two well-regarded aspirations for our classes are meaningful learning and authentic learning.

MEANINGFUL LEARNING

Meaningful learning is described as an active, constructive, intentional, authentic, and cooperative educational process (Jonassen et al., 2008). Active learning results from manipulating the environment and observing the effects. Constructive learning encompasses reflecting on experience and articulating the results. Intentional learning is a consequence of setting goals and regulating behavior to achieve those goals. Cooperation in educational settings involves conversing with others and collaborating to achieve aligned endeavors. Authentic learning is said to result from complex tasks that have real-world contextual relevance (Jonassen et al., 2008). The interrelated attributes of meaningful learning are shown in Figure 3.6.

Meaningful learning attempts to shift students beyond merely remembering knowledge to making sense of what they have learnt so that they can apply it in other contexts (Mayer, 2002). Jonassen (2007) proposes that the most meaningful learning occurs through problem solving, for instance, through decision-making problems, diagnosis problems, policy analysis problems, planning problems, and design problems. Problem solving derives its meaning from its authenticity, its purposefulness, its contextuality, and the depth of learning that occurs (Jonassen, 2007). Design tasks are among the most complex and ill-structured problem-solving tasks (Jonassen et al., 2008). Technology can facilitate meaningful learning by supporting investigation, experimentation, documentation,

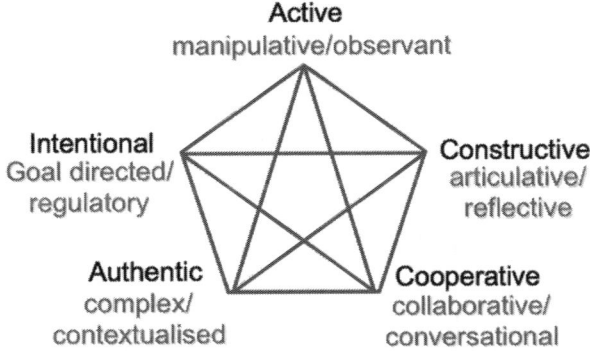

Figure 3.6.   Attributes of Meaningful Learning (Jonassen et al., 2008).

modeling, community building, communication, design, and visualization processes (Jonassen et al., 2008).

AUTHENTIC LEARNING

Authentic learning is based on research and development that occurred in higher education, but is relevant to learning at all levels. The 10 features that define authentic learning are (1) authentic context, (2) authentic activities, (3) expert performance, (4) multiple roles and perspectives, (5) reflection, (6) collaboration, (7) articulation, (8) coaching and scaffolding, (9) integrated authentic assessment, and (10) professional learning (Herrington & Kervin, 2007). Herrington and Oliver (2000) suggest that design guidelines for authentic learning environments that integrate learning with context appear to help create environments that supported the acquisition of advanced knowledge.

Technology can be used to enable authentic learning. The emergence of communication, visualization, and simulation technologies via the Internet offers students the opportunity for experimentation and real-world problem solving (Lombardi, 2007). Herrington, Reeves, and Oliver (2007) argue that visual realism is less important than facilitating realistic problem-solving processes (i.e., 'cognitive realism') when it comes to promoting authentic learning in digital environments.

Concluding Remarks

Which pedagogical perspectives, approaches, and strategies should educators choose? Some teachers decide to frame all of their learning designs using one pedagogy, arguing that it is more appropriate or effective in terms of achieving their desired learning outcomes. A potentially more balanced and synergistic tact is to adopt a multi-paradigmatic approach. This may mean drawing upon the appropriate pedagogy depending on the particular learning activities at stake (for instance, behaviorist pedagogies for learning factual knowledge versus more constructivist pedagogies for learning scientific concepts). It may also mean integrating pertinent elements of different pedagogical perspectives for a particular learning activity (for instance, adopting cognitivist pedagogies to developing multimedia instructional resources but social constructivist pedagogies to having students reflect upon and evaluate the content). Some educators and researchers recommend this more multi-theoretic and context-sensitive approach (Hung, 2001; Sherry, 1998). Meta-analyses reveal that the use of technology is more effective when a variety of teaching strategies are used (Hattie, 2008).

In any case, the many pedagogical perspectives offer referents with which educators and researchers can reflect upon practice. Do teachers use purely behaviorist pedagogies, or solely constructivist pedagogies, or exclusively constructionist pedagogies, without ever intending to do so? If so, it may prompt us to think through why the same pedagogies are always being used, and whether it might be possible to expand the repertoire of pedagogies in order to better cater to student learning needs and add variety to the curriculum.

The critical point is that the sort of pedagogy adopted will influence the type of technology that is needed — for instance, drill and practice tools for behaviorist pedagogies, online tutorials for cognitivist pedagogies, simulation tools for constructivist pedagogies, and communication tools for social constructivist pedagogies (Hung, 2001). The next chapter examines in detail how to think about the various potentials of technologies for learning and the subsequent implications for designing lessons.

References

Adams, P. (2006). Exploring social constructivism: Theories and practicalities. *Education*, *34*(3), 243–257.

Apedoe, X. S., Reynolds, B., Ellefson, M. R., & Schunn, C. D. (2008). Bringing engineering design into high school science classrooms: The heating/cooling unit. *Journal of Science Education and Technology*, *17*(5), 454–465.

Beetham, H., & Sharpe, R. (2013). An introduction to rethinking pedagogy. In H. Beetham & R. Sharpe (Eds.), *Rethinking pedagogy for a digital age – Designing for 21st century learning* (pp. 1–15). New York, NY: Routledge.

Bell, F. (2010). Connectivism: Its place in theory-informed research and innovation in technology-enabled learning. *The International Review of Research in Open and Distance Learning, 12*(3), 98−118.

Bower, M. (2008). *Designing for interactive and collaborative learning in a web-conferencing environment.* PhD thesis. Retrieved from http://hdl.handle.net/1959.14/26888

Bruckman, A., Edwards, E., Elliott, J., & Jensen, C. (2013). Uneven achievement in a constructionist learning environment. Paper presented at the International Conference of the Learning Sciences: Facing the Challenges of Complex Real-World Settings.

Bruner, J. (1990). *Acts of meaning.* Cambridge, MA: Harvard University Press.

Buzzetto-More, N. A. (2012). Social networking in undergraduate education. *Interdisciplinary Journal of Information, Knowledge, and Management, 7*(1), 63−90.

Byrnes, J. P. (2001). *Minds, brains and learning.* New York, NY: The Guilford Press.

Caulatta, R. (2015). Constructivist theory (J. Bruner). Retrieved from http://www.instructionaldesign.org/theories/constructivist.html. Accessed on 28 February, 2017.

Clark, R. C. (2003). *Building expertise.* Silver Spring, MD: International Society for Performance Improvement.

Clark, R. C., & Lyons, C. (2004). *Graphics for learning.* San Francisco, CA: Pfeiffer.

Conole, G., Dyke, M., Oliver, M., & Seale, J. (2004). Mapping pedagogy and tools for effective learning design. *Computers & Education, 43*(1−2), 17−33.

Cooper, P. A. (1993). Paradigm shifts in designed instruction: From behaviorism to cognitivism to constructivism. *Educational Technology, 33*(5), 12−19.

Cormier, D. (2008). Rhizomatic education: Community as curriculum. *Innovate: Journal of Online Education, 4*(5), n5.

Dillenbourg, P. (1999). What do you mean by collaborative learning? *Collaborative-Learning: Cognitive and Computational Approaches,* 1−19.

Doppelt, Y., Mehalik, M. M., Schunn, C. D., Silk, E., & Krysinski, D. (2008). Engagement and achievements: A case study of design-based learning in a science context. *Journal of Technology Education, 19*(2), 22−39.

Downes, S. (2006). *Learning networks and connective knowledge.*

Downes, S. (2008). Places to go: Connectivism & connective knowledge. *Innovate: Journal of Online Education, 5*(1).

Edelson, D. C., Gordin, D. N., & Pea, R. D. (1999). Addressing the challenges of inquiry-based learning through technology and curriculum design. *Journal of the Learning Sciences, 8*(3−4), 391−450.

Gagné, R. (1985). *The conditions of learning* (4th ed.). New York, NY: Holt, Rinehart & Winston.

Garcia, E., Elbeltagi, I., Brown, M., & Dungay, K. (2015). The implications of a connectivist learning blog model and the changing role of teaching and learning. *British Journal of Educational Technology, 46*(4), 877−894.

Gee, J. P. (2005). Good video games and good learning. Paper presented at the Phi Kappa Phi Forum.

Gilakjani, A. P., Lai-Mei, L., & Ismail, H. N. (2013). Teachers' use of technology and constructivism. *International Journal of Modern Education and Computer Science*, *5*(4), 49–63.

Girvan, C., & Savage, T. (2010). Identifying an appropriate pedagogy for virtual worlds: A communal constructivism case study. *Computers & Education*, *55*(1), 342–349.

Goodyear, P. (2005). Educational design and networked learning: Patterns, pattern languages and design practice. *Australasian Journal of Educational Technology*, *21*(1), 82–101.

Guo, Z., & Stevens, K. J. (2011). Factors influencing perceived usefulness of wikis for group collaborative learning by first year students. *Australasian Journal of Educational Technology*, *27*(2).

Hattie, J. (2008). *Visible learning: A synthesis of over 800 meta-analyses relating to achievement*. London: Routledge.

Herrington, J., & Kervin, L. (2007). Authentic learning supported by technology: Ten suggestions and cases of integration in classrooms. *Educational Media International*, *44*(3), 219–236.

Herrington, J., & Oliver, R. (2000). An instructional design framework for authentic learning environments. *Educational Technology Research and Development*, *48*(3), 23–48.

Herrington, J., Reeves, T. C., & Oliver, R. (2007). Immersive learning technologies: Realism and online authentic learning. *Journal of Computing in Higher Education*, *19*(1), 80–99.

Hung, D. (2001). Theories of learning and computer-mediated instructional technologies. *Educational Media International*, *38*(4), 281–287.

Jonassen, D. H. (1991). Objectivism versus constructivism: Do we need a new philosophical paradigm? *Educational Technology Research and Development*, *39*(3), 5–14.

Jonassen, D. H. (2007). A taxonomy of meaningful learning. *Educational Technology*, *47*(5), 30–35.

Jonassen, D. H., Howland, J., Marra, R., & Crismond, D. (2008). *Meaningful learning with technology*. Upper Saddle River, NJ: Pearson/Merrill Prentice Hall.

Kanselaar, G. (2002). *Constructivism and socio-constructivism*. Article published on July 16, 2002. Retrieved from http://www.unhas.ac.id/hasbi/LKPP/Hasbi-KBK-SOFTSKILL-UNISTAFF-SCL/MentalModel/Constructivism-gk.pdf

Kay, J., Barg, M., Fekete, A., Greening, T., Hollands, O., Kingston, J. H., & Crawford, K. (2000). Problem-based learning for foundation computer science courses. *Computer Science Education*, *10*(2), 109–128.

Kirschner, P. A., Sweller, J., & Clark, R. E. (2006). Why minimal guidance during instruction does not work: An analysis of the failure of constructivist, discovery, problem-based, experiential, and inquiry-based teaching. *Educational Psychologist*, *41*(2), 75–86.

Kop, R. (2011). The challenges to connectivist learning on open online networks: Learning experiences during a massive open online course. *The International Review of Research in Open and Distance Learning*, 12(3), 19–38.

Kop, R., & Hill, A. (2008). Connectivism: Learning theory of the future or vestige of the past? *The International Review of Research in Open and Distance Learning*, 9(3).

Kuhn, D. (2007). Is direct instruction an answer to the right question? *Educational Psychologist*, 42(2), 109–113.

Laurillard, D. (2012). *Teaching as a design science — Building pedagogical patterns for learning and technology*. New York, NY: Routledge.

Li, X., Chu, S. K. W., & Ki, W. W. (2014). The effects of a wiki-based collaborative process writing pedagogy on writing ability and attitudes among upper primary school students in Mainland China. *Computers & Education*, 77, 151–169.

Lombardi, M. M. (2007). Authentic learning for the 21st century: An overview. *Educause Learning Initiative*, 1(2007), 1–12.

Mayer, R. E. (2002). Rote versus meaningful learning. *Theory into Practice*, 41(4), 226–232.

Mayer, R. E. (2005). Introduction to multimedia learning. In R. E. Mayer (Ed.), *The Cambridge handbook of multimedia learning* (pp. 1–17). New York, NY: Cambridge University Press.

Mayes, T., & De Freitas, S. (2013). Technology-enhanced learning — The role of theory. In H. Beetham & R. Sharpe (Eds.), *Rethinking pedagogy for a digital age — Designing for 21st century learning* (pp. 17–30). New York, NY: Routledge.

McLeod, G. (2003). Learning theory and instructional design. *Learning Matters*, 2(2003), 35–43.

Miller, G. A. (1956). The magical number seven, plus or minus two: Some limits on our capacity for processing information. *Psychological Review*, 63, 81–97.

Miller, P. (1993). *Theories of developmental psychology*. (3rd ed.). New York, NY: W. H. Freeman.

Milligan, C., Littlejohn, A., & Margaryan, A. (2013). Patterns of engagement in connectivist MOOCs. *MERLOT Journal of Online Learning and Teaching*, 9(2).

Naidu, S., & Järvelä, S. (2006). Analyzing CMC content for what? *Computers & Education*, 46(1), 96–103.

Neville, M. (2010). Meaning making using new media: Learning by design case studies. *E-Learning and Digital Media*, 7(3), 237–247.

Ott, M., Popescu, M. M., Stănescu, I. A., & de Freitas, S. (2013). Game-enhanced learning: Preliminary thoughts on curriculum integration. In S. de Freitas, M. Ott, M. M. Popescu, & I. Stănescu (Eds.), *New pedagogical approaches in game enhanced learning: Curriculum integration*. Hershey, PA: IGI Global.

Papert, S., & Harel, I. (1991). Situating constructionism. *Constructionism*, 36, 1–11.

Peterson, L., & Peterson, M. J. (1959). Short-term retention of individual verbal items. *Journal of Experimental Psychology*, 58(3), 193.

Pettenati, M. C., & Cigognini, M. E. (2007). Social networking theories and tools to support connectivist learning activities. *International Journal of Web-Based Learning and Teaching Technologies (IJWLTT)*, 2(3), 42–60.

Piaget, J. (1970). *The science of education and the psychology of the child*. New York, NY: Grossman.

Prensky, M. (2008). Students as designers and creators of educational computer games: Who else? *British Journal of Educational Technology*, 39(6), 1004–1019.

Richardson, V. (1996). From behaviorism to constructivism in teacher education. *Teacher Education and Special Education*, 19(3), 263–271.

Savery, J. R. (2006). Overview of problem-based learning: Definitions and distinctions. *Interdisciplinary Journal of Problem-Based Learning*, 1(1), 3.

Seidenberg, M. S., & McClelland, J. L. (1989). A distributed, developmental model of word recognition and naming. *Psychological Review*, 96, 523–568.

Sherry, A. C. (1998). Evaluation of multimedia authoring instruction based in a behaviorist-cognitive-constructivist continuum. *International Journal of Instructional Media*, 25(2), 201–216.

Siemens, G. (2005). Connectivism: A learning theory for the digital age. *International Journal of Instructional Technology and Distance Learning*, 2(1), 3–10.

Siemens, G. (2012). MOOCs are really a platform. Retrieved from http://www.elearnspace.org/blog/2012/07/25/moocs-are-really-a-platform

Skinner, B. F. (1974). *About behaviourism*. London: Penguin.

Squire, K. (2006). From content to context: Videogames as designed experience. *Educational Researcher*, 35(8), 19–29.

Sylwester, R. (1995). A celebration of neurons. Association for Supervision and Curriculum Development, Alexandria.

Tan, S. M., Ladyshewsky, R. K., & Gardner, P. (2010). Using blogging to promote clinical reasoning and metacognition in undergraduate physiotherapy fieldwork programs. *Australasian Journal of Educational Technology*, 26(3), 355–368.

Teles, L. (1994). Cognitive apprenticeship on global networks. In L. Harasim (Ed.), *Global networks: Computers and international communications* (pp. 271–282). Cambridge, MA: The MIT Press.

van Haren, R. (2010). Engaging learner diversity through learning by design. *E-Learning and Digital Media*, 7(3), 258–271.

Vygotsky, L. S. (1978). *Mind in society*. Cambridge, MA: Harvard University Press.

Willis, E. M., & Tucker, G. R. (2001). Using constructionism to teach constructivism: Modeling hands-on technology integration in a preservice teacher technology course. *Journal of Computing in Teacher Education*, 17(2), 4–7.

Woo, Y., & Reeves, T. C. (2007). Meaningful interaction in web-based learning: A social constructivist interpretation. *The Internet and Higher Education*, 10(1), 15–25.

Yilmaz, K. (2011). The cognitive perspective on learning: Its theoretical underpinnings and implications for classroom practices. *The Clearing House: A Journal of Educational Strategies, Issues and Ideas, 84*(5), 204–212.

Zahn, C., Pea, R., Hesse, F. W., & Rosen, J. (2010). Comparing simple and advanced video tools as supports for complex collaborative design processes. *Journal of the Learning Sciences, 19*(3), 403–440.

4

Technology Affordances and Multimedia Learning Effects

ABSTRACT

This chapter provides an overview of two generally applicable frameworks relating to the use of technology-enhanced learning — 'affordances' and multimedia learning effects. First, the concept of 'affordances' as action potentials of technologies is identified as a way to think through technology-enhanced learning design possibilities, so as to help make technology selection decisions. Second, multimedia learning effects including the multimedia effect, the modality effect, the redundancy effect, the split-attention effect, and the personalization effect are presented as a scientific basis for understanding how to create cognitively effective learning experiences using text, images, sound, and video. Both affordances and multimedia learning effects are characterized as ongoing areas of research that are somewhat related, with the successful utilization of each depending on critical application by the designer.

Establishing Conceptual Foundations for the Analysis of Learning Technologies

If educators and researchers are to use technology in discerning and impactful ways, then they need to have frameworks for conceptualizing technologies and understanding their effects. In the previous chapter, we explored various pedagogical paradigms that can be used for educative purposes, and in this chapter we investigate technological features and implications. In the next chapter, we will reflect upon content-based issues, so that we can establish analytical foundations in all of the TPACK dimensions.

This chapter is divided into roughly two halves. In the first half, the concept of 'affordances' is introduced as a means for thinking through the potentials of different technologies in a way that is resilient to changes over time. It is important that we can penetrate past the glossy look-and-feel of technologies to understand what they actually have to offer in terms of educational benefit – that way we can make discerning decisions about which tools are the most appropriate for a given context. Thinking through the action potentials of different technologies allows selection to be based upon explicitly identified learning needs rather than pure intuition or no reasoning at all.

The second half of the chapter provides an overview of multimedia learning effects, which are research-based findings about how different approaches to communicating information using text, images, audio, video, and so on, can impact upon comprehension and learning. It is critically important that we understand how different approaches to organizing information using technology will effect learning because educators and researchers are so often designing digital content for students to use. A strong understanding of multimedia learning effects means that we can use technologies in ways that promote cognitively effective learning.

Let's start by considering the idea of technology 'affordances' and how they might support technology-enhanced learning design.

Affordances

WHAT ARE AFFORDANCES?

'Affordance' is a frequently used term in education circles when talking about the potentials of technologies, but it is also one that has been used with several different meanings (Hartson, 2003;

McGrenere & Ho, 2000; Oliver, 2005). In order to understand the various nuances of the term 'affordance' it is helpful to briefly trace its etymology (i.e., its semantic history).

James Gibson (1979) first coined the term 'affordance' as follows:

> what it *offers* the animal, what it *provides* or *furnishes*, either for good or ill …. It implies the complementarity of the animal and the environment. (p. 127, italics by Gibson)

Under Gibson's definition an 'affordance' exists as long as the person can take the necessary actions to utilize it. For instance, a postbox is a 'letter-mailing-with-able' object whether or not a person recognizes it as such.

The other frequently cited proponent of the term 'affordances' is Donald Norman, who describes an affordance as a design aspect of an object that suggests how the object should be used:

> the term *affordance* refers to the perceived and actual properties of the thing, primarily those fundamental properties that determine just how the thing could possibly be used. A chair affords ('is for') support and, therefore, affords sitting. (Norman, 1988, p. 9)

Norman's usage emphasizes the idea of "perceived" affordances – that until an affordance is perceived, it is of no utility to the potential user (Norman, 1988).

Thus there is an important distinction between Gibson's and Norman's definition of affordances, because the interpretation determines whether or not the term 'affordance' encompasses usability or just utility (Kirschner, Strijbos, Kreijns, & Beers, 2004). Gibson's frame of reference focuses solely upon the fundamental characteristics of the object in relation to the user, which is a question of utility. Norman places greater emphasis on how an object is perceived, which relates to usability and not just utility.

This book will adopt a principally Gibsonian idea of 'affordance' so as to clearly distinguish usefulness from usability. For the purposes of the ensuing discussion and analysis, 'affordance' will be defined as:

> The action potentials inherent in an object (for instance a technology) that determine how it can be used.

Our core interest will be to discriminate between technologies for the purposes of determining their suitability for use in learning tasks. The Gibsonian use of 'affordances' as intrinsic potentials for the user means that in the first instance the underlying properties of technologies are the focal point for analysis, rather than evaluating the quality of the user interface. As McGrenere and Ho (2000) point out, the affordance should not be confounded with designing the information that specifies the affordance. In later works, Norman revises his original definition in order to distinguish between 'real' and 'perceived' affordances (Norman, 1999). None of this is to say that educators should avoid evaluating the usability of technologies − they should − but in the first instance we need to determine whether the technologies have the capacity to facilitate the desired task activities.

WHY IS IT IMPORTANT TO UNDERSTAND AND ANALYZE THE AFFORDANCES OF TECHNOLOGIES?

The success with which technology is utilized for learning and teaching depends on the educator's ability to appreciate the requirements within the learning context and subsequently select and use technologies in ways that meet those needs (Conole & Jones, 2010; John & Sutherland, 2005; Yoon, Ho, & Hedberg, 2005). Every class is different, and given this situatedness, it is imperative that the teacher has the ability to tailor the use of technology to meet the needs of their students and broader context (Mishra & Koehler, 2006). Much of the software available for educative purposes has not been designed for learning and teaching, and thus the teacher should analyze the affordances and constraints of such technologies to creatively repurpose them for the educational context (Mishra & Koehler, 2006).

A focus on the affordances underlying the technologies makes the analytic approach of educational designers adaptable to changes in technology. It is precisely because technology changes so rapidly that we must shift our focus from purely understand specific tools to also being able to analyze the educational utility of new tools based on their merits (Mishra & Koehler, 2006).

Constructing a general, relevant approach for supporting the selection and utilization of technologies for learning and teaching purposes is both difficult and subjective. Yet it is a worthwhile pursuit − being able to consciously identify and articulate the affordance requirements of learning tasks and how they can be satisfied by the inherent affordances of e-learning technologies draws educational designers' thinking closer to the underlying attributes of the technologies and tasks.

CLASSIFYING AFFORDANCES OF LEARNING TECHNOLOGIES

There have been several attempts throughout educational literature where researchers have defined categories of affordances. For instance, Conole and Dyke (2004) define the affordances of information and communication technologies as accessibility, speed of change, diversity, communication and collaboration, reflection, multimodal and nonlinear, risk, fragility and uncertainty, immediacy, monopolization, and surveillance. While this constitutes a broad list of properties and implications of ICTs, the mix of different types of elements has been seen by some to lack conceptual consistency and in some cases not actually refer to affordances at all (Boyle & Cook, 2004; Oliver, 2005).

In an attempt to provide a consistent approach to conceptualizing affordances, Bower (2008) presents a categorization framework that includes media affordances, spatial affordances, temporal affordances, navigational affordances, emphasis affordances, synthesis affordances, and access control affordances. Specific affordances within the different categories are expressed as 'abilities' to emphasize the action potentials they offer. The affordances are also distinguished in terms of the extent to which they generally support more receptive (static/instructive) learning in contrast to more active (collaborative/productive) learning. A summary of Bower's (2008) framework of affordances is represented in Table 4.1. Bower's (2008) affordance framework is pitched at a fundamental, pragmatic, and functional level in order to support analysis and selection of technologies for educational design purposes.

Kirschner et al. (2004) make the potentially useful distinction between technological affordances (as defined by their usability), as opposed to social affordances and educational affordances. The latter two classes of affordances are defined as follows:

- Educational affordances: characteristics of an educational resource that indicate if and how a particular learning behavior could possibly be enacted within the context
- Social affordances: aspects of the online learning environment that provide social-contextual facilitation relevant to the learner's social interaction.

Table 4.1.   Functional Affordances, Categorized by Type, and Degree of Interaction.

	Static/instructive		Collaborative/productive
Media Affordances:	read-ability view-ability listen-ability watch-ability		write-ability draw-ability speak-ability video-produce-ability
Spatial affordances:		resize-ability move-ability	
Temporal Affordances:	playback-ability	accessibility	record-ability synchronous-ability
Navigational affordances:	browse-ability search-ability	data-manipulation-ability	link-ability
Emphasis affordances:	highlight-ability		focus-ability
Synthesis affordances:		combine-ability integrate-ability	
Access-control affordances:			permission-ability share-ability

(Items on the center line fall into
both classifications)

Source: Updated from Bower (2008).

This extends the focus of affordances beyond the potentials of the technologies to how they may be used for educative and interactional purposes.

One of the problems with the idea of affordances is that there can be conceptual inconsistency regarding what is being examined (Oliver, 2005). For instance, in the area of mobile learning Klopfer and Squire (2008) suggest five affordances of mobile handheld computers, namely portability, social interactivity, context sensitivity, connectivity, and individuality. Churchill and Churchill (2008) suggest a different set of affordances: multimedia-access, connectivity, as well as the ability to capture, represent, and analyze. Cochrane and Bateman (2010) define the affordances of mobile devices as image capture, video capture, video streaming, mobile web experience text entry, GPS, touch screen, application availability, ease of user interface, 3G, wifi, cost, availability, screen size, video out, and portability (size and weight). We can see that between these three different lists of affordances that there is a degree of conceptual inconsistency, with different affordances being identified between researchers and at times researchers talk about the componentry of the technologies themselves rather than their affordances. Thus, for practical purposes when communication in design situations, educators may need to accept the term 'affordances' as a synonym for 'features' or 'benefits.'

Reflecting on the educational affordances of technologies is useful because they help the designer to consider how to take pedagogical advantage of the tools in question. However, care needs to be taken when attributing educational affordances to technologies – it is important to consider how much is really due to the technology as opposed to the task designs, the learners themselves, or other contextual factors.

AFFORDANCES IN PRACTICE – A BRIEF EXAMPLE

In order to illustrate the concept of affordances let's examine a technology called FlipSnack (http://flipsnack.com). FlipSnack allows users to upload PDF documents so that they can be viewed as online flip-the-page books through an appealing and easy to use interface. The tool also includes an editor that enables text, captions, tags, hyperlinks, and video to be added to the online books that are created (see Figure 4.1).

In terms of merely uploading a PDF document for online consumption, FlipSnack only affords the ability to read and view content. So teachers or students who merely upload their PDF

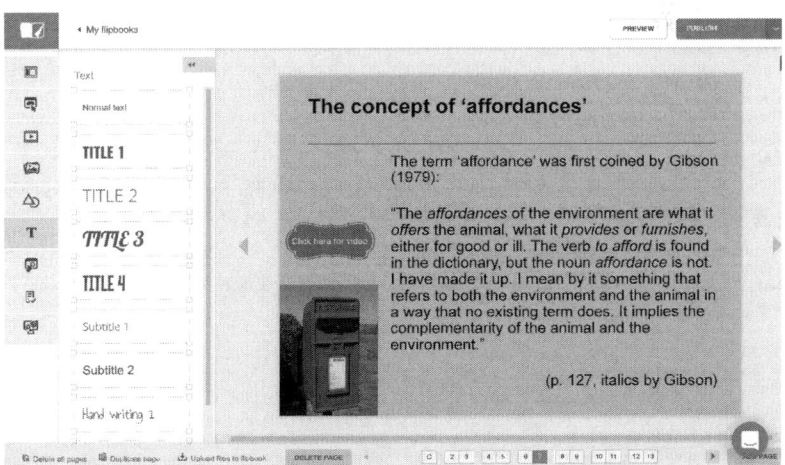

Figure 4.1.   Screenshot of the FlipSnack Editor Being Used to Create an Online Book (http://flipsnack.com).

documents to be viewed online are deriving little pedagogical value from the tool, other than to disseminate it. However, using the FlipSnack advanced editor enables students and teachers to annotate, qualify, categorize, link, and add multimedia, thus expanding out the sorts of thinking skills that can be engaged. For instance, students may be required to explain, summarize, classify, interrelate, and exemplify. This illustrates that while a technology may afford several educational potentials, the learning benefits subtended by those affordances will only be truly realized once the affordances are recognized and used.

Obviously there are literally thousands of technologies that educators have at their disposal to promote learning and it is not possible to review them all here. Nor is it argued as necessary to formally tabulate affordances of technologies to cross-check against the affordance requirements of tasks. The key point is to draw educators' attention beyond the superficial aspects of technologies to examine the true underlying features and how they may be used to promote learning.

HOW A FOCUS ON TECHNOLOGY AFFORDANCES CAN BE USED TO INFORM LEARNING DESIGN PROCESSES

Usually an educator will have one or more educational goals that they are aiming to have their students achieve (which are often defined by a syllabus or curriculum document). Given a series of educational goals they will generally postulate suitable tasks, drawing from their experience as educators, advice from colleagues, or personal inspiration. With an affordances perspective in mind they can then analyze these propositional tasks to derive the affordances needed to facilitate the desired representations and interactions. At the same time they can scrutinize technologies at their disposal to determine the extent to which the technologies will meet the required affordances of intended tasks.

Matching affordances of learning technologies with the affordance requirements of learning tasks is rarely a lock-step process. Educators should both select technologies that match the pedagogy of the tasks, as well as design tasks that take advantage of the technological tools (Jonassen, Lee, Yang, & Laffey, 2005). Frequently technologies will not immediately and directly meet the needs of the task at hand. Similarly, one or more technologies may have additional features that inspire new ideas about how the task could be redesigned to help students achieve the intended learning outcomes. Synergistic, integrative, and creative thinking is often necessary to iteratively derive the final e-learning task from the originally postulated tasks and the available technologies (Bower, 2008).

CONCLUDING COMMENTS ON AFFORDANCES

It should be noted that the use of 'affordances' with reference to educational technology has been criticized for being overly ambiguous, too broad in terms of attribution, and perpetuating a technologically deterministic view of education (Oliver, 2013). However, the capabilities of technologies determine what can be done with them, and what we do with them influences student learning, so it is important that we have a nomenclature to support conceptualization of learning technology features. Acknowledging the ontological limitations, affordances are the most commonly accepted and used approach to deconstructing the design possibilities of learning technologies. As such it is important to be aware of them (both in terms of interpreting prior work in the field and engaging in design practice).

It is proposed here that using affordances to support the technology selection process does not undermine the role of the designer – in fact, it increases it. The designer is needed to appropriately identify the affordance potentials of technologies for the educative goals at hand. As well, there are several contextual factors that need to be considered when analyzing and selecting technologies based on their affordances, such as student ability, group allocation, motivation, and assessment. Further, the subtle interactions between affordances and the details of how they operate can have a major impact on the learning experience. As such, the expertise and artistry of the designer are critical to account for all of these elements.

In the age of technology-based learning having a portfolio of approaches for identifying, describing, analyzing, and allocating technologies for deployment enables the educator to move beyond merely selecting tools based on intuition or convenience. There is no doubt that there are conceptual inconsistencies in the field and that further work will be required to resolve these. However, analyzing the affordances of technologies has the worthwhile consequence of concentrating the designer's focus directly on the critical aspects of the selection process: the underlying potentials of tools and the requirements of intended learning tasks. Thus, affordance analysis offers us a valuable means for conceptualizing the relevance of technologies for learning purposes.

Having established a means of thinking through the potentials of different technologies, the next section on multimedia learning provides an empirical basis for understanding the cognitive consequences of our technology selection, organization, and deployment decisions.

Multimedia Learning Effects

In the age of the Internet and multimedia, educators are often working with text, images, sound, and video in order to create learning resources and environments for their students. In order to assist this, research into cognition and cognitive load has led to the development of several principles related to the design of multimedia learning artifacts. Prominent expert in the field, Richard Mayer, defines multimedia as simultaneously "presenting words (such as printed text or spoken text) and pictures (such as illustrations, photos, animation, or video)" (Mayer, 2014c, p. 2). Multimedia learning is defined as building mental representations from both words and pictures (Mayer, 2014c). The success of learning technology usage depends on the effectiveness with which media facilitates the communication of concepts and ideas, and thus multimedia learning effects are crucial for educators to understand.

It is important to note that there is a related but somewhat separate field of study that investigates 'multimodality.' Modalities are defined as sets of representational resources for making meaning, including image, color, speech and sound-effect, movement and gesture, and gaze (Jewitt, 2006). In the multimodality field modalities are distinguished from 'media' (such as printed books, CD-Roms, and computer applications), the latter of which is how modalities are actually disseminated. Thus there is an unfortunate contradiction in nomenclature, where 'multimedia' in the multimedia learning field is referring more to multimodality in the multimodal learning field. Since this section draws upon findings from the multimedia learning field, we will adopt their terminology (i.e., refer to multimedia learning as learning through words, images, video, and so on). In other sections of this book, 'modalities' will be used to refer to words, images, video, and so on in order to distinguish them from the media by which they are disseminated, such as CD-Roms, printed books, software applications.

The scientific rigor of multimedia learning concepts that we are about to cover demonstrates the in-depth research activity in the area. There are at least three important reasons for people in the technology-enhanced learning field to understand multimedia learning effects: (i) if we want to use and contribute to the research basis of the field, then multimedia learning effects are the foundation for how people process technology-enhanced learning, (ii) without an understanding of multimedia learning effects educators and industry often design cognitively ineffective and confusing resources, and (iii) as professionals charged with the responsibility of promoting learning in society it is imperative that we understand how the human mind works. As Sylwester (1995) notes, an educator who has no understanding of how the mind works is like an auto-mechanic who chooses not to look under the bonnet! Fortunately, the study of multimedia learning effects is also quite fascinating.

ASSUMPTIONS UNDERPINNING MULTIMEDIA LEARNING

There are fundamental assumptions that help us to understand how humans process information for learning purposes.

> **Assumption 1:** Humans have separate information processing systems for visual and verbal information (Baddeley, 1992; Mayer, 2014b; Pavio, 1986).

People can process visual information and auditory information using separate parts of working memory, at least to some extent (Pavio, 1986). Words and sounds are initially processed in our auditory working memory, and written text and images are initially processed in our visual working memory (Mayer, 2014b). The items of information contained in these dual channels of working memory are then interrelated, not only with each other but often with existing knowledge structure stored in long-term memory (also known as 'schema') (Mayer, 2014b). If adequate memorization occurs, the newly acquired knowledge will be accommodated or assimilated with other schema in long-term memory. This chain of events is illustrated in Figure 4.2.

It should be noted that this description of information processing is a simplification – for more detailed models refer to sources solely focused on describing the information processing pipeline (for instance, Mayer, 2014b; Schnotz, 2014). However,

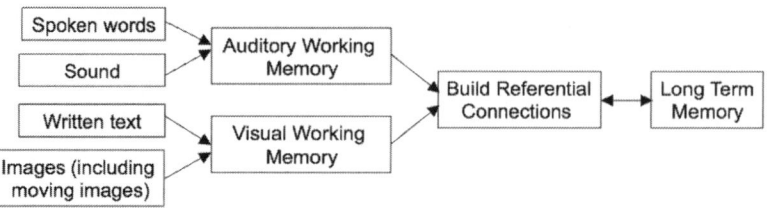

Figure 4.2. Schematic Representation of How Information Is Processed in Working Memory and Interacts with Long-Term Memory. *Source*: Adapted from Mayer (2005, p. 37).

the description does represent enough detail to explain the main multimedia effects we will be examining.

For instance, presenting words and pictures rather than solely words (or pictures) takes advantage of the full information processing capacity of humans rather than leaving one or other of the channels dormant (Mayer, 2014c). It also allows the two modes of information to complement one another to enhance learner understanding, and leverages the relative advantage of each mode for presenting different types of information (Mayer, 2014c).

Assumption 2: Humans have limited information processing capacity (Baddeley, 1992; Chandler & Sweller, 1991; Mayer, 2014b)

Every person only has a certain amount of information that they can process in working memory at any one time (Baddeley, 1986). 'Cognitive load' refers to "the load imposed on working memory by information being presented" (Paas & Sweller, 2014, p. 40), and each person has a maximum cognitive load that they can assume at any instant. For instance, most people can only store around seven unrelated items of information in working memory at any one time (Miller, 1956), and can only simultaneously interrelate between two and four items of information (Paas & Sweller, 2014).

The cognitive load imposed in any learning situation is dependent on how information is presented and how the person processes that information. Without taking into account cognitive aspects of information processing, such as the relationship between working memory and long-term memory, the effectiveness of learning designs may be severely impaired (Paas & Sweller, 2014). For instance, if information processing requirements exceed a person's maximum cognitive load, they reach a state of 'cognitive overload' where they do not have the mental resources to sufficiently interrelate items of information.

It is important to note that findings about effective use of multimedia learning relate to situations where learners are approaching the limits of their cognitive load (Paas & Sweller, 2014). That is to say, if learning the information is simple, then presenting it in cognitively inefficient forms may not impact on learning because unused cognitive load can be used to perform any additional information processing that is required (Paas & Sweller, 2014).

Assumption 3: Learning results from active processing of information through cognitive activities such as selection, organization, and integration (Mayer, 2014b; Wittrock, 1989).

Active learning occurs when a learner utilizes cognitive processes to make sense of incoming material (Mayer, 2014b). Successful learning occurs when learners make coherent 'mental models,' that is, knowledge structures that have consistent explanatory power of the phenomena being considered (Mayer, 2014b). 'Mental models' will be addressed in more detail in the next chapter.

Three cognitive processes essential for active learning are selection (choosing information that is relevant to the task or phenomena at hand), organization (mentally arranging selected information into a coherent and consistent structure within working memory), and integration (connecting new knowledge structures with existing knowledge in long-term memory) (Mayer, 2009, 2014b; Wittrock, 1989). Active processing can be used to explain the quality of learning that occurs. For instance, when students exercise extensive cognitive effort to synthesize pictorial and verbal representations and relate it to existing schema (mental models), more complete and meaningful learning can occur (Mayer, 2014c).

These three assumptions – dual channel processing, limited processing capacity, and active processing – provide a basis for understanding most of the main effects that have been observed by multimedia learning researchers. A summary of key effects is provided below, along with the explanation of each based on the three assumptions above. Note that many of the findings are alternately described as 'effects' and 'principles,' though we will distinguish these by referring to the occurrence of the multimedia learning phenomena as an 'effect' and the corresponding implications for design as the 'principle.' Also note that there are many more effects that have been observed – this section focuses on several fundamental ones. Limitations of multimedia learning principles in practice are then discussed.

THE MULTIMEDIA EFFECT

An effect in multimedia learning that has been repeatedly validated is the so-called multimedia effect – that people learn more effectively from words and pictures than from words alone (Butcher, 2014; Fletcher & Tobias, 2005). Note that this is also referred to as 'the' multimedia effect, not to be confused with multimedia learning effects generally, which refers to the broad class of effects in this section.

The explanation for the multimedia effect is that the mental processing of words and images involves processes that are to a significant degree both independent insofar as they involve separate cognitive units, but also additive insofar as they are capable of interacting with and complementing one another (Pavio, 1986). For example, consider learning about photosynthesis from the following words alone, compared to learning about photosynthesis from the words and diagram shown in Figure 4.3.

The effect is supported by other studies reporting superior transfer of learning when narration is accompanied by animation

Words: The sun's light energy is captured by chlorophyll in leaves. This is then combined with carbon dioxide absorbed through leaves as well as water absorbed through leaves and roots. The resulting chemical reaction produces sugar for the plant to grow and as a byproduct the oxygen that we need to breathe.

Figure 4.3.   Example of the Multimedia Learning Effect – Combining Words and Image in Order to Enhance Learning.

compared to narration or animation deployed in isolation (Fletcher & Tobias, 2005, p. 117). It should be noted that the multimedia principle has come to refer generally to the positive impact of both verbal and visual information in any form; however, other principles (some of which are discussed below) provide further details about the nuances of combining words and pictures to enhance learning (Butcher, 2014). A meta-analysis of nine studies involving the multimedia learning effect found a relatively large median effect size of 1.5 (Mayer, 2009).

MODALITY EFFECT

Closely related to the multimedia principle in understanding how different presentation media interact is the 'modality effect.' The modality principle states that presenting some instructional content that can be processed visually and other parts of the material in auditory mode can lead to more effective learning than using purely visual or auditory representation alone (Low & Sweller, 2014). This differs from the previous 'multimedia effect' in that verbal information is in auditory mode. So whereas the multimedia effect related to presentation of images and written text, the modality effect typically relates to combining images and auditory information.

As an example, imagine the diagram in Figure 4.4 is complemented by narration of the words rather than text. The learner only needs to process one source of visual material and one source of auditory materials, rather than two sources of visual material. Thus the explanation for the improvement in comprehension by using one visual and one auditory mode is once again based upon the dual coding theory of information processing (Pavio, 1986). Because visual and auditory information can be processed independently and simultaneously by different areas of working memory (at least to some extent), presenting some information in auditory mode to complement a diagrammatic representation can reduce cognitive load as compared to presenting all of the material in just one form (Low & Sweller, 2014). It is important to note that the multimodal effect applies in situations where both sources of information (visual and auditory) are required to understand one another, and cannot each be learned in isolation (Low & Sweller, 2014). An analysis of 61 studies involving the modality effect found that it was supported in 53 cases with a median effect size of 0.76 (Mayer & Pilegard, 2014).

Narration: The sun's light energy is captured by chlorophyll in leaves. This is then combined with carbon dioxide absorbed through leaves as well as water absorbed through leaves and roots. The resulting chemical reaction produces sugar for the plant to grow and as a byproduct the oxygen that we need to breathe.

Figure 4.4.   Example of the Modality Effect – Combining Images and Narration to Enhance Learning.

REDUNDANCY EFFECT

The redundancy effect suggests that inclusion of redundant information interferes with rather than facilitates learning (Kalyuga & Sweller, 2014). Redundancy occurs when information is unnecessarily repeated in different forms or where unnecessary information is included (Kalyuga & Sweller, 2014). For instance, if a visual presentation includes some auditory explanation, then repeating the auditory information using text can hinder learning. The effect is also observed for unnecessarily elaborated information within one modality, for instance overly verbose explanations that do not contain extra knowledge value or images that distract learners rather than contributing new information about the material being learnt (Kalyuga & Sweller, 2014). For example, consider a situation in Figure 4.5 where the same written words and spoken words are used to explain photosynthesis, and extra unnecessary information is included in the written explanation. Learning would be more efficient if the redundant information was excluded.

The explanation for the negative impact of redundant information lies in the limited processing capacity assumption. The extra cognitive load is imposed by having to process and coordinate the unnecessary information could have otherwise been deployed to learn concepts intrinsically related to the task (Kalyuga & Sweller, 2014). The redundancy effect is sometimes referred to as the 'coherence effect' (Mayer & Moreno, 2003), and in some cases refers to the specific situation when text is used to unnecessarily

Written text: *The sun's light energy is captured by chlorophyll in leaves. This is then combined with carbon dioxide absorbed through leaves as well as water absorbed through leaves and roots. The resulting chemical reaction produces sugar for the plant to grow and as a byproduct the oxygen that we need to breathe. Plants are often green and usually soft to touch. But sometimes they can be prickly.*

Narration: *The sun's light energy is captured by chlorophyll in leaves. This is then combined with carbon dioxide absorbed through leaves as well as water absorbed through leaves and roots. The resulting chemical reaction produces sugar for the plant to grow and as a byproduct the oxygen that we need to breathe.*

Figure 4.5. Example of the Redundancy Effect – Providing the Same Information in Two Different Forms or Irrelevant Information Detracts from Learning.

elaborate graphics and auditory narration (Mayer & Fiorella, 2014). Like the modality effect, it only applies when the task imposes high levels of cognitive load on the learner, often in cases of high element interactivity (Kalyuga & Sweller, 2014). The more interesting the redundant information, the more it can impede learning (Mayer, Griffith, Jurkowitz, & Rothman, 2008). An analysis of 39 experimental tests involving the redundancy principle found a median effect size of 0.86 (Mayer & Fiorella, 2014).

SPLIT-ATTENTION EFFECT

The 'split-attention effect' describes how people learn more effectively when words and pictures are physically and temporally integrated (Ayres & Sweller, 2005). Placing related information in close time or space proximity reduces the cognitive load caused by learners having to mentally integrate multiple sources of information that would otherwise be 'split.' For instance, compare the diagram shown in Figure 4.6 and the written words and image in Figure 4.3 that were used to introduce the multimedia learning effect.

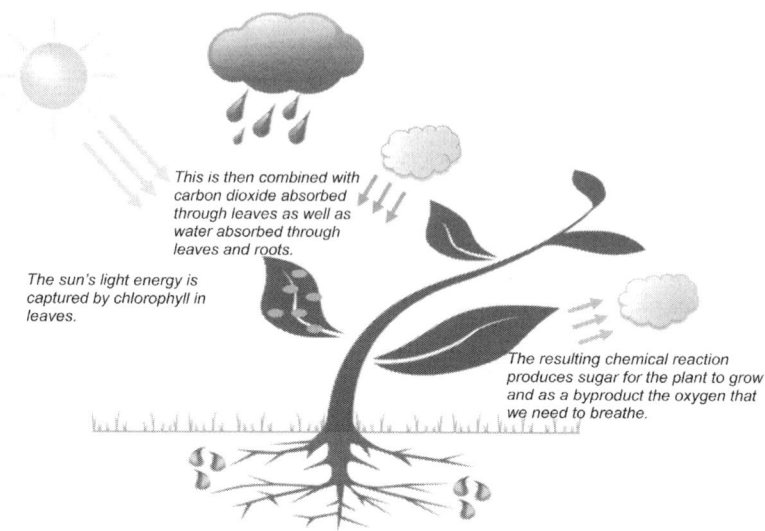

Figure 4.6.   Example of the Split-Attention Effect — Placing Words and Pictures
in Close Proximity Enhances Learning.

The explanation for the split-attention effect again lies in the limited processing capacity assumption. Separating information physically requires students to determine which elements relate to one other and how. Separating information by time imposes an added burden of requiring students to accurately store a representation of an element in memory (at a stage where that representation may be unfamiliar or not be fully formed) and then relate it to material presented at a later stage (Ayres & Sweller, 2014). These two forms of the split-attention effect are also known as the physical contiguity and temporal contiguity effects, respectively (Ayres & Sweller, 2014). Like the modality effect, the split-attention effect only applies when the multiple sources of information are required to understand one another, and cannot each be learned in isolation (Ayres & Sweller, 2014). If information needs to be separated for logistical reasons, then strategies to overcome split attention include directing the focus of learner attention to the correct places (for instance, using color) and using links (such as hypertext) so that learners can quickly move between sources (Ayres & Sweller, 2014). A meta-analysis of the split-attention effect across over 50 studies found a large effect size of 0.85 (Ginns, 2006). More recent analysis of the spatial contiguity and temporal contiguity found even larger median effect sizes of 1.10 (n = 22) and 1.22 (n = 9) respectively (Mayer & Fiorella, 2014).

SIGNALING (OR CUEING) EFFECT

According to the signaling (or cueing) effect, guiding the learner's attention to the relevant elements of materials highlighting the organization of the material can lead to improved learning (van Gog, 2014). Cues may take several forms, including text that directs attention to particular parts of an image, color, and shading in diagrams, intonation in spoken text, or arrows in pictures (van Gog, 2014). As a simple demonstration of the cueing effect, consider the situation illustrated in Figure 4.7 where numbers are added to the written text below to help the learner sequence their attention. A more impactful example that is not possible in a book would be to use a highlighter pen to circle relevant parts of the diagram as a narration discussed them.

Once again, the explanation of the signaling effect lies in the limited processing capacity assumption. Select pertinent elements of the resources for learners to focus upon reduces the cognitive load that would otherwise be imposed if they were required to deduce relevant items for themselves (van Gog, 2014). Using cues can mean that students both select relevant information for

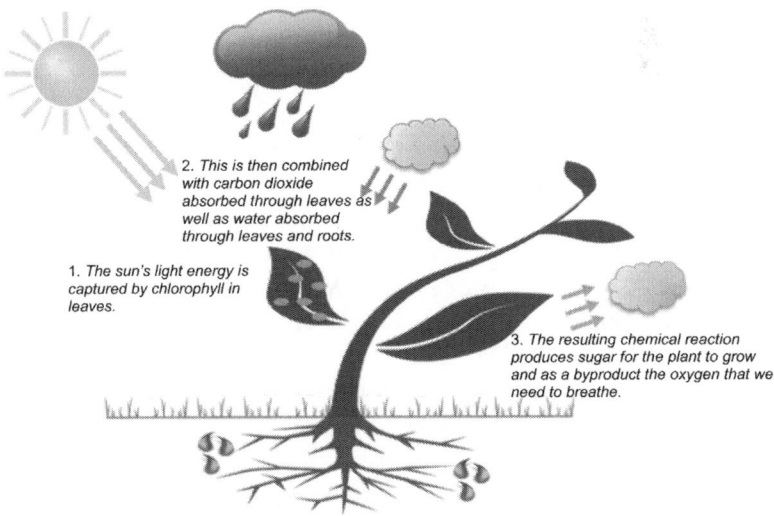

Figure 4.7.   Example of the Signaling Effect — Highlighting Where the Learner Should Focus Attention Enhances Learning.

processing in working memory and do not process less relevant information, both of which contribute to learning (van Gog, 2014). Signaling may also assist in mental organization and integration of information, not just selection (van Gog, 2014). An analysis of 28 experimental tests involving the signaling principle found that it was supported in 24 cases, yielding a median effect size of 0.41 (Mayer & Fiorella, 2014).

PERSONALIZATION EFFECT

The personalization effect proposes that people learn more deeply when the words in a multimedia presentation are in a conversational style rather than a formal style (Mayer, 2014d). For instance, personalization may take the form of using words like 'you' and 'I' rather than merely third person grammatical tenses. As a simple example, consider the two passages below:

> Photosynthesis is a requirement for human existence. It produces the oxygen that people need to breathe and the sugars that the plants eaten by humans need in order to grow.

> You need photosynthesis to stay alive! It gives you the oxygen you need in order to breathe and the plants you eat the sugars they need in order to grow.

The premise of the personalization effect is that when the writing or talking is related to you – yes you – you tend to take more notice and relate the material more to yourself. Rather than enhancing learning through more cognitively efficient representation of information, the personalization principle relies on the ability of social cues in multimedia instruction to prime a social response in learners that increases attention, motivation, and deeper cognitive processing (Mayer, 2014d). Thus, the personalization effect is explained by the active processing assumption.

An analysis of 17 experimental tests involving the personalization principle found that it was supported in 14 cases, yielding a median effect size of 0.79 (Mayer, 2014d). Note that research into applying personalization in manners not directly associated to the information being broadcast (for instance, having the image of the speaker showing on the screen) have not borne any substantial educational gains (Mayer, 2014d).

SYMBOL SYSTEM THEORY AND TRANSFER-APPROPRIATE PROCESSING

Symbol System Theory advocates the appropriate matching of the representational form to the nature of the information being communicated (Salomon, 1994). For instance, if students need to know how to perform a reasonably complex computer-based process, then presenting a series of written steps or verbal instruction is a far less cognitively effective means of teaching than an audio-annotated desktop recording.

Symbol system theory frames all media in terms of the contents they convey, the technologies used to convey contents, the social situation in which they are applied, and the symbol systems in which information is encoded (Salomon, 1994). Empirical evidence suggests that presenting information using a symbol system (representational form) that appropriately matches (for instance, is similar to) that of the underlying skill or concept being taught results in more effective learning (Salomon, 1994).

The explanation for this effect is underpinned by the limited processing capacity assumption. If information is presented to learners in a form that matches the actual nature of the information, then it reduces the degree of elaboration and recoding required for learner comprehension (Salomon, 1994). It means that the encoded information is more easily transferred to the context in which it needs to be used, which is also referred to as 'transfer-appropriate processing' (Bransford, 1979). Though not typically classed as a multimedia learning effect, it is included here because it contributes an important design principle not represented in the other effects that have been described.

Summary of Multimedia Learning Principles

In simple summary, the multimedia learning effects that have been described imply the following principles for multimedia learning (the first six of which are from Mayer, 2014c):

- *Multimedia principle*: People learn better from words and pictures than from words alone.
- *Modality principle*: People learn better from graphics and narration than from graphics and printed text.

- *Redundancy principle*: People learn better when the same information is not presented in more than one format.
- *Split-attention principle*: People learn better when words and pictures are physically and temporally integrated.
- *Signaling principle*: People learn better when cues are added that highlight the key information and its organization.
- *Personalization principle*: People learn better when the words of a multimedia presentation are in conversational style rather than formal style.
- *Transfer-appropriate processing principle*: People learn better when the information to be learnt is represented in a form that matches (resembles) the nature of information itself.

There are several other principles of multimedia learning that researchers have identified relating to approaches to learning, such as guided discovery and self-explanation. However, as these extend beyond how the technologies are used to represent information they will not be covered here. It is also important to note that this has only been a basic introduction to a quite intensively researched and nuanced area of study, in order to provide an understanding of the basic principles. For further details of effects and explanations, please see Mayer (2014a).

Caveat to Application of Multimedia Learning Principles

While it is useful for educational designers and researchers to understand how and why multimedia learning effects impact on learning, it is important not to over-attribute learning to multimedia learning effects and also to understand their context sensitivity. Multimedia learning effects have generally been studied under tightly constructed experimental conditions using very specific instructional materials. In real classrooms, many other factors (for instance, behavioral, environmental, and affective factors) can influence learning far more than the way in which multimedia is used. Also, for any multimedia learning effect there are a range of effect sizes that have been measured, and a range of subtle differences in the ways they are applied can lead to different levels of learning. Further research into multimedia learning will undoubtedly uncover new insights into the conditions under which educational resources and environments are most cognitively efficient.

Each individual will respond to multimedia learning materials and environments differently, noting that various multimedia effects only apply where people are operating at close to maximum cognitive load (Ayres & Sweller, 2014). Thus, students with high levels of prerequisite knowledge and ability may not benefit from well-designed instructional materials as much as a less knowledgeable and able learner. Moreover, there are times that it may be appropriate to design in ways that are counter to multimedia principles, for instance, provide text and auditory instructions along with visual materials as a matter of accessibility. The personalization principle also highlights that cognitive efficiency is not the only influence on the effectiveness of learning – for instance, motivation can play an important role in increasing learning outcomes. As well, multimedia learning effects relating to instantaneous aspects of learning, but do not accounting for longer term learning effects of self-regulation, development of problem-solving capabilities, or the importance of learning collaborative skills. Consequently, educators are advised to understand multimedia learning effects, take them into account in their designs, but never apply them blindly or without consideration of other educational factors.

Concluding Remarks about Conceptualizing Technologies and Their Use

In this chapter, we have laid overarching conceptual foundations for the study and use of technology in learning. Affordances provide us with a focus on the action potentials of learning technologies so that we can make conscious design and selection decisions based on the requirements of tasks. Multimedia learning research provides us with an understanding of how combinations of text, images, audio, and video in learning environments may impact on cognition and knowledge acquisition.

The application of both the affordances and multimedia paradigms depends on educators adopting a critical approach. Using affordances to help with the more deliberate selection of technologies is by no means a mechanistic process and educators need to take a range of contextual factors into account (student attributes, technology availability, usability, support). Similarly, the use of multimedia learning effects can enhance educational outcomes if applied appropriately and sensibly, but should only be seen as one input among a broader context of factors that influences the design and effectiveness of technology-enhanced learning.

There has been a tendency in the technology-enhanced learning design field to treat affordances and multimedia learning effects as somewhat unrelated areas. While the two areas are relatively distinct bodies of research and development, they should not be seen as unconnected. The affordances of technologies may incorporate particular multimedia, and the way that multimedia is arranged may subtend certain affordances. Accordingly, both affordances and multimedia learning effects are important to take into account during technology-enhanced learning design and research, not only separately but also how they mutually influence each other. They both have a fundamental and interconnected role to play in analyzing how technology usage can impact on learning, for instance, in the Web 2.0, social networking, mobile learning, and virtual worlds topics to follow.

However, we will not be taking an in-depth look at the application of specific technology-enhanced learning platforms just yet. Having previously considered the different pedagogies at our disposal and now having a means to analyze the potentials and usage of technologies, in the next chapter we turn our attention to the third dimension of the TPACK model – the 'content' to be learned.

References

Ayres, P., & Sweller, J. (2005). The split-attention principle in multimedia learning. In R. E. Mayer (Ed.), *The Cambridge handbook of multimedia learning* (pp. 135–146). New York, NY: Cambridge University Press.

Ayres, P., & Sweller, J. (2014). The split-attention principle in multimedia learning. In R. E. Mayer (Ed.), *The Cambridge handbook of multimedia learning* (pp. 206–226). New York, NY: Cambridge University Press.

Baddeley, A. (1986). *Working memory*. New York, NY: Oxford University Press.

Baddeley, A. (1992). Working memory. *Science, 255*(5044), 556–559.

Bower, M. (2008). Affordance analysis – Matching learning tasks with learning technologies. *Educational Media International, 45*(1), 3–15.

Boyle, T., & Cook, J. (2004). Understanding and using technological affordances: A commentary on Conole and Dyke. *Research in Learning Technology*, 12(3).

Bransford, J. D. (1979). *Human cognition: Learning, understanding, and remembering.* Belmont: Wadsworth.

Butcher, K. (2014). The multimedia principle. In R. E. Mayer (Ed.), *The Cambridge handbook of multimedia learning* (pp. 174–205). New York, NY: Cambridge University Press.

Chandler, P., & Sweller, J. (1991). Cognitive load theory and the format of instruction. *Cognition and Instruction*, 8(4), 293–332.

Churchill, D., & Churchill, N. (2008). Educational affordances of PDAs: A study of a teacher's exploration of this technology. *Computers & Education*, 50(4), 1439–1450.

Cochrane, T., & Bateman, R. (2010). Smartphones give you wings: Pedagogical affordances of mobile Web 2.0. *Australasian Journal of Educational Technology*, 26(1), 1–14.

Conole, G., & Dyke, M. (2004). What are the affordances of information and communication technologies? *Association for Learning Technology Journal*, 12(2), 113–124.

Conole, G., & Jones, C. (2010). Sharing practice, problems and solutions for institutional change. In P. Goodyear & S. Retalis (Eds.), *Technology-enhanced learning: Design patterns and pattern languages* (pp. 277–296). Rotterdam: Sense Publishers.

Fletcher, J. D., & Tobias, S. (2005). The multimedia principle. In R. E. Mayer (Ed.), *The Cambridge handbook of multimedia learning* (pp. 117–133). New York, NY: Cambridge University Press.

Gibson, J. (1979). *The ecological approach to human perception.* Boston, MA: Houghton Mifflin.

Ginns, P. (2006). Integrating information: A meta-analysis of the spatial contiguity and temporal contiguity effects. *Learning and Instruction*, 16, 511–525.

Hartson, H. R. (2003). Cognitive, physical, sensory, and functional affordances in interaction design. *Behaviour and Information Technology*, 22(5), 315–338.

Jewitt, C. (2006). *Technology, literacy and learning – A multimodal approach.* Oxon: Routledge.

John, P., & Sutherland, R. (2005). Affordance, opportunity and the pedagogical implications of ICT. *Educational Review*, 57(4), 405–413.

Jonassen, D. H., Lee, C. B., Yang, C.-C., & Laffey, J. (2005). The collaboration principle in multimedia learning. In R. E. Mayer (Ed.), *The Cambridge handbook of multimedia learning* (pp. 247–270). New York, NY: Cambridge University Press.

Kalyuga, S., & Sweller, J. (2014). The redundancy principle in multimedia learning. In R. E. Mayer (Ed.), *The Cambridge handbook of multimedia learning* (pp. 247–262). New York, NY: Cambridge University Press.

Kirschner, P., Strijbos, J.-W., Kreijns, K., & Beers, P. J. (2004). Designing electronic collaborative learning environments. *Educational Technology Research & Development*, 52(3), 47–66.

Klopfer, E., & Squire, K. (2008). Environmental detectives – The development of an augmented reality platform for environmental simulations. *Educational Technology Research and Development*, 56(2), 203–228.

Low, R., & Sweller, J. (2014). The modality principle in multimedia learning. In R. E. Mayer (Ed.), *The Cambridge handbook of multimedia learning* (pp. 227–246). New York, NY: Cambridge University Press.

Mayer, R. E. (2009). *Multimedia learning* (2nd ed.). New York, NY: Cambridge University Press.

Mayer, R. E. (2014a). *The Cambridge handbook of multimedia learning*. New York, NY: Cambridge University Press.

Mayer, R. E. (2014b). Cognitive theory of multimedia learning. In R. E. Mayer (Ed.), *The Cambridge handbook of multimedia learning* (pp. 43–71). New York, NY: Cambridge University Press.

Mayer, R. E. (2014c). Introduction to multimedia learning. In R. E. Mayer (Ed.), *The Cambridge handbook of multimedia learning* (pp. 1–24). New York, NY: Cambridge University Press.

Mayer, R. E. (2014d). Principles based on social cues in multimedia learning: Personalization, voice, image, and embodiment principles. In R. E. Mayer (Ed.), *The Cambridge handbook of multimedia learning* (pp. 345–368). New York, NY: Cambridge University Press.

Mayer, R. E., & Fiorella, L. (2014). Principles for reducing extraneous processing in multimedia learning: Coherence, signaling, redundancy, spatial contiguity, and temporal contiguity principles. In R. E. Mayer (Ed.), *The Cambridge handbook of multimedia learning* (pp. 279–315). New York, NY: Cambridge University Press.

Mayer, R. E., Griffith, E., Jurkowitz, I. T., & Rothman, D. (2008). Increased interestingness of extraneous details in a multimedia science presentation leads to decreased learning. *Journal of Experimental Psychology: Applied*, 14(4), 329.

Mayer, R. E., & Moreno, R. (2003). Nine ways to reduce cognitive load in multimedia learning. *Educational Psychologist*, 38, 43–52.

Mayer, R. E., & Pilegard, C. (2014). Principles for managing essential processing in multimedia learning: Segmenting, pre-training, and modality principles. In R. E. Mayer (Ed.), *The Cambridge handbook of multimedia learning* (pp. 316–344). New York, NY: Cambridge University Press.

McGrenere, J., & Ho, W. (2000, May 15–17). Affordances: Clarifying and evolving a concept. Paper presented at the Graphics Interface 2000, Montreal, Quebec, Canada.

Miller, G. A. (1956). The magical number seven, plus or minus two: Some limits on our capacity for processing information. *Psychological Review*, 63, 81–97.

Mishra, P., & Koehler, M. J. (2006). Technological pedagogical content knowledge: A framework for teacher knowledge. *Teachers College Record*, 108(6), 1017–1054.

Norman, D. A. (1988). *The psychology of everyday things*. New York, NY: Basic Books.

Norman, D. A. (1999). Affordance, conventions, and design. *Interactions*, 6(3), 38–43.

Oliver, M. (2005). The problem with affordance. *E-Learning*, 2(4), 402–413.

Oliver, M. (2013). Learning technology: Theorising the tools we study. *British Journal of Educational Technology*, 44(1), 31–43.

Paas, F., & Sweller, J. (2014). Implications of cognitive load theory for multimedia learning. In R. E. Mayer (Ed.), *The Cambridge handbook of multimedia learning* (pp. 27–42). New York, NY: Cambridge University Press.

Pavio, A. (1986). *Mental representations: A dual coding approach*. New York, NY: Oxford University Press.

Salomon, G. (1994). *Interaction of media, cognition, and learning*. Mahwah, NJ: LEA.

Schnotz, W. (2014). Integrated model of text and picture comprehension. In R. E. Mayer (Ed.), *The Cambridge handbook of multimedia learning* (pp. 72–103). New York, NY: Cambridge University Press.

Sylwester, R. (1995). *A celebration of neurons*. Alexandria: Association for Supervision and Curriculum Development.

van Gog, T. (2014). The signaling (or cueing) principle in multimedia learning. In R. E. Mayer (Ed.), *The Cambridge handbook of multimedia learning* (pp. 263–278). New York, NY: Cambridge University Press.

Wittrock, M. C. (1989). Generative processes of comprehension. *Educational Psychologist*, 24(4), 345–376.

Yoon, F. S., Ho, J., & Hedberg, J. G. (2005). Teacher understandings of technology affordances and their impact on the design of engaging learning experiences. *Educational Media International*, 42(4), 297–316.

5 Representing and Sharing Content Using Technology

ABSTRACT

Having considered various types of pedagogy as well as technology affordances and multimedia learning principles, this chapter focuses on issues surrounding the representation and sharing of content using technology. Anderson & Krathwohl's (2001) Taxonomy of Learning, Teaching and Assessing is examined as a means of conceptualizing different types of thinking processes in a way that can be applied across discipline areas. The representational requirements of different subject areas (English, mathematics, science, history, geography, and computing) are explored by means of examples, with reference to the role of technology and the range of possible tasks that may be utilized. Assessment issues as they relate to the representation of content are also considered. The broader contextual shift toward open education and sharing is discussed, including key drivers such as learning object repositories, open educational resources, Creative Commons licensing, and massive open online courses.

Introduction to Representing Content Using Technology

One of the fundamental ways that technology is used to promote learning is by representing content. Digital technologies enable facts, concepts, and skills to be represented across a range of disciplines using multimodal and interactive techniques. This chapter will examine some of the ways in which content can be represented and conceptualized in order to underpin the effective design of lessons and use of learning materials. This is of particular importance because the way content is represented and shared influences the thinking and learning that occur as a result.

As in previous chapters, this chapter's focus is upon underlying frameworks and thinking skills that can guide the design of technology-enhanced learning. For instance, how can we conceptualize the type of content that needs to be represented and shared? What is the role of technology in supporting knowledge representation and thinking processes? What are the different representational requirements of different discipline areas and how can technology be used to support them? What are the implications of using technology for representing content as part of assessment processes? How does and should the shifting landscape of content sharing and open educational resources influence teacher practice?

We will begin by considering how different sorts of content can be conceptualized in general terms before considering how technology can be used to represent content within the disciplines. Note that because this chapter is focused on the nexus between content and technology (TC Knowledge according to the TPACK model) it will not address more social pedagogies or technologies in any detail. These will be discussed in an integrated sense in later chapters.

Conceptualizing Content Using Anderson & Krathwohl's Taxonomy of Learning, Teaching and Assessing

With so many different representational demands across a range of disciplines, one challenge is how to best conceptualize to-be-learnt content in way that encompasses a variety of different learning areas. One possible way to think about content is by means of

Anderson and Krathwohl's (2001) Taxonomy of Learning, Teaching and Assessing. Their framework incorporates a Knowledge dimension and cognitive process dimension that are not bound to specific discipline areas. An advantage of using Anderson and Krathwohl's (2001) taxonomy for conceptualizing content is that it retains a focus on learning (knowledge types and cognitive processes) rather than on technology, and thus offers a framework for thinking about the representation of content that is somewhat resilient to changes in technologies over time. A summary of Anderson & Krathwohl's Taxonomy of Learning, Teaching and Assessing is shown in Table 5.1.

The Knowledge dimension of Anderson and Krathwohl's (2001) taxonomy relate to the sorts of subject matter content being addressed and incorporates the following four categories:

1. Factual knowledge – discrete pieces of elementary information, required if people are to be acquainted with a discipline and solve problems within it
2. Conceptual knowledge – interrelated representations of more complex knowledge forms, including schemas, categorization hierarchies, and explanations
3. Procedural knowledge – the skills to perform processes, to execute algorithms, and to know the criteria for their appropriate application
4. Metacognitive knowledge – knowledge and awareness of one's own cognition as well as that of other people (Anderson & Krathwohl, 2001, pp. 27–29).

Table 5.1.   Anderson & Krathwohl's (2001) Taxonomy of Learning, Teaching and Assessing

Knowledge Dimension	Cognitive Process Dimension					
	Remember	Understand	Apply	Analyze	Evaluate	Create
Factual Knowledge						
Conceptual Knowledge						
Procedural Knowledge						
Metacognitive Knowledge						

The levels of the cognitive process dimension of Anderson and Krathwohl's (2001) model are Remember, Understand, Apply, Analyze, Evaluate, and Create, which represent a refinement of Bloom's (1956) taxonomy. These cognitive processes represent a continuum from lower order thinking skills to higher order thinking skills, with lower level thinking capacities being a necessary prerequisite for corresponding higher order thinking skills to occur. Anderson and Krathwohl's (2001) model outlines a number of subprocesses that comprise each level, and Churches (2008) extended these to incorporate the sorts of cognitive processes that specifically relate to digital learning (examples of Churches' additional digital processes listed in italics):

- *Remember* – Recognizing, listing, describing, identifying, retrieving, naming, locating, finding, *highlighting, bookmarking, social bookmarking*
- *Understand* – Interpreting, summarizing, inferring, paraphrasing, classifying, comparing, explaining, exemplifying, *blog journaling, commenting, annotating*
- *Apply* – Implementing, carrying out, using, executing, *running, operating, editing*
- *Analyze* – Comparing, organizing, deconstructing, attributing, outlining, finding, structuring, integrating, *tagging, validating, reverse-engineering*
- *Evaluate* – Checking, hypothesizing, critiquing, experimenting, judging, testing, detecting, monitoring, *blog/vlog commenting, moderating, alpha/beta testing*
- *Create* – designing, constructing, planning, producing, inventing, devising, making, *programming, publishing, directing/producing.*

It is important to note that each of these processes (or 'verbs') are generalizations, and the extent to which students actually engage the level of thinking of the cognitive process category depends on the task itself and the students' level of cognitive engagement with it.

How does Anderson and Krathwohl's (2001) taxonomy support technology enabled design? The point is this – based on the type of knowledge and the intended cognitive processes different technologies will be more or less suitable for representing the task at hand. For instance, a text chat tool such as Twitter may be perfectly reasonable tool for sharing a definition of cardio pulmonary resuscitation, but video may be more appropriate for teachers (or students) to demonstrate application of the process. A presentation tool such as Prezi may be useful for explaining concepts underpinning the events leading up to World War I, but a blog may be better for students to evaluate how they have engaged with learning modern historical concepts in a metacognitive sense. Reflecting upon the knowledge types and cognitive processes intended for the content being addressed can lead to more appropriate selection and utilization of technologies.

On another level, Anderson and Krathwohl's (2001) taxonomy can provide a useful planning and reflection tool for curriculum design. Firstly, do the tasks that make up a module of work focus more on some knowledge types or cognitive processes more than others? If so, then there may be a need to diversify the sorts of tasks being applied. Secondly, is there alignment between the learning outcomes, the tasks that have been set, and the way that students will be assessed? Biggs and Tang (2011) refer to this as 'constructive alignment,' and note that in education the learning tasks often do not match the sorts of knowledge or cognitive processes prescribed in the pre-identified outcomes, and these may also be misaligned with the nature of the assessment tasks. Thus, Anderson and Krathwohl's (2001) Taxonomy of Learning, Teaching and Assessing provides a generally applicable starting point for analyzing and evaluating digital content representation.

Disciplines and Their Different Representational Demands

Although Anderson and Krathwohl's (2001) taxonomy offers a generic framework for considering content, it is important to also recognize that different disciplines have different representational demands (Hedberg & Van Bergen, 2008). In each discipline area there may be different technologies that better support the particular representational requirements of the subject matter. While some of these technologies may fulfill needs of other disciplines, often they are more appropriate or frequently used in a particular discipline, or are in fact unique to a discipline. While it is not the purpose of this book to provide an in-depth expose of how different technologies cater to different disciplinary needs (for each discipline it would be possible to write a book about how technology facilitates subject specific content representation), some are mentioned here as a way of highlighting the variety of representational demands and technology uses in different learning areas. Possible student tasks are also postulated in order to demonstrate the types of learning that may be encouraged.

ENGLISH

In English, it is often useful to represent key language forms and features of a text. One popular way of extracting the key issues and themes from a piece of writing is to use a word cloud, for instance using Wordle™ (http://wordle.net). After entering the URL of the text under consideration, a visual representation of the key words from the text are organized as an image, with more frequent words in larger font sizes (see Figure 5.1). This enables rapid identification of the language elements being most frequently used, and the capacity to perform some surface level analysis of the constitution and focus of a text. Accordingly, students could be asked to perform an initial analysis of how language is used to emphasize key themes in a given composition, or evaluate whether their own writing may be weighted toward certain sorts of vocabulary. In these cases, technology takes the role of rapidly representing a summary of the content in a different form for the purposes of analysis.

Figure 5.1. Example of a Wordle™ Word Cloud Based on the Text from This Chapter.

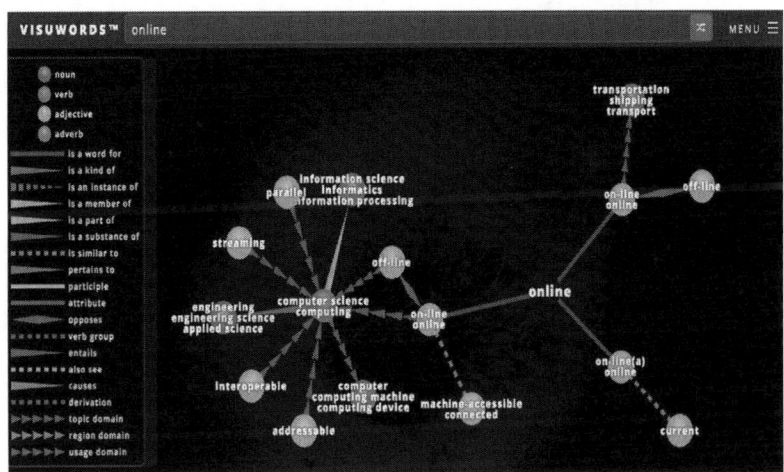

Figure 5.2.   A Visuwords™ Word Map for the Word 'Online.'

Another example of the technological representation of content in English is the Visuwords™ visual dictionary and thesaurus (http://visuwords.com). After the user enters the word of interest Visuwords™ will visually map semantically related words (such as instances, synonyms, antonyms, as well as different grammatical forms) as an ontological network (see Figure 5.2). This enables learners to develop a better understanding of the meaning of words and to evaluate the appropriateness of the words that they and their peers are using. For instance, students may be asked to check the meaning of new vocabulary they are learning, to diversify the language they are using in their writing, or to critique the representation of a particular word based on their developing subject matter expertise. In these cases technology facilitates rapid retrieval of subject matter information and representation of interrelationships.

SCIENCE

In science technology can help to represent phenomena such as the structure of molecules, the laws of physics, or biological processes that would not be possible or as easily achieved by other means. For example, the PhET Interactive Simulation collection from the University of Colorado allows students to perform experiments in physics, biology, chemistry, and earth sciences (http://phet.colorado.edu). A screenshot of a masses and springs

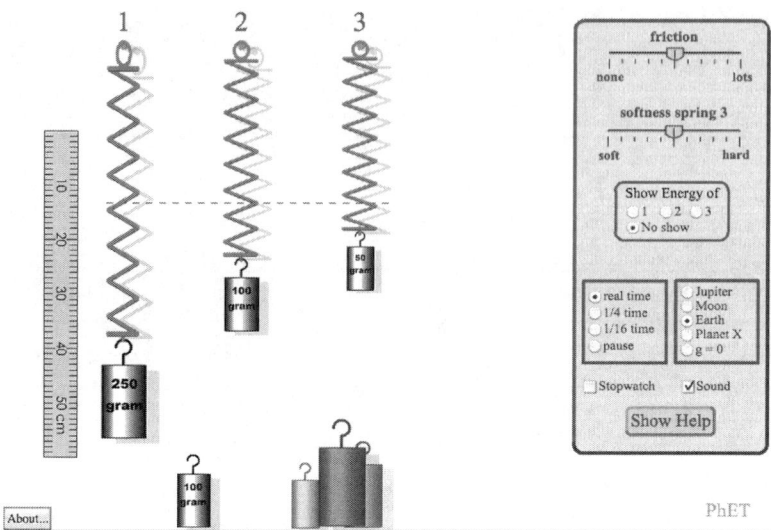

Figure 5.3. Masses and Springs Interactive Simulation from the University of Colorado Allowing Students to Deduce Physics Properties. PhET Interactive Simulations, University of Colorado Boulder https://phet.colorado.edu.

simulation is shown in Figure 5.3. The simulations enable learners to simulate and analyze scientific concepts so that they can observe and deduce an understanding of the principles for themselves. For instance, students could be asked to apply formulas that determine the frequency of oscillation based on the weight of a spring, or through simulation derive the formula for themselves.

Sometimes information can be cleverly organized using technology so as to spatially represent the relationship between content. One example in the science discipline is the Periodic Table of Videos produced by The University of Nottingham (http://www.periodicvideos.com). Each element in the periodic table is hyperlinked to a video explaining the properties of the element as well as information regarding how it can be used (see Figure 5.4). In this way, students have an organizing structure with which to consider how the atomic composition of elements may affect their properties in relation to other elements. Students in a class could be asked to each review one element and through report-back see if they can determine patterns among the atomic values and elemental properties. Alternately, the videos could be used as an introduction to provide salient information about an element before an in-class experiment. In this example, technology plays an organizing role in accessing and providing information.

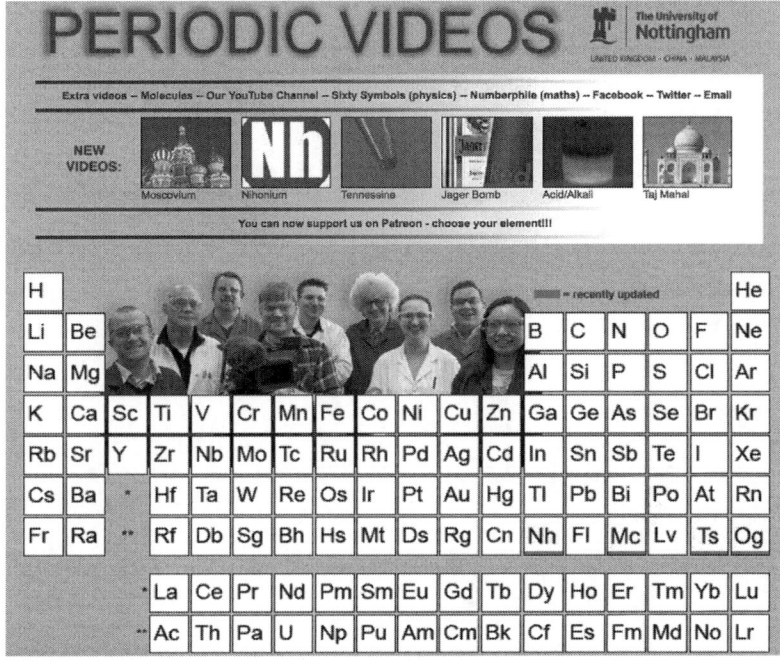

Figure 5.4.   Periodic Table of Videos, with a Video Hyperlink from Each Element in the Periodic Table.

MATHEMATICS

In mathematics, there is a frequent need to represent algebraic notation, graphs, shapes, and at times dynamic concepts such as those involving limits or geometric theorems. There is a myriad of tools that support these functions. For instance, the Utah State University National Library of Virtual Manipulables offers a range of mathematics tools that support dynamic visualization of mathematical concepts (http://nlvm.usu.edu). Figure 5.5 shows a 'virtual manipulable' that traces the construction of a Golden Spiral. This allows learners to more rapidly acquire an understanding of the shape and how it is constructed than if they or the teacher drew it themselves. Technology here supports rapid visualization.

Other mathematics software such as *GeoGebra*, *Geometer's Sketchpad*, and *Mathematica* provide learners with the capacity to draw, graph, calculate, manipulate, and examine differences according to their own input based on the mathematical problem at hand. A screenshot of *GeoGebra* in action is shown in

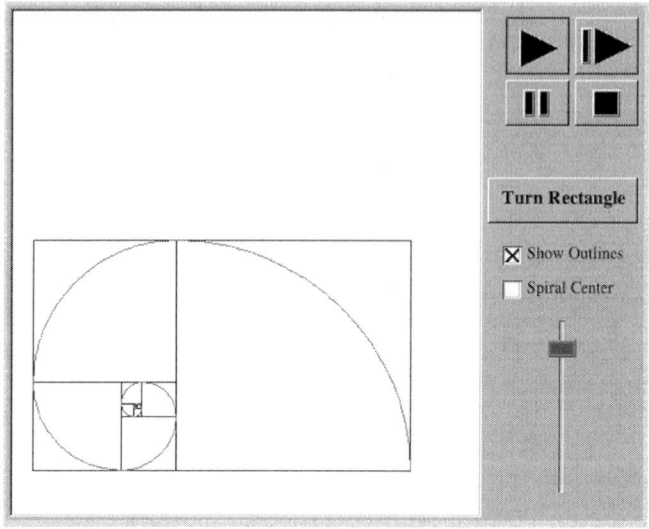

Figure 5.5.   'Virtual Manipulable' Tracing the Construction of the Golden Spiral.

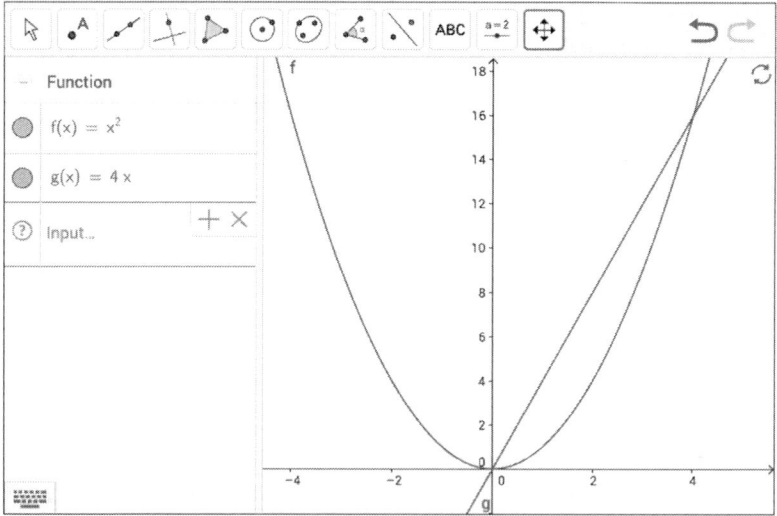

Figure 5.6.   Graphs of Curves Shown in *GeoGebra*.

Figure 5.6. Students can be asked to graph relationships, represent geometric patterns, construct algebraic equations, deduce theorems, and solve real world problems. The flexibility of this sort of mathematical software means it can be used for basic tasks where students learn the essential nature of different mathematical constructs as well as for more authentic problem-solving tasks. For instance, students could use the graphs in Figure 5.6 to learn the basic shape of linear and quadratic functions, or to find the side length of a square that has area the same as its perimeter length. In this example, technology becomes a tool to support calculation, visualization, and abstraction.

HISTORY

In history educators and learners often want to represent timelines, upload and share artifacts for review, and represent scenes or models that portray historical events. Using Tiki-Toki™ they can create timelines in three dimensions (http://tiki-toki.com), for instance, the timeline representing the history of the Tower of London shown in Figure 5.7. The use of two dimensions enables different themes to be plotted beside one another, and hyperlinking facilities allow more in-depth rich-media information to be nested at each point. Students could be asked to learn a chronology of events created by the teacher and consequently explain what caused key occurrences to eventuate. Alternately they could be asked to research and create timelines for themselves. Technology becomes a tool for organizing, documenting, and sharing information.

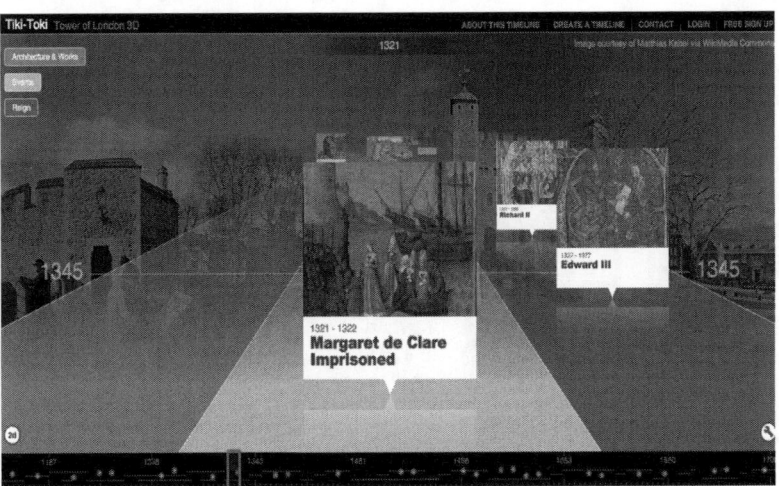

Figure 5.7. Timeline Representing the History of the Tower of London Created Using Tiki-Toki™.

GEOGRAPHY

Geographical Information Systems (GISs) have almost redefined the geography field. GISs enable data across a geographic region to be represented visually, and information sets to be layered on top of one another. Figure 5.8 shows a screenshot of the IDRISI GIS system showing seasonal trends in Europe. GISs constitute powerful tools for developing higher order thinking capabilities through analysis of data, evaluation of strategies, and designing courses of action. For instance, students can be asked to analyze time-series data of geographic information to predict the possible impact of global warming over time. Technology becomes a tool for summarizing, organizing, manipulating, and visualizing.

COMPUTING

In computing we often wish to represent programming logic and have students share it with other learners. As one example the *Scratch* visual programming application shown in Figure 5.9 allows students to drag and drop computing constructs and 'play' their programs within the interface without having to write programming code (http://scratch.mit.edu). By removing the need to write programming code, learners can represent programming constructs and apply programming processes without being

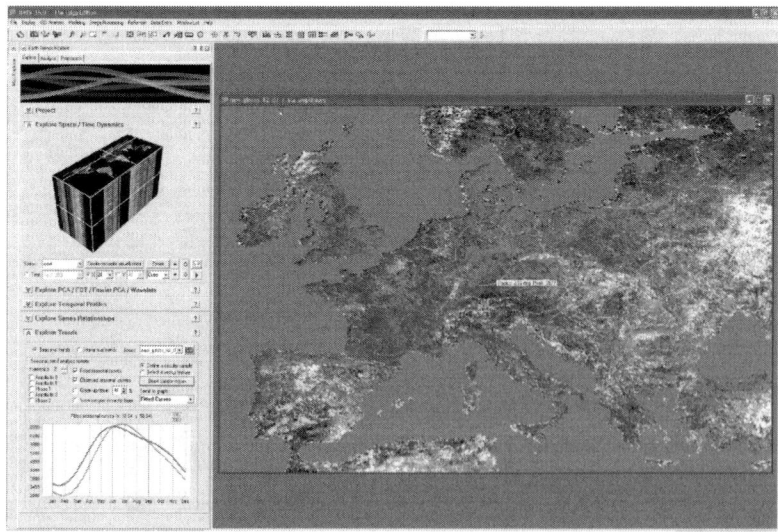

Figure 5.8.   IDRISI GIS Seasonal Trends (CC-BY Shankar Dayal).

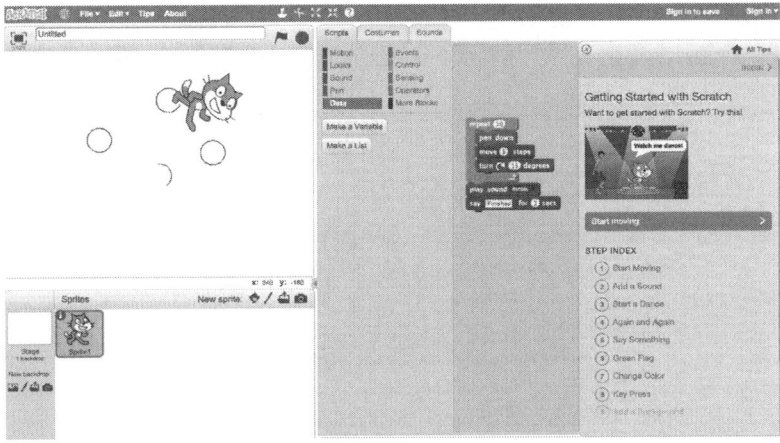

Figure 5.9. The Scratch Visual Programming Interface Supporting the Development of Computing Concepts through Drag and Drop Controls.

concerned about making syntactical errors. The system also incorporates a facility for the sharing of programs, as a means for users to source creative ideas and learn from each other. Students could be asked to create a digital story using *Scratch* based on a topic being studied in class, or evaluate the quality of programs uploaded to the Scratch Community website. Technology provides a means of scaffolding scripting and sharing programs in a way that removes some of the complexity inherent in higher level computing practice.

REFLECTIONS UPON THE REPRESENTATION OF CONTENT USING TECHNOLOGY

There are many other subject areas in which content has particular representational requirements that are satisfied by discipline-specific technologies, and it is not possible to provide a comprehensive review of all such tools here. However, it is useful to reflect upon how, even among the small number of examples provided above, a broad range of knowledge types and cognitive processes can be supported. These have been mapped within Table 5.2 based on the very brief postulations of learning tasks, noting there are many other cognitive processes and knowledge types that could be addressed in each discipline area using the aforementioned (and other) technologies. It is also important to point out that tasks

Table 5.2.   Different Types of Discipline-Specific Technology-Enhanced Learning Tasks Organized according to Anderson and Krathwohl's (2001) Taxonomy of Learning, Teaching and Assessing.

Knowledge Dimension	Cognitive Process Dimension					
	Remember	Understand	Apply	Analyze	Evaluate	Create
Factual Knowledge	Use a timeline to help remember when events occurred	Understand what led to a particular historical event occurring	Use Visuwords to diversify the language usage in a passage	Analyze the content of a given text using a word cloud	Evaluate vocabulary of own writing using a word cloud	Create a timeline of key events for a historical period
Conceptual Knowledge	Use graphing software to help remember the shape of different curves	Understand relationship between word meanings using Visuwords	Use graphs in order to solve authentic problems	Use videos to analyze how the properties of elements relate to their atomic value	Critique how a word meaning is represented in Visuwords	Use a simulation to derive a formula for oscillation of a spring
Procedural Knowledge	Use videos to learn safety information about how to handle chemical elements	Use plotting tool to understand how a Golden Spiral is constructed	Apply a formula to predict oscillation in a spring simulation	Analyze time-series data using GIS to predict impact of global warming	Evaluate the way in which peers created their computer programs	Create a digital story using Scratch

Note: metacognitive knowledge is not represented in the table because the technologies that typically support it tend not to be discipline specific (for instance, blogs and mindmapping tools).

(including those that relate to technology-enhanced learning) do not neatly and completely fall into knowledge and cognitive process dimensions. A range of knowledge dimensions and cognitive processes are often engaged as part of a learning activity. However, it can be helpful to reflect upon what sort of knowledge and cognitive processes are being centrally targeted, in order to promote conscious design practices that align outcomes, tasks, technology, and assessment.

Table 5.2 highlights some important aspects of using technology to represent content. In terms of design, the cognitive processes that are encouraged are less bound to the technology being used, and are more related to the sorts of tasks teachers design.

For instance, a timeline tool can be used to help remember factual knowledge or create factual knowledge. Of course, whether or not any of the targeted cognitive processes occur depends greatly on the learning environment and how students engage with the task (this will be discussed in more detail in the next chapter).

Technologies often do tend to lend themselves to the representation of certain sorts of knowledge types. For example, the timelines and the summaries provided by word clouds lend themselves to the representation of factual knowledge, simulations, and pattern representations enabled by mathematics and science software helps to develop conceptual understanding, and the ability to practice scripting means that programming tools support the development of procedural knowledge. The reason for these relationships is because of the nature of the knowledge types and the technologies themselves. Factual knowledge involves discrete chunks of information, conceptual knowledge involves interrelationships between items of information, and procedural knowledge involves sequenced information. Accordingly, technologies that facilitate representation of each (for instance, those based on text, diagrams, and videos, respectively) may provide more appropriate representation. However, once again, there are no hard-and-fast rules, with technologies often representing and developing multiple knowledge types (as shown in Table 5.2).

What we can conclude is that technology, within different disciplines and for different content, plays an important role in mediating learning through rapid access, retrieval, representation, organization, summarization, visualization, simulation, calculation, documentation, manipulation, programming, and sharing of information. Therefore, it critical that educators and researchers understand the nuanced praxis of their disciplines and how different tools can be used to support knowledge representation and learning processes. This is particularly important for assessment, where students deserve the opportunity to be provided with tools that enable them to accurately and fully demonstrate what they have learnt.

Considering the Assessment of Learning Using Technology

Technology not only plays an important role in representing and sharing content for instructional purposes and as part of learning tasks, but also for assessment. The primary objective of representing and sharing content is so that people can develop accurate and comprehensive schema or 'mental models,' so it is critical that technologies provide learners with the capacity to represent their mental models in order for teachers to gauge students' understanding and provide appropriate feedback. This is fundamental to Laurillard's Conversational Framework (Laurillard, 2002), as we will see in the next chapter. However, it can be challenging to select technologies for assessment purposes when there are so many at the educator's disposal, and so many different types of content that may require representation. As well, teachers may have different pedagogical intentions when they assess students as they learn (formatively) as compared to when they are assessing learning outcomes at the end of a term or course (summatively). At a higher level, on what basis can educators and researchers conceptualize the extent to which students have learnt the desired knowledge and skills?

One well-established and general framework for considering the structure and sophistication of student representations of their mental models is SOLO taxonomy (Biggs & Collis, 1982). It is a long-standing and well-renown constructivist model that classifies the completeness of information that has been provided in a student's representation of their mental model and the extent to which it has been interrelated. The SOLO taxonomy has five levels:

1. Prestructural – the learner does not understand any aspects of the concept or target system
2. Unistructural – the learner is able to present one correct element regarding the concept or target system
3. Multistructural – the learner can provide several correct responses regarding the concept or target system but presents incorrect responses on other aspects and the correct responses are not entirely interrelated with one another to form a complete mental model
4. Relational – the learner presents a complete understanding of all of the elements of the concept and target system and these are all logically and consistently interrelated with one another
5. Extended abstract – the learner not only demonstrates a completed understanding of all of the elements of a target system and how they relate, but can also relate it to concepts outside the target system.

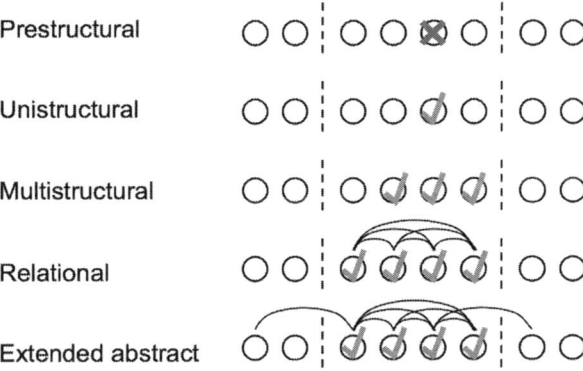

Figure 5.10. A Schematic Representation of Knowledge Structures at Different Levels of the SOLO Taxonomy.

The different levels of the SOLO taxonomy are illustrated in Figure 5.10. The taxonomy is not an attempt to box responses into one level or another. Rather, by defining levels of responses in terms of the features of the response educators are provided with a somewhat consistent means of describing different levels of mental model development, and thinking through how technologies might be used to assess them. From a technological point of view, the SOLO taxonomy sheds light on how different tools may or may not support the sharing and assessment of students' mental models. For instance, it may be possible to assess that students have a unistructural understanding using online multiple-choice quizzes or single line text responses. However, if a relational or even extended abstract understanding is to be assessed, then it may be necessary to provide students with diagramming or extended text response tools. This may differ according to when in the learning cycle knowledge formation takes place – when assessing prior knowledge or formatively assessing students during a module of work teachers may be more interested in gauging unistructural or multistructural understanding, whereas summative assessment at the end of a unit may focus upon relational or extended abstract understanding.

Thus, we can see that there is a lot to consider when representing content for learning, teaching, and assessment purposes, from the type of knowledge being shared, to the discipline-specific representational requirements, to the sophistication and elaborateness of the knowledge and skills being assessed. Furthermore, it can be immensely time consuming to evaluate technologies and develop resources. While individuals can undoubtedly make substantial progress in design of technology-enhanced tasks and resources to support learning and assessment, the greatest transformation (individually and societally) can only occur through a communal culture of open collaboration.

The Open Education Revolution

Open education is a rapidly evolving modus operandi for sharing content and resources in the learning and teaching field. Before this century 'copyright' was the only major legal paradigm for the distribution of resources. The underlying assumption of copyright is that the creators of a resource will want to own all rights to it and prevent others from using or benefiting from their efforts. Copyright does not cater for the possibility that people may be willing to share their work, either openly or under certain conditions.

In September of 2007, approximately thirty influential educators from around the world joined forces to form the Capetown Declaration – a decree promoting the open sharing of resources, technologies, and teaching practices in education. The declaration can be found at http://www.capetowndeclaration.org. It reads:

> This emerging open education movement combines the established tradition of sharing good ideas with fellow educators and the collaborative, interactive culture of the Internet. It is built on the belief that everyone should have the freedom to use, customize, improve and redistribute educational resources without constraint. Educators, learners and others who share this belief are gathering together as part of a worldwide effort to make education both more accessible and more effective. (Cape Town Open Education Declaration, 2007, para 2)

The declaration drew over 2,500 signatories from around the world, with the intention of encouraging educators to create openly available resources, to champion a sharing orientation, and to work toward policy that embraces international collaboration. Benefits of open education for society include greater access to learning resources for students and teachers, sharing of pedagogical and curriculum knowledge by teachers, the ability to adapt and collaboratively improve upon existing resources, greater efficiencies within the education field, and emergent networks of educators with common interests (Cape Town Open Education Declaration, 2007).

Initially, the open education movement was best encapsulated through the development and sharing of modular and reusable 'learning objects' that teachers could embed within their lessons. In very general terms, this was followed by a shift toward more 'open educational resources,' which were more varied in nature and more likely to reside outside dedicated online repositories. Open educational resources and the rise of open courseware were both facilitated through the development of Creative Commons licenses. More recently, open education has manifest itself through the emergence of Massive Open Online Courses (MOOCs). Each of these phenomena are briefly discussed below.

LEARNING OBJECTS

Some of the examples of discipline-specific tools described above that have very focused applications can be described as 'learning objects.' For instance, the interactive spring and mass simulation in Figure 5.3 and the virtual golden spiral manipulable in Figure 5.5 can both be considered to be learning objects. Learning objects have been defined as "discrete chunks of reusable learning materials or activities that can articulate with other learning objects to build a learning environment" (Koppi, Bogle, & Bogle, 2005, p. 84). While the term 'learning object' can be used loosely to describe any reusable learning material whether physical or computer based, it is frequently used to describe digital learning objects. To this extent, the Wisconsin Online learning object repository defines learning objects as "web-based, self-contained, small chunks of learning ... [that] are small enough to be embedded in a learning activity, lesson, unit, or course" (Wisc-Online, 2017).

Learning objects may be assessments, animations, simulations, case studies, drill and practice activities, or templates (Wisc-Online, 2017). Characteristics of learning objects include the extent to which a learning object may be reused (reusability), the size of a learning object (granularity), the information that describes a learning object (metadata), the extent to which the learning object contains content versus promotes learning (content and structure), whether a learning object supports collection of data from learners (tracking), the degree to which the learning object can be integrated with other learning objects (standards), and the extent to which the learning object can be used in different learning and content management systems (interoperability) (Churchill, 2007). The utopian vision is that any learning object should be perfectly portable and reusable so that the amount of work required by educators is minimized. This requires that learning objects are easily locatable, sufficiently adaptable, and interoperable in order for educators to efficiently harness their power.

Learning objects are often organized into repositories, for instance:

- Merlot: http://www.merlot.org
- Wisconsin Online: http://www.wisconline.org
- Scootle (by Educational Services Australia): http://scootle.edu.au

Each repository has its own criteria for sourcing, accepting, organizing, and describing learning objects. Not all repositories make their learning objects freely available, though many do. For a more comprehensive list of learning object repositories, see: http://edutechwiki.unige.ch/en/Learning_objects_repositories.

The attempt to transform the educational field by creating learning object repositories has been criticized by some, firstly because of the variable pedagogy inherent in many learning objects that is often decontexualized, transmissionist, and reductionist (Jonassen & Churchill, 2004), and secondly because in practice teachers often do not utilize learning object repositories to their full advantage (Parrish, 2004; Pegler, 2013).

OPEN EDUCATIONAL RESOURCES

While there was a strong push to set up and embed learning object repositories in the 2000s, in more recent years the international drive seems to have been utilization of the exponentially increasing amount of resources available outside of repositories. Educators often draw from open websites, blogs, YouTube, and a range of other online resources that have not necessarily been created for educational purposes let alone a specific learning activity. The underlying philosophy of learning objects and their extensively designed nature constitute noble and valuable ideals, and there is no doubt that learning object repositories are a useful source of resources for educators. Nonetheless, it is important to understand the limitations of learning objects and the potential of freely available content beyond their archives, that is, to consider 'open educational resources.'

Open Educational Resources (OERs) can be defined as "digitized materials offered freely and openly for educators, students, and self-learners to use and reuse for teaching, learning, and research" (Bissell, 2009, p. 97). There are many open education initiatives that release and support the use of Open Educational Resources (OERs). Well-known initiatives that offer OERs including OER Commons (http://oercommons.org), Curriki (http://curriki.org), The Open Education Consortium (http://www.oeconsortium.org), and the CK-12 Foundation (http://www.ck12.org). In some cases, resources are organized into entire courses with well-known instances including Massachusetts Institute of Technology Open Courseware (http://ocw.mit.edu), Khan Academy (http://khanacademy.org), and Connexions (http://cnx.org). However, as previously identified, many freely available educational resources that fall under the banner of OERs do not reside in custom-built repositories, but rather are sourced from the Internet at large. In order to find OERs, Google advanced search (http://www.google.com.au/advanced_search) allow users to filter by usage rights, or the Creative Commons website Search tool (http://search.creativecommons.org) searches for materials that can be used under their licenses (discussed in more detail below). Alternately, people often search on websites that they know contain OERs, such as Wikimedia Commons (http://commons.wikimedia.org). For further support in finding OERs see the Open Professionals Education Network (http://open4us.org/find-oer) that has a directory of OER sites and search strategies, or the WikiEducator OER Handbook (http://wikieducator.org/OER_Handbook/educator_version_one). Another valuable source of information about OERs is the Creative Commons website itself (see https://creativecommons.org/education and https://wiki.creativecommons.org/wiki/What_is_OER?) with Creative Commons being the engine that enables clear and explicit sharing agreements for open education to occur.

CREATIVE COMMONS LICENSES

Practices underpinning the effective utilization of OERs are the ability to reuse, redistribute, revise, and remix (Hilton, Wiley, Stein, & Johnson, 2010). Creative Commons licenses are the way in which people and organizations specify the conditions under which they are willing to share their work. They enable release of intellectual property with less stringent conditions than a full

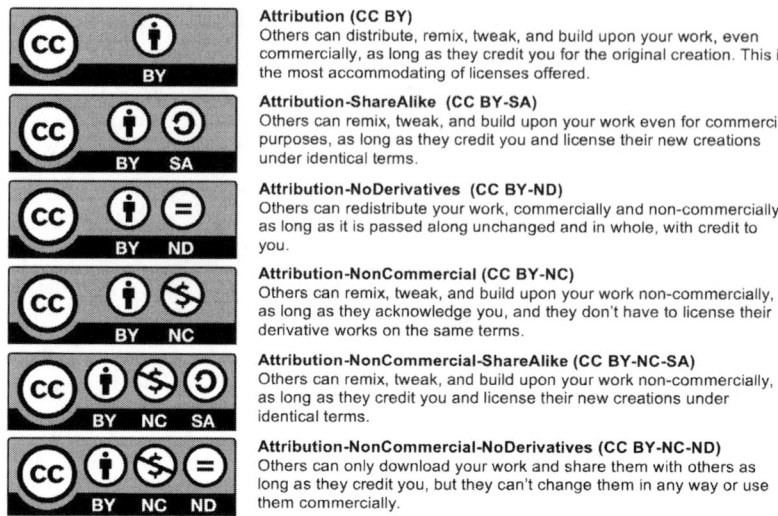

Attribution (CC BY)
Others can distribute, remix, tweak, and build upon your work, even commercially, as long as they credit you for the original creation. This is the most accommodating of licenses offered.

Attribution-ShareAlike (CC BY-SA)
Others can remix, tweak, and build upon your work even for commercial purposes, as long as they credit you and license their new creations under identical terms.

Attribution-NoDerivatives (CC BY-ND)
Others can redistribute your work, commercially and non-commercially, as long as it is passed along unchanged and in whole, with credit to you.

Attribution-NonCommercial (CC BY-NC)
Others can remix, tweak, and build upon your work non-commercially, as long as they acknowledge you, and they don't have to license their derivative works on the same terms.

Attribution-NonCommercial-ShareAlike (CC BY-NC-SA)
Others can remix, tweak, and build upon your work non-commercially, as long as they credit you and license their new creations under identical terms.

Attribution-NonCommercial-NoDerivatives (CC BY-NC-ND)
Others can only download your work and share them with others as long as they credit you, but they can't change them in any way or use them commercially.

Figure 5.11.   Six Popular Creative Commons Licenses.

copyright license. While the range of possible licenses has undergone some changes since their introduction in 2002, there are currently six popular licenses available under the Creative Commons 4.0 scheme (Creative Commons, 2017), as shown and explained in Figure 5.11.

Creative Commons licenses give educators much greater flexibility when sharing the fruits of their labor, because they can decide whether they wish to be attributed as the owner, whether they are willing to permit derivative works, whether other people can make money from their work, and whether they want people to share under the same conditions that they have. For more information about the Creative Commons licenses, see the Creative Commons website (2017) at http://creativecommons.org/licences. In any case, it is important to check the usage rights of any resources being drawn from the Internet because they vary case-by-case. It is also crucial that teachers understand intellectual property laws in their jurisdiction because fair usage rights for education can vary between countries.

MASSIVE OPEN ONLINE COURSES

While arguably edging beyond the focus of the chapter, it is hard not to at least briefly mention MOOCs when talking about open education and representation of content using technology. MOOCs are 'massive' insofar as there are virtually no limits to numbers of enrollments, 'open' because anyone from the public can freely enroll, 'online' by virtue of requiring no physical attendance, and 'courses' insofar as they provide structured resources and activities with an aim of helping students achieve specific learning outcomes (Educause, 2011). Building upon the idea of open courseware as freely available and organized course resources, MOOCs additionally incorporate teacher guidance and interaction with other learners from around the world as people complete online courses together. Well-known MOOC providers include Coursera (http://coursera.org), edX (http://edx.org), and Udacity (http://udacity.com), with Coursera and edX being affiliated with higher education institutions and Udacity having an industry emphasis. For a list of MOOC and open course providers, see http://www.mooc.ca/providers.htm. For a directory of MOOCs on offer around the world, see https://www.mooc-list.com.

MOOCs have received a great deal of popular attention when they first emerged into the mainstream, with the *New York Times* labeling 2012 the "Year of the MOOC" (Pappano, 2012). However, the pedagogical quality of MOOCs has been called into question, as they tend to adopt more transmissionist, decontextualized, and individualistic approaches to teaching as opposed to more constructivist, authentic, and social approaches to learning (Margaryan, Bianco, & Littlejohn, 2015; Toven-Lindsey, Rhoads, & Lozano, 2015). As well, completion rates of MOOCs are usually very low — typically at around 10% of enrollments — due to factors such as lack of incentive, assistance, understanding, and time (Hew & Cheung, 2014). Nevertheless, the freely available nature of MOOCs means that educators are able to use them as a source of resources and as inspiration for ideas. Teachers can even have students access MOOCs as part of their own classes. So while the effectiveness of MOOCs generally may still be under question, they undoubtedly form an important part of the digital content ecology.

Summary of Issues Surrounding the Representation of Content Using Technology

This chapter has established foundations for thinking about the representation and sharing of content using technology.

Anderson and Krathwohl's (2001) Taxonomy of Learning, Teaching and Assessing reminds us that there are a wide range of knowledge types and cognitive processes that may need to be represented for learners and supported by teachers. Tabulating some examples demonstrated that the type of knowledge represented may influence the sort of technology we use, though the type of thinking encouraged will depend heavily on the task educators prescribe.

Different disciplines have different representational requirements, and it is critical that educators come to understand how technologies support cognitive development and sharing within the fields they teach. Technology can play an important mediating role in the representation and sharing of content by enabling rapid access, retrieval, representation, organization, summarization, visualization, simulation, calculation, documentation, manipulation, programming, and sharing of information. When using technology for assessment purposes it is important that students have the opportunity to represent the complexity of their understanding, which may vary according to whether assessment is taking place during the learning process (formatively) or at the end of a unit of work (summatively).

On a contextual level, it is important to understand the relatively recent and rapid open education movement. Learning object repositories provide a source of topic-specific digital resources for educators to consider when designing their learning activities. However, these need to be evaluated for appropriateness and pedagogical quality. Open Educational Resources may be considered for less structured media that can be used as inputs into modules, with open courseware and MOOCs providing educators with additional resources, activities, and ideas that they can utilize when designing technology-enhanced learning. Creative Commons licenses play an important role in providing the platform via which unambiguous and efficient sharing of resources can take place.

Concluding Remarks

With the proliferation of the Internet in the last two decades, we are now living at a time when high-quality resources are widely available to many. Novel discipline-specific technologies and practices provide new ways for teachers to help students understand the key concepts and skills of their subjects. Yet some see the uptake of open education to be disappointing, perhaps in part because it has not been supported by widespread Open Educational Practices (OEPs) such as institutional and systemic policies that encourage reuse (Pegler, 2013). There are undoubtedly pedagogical issues that need to be considered, such as the pedagogical quality of the resources on offer (Jonassen & Churchill, 2004; Margaryan et al., 2015; Toven-Lindsey et al., 2015). Care needs to be exercised when utilizing OERs, so as to respect the conditions of use that have been stipulated by the creator. Yet the shift toward open education and content provides a foundation to achieve international aspirations of access to quality education for all human beings (UNESCO et al., 2015).

What the proliferation of freely available digital content does mean is that the role of the educator changes. Whereas previous generations of educators quite often spent inordinate hours laboriously designing all their educational content on their own, they now need to be savvy content locators, with the ability to adapt and remix resources to suit their educational context. In a world where content is most likely available somewhere online, educators need to guide and support students to navigate, interpret, critique, and utilize digital content for themselves. And teachers need to be able to structure, sequence, and scaffold learning activities and environments in a way that optimizes learning and empowers students to take control.

Thus, educators of today need to be learning designers. While technology can play an important role in shaping the learning environment, it is simply the mediator of representation and collaboration. It is the type of task, thinking processes, and broader context in which students engage that determines the quality of learning. All of these are dependent on how the teacher designs the learning environment. This is the focus of the next chapter.

References

Anderson, L., & Krathwohl, D. (2001). *A taxonomy for learning, teaching and assessing: A revision of Bloom's taxonomy of educational objectives*. New York, NY: Longman.

Biggs, J., & Collis, K. (1982). *Evaluating the quality of learning: The SOLO taxonomy*. London: Academic Press.

Biggs, J., & Tang, C. (2011). *Teaching for quality learning at university* (3rd ed.). Maidenhead: McGraw-Hill.

Bissell, A. N. (2009). Permission granted: Open licensing for educational resources. *Open Learning, 24*(1), 97−106.

Bloom, B. S. (1956). *Taxonomy of educational objectives, handbook I: The cognitive domain*. New York, NY: David McKay Co Inc.

Cape Town Open Education Declaration. (2007). Cape Town Open Education Declaration: Unlocking the promise of open educational resources.

Churches, A. (2008). Bloom's taxonomy Blooms digitally. *Educators' eZine*. Retrieved from http://www.techlearning.com/article/8670. Accessed on February 22, 2011.

Churchill, D. (2007). Towards a useful classification of learning objects. *Educational Technology Research and Development, 55*(5), 479−497.

Creative Commons. (2017). About the licenses. Retrieved from https://creativecommons.org/licenses/. Accessed on January 1, 2017.

Educause. (2011). Seven things you should know about MOOCs. Retrieved from: https://library.educause.edu/resources/2011/11/7-things-you-should-know-about-moocs

Hedberg, J., & Van Bergen, P. (2008). Transforming through technologies the modalities of learning: New life sciences in secondary schooling. Paper presented at the World Conference on Educational Multimedia, Hypermedia and Telecommunications.

Hew, K. F., & Cheung, W. S. (2014). Students' and instructors' use of massive open online courses (MOOCs): Motivations and challenges. *Educational Research Review, 12*, 45−58.

Hilton, J., Wiley, D., Stein, J., & Johnson, A. (2010). The four 'R's of openness and ALMS analysis: Frameworks for open educational resources. *Open Learning, 25*(1), 37−44.

Jonassen, D. H., & Churchill, D. (2004). Is there a learning orientation in learning objects? *International Journal on E-Learning, 3*(2), 32−41.

Koppi, T., Bogle, L., & Bogle, M. (2005). Learning objects, repositories, sharing and reusability. *Open Learning: The Journal of Open, Distance and e-Learning, 20*(1), 83−91.

Laurillard, D. (2002). *Rethinking university teaching − A framework for the effective use of learning technologies*. Oxford: RoutledgeFalmer.

Margaryan, A., Bianco, M., & Littlejohn, A. (2015). Instructional quality of massive open online courses (MOOCs). *Computers & Education, 80*, 77−83.

Pappano, L. (2012). The Year of the MOOC. *The New York Times*. Retrieved from http://www.nytimes.com/2012/11/04/education/edlife/massive-open-online-courses-are-multiplying-at-a-rapid-pace.html

Parrish, P. E. (2004). The trouble with learning objects. *Educational Technology Research and Development, 52*(1), 49−67.

Pegler, C. (2013). The influence of open resources on design practice. In H. Beetham & R. Sharpe (Eds.), *Rethinking pedagogy for a digital age - Designing for 21st century learning* (pp. 306−333). New York, NY: Routledge.

Toven-Lindsey, B., Rhoads, R. A., & Lozano, J. B. (2015). Virtually unlimited classrooms: Pedagogical practices in massive open online courses. *The Internet and Higher Education, 24*, 1−12.

UNESCO et al. (2015). Incheon Declaration Education 2030: Towards inclusive and equitable quality education and lifelong learning for all. Retrieved from: http://www.unesco.org/new/en/education/themes/leading-the-international-agenda/ education-for-all/education-2030-framework-for-action/

Wisc-Online. (2017). About learning objects. Retrieved from https://www.wisc-online.com/about-learning-objects. Accessed on January 1, 2017.

6 Design Thinking and Learning Design

ABSTRACT

This chapter unpacks 'design thinking' as it relates to educational design, and highlights how developments in the field of Learning Design may be of assistance to educators. Design is defined as a creative, scientific, and complex process, underpinned by several design thinking qualities. Teaching, it is argued, should be positioned as a design science, based on its nature, practice, and intentions. Learning to design is characterized as a challenging pursuit that is supported through practice, refection, examples, and expert guidance. Based on the literature, the pursuit of designing for learning is explained as a process involving the creation of accessible and aligned designs that cater to students in order to achieve desired learning outcomes. Educational design models by Laurillard, Siemens, and Conole are contrasted and evaluated in order to critically reflect on the general utility of such models. The field of Learning Design is introduced as a discipline area that aims to help educators develop and share great teaching ideas. Six approaches that support the description and sharing of learning designs are briefly described (technical standards, pattern descriptions, visualizations, visualization tools, pedagogical planners, and the Learning Activity Management System) so as to illustrate how the Learning Design field has evolved and how educators can capitalize upon it. Directions forward are recommended, which center around reflection, collaboration, and a design orientation.

Introduction to Design Thinking and Learning Design

The design phase is where educators draw together their technological, pedagogical, content, and contextual knowledge to create synergistic solutions to educational problems. But the million dollar questions are how should educators go about design, and what does it involve? In order to address these questions we will be taking a broad look at design both generally and with relation to education.

This chapter starts by examining what design actually is and what design thinking involves. This is useful because it enables us to draw from what is known about design across the disciplines and utilize it in education. We will also consider why design is particularly hard to learn and what is known about how design capabilities are most effectively developed. After having laid these general foundations, we will turn our attention to the field of education to scrutinize what designing for learning involves based on design models and conventional wisdom from the field. The field of Learning Design is then introduced, and techniques for representing learning designs critiqued. This allows us to learn from the developments and thinking approaches of the field and critically understand how it can be best utilized in practice.

A reflective rather than accepting approach is adopted and encouraged, based on the assumption that all design knowledge needs to be applied in context. That is, this book resists the temptation to provide a lock-step set of algorithms for design. Why? Because that's not how either good science or good art occurs. Good design is neither linear nor mechanistic – otherwise we would get robots to do it. Rather than adopting a paint-by-numbers approach to design, this book acknowledges the educator as the situated expert who, with a deep understanding of the design issues and context is perfectly positioned to create the right tasks for their students. But in order for this to occur educators need to have a deep understanding of design generally and as it relates to education.

So let's start by asking: what exactly is design all about?

What Is Design?

Design has been simply and seminally defined as devising "courses of actions aimed at changing existing situations into preferred ones" (Simon, 1996, p. 111). Although concisely stated, this definition encapsulates key aspects of design, namely that design involves purposeful activity, it involves some form of creative transformation, and it is a value-laden pursuit. Alternately, Charles Burnette, a forefather of the Design-Based Education movement, defines design as:

> ... a process of creative and critical thinking that allows information and ideas to be organized, decisions to be made, situations to be improved, and knowledge to be gained. (Burnette, 2005, para. 2)

In contrast to the more behaviorist definition of Simon, Burnette's definition places greater emphasis on the fundamental thinking processes that underpin design practice and its intrinsically constructive nature for the designer.

Design encompasses both art and science. Löwgren (2005) distinguishes between creative design and engineering design, stating that creative design is a more personal and unpredictable process resulting in the creation of many parallel ideas and concepts, whereas engineering design involves finding solutions to precisely defined problems. Importantly, in an attempt to dispel negative connotations associated with creative design processes and promote its intellectual rigor, Wolf, Rode, Sussman, and Kellogg (2006) point out that rather than being diametrically opposed, engineering design often involves elements of divergent and artistic production while creative design often contains structured practice and scientific reflection. That is to say, no matter the domain we should always expect design pursuits to involve both creative and scientific thinking.

Design tasks are ill-structured or even 'wicked' in nature. The aim of design is to find an optimal solution to satisfy multiple criteria within determined constraints, yet in reality goals and parameters of the design problem are rarely completely defined (Jonassen, Howland, Marra, & Crismond, 2008). The ill-structured nature of the problem means that the problem and the solution actually co-evolve, with the information designers need to know about a problem only revealing itself as they try to solve it (Cross, 2006; Dorst, 2006). Another challenge of design is that because design problems have multiple solutions rather than a single 'right' answer it is not possible to verify a design as being 'correct,' meaning that there is no inbuilt condition under which a designer knows they must stop (Jonassen et al., 2008).

Yet, design problems are among the most common problems that confront us every day, with literally millions of possible design tasks of many different levels of scale. In our daily lives we may need to design an invitation, or a room layout, or a way to stop a tap from leaking. In industries outside education people design products, systems, processes, models, or more tangibly items such as a software program, advertising campaign, or lunch order system (Jonassen et al., 2008). In education we may design a new lesson resource, or module of work, or curriculum, or school system. Design problems abound.

Design solutions typically attempt to please the recipients of the design, making design a highly interpersonal phenomenon (Jonassen et al., 2008). The designer's interpretation of the aims and context of a design task may not directly align with the value system of the reviewer of a design, and thus objective assessment of designs is often difficult. Yet, tantalizingly, there can be a large degree of alignment between judges of design (Greg Kress & Sadler, 2014). That is to say, even though good design is often hard to describe and quantify, we often know it when we see it.

Design can be characterized, conceptualized, experienced, and valued in many different ways. Design has been characterized as an exploratory, emergent, ambiguous, opportunistic, abductive, risky, reflective, and persuasive practice (Cross, 2006). Design processes can be conceptualized and experienced as evidence-based decision making, organized translation, personal synthesis, intentional progression, directed creative exploration, and creative freedom (Daly, 2008). Values that underpin design include ingenuity, practicality, empathy, and a concern for appropriateness (Cross, 2006). Thus, design is a complex phenomenon that may take on many different forms and functions depending on the context.

Designing and Design Thinking

'Design thinking' constitutes a focus on the fundamental thinking skills that underpin design. Recently, there has been considerable interest in developing the creative problem solving capabilities of people in ways that can be applied across disciplines. Research and inquiry in the area of design has shed light on the nature of design thinking, which can be summarized as follows:

1. *Design thinking is solution focused.* While attempting to solve 'ill-defined' problems designers use constructive

modes of thinking that focus more on the solution than the problem (Cross, 2006).

2. *Design thinking is user focused.* Designing inherently involves anticipating the tastes of the user in an attempt to provide them with an aesthetically pleasing and satisfying experience (Tonkinwise, 2011).

3. *Design thinking requires frequent reframing of the problem.* The frame of the problem, which can be thought of as the mental scaffolding around which designers build their solution (Greg Kress & Sadler, 2014), is frequently adjusted according to emergent criteria, priorities, foci, and constraints of the problem and solution space (Dorst, 2006; Dorst & Cross, 2001; Tonkinwise, 2011).

4. *Design thinking leverages previous design knowledge.* All design involves a degree of re-design insofar as it builds upon design knowledge from the past, meaning that in order to optimize design performance we should aim to understand previous design efforts (Meinel & Leifer, 2014).

5. *Design thinking necessitates prototyping.* Making tangible design artifacts, for instance prototypes, is crucial in order develop design ideas and to communicate our thinking (Meinel & Leifer, 2014).

6. *Design thinking involves exploring for creative bridges.* Design involves a creative search for mental bridges between previously unrelated elements of the problem space and solution space, often resulting in 'aha' moments of resolution (Cross, 2006; Dorst, 2006; Dorst & Cross, 2001).

7. *Design thinking requires flexibility.* Good designers are less likely to become fixated on a poor solution, are opportunistic, and are able to move fluently between design activities (Cross, 2004).

8. *Design thinking demands a tolerance for ambiguity.* Preserving a sense of ambiguity throughout the design process is important in order for new and potentially better ideas to emerge (Meinel & Leifer, 2014).

9. *Design thinking involves learning.* Because the problem is never entirely defined and the solution is not initially known design thinking necessarily involves learning (Dorst, 2006).

10. *Design thinking is ultimately social.* Even if design does not occur in teams it is ultimately social because design activities inevitably return to a human-centric point of view (Meinel & Leifer, 2014).

Researchers have noticed some other interesting phenomena surrounding design. One may suspect that good design involves the ability to manifest an almost endless array of design ideas, but actually too many solutions (as well as too few) appear to constrain the quality of creative design (Cross, 2004). Good designers will often arrive at an overall principal solution concept (but not solution) that drives the design process (Cross, 2004). Often designers, particularly expert designers, will base their solution concept upon apparent paradoxes within the design problem (Cross, 2004; Dorst, 2006). Thus, good design appears to involve striking the right balance, embracing challenge, and identifying promising lines of inquiry.

Why Conceptualize Teaching as Design?

Design fields such as engineering, computer science, and architecture can be distinguished from the natural or social sciences by virtue of their purposefulness — whereas natural sciences are concerned with how thing are, design sciences focus on how things should be (Laurillard, 2012; Simon, 1996). Noteable educational scholars provide articulate arguments for why teaching should be conceptualized as design. For instance, Laurillard explains:

> A design science uses and contributes to theoretical science, but it builds design principles rather than theories, and the heuristics of practice rather than explanations, although like both the sciences and the arts, it uses what has gone before as a platform or inspiration for what it creates. Teaching is more like a design science because it uses what is known about teaching to attain the goal of student learning, and uses the implementation of its designs to keep improving them. (2012, p. 1)

So for Laurillard (2012), teaching is a design science because its fundamental nature involves moving beyond what is known to purposefully and analytically reify what should be.

Kimber and Wyatt-Smith (2006) describe this role of teacher as designers more specifically through analogy with architecture:

> Through the metaphor of design … teachers are positioned as architects of classroom experiences, balancing the development of multiple literacies and designing a learning environment where appropriate computer-based

cognitive tools are applied imaginatively to collaborative, student-focused, reflective, problem-based approaches to learning .... (Kimber & Wyatt-Smith, 2006, p. 28)

From Kimber and Wyatt-Smith (2006) we can see how the actual day-to-day practice of teaching constitutes design.

Taking a big picture view, Gunther Kress (2000) sees design as a means of engaging social transformation:

Design shapes the future through deliberate deployment of representational resources in the designer's interest. Design is the essential textual principle and pedagogic/political goal for periods characterized by intense and far-reaching change. (Kress, 2000, p. 160)

According to Kress (2000), while educators are designing in the moment they are working toward preferred futures, potentially on a grand scale. Taken together these three perspectives highlight how teaching is a design science in nature, practice, and intentions.

The Challenge of Developing Design Thinking

Conceptualizing education as design is useful insofar as it can inform how we approach and think through our practice. However, if we are to consider teaching as design there are several conundrums we must confront when attempting to develop design capabilities, as originally outlined by Schon (1987) and more recently argued by Koehler and Mishra (2005):

1. Design is an holistic skill
2. Design depends on recognition of design qualities
3. Design is a creative process whereby the designer arrives at novel ways of seeing and doing, meaning that no prior description can take the place of learning by doing
4. Descriptions of designing may be initially perceived as confusing, vague, ambiguous, or incomplete
5. There are usually multiple gaps between the initial design conception and the process of achieving the final design.

Given these complexities, how should people go about developing their technology-enhanced learning design capabilities? The perhaps obvious answer, which accords with themes raised in Chapter 2, is that the most direct way to learn about design is through design. Design tasks that require educators to develop an understanding of the complex interrelationships between artifacts, users, tools and practices help teachers to develop a more flexible understanding of how technology can be used for learning and teaching (Koehler & Mishra, 2005). Through design, educators learn about the affordances and constraints of technologies and their context sensitivity (Mishra & Koehler, 2006). When designing, educators learn about the eclectic and complex nature of design, in an experiential way that cannot be taught purely by lectures and demonstrations (Koehler & Mishra, 2005).

Exposure to examples can also support design by enhancing creativity. For example in one study, Kulkarni, Dow, and Klemmer (2014) found that early exposure to examples significantly increased the creativity of novice designers. Additional exposure to examples in-between prototyping activities further increased creativity. Though it should be noted that exposure to examples can increase conformity of thinking, so designers and design educators should apply this strategy judiciously (Kulkarni et al., 2014).

Reflection plays a key role in influencing how much can be learned through design processes. Schön (1987) famously analyzed and conceptualized design-based learning through observations upon an architectural design studio, and argued that design skills are best developed through 'reflection-in-action.' Whereas 'knowing-in-action' refers to the sorts of everyday know-how that we reveal in our intelligent action, and 'reflection-on-action' involves thinking about our actions (either past or present) without influencing them, 'reflection-in-action' is where in-situ events cause us to reflect upon our knowing-in-action and adjust our activity so as to explore, test, or affirm our evolving understanding (Schön, 1987). In order to learn to design, we need to reflect while we design, so as to take advantage of the intrinsic learning and optimization opportunities embedded within our moment-by-moment design practices.

Additionally, Schön (1987) points out that we also learn about design by observing and working with expert designers. Working with good designers allows us to move beyond superficial processing of design knowledge, to internalize design principles, and develop an embodied understanding of what it is to be a designer. This process often requires learners to assume an open-minded stance where they temporarily suspend disbelief and explore the value of views express by others during design conversations (Schön, 1987). This social and constructive view of learning how to design is in contrast to the more rational and reductionist approach to design proposed by Simon (1996; see Cross, 2006, for an elaboration of this point). In practice, all the strategies above (undertaking authentic design tasks, drawing from design examples, adopting a reflective approach and consultation with experts) can be applied together in order to enhance design performance.

Designing for Learning

So if teaching is a design science, what does conventional wisdom say that designing for learning actually involves? First, let's clarify what we mean by 'designing for learning.' Beetham and Sharpe (2013a) define 'designing for learning' as:

> a process by which [educators] arrive at a plan or structure or designed artifact for a learning situation or setting. The situation may be as small as a single task, or as large as a degree course. In a learning situation, any of the following may be designed with a specific pedagogic intention: learning resources and materials; the learning environment; tools and equipment; learning activities; the learning program or curriculum. (Beetham & Sharpe, 2013a, p. 8)

The phrase 'designing for learning' is appropriate to use because it maintains the focus on the learner and our intentions to create designs that provide the optimal conditions for learning to occur (Dalziel et al., 2016; Laurillard, 2012).

Designing for learning is chiefly concerned with the design of good learning tasks – suggestions of what people should do in order to achieve intended learning outcomes (Goodyear & Carvalho, 2013). At this point it is important to make the distinction between a learning *task* and learning *activity*. A learning task is what educators design in advance for learners to do, whereas a learning activity is what actually takes place during the course of a lesson (Goodyear, 2005). It is critical to recognize that design works indirectly – although educators may design tasks in ways to promote certain sorts of activity, learners have scope to act in unintended ways during learning activities (Conole & Jones, 2010; Goodyear & Retalis, 2010). Thus, learning can never be wholly designed, only designed *for* (Beetham & Sharpe, 2013a; Laurillard, 2012).

Good design is a complex, skillful, and time-consuming pursuit that requires synergistic consideration of people, tasks, and tools as inputs into activities (Goodyear & Retalis, 2010). Good design is crucial in education because much of the learning that students undertake is without direct supervision, meaning that learners only have designed instructions, artifacts, and scaffolding to guide their activity (Goodyear & Carvalho, 2013). The scope of educational design is quite broad, because it not only involves designing learning tasks but also supportive learning environments (Goodyear & Retalis, 2010). Good educational design incorporates all of the design thinking skills identified earlier in this chapter, but also builds upon and customizes that knowledge to directly relate to learning and teaching.

As well, deep consideration of the context is essential in order to design for high-quality learning (Boyle & Ravenscroft, 2012). This is problematic when generally discussing designing for learning because it is not possible to discuss every learning context (although the chapters to follow examine specific learning environments and example tasks). As a general grounding, four high-level concerns that relate to any educational design context are discussed below.

UNDERSTANDING AND CATERING TO STUDENTS

One of the challenges of designing for learning is that while there are general principles and theories from which educators can draw, the remit of the teacher is to create the conditions for learning that are specific to their students in their particular context (Laurillard, 2012). This involves imagining other people's learning and how they will respond to tasks (Goodyear & Retalis, 2010).

Learners have a range of attributes that warrant consideration. These include their subject-specific understanding, experience, motivations, expectations, preferences, interpersonal dispositions, access needs (including due to disabilities), familiarization with learning mode, and digital literacies (Beetham, 2013). These characteristics are intrinsically interlinked, for instance, learners of different dispositions and familiarities experience tasks quite differently when different technologies are involved (Beetham, 2013). The range of different learner attributes and their interconnected nature makes catering to learner variance a considerable challenge (Beetham, 2013). In order to understand the characteristics of learners and the efficacy of previous designs, student learning data can become an important input into the design process (Sharpe & Oliver, 2013).

A core way that educators can cater to the multiplicity of different learner needs and interests in any class is by providing a variety of different tasks (i.e., 'differentiation'). The aim of differentiation is to provide appropriate levels of challenge and choice in order to optimize learning and motivation. Differentiation can be in terms of the content addressed (in terms of complexity and resources used), the processes applied (degree of interaction and student independence based on different pedagogies), and the products students produce (for instance using different media) (Fogarty & Pete, 2007). Technology can play a key role in facilitating the design and development of different learning pathways for students (Bower, 2012; Fogarty & Pete, 2007).

DESIGN OF TASKS ACCORDING TO INTENDED LEARNING OUTCOMES

Once the range of student needs have been identified and understood, educators can start to consider the sorts of tasks that they might design for learners. In formal learning contexts such as schools and universities, learning outcomes are often used as a starting point for design (Beetham, 2013). Based on the attributes of the students and the broader learning context, high-quality task designs promote learner engagement and challenge within a nurturing practice environment (Boud & Prosser, 2002). Effective designs foster both individual and social processes and outcomes (Laurillard et al., 2013).

Tasks may take many forms depending on the outcomes that need to be achieved. They may be *rule*-based (where students are required to learn a standard procedure), *incident*-based (where exposure to an authentic event helps to develop decision-making abilities), *strategy*-based (requiring courses of action to be planned), and *role*-based (where learning is achieved through assuming a role in a scenario-based activity) (Oliver, Harper, Wills, Agostinho, & Hedberg, 2013). Tasks can also vary according to their authenticity, formality, and structure, whether they require retention and reproduction versus reflection and internalization, the roles and significance of other people, and the locus of control regarding who makes decisions about learning activities and pathways (Beetham, 2013). Accordingly, there are many ways that tasks may be actualized within different discipline areas depending on the learning requirements of the context.

ALIGNMENT WITHIN DESIGNS

Designing for learning operates at various levels of scale, from micro-level considerations of items such as specific technologies up to macro-level considerations such as institutional infrastructure (Conole & Jones, 2010; Goodyear & Retalis, 2010). Design is an iterative and multifaceted process whereby designers frequently switch between different levels and focus on different elements (Conole & Jones, 2010; Goodyear & Carvalho, 2013). While design may focus on different levels and elements at different stages of the design process, alignment between these levels and elements is critical for coherence and effectiveness (Conole & Jones, 2010; Goodyear & Retalis, 2010). For instance, it is important that the high-level pedagogy being applied aligns with the pedagogical strategies and tactics being used (Goodyear, 2005). Additionally, there needs to be an alignment between the learning outcomes, the learning tasks, and the approach to assessment (in accordance with Biggs & Tang, 2011, and as outlined in the previous chapter).

PROMOTING ACCESSIBILITY

Design needs to attend to the social and physical setting to ensure learners have effective access to resources (Goodyear & Carvalho, 2013). In accordance with the idea of differentiation, an important part of access involves considering students with disabilities or special needs. Building on the general concept of universal design (for instance, see Iwarsson & Ståhl, 2003), Universal Design for Learning (UDL) guidelines aim to provide all individuals including those with special needs equal opportunity to learn (Rose, Harbour, Johnston, Daley, & Abarbanell, 2006). Drawing upon findings from neuroscience, UDL is based on three principles:

1. *Providing multiple means of engagement* – through options for self-regulation, for sustaining effort and persistence, and for cultivating interest
2. *Providing multiple means of representation* – through options for comprehension, for language, mathematical expression and symbols, and for perception

3. *Providing multiple means of action and expression* – through options for executive function, expression and communication, and physical action.

There has been some initial work to integrate UDL and the TPACK model so that teachers understand how to synergistically integrate technology, pedagogy, and content in a way that caters to students with special needs (Benton-Borghi, 2013). For more information about UDL and designing accessible education generally, see the National Center on Universal Design for Learning website at http://udlcenter.org.

Understanding and catering to students, design of tasks according to outcomes, alignment within designs, and promoting accessibility constitute four foundational pillars of design thinking as it relates to education. Yet these pillars do not make any commitment about how an educational designer should go about the process of design. There are several design models that have been proposed in order to provide educators with guidance.

Educational Design Models

There are actually many models that have been created in order to support the design, development, and implementation of learning tasks and activities (we will refer to these as 'educational design models'). This section contrasts three of these by way of exemplification. While the summaries presented below are by necessity simplifications that do not attend to the detail contained within the models, they do serve to illustrate the range of possible considerations and approaches, as well as the variety of forms that guidance can take. Critical reflections on the models will be reserved until after all three have been presented.

THE CONVERSATIONAL FRAMEWORK

According to Laurillard's (2002) Conversational Framework, teaching involves facilitating an iterative dialogue with students that is discursive, adaptive, interactive, and reflective. Through iterative learning conversations, teachers describe theories and ideas that students describe back to them (discursive). Teachers also set goals for learning and students act upon those goals (interactive). Teachers will adapt the learning tasks in light of student ability, and students will adapt their actions in response to the ideas put

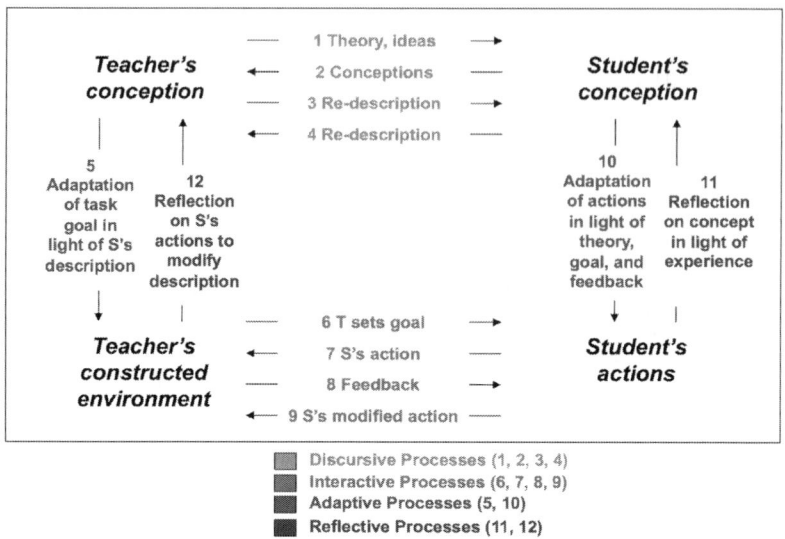

Figure 6.1. The Discursive, Adaptive, Interactive and Reflective Nature of Learning According to the Conversational Framework (Laurillard, 2002, p. 87).

forward by the teacher (adaptive). Students ideally reflect on their conceptions in light of their experiences, just as teachers preferably reflect on learner actions in order to modify the initial descriptions put forward (reflective). These transactions between students (S) and teachers (T) are shown in Figure 6.1, with numbering provided in order to help identify the nature of each process.

Laurillard (2002) proposes that different sorts of technologies can help to facilitate different types of activity. For instance, *narrative media* such as video broadcast and *communicative media* such as video conferencing can be used to support discursive processes, *interactive media* such as web and hypermedia resources can be used to support interactive processes, *adaptive media* such as simulations can be used to facilitate adaptive processes, and *productive media* such as modeling environments can be used to promote reflection. Note that according to the Conversational Framework multiple media types may support different types of learning processes, depending on the specific tools that are used.

THE LEARNING DEVELOPMENT CYCLE

Siemens (2005) suggests a Learning Development Cycle to cater for the more networked and ecological nature of contemporary

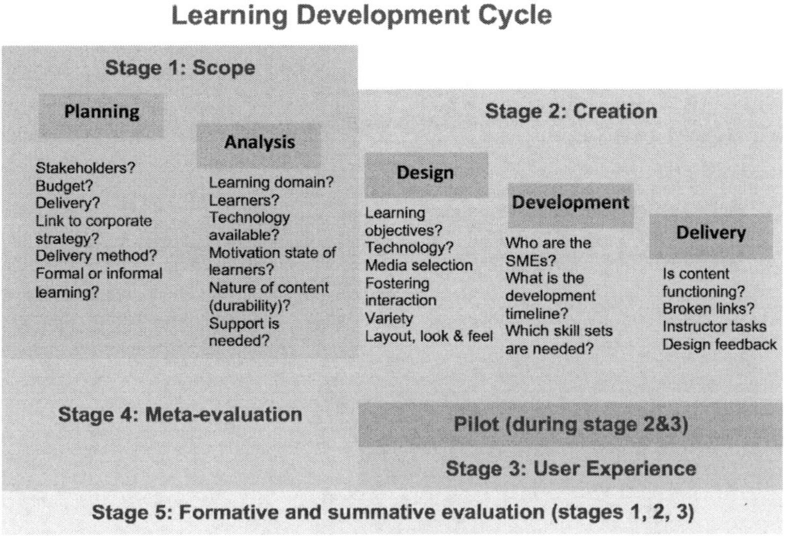

Learning Development Cycle

Stage 1: Scope

Planning   **Stage 2: Creation**

Analysis

Stakeholders?   Learning domain?   **Design**
Budget?   Learners?
Delivery?   Technology   **Development**
Link to corporate   available?   Learning
strategy?   Motivation state of   objectives?   Who are the   **Delivery**
Delivery method?   learners?   Technology?   SMEs?
Formal or informal   Nature of content   Media selection   What is the   Is content
learning?   (durability)?   Fostering   development   functioning?
                       Support is   interaction   timeline?   Broken links?
                       needed?   Variety   Which skill sets   Instructor tasks
                                             Layout, look & feel are needed?   Design feedback

Stage 4: Meta-evaluation   **Pilot (during stage 2&3)**

                                        Stage 3: User Experience

Stage 5: Formative and summative evaluation (stages 1, 2, 3)

Figure 6.2.   The Learning Development Cycle (Siemens, 2005).

learning. Learning is proposed to occur through teacher *transmission*, student-directed *acquisition*, reflective and reasoned *emergence*, and through situated and networked connectivist *accretion*. The Learning Development Cycle aims to provide a meta-model that accommodates the different approaches, intents, and desired aims of each of the ways of learning. It involves stages of Scoping (planning and analysis), Creation (design, development and delivery), User Experience (piloting and implementation), Meta-evaluation (reflecting on the effectiveness of the learning design process), and Evaluation of student learning and satisfaction (see Figure 6.2).

THE SEVEN CS MODEL

Conole (2015) proposes a 7Cs learning design framework that aims to shift the focus away from content provision to active and student-centered learning. It involves Conceptualizing the course in terms of forming a vision that is learner focused, thinking about how Communication will be facilitated, fostering mechanisms for group Collaboration, establishing ways for students to Consider and reflect upon their learning as well as enable teachers to assess student learning, Combining the different elements and perspectives cultivated throughout the design process, and

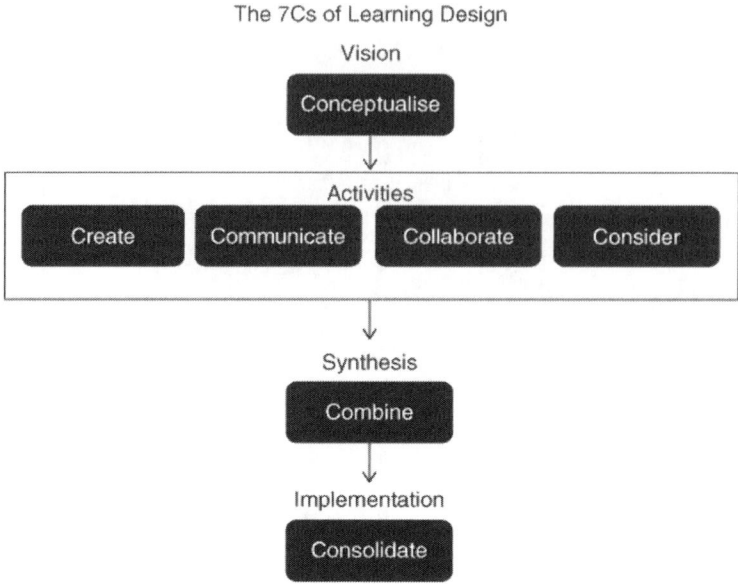

Figure 6.3.   The Seven Cs Model (Conole, 2015, p. 119).

Consolidating the design in a real-life context and evaluate its effectiveness (Conole, 2015). The arrangement of these components is shown in Figure 6.3. A variety of established educational theories, principles, practices and examples are suggested in the detailed explanation of each 'C.' Reference to technology throughout the model stages occurs at the Create stage.

The models presented above are but three of numerous educational design models that have been proposed over the last two decades. Other model include the 4 Component Instructional Design Model (Van Merriënboer, Clark, & De Croock, 2002), Design Thinking for Educators (IDEO, 2012), The Practitioners Guide to Technology Pedagogy and Content Knowledge (Hofer et al., 2015), to name but a few and to illustrate the very different orientations that educational design models can assume (instructivist, design thinking, and TPACK, respectively).

Critical Reflections on Design Models

Firstly, let's reflect on the three educational design models summarized above. The Conversational Framework (Laurillard, 2002) distinguishes itself from other models by being based on a model of how people learn and providing detailed guidance about how technologies might play a facilitative role. However, the convergence of information and communication media and the availability of multiple web services on a common platform means that it is difficult to maintain Laurillard's distinction between media (technology) types as they map to the processes in the Conversational Framework (Beetham, 2013). Also, the type of processes that technologies facilitate can depend more on the tasks that are set than the technologies themselves, as we saw in the previous chapter.

The Learning Development cycle (Siemens, 2005) flexibly caters to a range of different contemporary ways of learning, and is centered around the process that designers may undertake in order to develop learning tasks and modules. However, the model operates at quite an abstract level that means that it may be difficult for some designers to use in practice. Possible technologies that could be utilized in the creation phase are only briefly suggested and with no real mapping to any elements of the model.

The Seven Cs model (Conole, 2015) aims to support design activities as a process and does include numerous references to relevant theories and examples for designers to consider. However, to unpack all the elements of the model requires prolonged engagement, meaning that it perhaps lends itself more to professional learning than immediate application. The integration of learning technologies into the model could possibly be more comprehensive (at least in terms of the way the model is described).

This is not to be critical of these modeling attempts by three of the most eminent experts in our field — rather it is to point out that creating a comprehensive, generally applicable and useful educational design models is a fundamentally intractable problem. This is because educational design models can only ever struggle to account for all of the considerations along all of the numerous dimensions of variation that influence designing for learning. A model that strives to be too comprehensive or too generally applicable must inevitably compromise on usability. We have already established the wicked nature of design problems, and attempts to create an all-encompassing educational design model can only ever result in something that is too large, prescriptive, and unwieldy, or too general to be of any great assistance.

There are other notable issues with educational design models and design methodologies generally. Rational approaches to educational design that prescribe logical sequences of design steps are rarely used in practice because they do not account for the social and political context, the degree of artistry that design involves, and the wide range of flexible ways that technologies can be applied (Sharpe & Oliver, 2013). Design methodologies have also been broadly criticized for providing little support for the realistic and actual processes that design practitioners undertake (Cross, 2001, 2006). Seeing educational design as a rational problem solving process is also problematic because of the complex and frequently changing educational and technological context (Holmberg, 2014).

Educational design models can be a useful point of reference against which educators can compare to their practice (Sharpe & Oliver, 2013). Some studies have also supported the idea that design methodologies can help novice designers adopt a more efficient design process that results in better quality and quantity of design outputs (Cross, 2006). However, a design methodology can have no effect or even a negative effect if it is too rigidly prescriptive (Cross, 2006). A key part of the organic nature of design is that good designers are willing to deviate from typical design methodologies based on emergent findings and ideas (Cross, 2004). For reasons such as these, the search for general design models has largely been overtaken by attempts to better share teacher practice (Beetham & Sharpe, 2013b). Fortunately, the new and growing field of Learning Design is dedicated to this very pursuit.

The Learning Design Field

LEARNING DESIGN DEFINITIONS

The term 'learning design' has been defined in a number of ways by different educational researchers over time (for discussions of this see Agostinho, 2008; Conole & Jones, 2010; Dalziel et al., 2016; Dobozy, 2013; Goodyear & Retalis, 2010; Mor, Craft, & Maina, 2015). According to a recent symposium of international learning design experts (see Dalziel et al., 2016) the field of Learning Design is principally concerned with how to help educators describe, design and share great teaching ideas. It constitutes the descriptive frameworks, learning and teaching concepts, and educator practices surrounding the creation of learning tasks that are increasingly technologically enhanced. Learning Design maintains a greater emphasis on the design of learning *tasks* rather than the enactment of learning *activities*. Whereas the older field of Instructional Design has traditionally emphasized the science of cognitively efficient information delivery, the relatively new field of

Learning Design encompasses more of a focus upon collaborative and student-centered learning (Mor et al., 2015). Learning Design is also more concerned with how designs are described and shared. For a timeline of key events, initiatives, tools and publications emerging from the Learning Design field see Dalziel et al. (2016).

You may have noticed that when referring to the field of Learning Design the 'L' and 'D' are capitalized. This is an important point of distinction because 'learning design' (lowercase) can denote the process of designing learning experiences (verb) as well as the product that is the outcome of the design process (noun) (Agostinho, 2008). The *process* of learning design can be defined as "the creative and deliberate act of devising new practices, plans of activity, resources and tools aimed at achieving particular educational aims in a given context" (Mor & Craft, 2012, p. 86). So, in a sentence, one might declare that 'learning design requires careful reflection.' Often the phrase 'designing for learning' is used to denote the process of learning design in order to avoid confusion between the noun and verb forms (Agostinho, 2008; Beetham & Sharpe, 2013a).

A learning design as a *product* can be defined as "a representation of the learning experience to which students are exposed" (Oliver et al., 2013, p. 103), or alternately "representations of the design process and its outcomes, allowing for aspects of design to be shared" (Beetham & Sharpe, 2013a, p. 9). In a sentence one might state 'I created a new learning design for my class.' Historically and strictly speaking, a 'learning design' has referred only to the intermediary design artifact (such as a diagram or blueprint that represents a plan for the lesson sequence) and not the final resources and learning environment that are developed. However, in practice, design work often takes place in the targeted virtual learning environment[2] such as a learning management system (Goodyear, 2005) and the term 'learning design' has become a common part of the language that teachers use to describe their approach to designing learning experiences for students (McAndrew & Goodyear, 2013). As such, it has become sufficiently common practice to refer to any sequence of teaching and learning tasks that have been constructed using the

---

[2]In line with Laurillard (2002), a Virtual Learning Environment can be described as an online technological platform that educators can use to provide students with resources and support facilities that they need in order to learn.

ideas of Learning Design as a 'learning design' (uncapitalized), or more simply a 'design' (Dalziel et al., 2016).

A LEARNING DESIGN CONCEPTUAL MAP

Dalziel et al. (2016) describe the key concepts of the Learning Design field and how they interrelate in a Learning Design conceptual map (see Figure 6.4). The core concepts of learning design center around guidance, representation and sharing. Designs may be aligned to any educational philosophies, may be informed by any theories and methodologies, and may occur within any type of learning environment. Within their context, teachers design and plan, engage with students, reflect and often undertake professional learning. These phases of the teaching cycle may occur at a number of levels of granularity, from specific learning activities, to sessions (lessons), modules of work or indeed entire programs. Teachers employ tools and resources to implement their designs, and draw upon a range of feedback, assessment, learner analytics and evaluation to refine their teaching approaches. Within this framework the challenge for educators is to create learning experiences that achieve the desired learning outcomes.

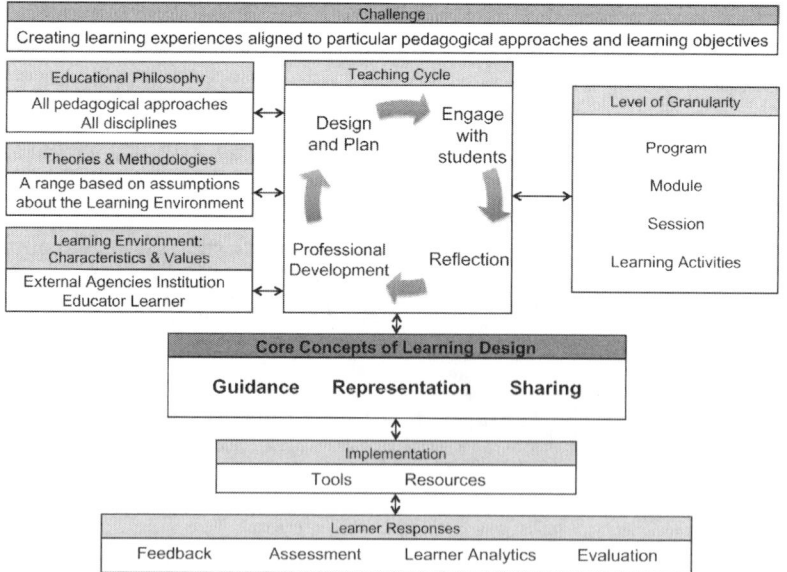

Figure 6.4.   A Learning Design Conceptual Map (Dalziel et al., 2016, p. 17).

You may note that while the Learning Design conceptual map in Figure 6.4 explains the descriptive framework and concepts of Learning Design, it provides little direct guidance on *how* to design. The reason for this lack of direct guidance is that from a descriptive point of view the Learning Design field aims to provide a general framework to describe any design, and thus avoids any prescription, bias or values. Yet, as previously noted, the intention of the Learning Design field is to support the development and sharing of great teaching ideas. The tension between these two goals seems at first paradoxical, because Learning Design is attempting to be at the same time pedagogically neutral and selective. However, this tension can co-exist within the field by using pedagogically inclusive frameworks to describe learning designs, and allowing people to separately make judgments about the efficacy of the designs (Dalziel et al., 2016). So the Learning Design conceptual map in Figure 6.4 is not an educational design model insofar as it does not provide any direct guidance about how to design, makes no commitments about how people learn, and offers no recommendations about how technologies should be used. Nevertheless, the clear identification of learning design components does make it a useful referent for designers upon which they can apply their own value systems.

Describing Learning Designs

For educators to share learning designs they must be able to describe their designs. Learning designs, when represented well, are readily interpretable, can be used as a source of design ideas, and can even potentially support the integration of technology, pedagogy and content (Agostinho, Bennett, Lockyer, Jones, & Harper, 2013). Formally describing designs rather than immediately creating the actual learning resources and environments also has advantages, such as providing an initial representation that can be used as a basis for self or collaborative reflection, and providing the opportunity to share designs as abstractions for re-use with potentially different content (Conole & Jones, 2010). Because design is cognitively demanding, external tools are often used to offload and store parts of the problem as well as assist in creation of design solutions (Goodyear & Retalis, 2010).

There have been a number of initiatives within the Learning Design field to develop languages and tools to support the description and design of learning. Six approaches along with an exemplar of each will be briefly described in order coarsely trace the evolution of learning design description in the Learning Design field. The six approaches are (i) the use of technical standards (IMS-LD), (ii) the use descriptive templates (pedagogical patterns), (iii) visualization approaches (AUTC LDVS), (iv) visualization tools (CompendiumLD), (v) pedagogical planner tools (the Learning Designer), and (vi) the Learning Activity Management Systems (LAMS). These examples also serve to illustrate the wide range of possible approaches that can be used to conceptualize, describe, create, and share learning designs.

TECHNICAL STANDARDS (IMS-LD)

Early efforts in the Learning Design field focused upon creating technical standards in order to support the description and sharing of learning designs. The logic behind these technical standards was that if learning designs could be described using a common technical framework then they could be more easily shared between people, platforms and contexts. There have been substantial initiatives to standardize the technical description of digital learning objects to make them more accessible, reusable and interoperable, for instance the Shareable Content Object Reference Model (SCORM). However, the most evolved and widespread set of technical standards for education is IMS Learning Design (IMS-LD).

IMS-LD is an open XML-based standard that can be used to specify a wide range of pedagogical strategies in the form of computer-interpretable models (Koper & Miao, 2008). This enables the models to be 'played' in any compatible execution environment (for instance, in learning management system such as Moodle). In comparison to other e-learning technical specifications like SCORM, IMS-LD provides strong support for the wide range of modern pedagogical approaches that are in use today, such as active learning, collaborative learning and competency-based learning (Koper & Miao, 2008). For IMS-LD guides and examples see https://www.imsglobal.org.

Despite the initial promise of the idea that technical standards could promote standardization, interoperation and sharing of learning designs across the education field, IMS-LD has not become as widely used as was initially hoped. One reason for the limited uptake of IMS-LD is that although there are freely available tools to support creation of IMS-LD designs, there is little incentive for coal-face educators and institutions to expend the extra effort to adopt it in their designs (Goddard, Griffiths, & Mi, 2015). Another possible reason is that the specification doesn't necessarily cater for all sorts of learning designs, such as those involving run-time adaptation dependent on context (Burgos, 2015).

PATTERN DESCRIPTIONS (PEDAGOGICAL PATTERNS)

Based on the general concept of design patterns emanating from the field of architecture (Alexander, 1979), pedagogical patterns (or 'learning patterns') are proposed to provide a good way of capturing and sharing design knowledge in education because of the low technical threshold required to specify them (Goodyear, 2005; McAndrew & Goodyear, 2013). Patterns are specified in human readable form using the following format:

1. A picture showing an epitomic example of the pattern
2. An introductory paragraph explaining the context for the pattern
3. A problem headline to briefly describe the essence of the problem
4. The problem body that explains the empirical background and variants of the problem
5. The solution stated as an instruction to promote application
6. A diagrammatic representation of the solution
7. A paragraph linking the pattern to smaller patterns that can be used to complete it (McAndrew & Goodyear, 2013).

Sharing design knowledge using pattern descriptions is proposed to offer educators good design ideas in an easy to create and structured way that clarifies the context and emphasizes the relationship between patterns (Goodyear, 2005). The Pedagogical Patterns Project (http://www.pedagogicalpatterns.org) provides an example repository of pedagogical patterns. There has not been a wide proliferation in use of pedagogical patterns among educators, potentially because the approach is not closely integrated into the way they practice design.

VISUALIZATION APPROACHES (AUTC LD)

Based on funding from the former Australian Universities Teaching Committee (AUTC) the *ICTs and Their Role in Flexible Learning* project (known as the LD project) aimed to identify, evaluate, document and disseminate high-quality learning designs that involved the use of technology (Agostinho et al., 2013). As part of the project a graphical representation called the Learning Design Visual Sequence (LDVS) was developed to facilitate descriptions of designs. LDVS describes learning designs in terms of the resources, tasks and supports that were required to implement them. A 'jigsaw' learning design (whereby teams of students research different topics and then individuals from teams share the findings with other groups) is shown in Figure 6.5. All visualizations were complemented by textual descriptions of the

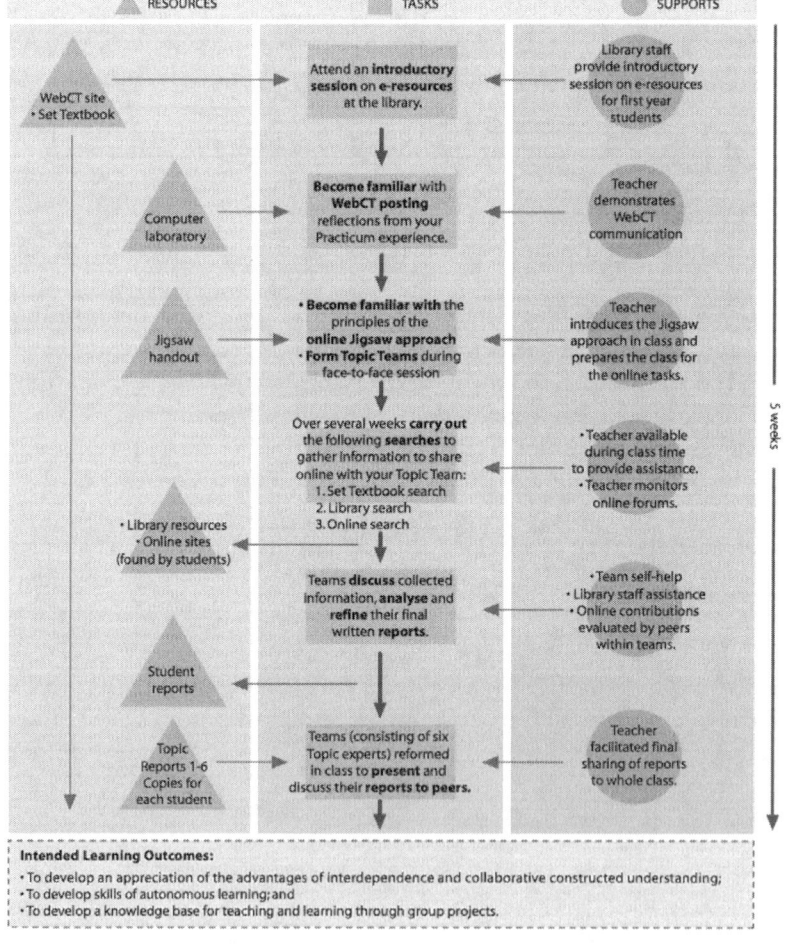

Figure 6.5. Representation of a 'Jigsaw' Learning Design Using an AUTC Learning Design Visualization Sequence.

implementation context (setting, outcomes, assessment and ICT contribution) and designers' reflections (pedagogical notes, history and evaluation).

Studies by Agostinho et al. (2013) report that educators found the designs to be particularly useful for sourcing design ideas and benchmarking good practice. The contextual descriptions that accompanied the LDVS visualizations were particularly important in supporting use and reuse of the designs. There was small-scale evidence that using the learning designs could improve TPACK understanding and that the system was used beyond the project. The repository of learning design descriptions and other supporting resources can be found at http://learningde-signs.uow.edu.au.

VISUALIZATION TOOLS (*COMPENDIUM LD*)

Compendium LD is a learning design visualization tool based on mindmapping paradigm (Brasher & Cross, 2015; Conole, 2013; Conole & Jones, 2010). It enables users to show connections between learner and teacher tasks and resources in a diagrammatic manner. Built using mindmapping software, custom icons enable representation of outcomes, tasks, resources, tools, roles, and learner. The designs can be exported in different formats including HTML and JPG. A visualization for a simple task is shown in Figure 6.6.

Conole (2013) reports that *Compendium LD* enabled those in the study to visualize design structure, as well as identify gaps and flaws in a way that textual descriptions could not. However some users found the tool frustrating and time consuming to learn and use, and also too rigid to represent all types of designs. The tool was considered by users as useful for articulating key steps and interdependencies within a learning design, planning logistics, and sharing practice. The *CompendiumLD* software along with associated documentation is freely available for download from http://compendiumld.open.ac.uk.

PEDAGOGICAL PLANNER TOOLS (THE *LEARNING DESIGNER*)

Whereas visualization tools provide a means for describing learning designs, pedagogical planners provide more structured guidance on the design process that accounts for the sorts of elements that need to be considered if a design is to be successful. The *Learning Design Support Environment* is an

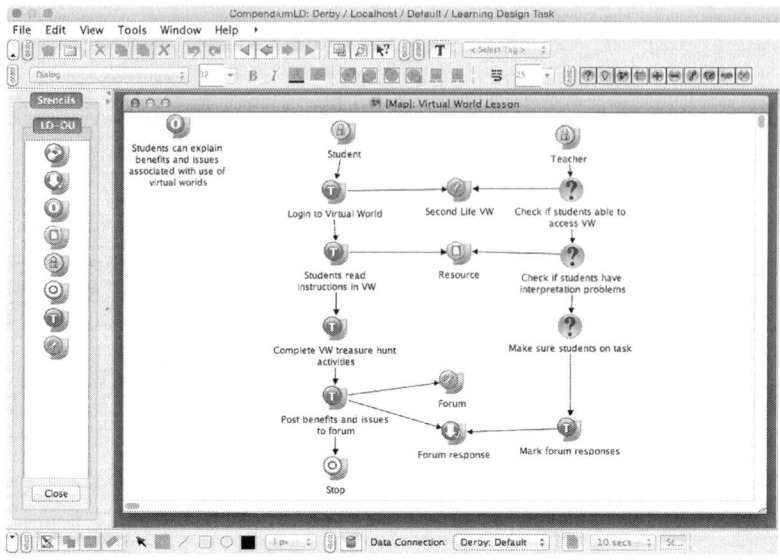

Figure 6.6. A simple Virtual World Task Represented Using CompendiumLD.

interactive tool and set of resources to scaffold teachers' technology-enhanced learning design thinking (Laurillard, Masterman, Magoulas, Boyle, & Manton, 2017). Using the main design tool (called the *Learning Designer*) educators can select from a range of teaching and learning activities and schedule them along a timeline. Activities have default levels of cognitive activity (acquisition, inquiry, discussion, practice, and production) and social nature (personalized, social, one-size-fits-all), which can be adjusted by the user. The design interface is shown in Figure 6.7.

Once learning modules and sessions have been drafted, the *Learning Designer* can provide an overarching analysis of the learning experience in terms of the different proportions of cognitive activities and social structure. The system is also integrated with an intelligent database feature that enables it to offer context sensitive scaffolding for the design process. This demonstrates how learning design descriptive frameworks can interweave with learning design concepts to assist learning design practice (Laurillard et al., 2013). The *Learning Designer* and associated systems are freely available for download and use from https://sites.google.com/a/lkl.ac.uk/ldse/.

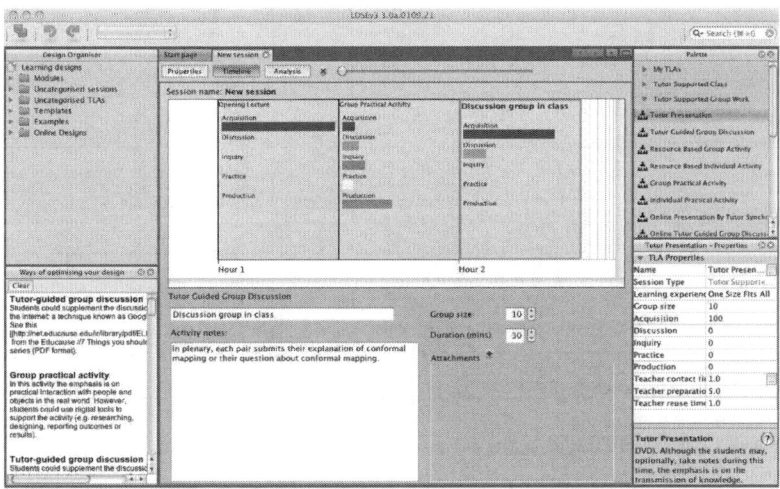

Figure 6.7.   The Design View of the Learning Designer.

THE LEARNING ACTIVITY MANAGEMENT SYSTEMS (*LAMS*)

The Learning Activity Management System (*LAMS*) is an online platform that provides a drag-and-drop interface so that users can organize their lessons on a canvas (Dalziel, 2013). Users can choose from a range of 'activities' such as chat, forum, mindmap, Q&A, voting, wiki, and so on, and either linearly sequence them or use a range of more sophisticated control flow tools such as branching and conditional logic. A distinguishing feature of *LAMS* is that it allows each activity to be populated with actual content so that educators can actually run their designs with real classes. A screenshot of a basic *LAMS* sequence is shown in Figure 6.8.

LAMS first emerged in 2003 and over time has grown substantially in terms of its features and user-base. Sequences can be exported and uploaded to the *LAMS* Community (http://lams-community.org) so that educators can download, adapt, deploy and re-share designs. There are over three thousand freely available sequences available on the *LAMS* community that have been downloaded tens of thousands of times by several thousand users. The Lesson *LAMS* server enables educators to create a free account that they can use with their classes (see http://lessonlams.com). Alternately, the *LAMS* platform can be freely downloaded onto institutional servers from http://lamsfoundation.org.

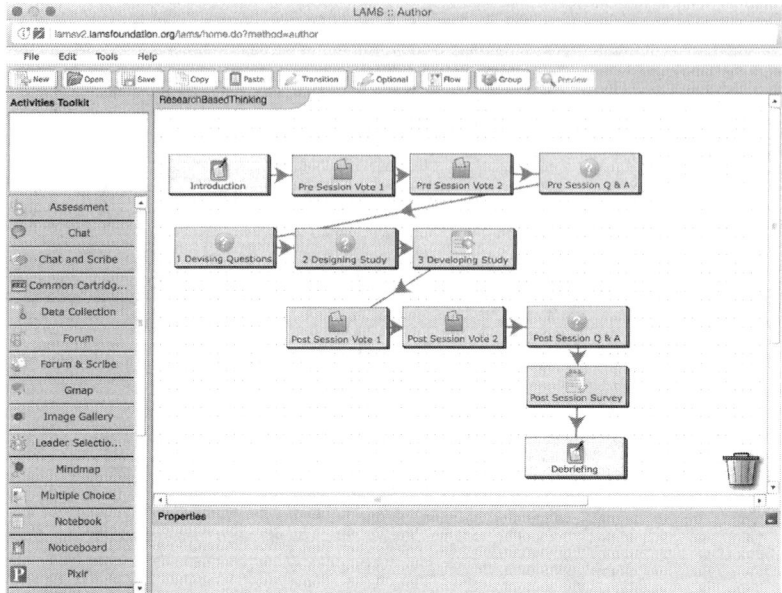

Figure 6.8.   An LAMS Sequence in Author Mode.

REFLECTIONS ON REPRESENTATION AND SHARING OF LEARNING DESIGNS

As you can see, there are many ways that learning designs can be represented, constructed and shared. These learning design representations can vary according to the form of notation system, the formality of the language, the level of contextuality supported, whether the pedagogy is made explicit, what can be reused, how reuse is facilitated (Agostinho, 2008). Each approach addresses some of the needs of the field and practitioners, but also has limitations.

The IMS-LD technical standards constitute machine representations to facilitate standardized description for interoperability, but have not been utilized widely by practitioners because of the extra technical effort required to use them (Goddard et al., 2015). Pedagogical patterns overcome the technical barriers for use by offering human readable and easy to create learning design descriptions (McAndrew & Goodyear, 2013), but likewise have had limited uptake in part because they do not integrate tightly with how coal-face educators design. Manual visualization systems such as AUTC LDVS help to clarify the key components of a design and how they are sequenced, and there is some evidence to suggest that it can help improve learning design thinking (Agostinho et al., 2013). While there are a few instances where LDVS has been used in practice beyond the scope of the project, such use is far from mainstream.

Moving beyond languages, the use of tools to represent learning designs has also had limited impact. Visualization tools such as *CompendiumLD* help educators to map out their designs in a flexible and somewhat portable way, but it can take users considerable time to learn the system and some are skeptical about the benefit as compared to the time commitment required (Conole, 2013). Pedagogical planner tools such as the *Learning Designer* do offer additional value add in terms of helping educators to analyze the efficacy of their designs, and the *Learning Designer* also integrates with an online repository and intelligent database to promote sharing. Yet as it stands, the *Learning Designer* has not yet infiltrated into general educational practice, perhaps because it is new but also again because teachers may not sufficiently value the return on investment for deviating from their current direct design approaches. *LAMS* is the learning design tool that has made the most impact on teaching practice, where people are able to plan their designs and then flesh-out the content so that they can run them with their classes. Yet, even the use of the LAMS Community is modest in comparison to the use of some learning object repositories (Dalziel, 2013).

Another important issue to consider is how much assistance design abstractions really offer. One of the key goals of learning design is to promote transfer of good teaching ideas (Dalziel et al., 2016). However, it is an open question whether general designs or patterns exist that make sense across a wide range of different learning contexts (Beetham & Sharpe, 2013a). Evidence suggests that educators prefer working with specific designs – even if they are from an unrelated context – rather than abstract designs (Agostinho et al., 2013; Masterman, 2013). Further, all intermediary design artifacts are once removed from actual artifacts and courses meaning that some of the detail is necessarily lost. What may be needed is for educators themselves to make abstractions about learning design, rather than being provided with them.

There is no doubt that each of the learning design representation approaches outlined above have made valuable conceptual contributions to the field of Learning Design, and can be used to advance practitioner thinking. When educators do take the time to use learning design tools and representations they often indicate it develops their design understanding (Agostinho et al., 2013;

Masterman & Manton, 2011). However, due to the general busy-ness of teaching work educators often struggle to find time for ped-agogical reflection and to think explicitly about design (Laurillard et al., 2013). For the same reason they may be reluctant to use intermediary learning design representations and tools rather than directly creating their designs in the target virtual learning environment.

Summarizing the Current State of Design Thinking and Learning Design

What can we conclude from the various areas of research and development that have been drawn together in this chapter? We have seen that design is the deliberate and purposeful practice of trying to solve ill-structured problems in order to create preferred futures. Design thinking requires frequent reframing of the prob-lem, involves a focus upon the solution, builds upon previous design knowledge, is centered around the user, necessitates proto-typing, involves exploring for creative bridges, requires flexibility, demands a tolerance for ambiguity, and is an intrinsically educa-tive practice.

Design is an excellent way to conceptualize teaching because how to educate is an ill-structured problem with practices and intentions that involve purposefully building upon prior knowl-edge to create preferred futures. Learning to design is challenging because design is an inherently ill-structured, synergistic, experi-ential, and ephemeral process. Adopting a reflective approach to design in combination with drawing upon expert guidance and examples is proposed as the most successful ways to develop design capabilities.

Quality designing for learning (or as we more recently agreed to call it, 'learning design') foundationally involves understanding and catering to students, designing tasks that accord in nature and focus with the desired learning outcomes, aligning the vari-ous levels of a design (from macro-level whole course concerns to micro-level strategies and tactics), and promoting accessibility. There are several educational design models (which we could just have easily called learning design models), including the Conversational Framework, the Learning Design Cycle, and the 7 Cs model, that aim to provide educators with guidance for the design of technology-enhanced learning. However, due to the intractable and contextual nature of design problems, these models struggle to be at the same time comprehensive, generally applicable and easily used.

The field of Learning Design aims to support the design of learning by helping educators to describe, design and share great teaching ideas. Several different approaches to describing and sharing designs have been proposed, including technical standards such as IMSLD, formalized pattern descriptions, visualization languages such as AUTC LDVS, visualization tools such as *Compendium LD*, pedagogical planner tools such as the *Learning Designer*, and the runnable learning design tool *LAMS*. While these have each made a considerable contribution to conceptualization and thinking in the field, the challenge has been for these approaches to impact on the practices of everyday educators.

Directions Forward for Learning Designers

So, given what is known about design thinking and the developments in the field of Learning Design, what strategies are likely to be most useful for learning designers going forward? Firstly, based on the work of Schön (1987), it is imperative that learning designers adopt a reflective approach to their practice (Holmberg, 2014). Design of high-quality technology-enhanced learning involves a great deal of artistic and reflective input from the educator, particularly for highly adaptive or cutting edge applications (Harding & Ingraham, 2013). Without periods of informed reflection it is hard for design practices to improve (Goodyear & Retalis, 2010). Holmberg (2014, via Schön, 1987) describes how in-action this involves learning designers have a "reflective conversation with the situation" (p. 294). That is to say, good design involves continual and conscious reflection in response to emergent conditions and observations.

Secondly, learning designers should strive to collaborate. Design itself occurs in a socio-cultural context, in which the community practices can have a marked impact upon the design process and outcomes (Masterman, 2013). Designing in teams provides opportunity for dialogue, brings together different sources of expertise, and enables peer learning through sharing of ideas (Sharpe & Oliver, 2013). At a practical level designing in teams allows complementary skills and knowledge to help solve the problem at hand (Goodyear & Retalis, 2010). Support from others, including administrators and personal learning networks plays a critical role in successful technology-enhanced learning design practices (Ertmer, Ottenbreit-Leftwich, Sadik, Sendurur, & Sendurur, 2012), so these should be utilized wherever possible. For instance, online communities formed through social networking tools such as Facebook and LinkedIn can offer an important source of support (Conole, 2013). Another more recent and exciting possibility is including students as participants in the design process (Sharpe & Oliver, 2013), for example, as outlined in the Students as Producers project at the University of Lincoln (http://studentasproducer.lincoln.ac.uk).

Thirdly, educators need to adopt a design mindset in order to truly become empowered and capable learning designers. Teacher beliefs play a critical role in determining how they design for learning (Kim, Kim, Lee, Spector, & DeMeester, 2013; Voogt, Fisser, Tondeur, & van Braak, 2016). A strong belief in the utility of student-centered and technology-based learning, as well as a problem solving mentality and a passion for technology all underpin exemplary technology-enhanced learning design and practice (Ertmer et al., 2012). Teachers' design dispositions (such as openness to new experiences, exploring conflicting ideas, deviating from established practices, comfort with productive failure) also influence the sorts of design practices that teachers use (Koh, Chai, Hong, & Tsai, 2015). Outstanding design is fueled by a personal commitment to high standards (Cross, 2004). It appears that for experienced designers, "design becomes a part of one's being because it involves so much that is personal, like your creativity, way of approaching the world's problems, your own history, learning style and view of the world" (Lawson & Dorst, 2009, p. 270). Sharing of teachers' orientations and beliefs has been associated with deeper levels of inquiry into technology-enhanced learning issues (Boschman, McKenney, & Voogt, 2015).

Final Comments

While there has been small sample self-report qualitative evidence from educators that working with learning design visualizations and tools can enhance learning design thinking (Agostinho et al., 2013; Masterman & Manton, 2011), the evidence to suggest that visualizations and tools result in better designs, or better student learning outcomes, is far from conclusive. Nor is there any strong evidence to suggest that educational design models result in better quality designs. Perhaps we do not have sufficient research data and they do in-fact lead to qualitatively better designs, or maybe difficulty objectively assessing designs makes improvements difficult to gauge. However, other reasons that descriptions, tools and models have not lead to convincing improvements in learning design could be that good design is an intrinsically complex, authentic and creative process, and that learning design tools and models do not fully capture and integrate the interconnected elements in a way that optimally supports design.

At the same time, the Learning Design Field is faced with a conundrum. It advocates the creation of generalized and transferable learning design patterns, while simultaneously recognizing that deep consideration of context is deemed essential for high-quality learning design. This means that no matter what sorts of abstractions that are provided to educators in the form of learning designs, it is up to individuals to make sense of designs and potentially significant adaptations depending on learner needs. Accordingly, out-of-context or generalized learning designs can only ever be sources of ideas, and significant responsibility and expertise necessarily needs to rest with the educator.

Thus, the best way to support technology-enhanced learning design may be to assist people to develop a deep understanding of the possibilities and issues so that they can make situated and empowered design decisions. Koh and Chai (2016) have shown that the design knowledge of teachers plays a large role in influencing their design processes. There is no doubt that learning design models, languages, tools and repositories can provide some support for educators. However, irrespective of the tools and resources provided, to create good technology-enhanced learning designs educators must move beyond surface processing of design to deeper and more analytical, yet still creative processes and production. Thus, instead of primarily aiming to provide educators with blueprints that are contextually void or inaccurate, or rational design prescriptions, the most realistic and promising approach to supporting design practices may be to help educators acquire contextually sensitive design principles (Holmberg, 2014; Sharpe & Oliver, 2013).

Empowering educators with contextually sensitive design principles and knowledge means that they can broach design as an in-context reflexive practice rather than naïvely, inaccurately or incompletely applying prescriptive approaches. It means that educators are more able to shift beyond what they are given and develop more creative and customized learning designs. That is the premise of this book, and the focus of the chapters to follow. The next four chapters provide an in-depth and evidence-based examination of different technologies, as design environments, in order to explore issues and potentials associated with the design of technology-enhanced learning, and to derive context sensitive principles for their use.

References

Agostinho, S. (2008). Learning design representations to document, model, and share teaching practice. In L. Lockyer, S. Bennett, S. Agostinho, & B. Harper (Eds.), *Handbook of learning design and learning objects: Issues, applications, and technologies* (Vol. 1, pp. 1−19). IGI Global.

Agostinho, S., Bennett, S., Lockyer, L., Jones, J., & Harper, B. (2013). Learning designs as a stimulus and support for teachers' design practices. In H. Beetham & R. Sharpe (Eds.), *Rethinking pedagogy for a digital age − Designing for 21st century learning* (pp. 119−132). New York, NY: Routledge.

Alexander, C. (1979). *The timeless way of building* (Vol. 1): New York, NY: Oxford University Press.

Beetham, H. (2013). Designing for active learning in technology-rich contexts. In H. Beetham & R. Sharpe (Eds.), *Rethinking pedagogy for a digital age − Designing for 21st century learning* (pp. 31−48). New York, NY: Routledge.

Beetham, H., & Sharpe, R. (2013a). An introduction to rethinking pedagogy. In H. Beetham & R. Sharpe (Eds.), *Rethinking pedagogy for a digital age − Designing for 21st century learning* (pp. 1−15). New York, NY: Routledge.

Beetham, H., & Sharpe, R. (2013b). Principles and practices of designing. In H. Beetham & R. Sharpe (Eds.), *Rethinking pedagogy for a digital age − Designing for 21st century learning* (pp. 13−15). New York, NY: Routledge.

Benton-Borghi, B. H. (2013). A universally designed for learning (UDL) infused technological pedagogical content knowledge (TPACK) practitioners' model essential for teacher preparation in the 21st century. *Journal of Educational Computing Research*, 48(2), 245−265.

Biggs, J., & Tang, C. (2011). *Teaching for quality learning at university* (3rd ed.). Maidenhead: McGraw-Hill.

Boschman, F., McKenney, S., & Voogt, J. (2015). Exploring teachers' use of TPACK in design talk: The collaborative design of technology-rich early literacy activities. *Computers & Education*, 82, 250−262.

Boud, D., & Prosser, M. (2002). Key principles for high quality student learning in higher education: A framework for evaluation. *Educational Media International*, 39(3), 237−245.

Bower, M. (2012). An ability approach to within-class curriculum differentiation using student response systems and Web 2.0 technologies: Analysing teachers' responsiveness. *Themes in Science and Technology Education*, 5(2), 5−26.

Boyle, T., & Ravenscroft, A. (2012). Context and deep learning design. *Computers & Education, 59*(4), 1224–1233.

Brasher, A., & Cross, S. (2015). Reflections on developing a tool for creating visual representations of learning designs – Towards a visual language for learning designs. In M. Maina, B. Craft, & Y. Mor (Eds.), *The art & science of learning design* (pp. 169–179). Rotterdam: Sense Publishers.

Burgos, D. (2015). A critical review of IMS learning design. In M. Maina, B. Craft, & Y. Mor (Eds.), *The art & science of learning design* (pp. 137–153). Rotterdam: Sense Publishers.

Burnette, C. (2005). What is design thinking? Retrieved from http://www.idesignthinking.com/01whyteach/01whyteach.html. Accessed on February 28, 2017.

Conole, G. (2013). Tools and resources to guide practice. In H. Beetham & R. Sharpe (Eds.), *Rethinking pedagogy for a digital age – Designing for 21st century learning* (pp. 78–101). New York, NY: Routledge.

Conole, G. (2015). The 7Cs of learning design. In J. Dalziel (Ed.), *Learning design: Conceptualizing a framework for teaching and learning online* (pp. 117–145). New York, NY: Routledge.

Conole, G., & Jones, C. (2010). Sharing practice, problems and solutions for institutional change. In P. Goodyear & S. Retalis (Eds.), *Technology-enhanced learning: Design patterns and pattern languages* (pp. 277–296). Rotterdam: Sense Publishers.

Cross, N. (2001). Designerly ways of knowing: Design discipline versus design science. *Design Issues, 17*(3), 49–55.

Cross, N. (2004). Expertise in design: An overview. *Design Studies, 25*(5), 427–441.

Cross, N. (2006). *Designerly ways of knowing*. London: Springer.

Daly, S. R. (2008). *Design across disciplines*. PhD. Purdue University, Indianapolis.

Dalziel, J. (2013). The LAMS community – Building communities of designers. In H. Beetham & R. Sharpe (Eds.), *Rethinking pedagogy for a digital age – Designing for 21st century learning* (pp. 230–243). New York, NY: Routledge.

Dalziel, J., Conole, G., Wills, S., Walker, S., Bennett, S., Dobozy, E., … Bower, M. (2016). The Larnaca declaration on learning design – 2013. *Journal of Interactive Media in Education, 2016*(1), 1–24.

Dobozy, E. (2013). Learning design research: Advancing pedagogies in the digital age. *Educational Media International, 50*(1), 63–76.

Dorst, K. (2006). Design problems and design paradoxes. *Design Issues, 22*(3), 4–17.

Dorst, K., & Cross, N. (2001). Creativity in the design process: Co-evolution of problem–solution. *Design Studies, 22*(5), 425–437.

Ertmer, P. A., Ottenbreit-Leftwich, A. T., Sadik, O., Sendurur, E., & Sendurur, P. (2012). Teacher beliefs and technology integration practices: A critical relationship. *Computers & Education, 59*(2), 423–435.

Fogarty, R. J., & Pete, B. M. (2007). *How to differentiate learning: Curriculum, instruction, assessment*. Thousand Oaks, CA: Corwin Press, A SAGE Publications Company.

Goddard, T., Griffiths, D., & Mi, W. (2015). Why has Ims learning design not led to the advances which were hoped for? *The Art & Science of Learning Design* (pp. 121–136). Springer.

Goodyear, P. (2005). Educational design and networked learning: Patterns, pattern languages and design practice. *Australasian Journal of Educational Technology, 21*(1), 82–101.

Goodyear, P., & Carvalho, L. (2013). The analysis of complex learning environments. In H. Beetham & R. Sharpe (Eds.), *Rethinking pedagogy for a digital age – Designing for 21st century learning* (pp. 49–63). New York, NY: Routledge.

Goodyear, P., & Retalis, S. (2010). Learning, technology and design. In P. Goodyear & S. Retalis (Eds.), *Technology-enhanced learning – Design patterns and pattern languages* (pp. 1–28). Rotterdam: Sense Publishers.

Harding, D., & Ingraham, B. (2013). The art of design. In H. Beetham & R. Sharpe (Eds.), *Rethinking pedagogy for a digital age – Designing for 21st century learning* (pp. 177–187). New York, NY: Routledge.

Hofer, M. J., Bell, L., Bull, G. L., Barry, R. Q., Cohen, J. D., Garcia, N., … Kim, R. (2015). *Practitioner's guide to technology, pedagogy, and content knowledge (TPACK): Rich media cases of teacher knowledge.* Association for the Advancement of Computing in Education.

Holmberg, J. (2014). Studying the process of educational design – Revisiting Schon and making a case for reflective design-based research on teachers' 'conversations with situations'. *Technology, Pedagogy and Education, 23*(3), 293–310.

IDEO. (2012). *Design thinking for educators.* Retrieved from http://designthinkingforeducators.com/

Iwarsson, S., & Ståhl, A. (2003). Accessibility, usability and universal design – Positioning and definition of concepts describing person-environment relationships. *Disability and Rehabilitation, 25*(2), 57–66.

Jonassen, D. H., Howland, J., Marra, R., & Crismond, D. (2008). *Meaningful learning with technology.* Upper Saddle River, NJ: Pearson/Merrill Prentice Hall.

Kim, C., Kim, M. K., Lee, C., Spector, J. M., & DeMeester, K. (2013). Teacher beliefs and technology integration. *Teaching and Teacher Education, 29*, 76–85.

Kimber, K., & Wyatt-Smith, C. (2006). Using and creating knowledge with new technologies: A case for students-as-designers. *Learning, Media and Technology, 31*(1), 19–34.

Koehler, M. J., & Mishra, P. (2005). Teachers learning technology by design. *Journal of Computing in Teacher Education, 21*(3), 94–102.

Koh, J. H. L., & Chai, C. S. (2016). Seven design frames that teachers use when considering technological pedagogical content knowledge (TPACK). *Computers & Education, 102*, 244–257.

Koh, J. H. L., Chai, C. S., Hong, H.-Y., & Tsai, C.-C. (2015). A survey to examine teachers' perceptions of design dispositions, lesson design practices, and their relationships with technological pedagogical content knowledge (TPACK). *Asia-Pacific Journal of Teacher Education, 43*(5), 378–391.

Koper, R., & Miao, Y. (2008). Learning design representations to document, model, and share teaching practice. In L. Lockyer, S. Bennett, S. Agostinho, &

B. Harper (Eds.), *Handbook of learning design and learning objects: Issues, applications, and technologies* (Vol. 1, pp. 41−86). IGI Global.

Kress, G. (2000). Design and transformation: New theories of meaning. *Multiliteracies: Literacy learning and the design of social futures*, 153−161.

Kress, G., & Sadler, J. (2014). Team cognition and reframing behavior − The impact of team cognition on problem reframing, team dynamics and design performance. In H. Plattner, C. Meinel, & L. Leifer (Eds.), *Design thinking research − Building innovation eco-systems* (pp. 35−48). Cham: Springer.

Kulkarni, C., Dow, S. P., & Klemmer, S. R. (2014). Early and repeated exposure to examples improves creative work. In H. Plattner, C. Meinel, & L. Leifer (Eds.), *Design thinking research − Building innovation eco-systems* (pp. 49−62). Cham: Springer.

Laurillard, D. (2002). *Rethinking university teaching − A framework for the effective use of learning technologies*. Oxford: RoutledgeFalmer.

Laurillard, D. (2012). *Teaching as a design science − Building pedagogical patterns for learning and technology*. New York, NY: Routledge.

Laurillard, D., Charlton, P., Craft, B., Dimakopoulos, D., Ljubojevic, D., Magoulas, G., ... Whittlestone, K. (2013). A constructionist learning environment for teachers to model learning designs. *Journal of Computer Assisted Learning, 29*(1), 15−30.

Laurillard, D., Masterman, L., Magoulas, G., Boyle, T., & Manton, M. (2017). Learning design support environment. Retrieved from https://sites.google.com/a/lkl.ac.uk/ldse/. Accessed on January 10, 2017.

Lawson, B., & Dorst, K. (2009). *Design expertise. 2009*. Oxford: Architectural Press.

Löwgren, J. (2005). Applying design methodology to software development. Paper presented at the Designing Interactive Systems.

Masterman, E., & Manton, M. (2011). Teachers' perspectives on digital tools for pedagogic planning and design. *Technology, Pedagogy and Education, 20*(2), 227−246.

Masterman, L. (2013). The challenge of teachers' design practice. In H. Beetham & R. Sharpe (Eds.), *Rethinking pedagogy for the digital age − Designing for 21st century learning* (pp. 64−77). New York, NY: Routledge.

McAndrew, P., & Goodyear, P. (2013). Representing practitioner experiences through learning design and patterns. In H. Beetham & R. Sharpe (Eds.), *Rethinking pedagogy for a digital age − Designing for 21st century learning* (pp. 133−144). New York, NY: Routledge.

Meinel, C., & Leifer, L. (2014). Introduction. In H. Plattner, C. Meinel, & L. Leifer (Eds.), *Design thinking research − Building innovation eco-systems* (pp. 3−10). Cham: Springer.

Mishra, P., & Koehler, M. J. (2006). Technological pedagogical content knowledge: A framework for teacher knowledge. *Teachers College Record, 108*(6), 1017−1054.

Mor, Y., & Craft, B. (2012). Learning design: Reflections upon the current landscape. *Research in Learning Technology, 20*.

Mor, Y., Craft, B., & Maina, M. (2015). Learning design — Definitions, current issues and grand challenges. In M. Maina, B. Craft, & Y. Mor (Eds.), *The art & science of learning design* (pp. ix—xxv). Rotterdam: Sense Publishers.

Oliver, R., Harper, B., Wills, S., Agostinho, S., & Hedberg, J. G. (2013). Describing ICT-based learning designs that promote quality learning outcomes. In H. Beetham & R. Sharpe (Eds.), *Rethinking pedagogy for a digital age — Designing for 21st century learning* (pp. 41—86). New York, NY: Routledge.

Rose, D. H., Harbour, W. S., Johnston, C. S., Daley, S. G., & Abarbanell, L. (2006). Universal design for learning in postsecondary education — Reflections on principles and their application. *Journal of Postsecondary Education and Disability, 19*(2), 135—151.

Schön, D. A. (1987). *Educating the reflective practitioner: Toward a new design for teaching and learning in the professions.* San Francisco, CA: Josey Bass.

Sharpe, R., & Oliver, M. (2013). Designing for learning in course teams. *Rethinking pedagogy for a digital age: Designing for 21st century learning* (pp. 163—176).

Siemens, G. (2005). Learning development cycle — Bridging learning design and modern knowledge needs. *Elearnspace Everything Elearning*, Retrieved from http://www.elearnspace.org/Articles/ldc.htm

Simon, H. A. (1996). *The sciences of the artificial* (3rd ed.). Cambridge, MA: The MIT Press.

Tonkinwise, C. (2011). A taste for practices: Unrepressing style in design thinking. *Design Studies, 32*(6), 533—545.

Van Merriënboer, J. J. G., Clark, R. E., & De Croock, M. B. M. (2002). Blueprints for complex learning: The 4C/ID-model. *Educational Technology Research and Development, 50*(2), 39—61.

Voogt, J., Fisser, P., Tondeur, J., & van Braak, J. (2016). Using theoretical perspectives in developing understanding of TPACK. *Handbook of Technological Pedagogical Content Knowledge (TPACK) for educators*, 33.

Wolf, T. V., Rode, J. A., Sussman, J., & Kellogg, W. A. (2006, April 22—27). Dispelling design as the 'Black Art' of CHI. Paper presented at the Computer Human Interaction 2006, Montréal, Québec, Canada.

7 Design of Web 2.0 Enhanced Learning

ABSTRACT

This chapter provides a comprehensive review of research and developments relating to the use of Web 2.0 technologies in education. As opposed to early educational uses of the Internet involving publication of static information on web pages, Web 2.0 tools offer a host of opportunities for educators to provide more interactive, collaborative, and creative online learning experiences for students. The chapter starts by defining Web 2.0 tools in terms of their ability to facilitate online creation, editing, and sharing of web content. A typology of Web 2.0 technologies is presented to illustrate the wide variety of tools at teachers' disposal. Educational uses of Web 2.0 technologies such as wikis, blogs, and microblogging are explored, in order to showcase the variety of designs that can be utilized. Based on a review of the research literature the educational benefits of using Web 2.0 technologies are outlined, including their ability to facilitate communication, collaborative knowledge building, student-centered activity, and vicarious learning. Similarly, issues surrounding the use of Web 2.0 tools are distilled from the literature and discussed, such as the possibility of technical problems, collaboration difficulties, and plagiarism. Two case studies involving the use Web 2.0 tools to support personalized learning and small group collaboration are detailed to exemplify design possibilities in greater detail. Finally, design recommendations for learning and teaching using Web 2.0 are presented, again based on findings from the research literature.

Introduction to Design of Web 2.0 Enhanced Learning

We have already established that teaching is a design science that is supported through reflection, exemplars, and expert guidance. While there are many design models and tools that can be used to help undertake design processes, contextually relevant understanding of design in the form of principles has been proposed as a primary way that educators can be assisted in their design pursuits. Moreover, it is argued that merely presenting design principles is nowhere near as powerful as grounding those principles in the evidence-base of the field, so that educators can understand how the principles were derived and appreciate their context sensitivity. This is in accordance with a 'scholarship of teaching' (Kreber & Kanuka, 2013; Trigwell, Martin, Benjamin, & Prosser, 2000) approach to learning design.

Correspondingly, this chapter analyzes learning design from within the context of Web 2.0 technology usage. Web 2.0 technologies have been selected for examination because they are easily accessed, afford a great deal of pedagogical flexibility in how they are used and have an extensive research base regarding their application. They also offer an interesting point of comparison to the educational use of social networking, mobile technologies and virtual worlds, which are investigated in the next three chapters. Comparing and contrasting these four different technological platforms will form the basis for abstracting technology-enhanced learning design principles in Chapter 11.

In order to effectively design Web 2.0 enhanced learning it is first necessary to form a clear understanding of the term 'Web 2.0,' the variety of Web 2.0 technologies that are available, the ways that the tools can be used for education, as well as their benefits, issues, and design implications. Consequently, this chapter addresses each of these concerns, based on a comprehensive and systematic analysis of the research literature.[3]

---

[3]See the Preface for an explanation of how the thematic analysis was conducted.

Let's start by examining what is meant by "Web 2.0" technologies.

WHAT ARE WEB 2.0 TECHNOLOGIES?

Arriving at a precise definition of Web 2.0 is an elusive goal (Cormode & Krishnamurthy, 2008). Tim O'Reilly, who is generally credited with popularizing the term 'Web 2.0,' essentially characterizes Web 2.0 as web-based platforms with simple to use interfaces that enable users to collectively contribute and share large amounts of information (O'Reilly, 2007). Specifically, he describes Web 2.0 technologies as those that enable:

> consuming and remixing data from multiple sources, including individual users, while providing their own data and services in a form that allows remixing by others, creating network effects through an 'architecture of participation' (O'Reilly, 2007, p. 17)

Thus, Web 2.0 technologies move beyond the original 'Web 1.0' incarnation of the Internet as purely an information delivery platform using static web pages that often required considerable technical knowledge to create (O'Reilly, 2007).

Alexander (2006) points out that ultimately the defining attributes of Web 2.0 technologies are far less important than the concepts and practices they encompass which include:

- Social software – connecting people via the Internet to boost their knowledge and capacity to learn
- Microcontent – typically short posts and contributions that are easily published and can be rapidly dispersed
- Openness – content can be instantly accessed by people and machines for more efficient sharing and knowledge formation
- Folksonomies – where people organize data by attaching keywords or 'tags' to it, rather than carefully arranging it in knowledge hierarchies.

Web 2.0 tools are often externally hosted whereby users self-register for an account, though some Web 2.0 platforms can be downloaded and hosted on institutional or individual servers (Franklin & Van Harmelen, 2007). Popular Web 2.0 technologies include blogs (e.g., Wordpress), wikis (e.g., Wikispaces), microblogging (e.g., Twitter), image sharing (e.g., Flickr), video sharing (e.g., YouTube), and social bookmarking (e.g., Diigo). More examples are provided in the next section.

Key pedagogical affordances of Web 2.0 technologies include the ability to establish connectivity and social rapport, the ability to collaboratively discover and share information, the ability to create content, and the ability to aggregate and remix information (McLoughlin & Lee, 2007). A critical feature underpinning the success of the Web 2.0 paradigm is that users willingly make public contributions so that concerns over intellectual property do not inhibit the distribution and reuse of online content (Beer & Burrows, 2007). Thus, through collective publishing, linking, tagging, commenting and rating it is possible to harness the intelligence of the crowd (McLoughlin & Lee, 2007).

The term 'Web 2.0' is sometimes used synonymously with 'social media' (Bennett, Bishop, Dalgarno, Waycott, & Kennedy, 2012; Manca & Ranieri, 2016) or 'cloud computing' (Stevenson & Hedberg, 2011), and the Web 2.0 paradigm is also known as the 'read-write' web (Richardson, 2006). To avoid confusion we will not refer to any of those terms in this chapter. For the purposes of having a working definition we will simply define Web 2.0 technologies in accordance with Bower (2016) as being:

> openly available online technologies that allow creation, editing and sharing of digital content between (often large) groups of people via a web-browser.

Examples of Web 2.0 Technologies

Historically, there have been several attempts to categories the different types of Web 2.0 tools available to educators (for instance, Bower, Hedberg, & Kuswara, 2010; Conole & Alevizou, 2010; Crook, 2008; Franklin & Van Harmelen, 2007; Kamel Boulos & Wheeler, 2007). Recently a typographical analysis of over 200 freely available Web 2.0 products by Bower (2016) found 37 distinct types of Web 2.0 technologies that can be classified into 14 different categories: text-based, image-based, audio, video, multimodal production, digital storytelling, website creation, knowledge organization and sharing, data analysis, timeline, assessment, social networking, and synchronous collaboration tools. The categories and their types are illustrated in Figure 7.1.

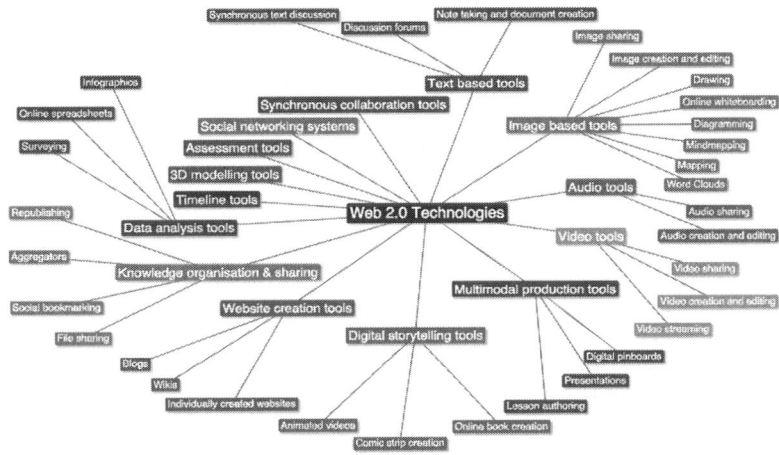

Figure 7.1. A Tree Diagram Outlining 37 Different Types of Web 2.0 Technologies (Bower, 2015).

For those interested in freely available tools, a description of the 212 different types of Web 2.0 products used to form the typology, organized into their 37 types and 14 categories, can be found in Bower (2015), available at http://bit.ly/educauseWeb2typology. A summary of the different types of Web 2.0 technologies, the sorts of interactions they enable, potential pedagogical use cases and two examples of each tool is provided in Table 7.1 (from Bower, 2016).

Thus, there is a colorful range of Web 2.0 technologies that educators can choose to use in the tasks they design.

Uses of Web 2.0 Technologies in Education

Perhaps because there is a wide array of Web 2.0 tools at the educator's disposal, there is large variety of ways that Web 2.0 technologies are used in education. Web 2.0 technologies can be used by students or educators as consumption tools where freely available knowledge is accessed via the web, or production tools where students or educators share digital artifacts and information that they created as part of an online community (Harris & Rea, 2009). While merely accessing information on the Internet is relatively straightforward, having students and teachers sharing

Table 7.1.   Types of Web 2.0 Technologies (Bower, 2016).

Type of Web 2.0 Tool	What They Enable	Pedagogical Use Cases	Examples
Text-based tools			
Synchronous text discussion	Exchange of text-based comments in real-time	Backchannels for in-class conversations	http://twitter.com http://todaysmeet.com
Discussion forums	Asynchronous text discussions organized by discussion threads	Reflective discussions and debate	http://forums.com http://proboards.com
Note taking & document creation	Collaborative authoring of documents in real-time and review of changes	Collaborative report writing	http://docs.google.com http://etherpad.org
Image-based tools			
Image sharing	Asynchronous public sharing of images	Sharing class images for analysis	http://flickr.com http://instagram.com
Image creation and editing	Individual creation and editing of images shareable via URL	Create an explanatory image	http://pixlr.com http://sumopaint.com
Drawing	Use of the mouse as a pen to create pictures which can be shared via URL	Capture of freestyle writing	http://flockdraw.com http://slimber.com
Online whiteboarding	Use of line, shape and text tools to structure illustrative processes	Collaborative brainstorm session	http://dweeber.com http://twiddla.com
Diagramming	Templates for creating diagrams and flowcharts	Creation of process diagram	http://creately.com http://gliffy.com
Mindmapping	Creation of images to represent a knowledge network	Representing conceptual knowledge	http://mind42.com http://coggle.it
Mapping	Creation of custom maps by marking up mapping information	Represent location of events	http://scribblemaps.com http://quikmaps.com
Word Clouds	Creation and sharing of visual arrangements of keywords	High level analysis of a text	http://wordle.net http://tagxedo.com
Audio tools			
Audio sharing	Upload and share audio recordings (for instance, podcasts)	Sharing an explanatory narrative	http://soundcloud.com http://chirbit.com
Audio creation and editing	Record and often remix audio directly through the browser	Creating a podcast overview	http://soundation.com http://vocaroo.com

Table 7.1. (*Continued*)

Type of Web 2.0 Tool	What They Enable	Pedagogical Use Cases	Examples
Video tools			
Video sharing	Share video content via public repositories	Sharing of video assignments	http://youtube.com http://vimeo.com
Video creation and editing	Create and edit videos through the browser	Creating a video response to a task	http://videotoolbox.com http://muvee.com
Video streaming	Publicly broadcast a live video stream from their video camera or webcam	Sharing a lecture series	http://livestream.com http://ustream.tv
Multimodal production tools			
Digital pinboards	Organization and sharing of notes, photos and files on a freeform canvas	Collecting assignment resources	http://padlet.com http://en.linoit.com
Presentations	Sequencing of multimodal content to create slides for an instructional narrative	Creating slides for a presentation	http://prezi.com http://haikudeck.com
Lesson authoring	Sequencing of content into learning modules with interactive elements	Creating a lesson for peers	http://lessonlams.org http://udutu.com
Digital storytelling tools			
Online book creation	Creation of online story books based on pictures and text, shared via URL	Creating a book to illustrate understanding	http://mixbook.com http://tikatok.com
Comic strip creation	Overlay of characters, text and backgrounds into comic strip templates	Creating a comic to show key steps	http://toondoo.com http://wittycomics.com
Animated videos	Creation an sharing of animated videos	Demonstrate a process via animated video	http://powtoon.com http://moovly.com
Website creation tools			
Individually created websites	Individual development of websites using point and click templates	Create a site to showcase topic understanding	http://sites.google.com http://wix.com
Wikis	Collaborative creation of multi-page interlinked web pages	Collaborative creation of project website	http://wikispaces.com http://pbworks.com
Blogs	Chronological posting of information on the web	Create an e-portfolio for a course	http://wordpress.org http://blogger.com

Table 7.1. (*Continued*)

Type of Web 2.0 Tool	What They Enable	Pedagogical Use Cases	Examples
Knowledge organization & sharing			
File sharing	Sharing of files (e.g., images documents, audio, video) via an online file system	Sharing project files between team members	http://dropbox.com http://mediafire.com
Social bookmarking	Storing, organizing and tagging of websites in a shareable repository	Creating a class repository of relevant sites	http://diigo.com http://delicious.com
Aggregators	Harvest Really Simple Syndication (RSS) information on a webpage	Creating a topic feed of news and events	http://flipboard.com http://feedly.com
Republishing	Scraping information from the web and re-sharing it with updates or comments	Creating a class annotated page of resources	http://scoop.it http://pinterest.com
Data analysis tools			
Surveying	Collection of data from participants via web forms	Collecting data from peers for analysis	http://surveymonkey.com http://polldaddy.com
Online spreadsheets	Collaborative editing of spreadsheets via URL	Collaborative analysis of numeric data	http://ethercalc.net http://smartsheet.com
Infographics	Representation and sharing of data via online templates	Creating an infographic to illustrate idea	http://infogr.am http://www.easel.ly
Other clusters			
Timeline tools	Visual arrangement of text and images on a webpage in chronological order	Provide a historical overview of events	http://tiki-toki.com http://capzles.com
3D modeling tools	3D Computer Aided Design model creation	Create a model to prototype a design	http://tinkercad.com http://shapeshifter.io
Assessment tools	Creation of online quizzes using a range of response types	Create a quiz in order to assess knowledge	http://quizlet.com http://cram.com
Social networking systems	Creation of a networked online profile for sharing photos, videos and text	Build a support network for study purposes	http://facebook.com http://edmodo.com
Synchronous collaboration tools	Synchronous sharing of audio-video, text-chat, and often other information	Hold an online meeting	http://zoom.us http://wiziq.com

knowledge they create is of particular interest from a learning design perspective because of the complexities that construction and collaboration introduce. Thus, this chapter will focus upon more productive and interactive uses of Web 2.0 technologies in education.

Due to the wide variety of Web 2.0 tools that educators can integrate into their classes and the large number of ways that those tools can be used, it is obviously not feasible to outline all possible uses in this chapter. In reality, some Web 2.0 technologies have attracted much greater attention from educators and researchers than others, with wikis and blogs being the most prevalently used tools. A summary of uses of wikis and blogs as detailed by the research literature is provided below, along with microblogging and some brief examples of other uses and combinations of tools. Social networking is acknowledged as a major category of Web 2.0 technology with complex features and issues, and as such is addressed exclusively in the next chapter.

WIKIS

Wikis can quite simply be defined as "websites that allow their users to create and edit content" (Grant, 2009, p. 105). People with sufficient access can use wiki pages to publish new content such as text, images and hyperlinks directly to the Internet, as well as edit existing content, and if necessary 'roll back' to a previous version using the 'page history' utility (Wheeler, Yeomans, & Wheeler, 2008).

A distinguishing feature of wikis is that they enable organization of content by linking pages to one another, making them suitable for forming knowledge bases such as Wikipedia (Ben-Zvi, 2007). Wikis also enable users to search for text, and in some cases attach files to pages (Raman, Ryan, & Olfman, 2005). Wiki pages often have a corresponding discussion page, which can provide a critical dialogic space for participants to negotiate a shared understanding of the content (Pifarré & Staarman, 2011). The inherent features of wiki technologies include incremental knowledge creation, multi-user authoring, and version management, all of which make them appropriate tools to support group learning processes (Cole, 2009). Figure 7.2 shows a PBWorks wiki being used in edit mode to create a whole class wiki.

Commonly used and freely available wikis for immediate online educational use include PBworks (http://pbworks.com) and Wikispaces (http://wikispaces.com). For a wiki that can be

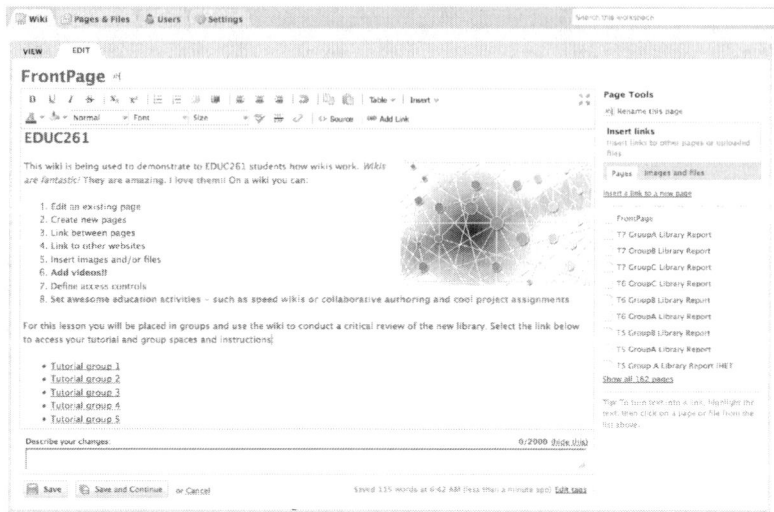

Figure 7.2.   A PBworks Wiki in Edit Mode Being Used to Create a Whole Class Collaborative Review Task.

downloaded onto a server an obvious candidate is the infamous MediaWiki (https://www.mediawiki.org), which is the technology that underpins Wikipedia. To compare the features of dozens of different wiki products see the WikiMatrix website (http://www.wikimatrix.org).

At school level wikis have been used to enable primary students to collaboratively draft, revise and edit their writing compositions (Li, Chu, & Ki, 2014; Li, Chu, Ki, & Woo, 2012), and to create their own science text-book together (Pifarré & Staarman, 2011). In high school contexts, wikis have been used for students to collaboratively form knowledge bases about culture (Lund & Smørdal, 2006) and recent technological innovations (Grant, 2009). Wikis have been also been used to enable middle school geography students located across different schools to complete collaborative research projects (Engstrom & Jewett, 2005). It should be noted that based on an analysis of publicly available wikis Reich, Murnane, and Willett (2012) concluded that school use of wikis is more often for teacher resource sharing and content delivery than for individual student assignments and student collaborative work.

There is an even wider variety of wiki uses documented in higher education contexts. Wikis have been used for entire classes to collaboratively create the course knowledge base, with discipline areas including information systems (Cole, 2009; Raman et al., 2005), mobile workforce technologies (Ruth & Houghton, 2009), media computation (Rick & Guzdial, 2006), statistics (Ben-Zvi, 2007), network technology and human resources development (Trentin, 2009), and the study of blended learning (Li, Dong, & Huang, 2011). Wikis have also been used to facilitate students' collaborative writing processes in foreign language classes (Jung & Suzuki, 2015), English composition (Rick & Guzdial, 2006), psychology (Judd, Kennedy, & Cropper, 2010), technology (Altanopoulou, Tselios, Katsanos, Georgoutsou, & Panagiotaki, 2015) and social work classes (Jones, 2007). They have sometimes been used as a platform to enable students to receive peer feedback on their individual compositions, for instance architectural design work (Rick & Guzdial, 2006), society and culture essays (Xiao & Lucking, 2008), and information technology assignments (Su & Beaumont, 2010).

There are also several documented uses of wikis to facilitate university students' group work collaboration on projects, for instance, in information systems classes (Elgort, Toland, & Smith, 2008; Guo & Stevens, 2011) and computing (Bower, Woo, Roberts, & Watters, 2006; Chou & Chen, 2008). Sometimes further sharing occurs by having students present their group wiki projects to the rest of the class, such as when groups of physiotherapy students present their analyses of patient cases (Snodgrass, 2011) or teams of software engineering students present their topic summaries (Tsai, Li, Elston, & Chen, 2011). In pre-service teacher education, wikis have often been used as a collaborative curriculum design space where groups of students create learning resources and tasks for prospective students (Biasutti & El-Deghaidy, 2012; Naismith, Lee, & Pilkington, 2011; Ng, 2016).

BLOGS

Blogs (short for 'web logs') have been defined as "online journals where an author (or authors) publishes a series of chronological, updateable entries or posts on various topics" (Farmer, Yue, & Brooks, 2008, p. 123). Users are typically able to embed images and videos into their posts in order to embellish text-based content (Harris & Rea, 2009). Another key feature of blogs is that they enable readers with sufficient access permissions to add their comments to other people's posts (Churchill, 2009). Blogs are commonly used as a means for student to keep electronic portfolios ('e-portfolios'), which have been described as "a form of authentic assessment with formative functions that include showcasing and sharing learning artifacts, documenting reflective learning processes, connecting learning across various stages and enabling frequent feedback for improvements" (Yang, Tai, & Lim, 2015, p. 1). A screenshot of a teacher education student e-portfolio is shown in Figure 7.3.

By far the most popular blogging tool is Wordpress. Users can sign up for a freely hosted Wordpress account at the Wordpress hosting site (http://wordpress.com), or the system can be sourced at no cost from the Wordpress download site (http://wordpress.org) for installation on institutional web servers. The downloadable version can be used for individual or multiple ('multisite') accounts. The Google owned Blogger platform (http://blogger.com) is a popular alternative that offers freely hosted blogs. For a comparison of the features of several blog products see the WeblogMatrix website (http://www.weblogmatrix.org).

Blogs have been used in schools as a publication and sharing platform in order to develop writing skills, cognitive abilities and confidence. For instance, in primary school, blogs have been used

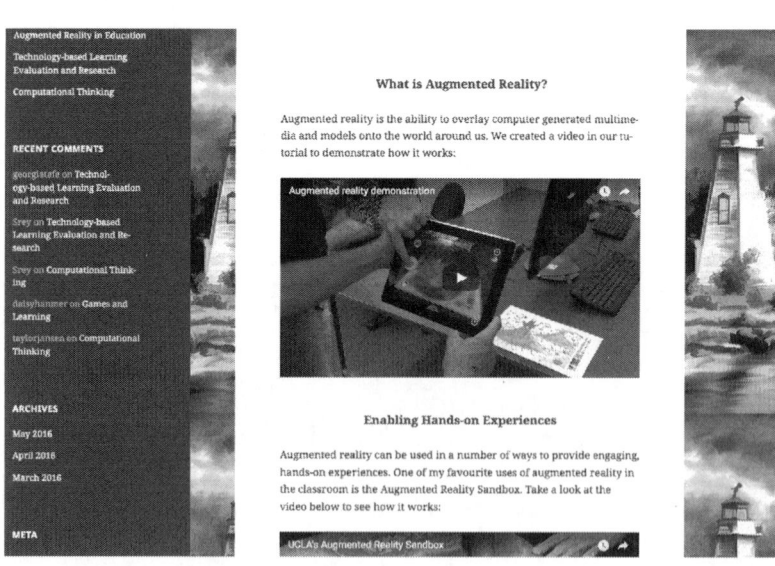

Figure 7.3.   A Teacher Education Student E-Portfolio Created Using Wordpress and Showcasing Video Documentary of Classroom Learning.

as a means for students to upload versions of their writing assignments and receive constructive feedback from their peers (Chen, Liu, Shih, Wu, & Yuan, 2011; Nicolaidou, 2013). Blogs have also been used in high school to enable students to post their thoughts about political events in order to develop their political awareness and political self-efficacy (Levy, Journell, He, & Towns, 2015), and to reflect upon web development projects over time (Chang, Liang, Shu, Tseng, & Lin, 2016).

In higher education, blogs are often used to promote reflective learning. Examples include molecular biology students reflecting upon submitted coursework and instructor feedback (Haave, 2016), and second language learners reflecting upon their language acquisition strategies (Hourigan & Murray, 2010). Reflection is often coupled with peer interaction, for example where pre-service teachers provide feedback to one another about their coursework and practicum experiences (Deng & Yuen, 2011; Yang, 2009), or where computer science students provide feedback to one another about their design diaries (Robertson, 2011). In some cases video blogging has been used to promote reflective and collaborative development of presentation capabilities for second language learners (Shih, 2010) and pre-service teachers (Bower, Cavanagh, Moloney, & Diao, 2011).

Still in higher education, blogs have been used as a platform for the creation of e-portfolios so that social work students could integrate theory and practice (Fitch, Peet, Reed, & Tolman, 2008), engineering students could develop life-long learning capabilities (Heinrich, Bhattacharya, & Rayudu, 2007) and English language teaching students could collaboratively develop their pedagogical competencies (Kabilan & Khan, 2012). In some cases, a single blog has been used by groups of students in order to facilitate collaboration, for instance so that undergraduate illustration students could share sketches, ideas and reflections (Garcia, Elbeltagi, Brown, & Dungay, 2015), undergraduate drama students could document group creative processes and discussion (Philip & Nicholls, 2009), and physiotherapy students could develop clinical reasoning skills, practice, reflective thinking and metacognition during their practicum experience (Ladyshewsky & Gardner, 2008; Tan, Ladyshewsky, & Gardner, 2010).

Blogs have also been used in university classes to enable interaction on writing tasks, for instance whereby English students received feedback about their compositions from their peers (Novakovich, 2016), second language learners receive feedback from peers and the teacher about their writing (Chen, 2014), or where computing students engage in 'jigsaw'-based collaborative activities to summarize topics they are learning (Huang, Huang, & Yu, 2011).

MICROBLOGGING

Microblogging services, most famously Twitter, allow users to "publish and share brief updates for real-time and asynchronous communication with no more than 140 characters" (Gao, Luo, & Zhang, 2012, p. 783). Globally, there are over 300 million active Twitter users each month (Statistica, 2017). In education, Twitter can support the development of formal and informal learning communities, collaborative learning, and reflective thinking (Shah, Shabgahi, & Cox, 2015), as well as process oriented learning (Ebner, Lienhardt, Rohs, & Meyer, 2010).

Twitter has been used in pre-health professional classes to foster engagement through academic and co-curricular instruction (Junco, Heiberger, & Loken, 2011), as an authentic platform for language students to practice their reading and writing (Ullrich et al., 2008), and as a means for research students to communicate formative course evaluations and questions to teachers (Chen & Chen, 2012). An alternative microblogging platform (Cirip) has been used to enable students to create digital narratives, share multimedia, and provide a live stream commentary of events (Holotescu & Grosseck, 2011).

OTHER APPLICATIONS, INTEGRATIONS, AND COMBINATIONS

Other examples of Web 2.0 in education include using the Prezi web-based presentation software to teach fifth grade geography concepts (Chou, Chang, & Lu, 2015), online spreadsheets for undergraduates to complete business computing tasks (Rienzo & Han, 2009), YouTube for undergraduate marketing students to showcase their academic and technological competencies (Orús et al., 2016), Google Docs so language learners could collaboratively help each other with comprehension tasks (Liu & Lan, 2016), and the Storybird digital storytelling platform for English language majors to compose narratives and provide feedback to their peers (Chwo, 2015).

Often Web 2.0 tools are used in combination to suit different phases of the learning cycle. For instance, groups of early high school students used a wide variety of Web 2.0 tools such as Mindmeister, Google Docs, Prezi, Twitter and blogging tools in order to create digital travel guides together (Rahimi, van den Berg, & Veen, 2015b). Group wiki projects, personal blog reflections, lecture podcasts, sharing video resources and web-conferencing were used in combination to support first-year high school mathematics students (Köse, 2010).

In higher education, wikis and blogs are often used in combination to often offer a foundation for collaboration and reflection. For instance, in undergraduates language learning classes wikis were used for collaborative translation tasks, blogs for free writing, and forums for discussion activities (Miyazoe & Anderson, 2010). Blogs, wikis and discussion forums were also used in doctoral level finance course, with tool selection depending on the types of questions being asked (Meyer, 2010). In order for pre-service teachers learn how technology can support design processes, podcasts were used for groups to present knowledge, wikis facilitated collaborative reflection on task progress, and blogs were used to enable inter-group critique (Chandra & Chalmers, 2010). As another example, sports management students used Facebook, YouTube, message boards and website creation tools as part of an authentic sports promotion task (Williams & Chinn, 2009). There are also instances where suites of Web 2.0 tools have been used to replace the traditional learning management system, for instance in a Master of Business course G Suite (formally known as Google Apps) including the Docs, photo, website and wiki tools was used to facilitate student tasks, and the Google calendar, announcements, file sharing and spreadsheet tools were used for course administration (Schneckenberg, Ehlers, & Adelsberger, 2011).

So hopefully we can agree that there are a wide variety of ways the Web 2.0 technologies can and have been used in education! The next section explores how these uses can actually *benefit* learning.

Benefits and Potentials of Web 2.0 in Education

A valuable attribute of Web 2.0 technologies is that they are commensurate with a wide variety of educational theoretical perspectives, including behaviorism through direct student feedback and guidance, constructivism through learner exploration and knowledge building, cognitivism through attention to stages of cognition and metacognitive reflection, and social constructivism through collaborative creation of meaning and learning with peers (Crook, 2008). For instance, wikis enable social constructivist learning as students develop knowledge bases together (Biasutti & El-Deghaidy, 2012). G Suite has been used to enhance self-directed and constructivist learning of students (Schneckenberg et al., 2011). Having people review each other's blog work and provide feedback to one another is a way of promoting connectivist learning (Garcia et al., 2015). By enabling students to learn through the creation of artifacts together, Web 2.0 tools are also suitable for facilitating constructionist learning (Franklin & Van Harmelen, 2007).

Based on a review of the research literature, benefits[4] of Web 2.0 technologies in education have been distilled into themes below. Using the findings and insights from the research allows us to move beyond our own personal intuitions about Web 2.0 learning and teaching, to form an understanding that is based on the evidence and observations of the field.

ENABLING COMMUNICATION

A key advantage of Web 2.0 technologies is that they enable communication of information. At a fundamental level, they facilitate conversations between learners and with the teacher as well as social feedback (Boyd, 2007). Because content is in digital form it can easily be shared, modified, or inserted into other Web 2.0 tools (for instance, a blog) so that peers and teachers can exchange ideas and build upon each other's understanding (Rahimi et al., 2015b). Web 2.0 technologies also enable a range of new web-based communication forms that were not previously possible, for instance commenting on one another's work, rating of shared content, and crowd sourcing of knowledge (Redecker, Ala-Mutka, Bacigalupo, Ferrari, & Punie, 2009).

---

[4]The term 'benefits' has been used rather than 'affordances', to avoid issues relating to attribution (as discussed in Chapter 4). Strictly speaking, benefits such as enabling reflection, student-centered learning, enhanced motivation and so on are not direct action potentials of the technology, but rather consequences of how the technologies used. Using the term 'benefits' rather than affordances avoids any nomenclatural complications, though in practice the term 'affordances' is often used to describe consequences such as these.

One positive aspect of communicating via Web 2.0 tools is that it often enables several simultaneous learner-directed discussions to occur at once (Crook, 2008). For example, with a wiki, multiple people and groups can upload their responses and then review each others' work more efficiently than if presenting to one another in face-to-face mode (Bower et al., 2006). Completing blog tasks enables students to share their ideas, solicit comments on their posts, and learning from the work of others (Churchill, 2009). Twitter can be used to promote continuity of class discussions, provide an informal means of asking questions, and enable students to receive prompt responses to their queries (Junco et al., 2011).

The teacher can also use Web 2.0 tools such as blogs to share content, post announcements, as well as solicit comments from students and respond to their ideas (Churchill, 2009). Synchronous tools like Twitter enable teachers to instantly disseminate up-to-date class and event reminders (Gao et al., 2012; Junco et al., 2011).

ACCESS EXTENDING THE BOUNDS OF THE CLASSROOM

One of the most frequently espoused benefits of Web 2.0 technologies is that they enable access to information and learning from any location (Harris & Rea, 2009). This opens up possibilities for blended, distance and informal learning by allowing students to undertake learning activities whether or not they are in the classroom (Project Tomorrow, 2016; Rahimi et al., 2015b; Redecker et al., 2009). The 'anytime-anywhere' availability of Web 2.0 can enhance learner autonomy and encourage extended learning through more open-ended and productive tasks (Crook, 2008). Anytime, anyplace access can also be used to facilitate more efficient team-based collaboration (Kam & Katerattanakul, 2014). Students value the capacity to flexibly collaborate on their compositions rather than all having to sit around a single computer (Rahimi et al., 2015b).

COLLABORATIVE KNOWLEDGE BUILDING

Web 2.0 environments enable the 'wisdom of the crowd' to be leveraged whereby users collaboratively build knowledge bases that are far more comprehensive than could be achieved individually (Grant, 2009; Ullrich et al., 2008). Students can share content such as images through online photo sites or written text via wikis in order to form a collaborative knowledge base about a topic (Bennett et al., 2012). Knowledge becomes decentralized, accessible, and co-constructed by a broad base of users thus facilitating collective intelligence and peer learning (Greenhow, Robelia, & Hughes, 2009; Kam & Katerattanakul, 2014). The process of collaboratively searching, reading, brainstorming, storytelling, mind mapping, analyzing, evaluating and creating digital artifacts can help students develop a range of cognitive abilities (Rahimi et al., 2015b). McLoughlin and Lee (2007) describe this new way of learning and teaching as 'collaborative remixability' – the ability to combine online media and information to create new ideas, designs and representations.

Research evidence and student feedback supports the value of collaborative knowledge building using Web 2.0 technologies. The process of externalizing knowledge through collaborative wiki tasks has been shown to result in significantly greater internalized knowledge of participants (Kump, Moskaliuk, Dennerlein, & Ley, 2013). The use of e-portfolios with peer feedback has been found to lead to significantly higher knowledge management capabilities (e.g., knowledge acquisition, application and sharing skills) than approaches where e-portfolios were not used (Chang, Tseng, Liang, & Chen, 2013). On an affective level, students who completed a statistics report writing task in groups using a wiki experienced significantly lower fear of asking for help and interpretation anxiety than students who completed the task individually in traditional mode (Neumann & Hood, 2009). In terms of qualitative feedback, students generally recognize the value of Web 2.0 tools for supporting collaboration (Chou & Chen, 2008; Elgort et al., 2008), and suggest that collaborative knowledge building enables them to learn more than if working alone (Lund & Smørdal, 2006).

FACILITATING FEEDBACK

When students complete tasks using Web 2.0 tools such as blogs, the teacher is able to monitor student work in progress and provide ongoing feedback to them (Churchill, 2009; Kabilan & Khan, 2012). Students appreciate how using blogs enables them to provide feedback to each other (Churchill, 2009) including from any location (Xiao & Lucking, 2008). Students also indicate that receiving feedback comments on their work from peers and the teacher contributes to their learning (Su & Beaumont, 2010). In some cases, students indicate greater comfort levels providing feedback online as opposed to face-to-face (Huang et al., 2011). University teachers also note that having students develop peer review and feedback skills is important in its own right (Waycott, Sheard, Thompson, & Clerehan, 2013).

One study of higher education students found that blog-mediated peer feedback led to significantly higher performance on writing tasks than traditional in-class paper-based approaches, with fewer trivial comments and significantly higher critical and suggestive comments (Novakovich, 2016). At primary school, peer feedback as part of a Web 2.0-based digital storytelling activity resulted in significantly more sophisticated stories and enabled students to form a more accurate appreciation of their creative capacities (Liu, Lu, Wu, & Tsai, 2016).

ENABLING VICARIOUS LEARNING

Teachers identify how the ability for students to view each other's work in itself provides vicarious learning opportunities (Waycott et al., 2013). Students also appreciate how posting work on Web 2.0 platforms makes the thinking of their peers visible, meaning they can learn from one another rather than working in isolation (Bennett et al., 2012). As an example, students can learn vicariously by reviewing peer blog posts and the feedback that those posts received (Churchill, 2009). Wikis also support vicarious learning by enabling students to compare their approach and progress with other groups (Zorko, 2009). This form of learning can enable less capable students to learn from more talented peers and thus reduce the burden on the teacher to be the source of all knowledge (Bower et al., 2006).

DEVELOPING MULTIMEDIA SKILLS

Web 2.0 technologies provide a platform for individual creativity through the production of posts, websites, audio recordings, videos and so on through simple to use interfaces (Ullrich et al., 2008). Students can embed or attach multimedia into their posts, which can potentially be motivating and enhance communication (Philip & Nicholls, 2009). For instance, in primary school teachers can encourage students to embed photos and graphics to embellish their topic descriptions (Woo, Chu, Ho, & Li, 2011). Having early high school students create personal learning environments using Web 2.0 technologies not only helped them to develop their technical and web skills, but also their understanding of how Web 2.0 technologies can be used to enhance their learning (Rahimi et al., 2015b). Web 2.0 technologies also enable students to become creators of course learning materials (Franklin & Van Harmelen, 2007). The multiple forms of contribution that Web 2.0 technologies enable (such as text, audio, image, video) also allow educators to design tasks that cater to a broad spectrum of learner preferences and needs (Franklin & Van Harmelen, 2007).

ENCOURAGING REFLECTION

The fact that Web 2.0 technologies often enable asynchronous contributions makes them suitable for tasks that involve student reflection (Bower et al., 2006; Huang et al., 2011). Students are able to view one another's contributions, for instance to a wiki, and have this lead to the reorganization and reconstruction of their thinking (Pifarré & Staarman, 2011). The ability for students to make posts to e-portfolios and revisit their thinking over time is another way that (self) reflection can be encouraged (Yang et al., 2015).

It seems that there is a reciprocal relationship between reflection, self-regulation and learning. Sustained use of blogs by high school political science students resulted in significantly increased levels of reflective thinking, and reflective thinking was in turn significantly correlated with improved performance (Xie, Ke, & Sharma, 2008). High school students who used e-portfolios to reflect upon their web design projects significantly improved their self-regulated learning capabilities, with greater levels of reflection correlated with higher self-regulated learning (Chang et al., 2016). Primary school students who used e-portfolios for eight months demonstrated significantly greater improvement in writing and self-regulated learning skills than control group counterparts, with gains attributed to the regular cycles of planning, doing and reflecting (Meyer, Abrami, Wade, Aslan, & Deault, 2010).

ENABLING STUDENT-CENTERED LEARNING

Web 2.0 technologies can be used to facilitate more active, personalized, self-regulated and student-centered environments (McLoughlin & Lee, 2010; Rahimi, Berg, & Veen, 2015a;

Rahimi et al., 2015b; Redecker et al., 2009; Williams & Chinn, 2009), constituting a shift from a focus on teaching to an emphasis upon learning (Schneckenberg et al., 2011). Web 2.0 tools enable self-regulated and personalized learning through their capacity for students to manage their information, interact and collaborate with others, as well as aggregate and summatively manage information (Dabbagh & Kitsantas, 2012). For instance, blog tasks can be used to encourage more self-directed learning where students generate goals, plan, estimate task difficulty, monitor progress, select between creative ideas, seek help and evaluate their performance (Robertson, 2011). Twitter has promoted more student-centered learning by enabling students to relate the course material to their own experiences (Junco et al., 2011) and to instantaneously record their emergent thinking (Gao et al., 2012). Web 2.0 tools also enable educators to apply more student-centered pedagogies by creating differentiated learning pathways for students of different abilities (Bower, 2013).

The use of Web 2.0 technologies to enable student-centered learning has been found to result in affective and attitudinal gains. The use of blogs as personal information management tools by primary school students led to significantly higher academic self-efficacy than for a control group (Yeo & Lee, 2014). Early high school students indicate that using a variety of Web 2.0 tools to work in teams endowed them with a sense of ownership over their learning (Rahimi et al., 2015b).

ENHANCING MOTIVATION AND ENGAGEMENT

Increased motivation and engagement is one of the commonly cited benefits of Web 2.0-based learning. In a collective case study by Redecker et al. (2009) students were generally motivated by the more active learning approaches that Web 2.0 technologies had enabled. In another study, school teachers observed that approaches using Web 2.0 technologies encouraged contribution by many learners who were otherwise tentative or who had special needs (Crook & Harrison, 2008). At university level, using Twitter in undergraduate classes led to significantly greater increases in student engagement as compared to control group classes (Junco et al., 2011). Students who completed a statistics report writing task using a wiki experienced higher levels of engagement than those working individually (Neumann & Hood, 2009). Significantly higher attitudinal scores have been observed when language learners use Google Docs for collaborative learning (Liu & Lan, 2016). Higher levels of student engagement have also been observed when a variety of Web 2.0 tools are integrated into the curriculum (Schneckenberg et al., 2011).

One of the key reasons for heightened student engagement when using Web 2.0 tools is the ability for them to publish work to a wide audience. This effect has been reported by primary school students completing collaborative writing tasks (Li et al., 2012), university students learning English as a second language (Zorko, 2009), and pre-service teachers using wikis to conduct research tasks (Wheeler et al., 2008). The positive impact that publishing to a wide audience has on student motivation has also been observed by school teachers (Crook & Harrison, 2008) and university educators (Waycott et al., 2013).

Increased motivation can in turn positively influence learner effort and attitude. Students in one study identified that the open and public audience encouraged them to write more accurate and relevant posts (Wheeler et al., 2008). Collaborative writing process using wikis resulted in significant higher increases in the writing attitude scores of primary school students as compared to traditional approaches (Li et al., 2014).

EASE OF USE

Generally speaking, students indicate that Web 2.0 tools are relatively straightforward to use (Chandra & Chalmers, 2010; E. Meyer et al., 2010). For instance, wiki's enable non-tech savvy students and teachers to create web pages without needing to know HTML or other technologies (Larusson & Alterman, 2009). As a student in one study commented about being able to make web pages using wikis: "While I have a basic understanding of HTML … [it's] great not having to deal too much with the 'technical' side" (Elgort et al., 2008). Students suggest that they are generally able to pick up the skills required to operate Web 2.0 technologies without any substantial problems (Zorko, 2009). Though it should be noted that perceived ease of use depends on the tool, task, context and individual (Bennett et al., 2012).

DEVELOPING COMMUNITY

Web 2.0 technologies can support the development of learning networks (Boyd, 2007). Having students share one another's work on the Web and provide feedback is seen by teachers to foster a sense of belonging and community (Waycott et al., 2013). For instance, students indicate that collective blogging in an illustration course helped them to develop a sense of learning community through constructive feedback and positive reassurance (Garcia et al., 2015). A content analysis of computing student design diaries found that 18% of all excerpts related to emotional expression and 24% to social support, illustrating the potential of blogs to facilitate social interaction and community building (Robertson, 2011). Using Twitter as a platform for collaboration during coursework was observed to catalyze interpersonal relationships across traditional social boundaries in a way that would have been difficult during regular class discussions (Junco et al., 2011). Twitter also enabled students to provide each other with emotional and affective support (Junco et al., 2011).

ENABLING NEW AND MORE EFFICIENT FORMS OF ASSESSMENT

With Web 2.0 technologies, assessment can take on new forms, from 'tweets' of critical reflections about course readings (Junco et al., 2011), to development and publication of visual media (Crook & Harrison, 2008). An advantage of assessment via Web 2.0 tools is that the teacher can usually access student work during the assessment process (Bower et al., 2006). This enables teachers to monitor student contributions as a means of formative assessment, and provide appropriate feedback (Kabilan & Khan, 2012; Woo et al., 2011). The page history and tracking features of Web 2.0 tools such as wikis enable teachers to observe and assess the learning process in retrospect (Trentin, 2009; Woo et al., 2011), and determine the contribution made by individuals as part of group work processes (Bower et al., 2006).

Publication online means that peer assessment can easily be facilitated (Crook & Harrison, 2008). Tasks that involve some form of collaborative assessment have been shown to result in significantly greater student review of their own work and significantly higher order comments to peers (Beckers, Dolmans, & van Merriënboer, 2016). Research has also shown that peer grading of work can provide a highly reliable form of assessment when compared with the grades awarded by teachers (Xiao & Lucking, 2008).

Issues and Limitations of Web 2.0 in Education

While there are many potential benefits of using Web 2.0 technologies in education, there are also a raft of issues and limitations that warrant consideration in order to design and implement effective Web 2.0 learning experiences. A summary of the main issues and limitations reported in the literature is presented below.

TECHNICAL CONSTRAINTS

Technical issues can arise when using Web 2.0 technologies for learning and teaching. Firstly, there may be problems with lost logins and forgotten passwords (Rahimi et al., 2015b), and students may be reluctant to create an account for yet another technology platform (Bennett et al., 2012). Often when students on different computers try to edit the same page at the same time it can result in work being lost or students being denied access (Engstrom & Jewett, 2005; Li et al., 2012; Wheeler et al., 2008; Woo et al., 2011). Depending on the product, the design of the Web 2.0 interface may be suboptimal and hence lead to frustration or technical problems (Bennett et al., 2012; Cole, 2009; Li et al., 2014).

In terms of infrastructure, use of Web 2.0 tools of course requires that students and teachers have adequate Internet access, so network issues can be a major impediment to learning (Crook & Harrison, 2008; Li et al., 2014). Students may not have sufficient access to physical devices, particularly in schools (Kale & Goh, 2014). Institutional firewall and filtering policies can act as a barrier to using Web 2.0 tools, particularly in schools (Crook & Harrison, 2008). There is a possibility that publically provided Web 2.0 technologies may change or disappear during the course of a task, which proposes issues for educational service provision, assessment and archiving (Albion, 2008; Redecker et al., 2009). There is also the sustainability issue of maintaining access to content and services over time, for instance after a course has finished (Franklin & Van Harmelen, 2007).

STUDENT DIGITAL SKILLS

In order to use Web 2.0 technologies as part of learning tasks, students require a range digital skills, for instance basic and more complex multimedia skills (Redecker et al., 2009). Although Web 2.0 tools are designed to be easily used, sometimes students lack the technological competence to operate the technologies, for instance knowing how to upload photos and format text (Beckers et al., 2016; Neumann & Hood, 2009). This can mean that the quality of student posts is compromised (Beckers et al., 2016; Redecker et al., 2009), or even that students inadvertently delete other students' work (Zorko, 2009). Another problem with low levels of digital literacy is that it may be correlated with low levels of motivation to undertake technology-based activities (Redecker et al., 2009). Alternately, students may be able to use the technology well but not understand how it can best be used to support their learning (Bennett et al., 2012; Rahimi et al., 2015b).

GROUP WORK AND COLLABORATION ISSUES

There are several challenges when attempting to use Web 2.0 to facilitate collaborative tasks. Group selection can be problematic, with group dynamics observed to have a substantial influence on team effectiveness (Naismith et al., 2011). When groups of early high school students used Web 2.0 tools to create a travel guide the teacher observed several group work issues relating to team disagreements, group coordination and task delegation (Rahimi et al., 2015b). In one study, the random allocation of group members was the most frequently mentioned complaint that students raised about their wiki assignment (Chou & Chen, 2008). Students also indicate that larger groups make teamwork more difficult to coordinate (Naismith et al., 2011).

Students may feel uncomfortable editing the work of others (Dohn, 2009; Karasavvidis, 2010; Lund & Smørdal, 2006; Wheeler et al., 2008). Likewise, students can become disgruntled when their work is edited, especially if revisions detract from the accuracy or quality of writing (Lund & Smørdal, 2006). Consequently, in some studies that explore the impact of peer editing, minimal collaboration has been observed, with many groups of students preferring to adopt a cooperative approach where work is divided between team members (Elgort et al., 2008; Grant, 2009; Naismith et al., 2011).

Alternately, there may be one primary author with collaborators only making minor revisions, rather than tightly integrated contribution and editing (Garcia et al., 2015; Lund & Smørdal, 2006). To put figures around this, one study of 772 undergraduate psychology students completing a collaborative writing wiki task found that one quarter of students completing the large majority (66%) of the work, while the least contributing quarter of the cohort contributed less than 5% of the content (Judd et al., 2010). This form of social loafing has also been observed at school level (Rahimi et al., 2015b). Another potential problem is that students may not take responsibility for the success of their group, for instance when completing wiki tasks (Zorko, 2009). Competitive or disorganized students may leave posts until the last moment, meaning that other students are unable to benefit from peer reviewing their work (Garcia et al., 2015). In one case, almost half of the contributions were made on the last day of the task, constraining the extent to which true collaboration could occur (Judd et al., 2010).

NEGATIVE STUDENT DISPOSITIONS

Students may not be familiar or comfortable with more student-directed approaches to learning enabled using Web 2.0 tools (Rahimi et al., 2015b), or may have negative attitudes toward new learning approaches generally (Karvounidis, Chimos, Bersimis, & Douligeris, 2014). Many students simply express a disinterest about using Web 2.0 technologies such as wikis to supplement course activity, or doubts about the quality of the contributions they would make (Cole, 2009). Several studies have found that students may be reluctant to post their assignment materials online because they are self-conscious or because they are competitive and do not want others to copy their work (Chou & Chen, 2008; Harris & Rea, 2009; Ruth & Houghton, 2009; Waycott et al., 2013; Yang et al., 2015). Students may be resentful that their peers do not contribute or their posts are of a quality that does not encourage discussion or debate (Kabilan & Khan, 2012).

PEER FEEDBACK CHALLENGES

Peer-based feedback can involve several challenges. In one study, primary school students were reluctant to provide feedback about their peers' writing because they did not know what to say and were not confident that their ideas were correct (Chen et al., 2011). In another study, undergraduate students indicate a reluctance to provide critical written feedback to their peers in case it jeopardized their friendships (Yang, 2009). One study found that peer feedback on blogs actually resulted in significantly lower levels of reflective thinking (Xie et al., 2008). Researchers posited that less reflective comments by peers could encourage lower quality reflective posts overall (Xie et al., 2008). Another issue is that students may find it frustrating if they do not receive peer feedback about their posts (Levy et al., 2015).

ASSESSMENT ISSUES

Students indicate that assessment is a strong driver for them to complete Web 2.0 tasks (Churchill, 2009). Consequently, if tasks are not assessable it can result in very low rates of participation (Divitini, Haugaløkken, & Morken, 2005). Then there is the inherent tension surrounding whether participation or the actual content contributed is to be assessed (Dohn, 2009). Popularity functions such as voting and 'liking' can potentially become proxies for correctness and quality, particularly in the case of peer assessment (Zhang, 2009). Students may also become more focused on the aesthetics of their Web 2.0 creations rather than the quality of the content (Rahimi et al., 2015b).

Assessment of group projects can be more complicated because, depending on the product used, it can be difficult to establish who authored each part of the submission (Harris & Rea, 2009). It may be difficult to determine contribution to group work based on page histories alone, for instance if one team member is designated to be the scribe (Zorko, 2009). Implementing peer assessment can also be problematic – in one study 40% of university students indicated that they were not comfortable grading the work of their peers (Tsai et al., 2011).

PLAGIARISM

Plagiarism is another major issue to consider when using Web 2.0 tools. The general accessibility of digital content can lead to students using a copy-paste approach to completing assignments rather than critically engaging with concepts or creatively authoring content for themselves (Crook, 2008; Heinrich et al., 2007). Alternately, there are observed instances where student copied work from their peers (Su & Beaumont, 2010). In its worst form, copying and pasting can constitute serious cases of plagiarism (Crook, 2008). It may even be that because of the nature of the Web, students actually believe that it appropriate to patch together information from other sources without appropriately referencing them (Dohn, 2009). Students identify plagiarism of information from the Internet by their peers as a serious issue (Kabilan & Khan, 2012).

STUDENT MISUSE

There are a number of ways that students may deliberately subvert the Web 2.0 learning process. Because they have access to the Internet, students may choose to play games or participate in non-educational activities using social media (Rahimi et al., 2015b). Because access to workspaces is often open (for instance on a wiki), students may vandalize or sabotage the work of other students (Boulos, Maramba, & Wheeler, 2006; Harris & Rea, 2009; Li et al., 2012), though it is noted that many Web 2.0 tools include rollback and restoration functions (Boulos et al., 2006). Less maliciously, students may become distracted when using open Web 2.0 tools such as Twitter that contain extraneous information from outside sources (Shah et al., 2015).

SAFETY AND PRIVACY

When teaching using Web 2.0 tools, there are several issues relating to safety, privacy, trust and identity that need to be considered (Redecker et al., 2009). In terms of safety, there are risks associated with the uncritical use of publically available Web 2.0 tools, such as cyber bullying and falling victim to predatory behavior, particularly for younger learners (Redecker et al., 2009). The very act of providing students with open access to the Internet exposes them to the risk of pornography, sites that encourage experimentation with drugs or explosives, and so on (Crook, 2008). As a matter of privacy, students may be reluctant to divulge and use their personal social networking accounts (such as Twitter) for learning purposes (Shah et al., 2015). University teachers have expressed concern about having student identities and work openly available on the Internet and see it as an important risk that needs to be managed (Manca & Ranieri, 2016; Waycott et al., 2013).

TEACHER DIGITAL SKILLS

Based on an analysis of eight Web 2.0 case studies, it was apparent that teachers also needed to develop appropriate digital skills so that they could design and manage learning experiences (Redecker et al., 2009). There are several digital challenges that educators need to address when teaching in Web 2.0 environments, for instance how to manage knowledge that is dispersed, and how to organize it in a way that supports learning (Zhang, 2009). It should also be noted that there are also a host of intellectual property rights issues relating to ownership, reuse and control that educators need to consider when designing technology-enhanced learning environments, particularly if they are using content that has been sourced online (Franklin & Van Harmelen, 2007). Teachers and institutions may be constrained by privacy and intellectual property policies, which make open and public use of Web 2.0 unfeasible (Bennett et al., 2012).

NEGATIVE STAFF PERCEPTIONS

While approximately 44% of open-ended question respondents in a large study of Spanish university teachers felt that using Web 2.0 tools was useful for teaching, 36% did not, with the remaining 20% being uncertain (Manca & Ranieri, 2016). Many teachers saw Web 2.0 technologies as being inferior to face-to-face teaching strategies and see the traditional Learning Management System as a more reliable and secure way to deliver a course (Manca & Ranieri, 2016).

INAPPROPRIATE TASK DESIGN

In some instances educators may design tasks that are inauthentic applications of Web 2.0 technologies (Albion, 2008; Bennett et al., 2012). For example, using e-portfolios as merely an alternative form of submission to an assignment dropbox was seen by students as not contributing anything to the learning process and actually detracting from it by increasing their logistical effort (Yang et al., 2015). In some cases students indicate that the scope and nature of tasks is overwhelming and overly time consuming

(Beckers et al., 2016; Karasavvidis, 2010). For example, under-graduates in one study indicated that posting regular and high-quality contributions to an e-portfolio imposed a substantial time burden (Kabilan & Khan, 2012). Alternately, the way in which a task is framed may leave students unclear about the purpose of the activity and the reason for using Web 2.0 technology (Wheeler et al., 2008).

INSTITUTIONAL AND EDUCATIONAL CULTURE

Many scholars discuss the cultural issues that need to be overcome when working toward effective Web 2.0 collaboration and learn-ing (Crook, 2008; Dohn, 2009; Grant, 2009; McLoughlin & Lee, 2008; Rick & Guzdial, 2006). In a Web 2.0 context learning is most often collaborative, distributed, and non-linear, which consti-tutes a fundamental paradigm shift for students and teachers from the more traditional individual, authoritative and sequential approaches to learning (Crook, 2008). For instance, schooling has historically cultivated an individualistic approach to writing and assessment that is not easily discarded or shifted, and thus tensions between individual and collective, as well as institutional and novel practices arise (Lund, 2008).

One higher education study across multiple disciplines found that 'cultural compatibility' of a wiki's application with the class-room and the discipline could critically impact on the success of the tool's application (Rick & Guzdial, 2006). Application of wikis in Science, Technology, Engineering and Mathematics (STEM) was disappointing because of staff and student resistance to the collaborative approach (Rick & Guzdial, 2006). Three cul-tural barriers to collaboration in STEM were observed: (1) com-petition and single answer assignments, (2) reluctance to seek help, and (3) staff attitudes and models of collaboration (Rick & Guzdial, 2006).

TEACHER SUPPORT

Adopting a Web 2.0 paradigm requires educators to shift their pedagogical thinking from information delivery and individual knowledge acquisition to facilitating collaborative knowledge integration (Huang & Behara, 2007; Redecker et al., 2009). Many teachers require guidance to shift from a more teacher-centered and instructive pedagogy to more student-centered and facilitative pedagogy (Redecker et al., 2009). School teachers have expressed concern about the lack of time for familiarization and planning of Web 2.0-based tasks (Crook & Harrison, 2008). University teachers report that lack of support both in terms of infrastructure and assistance are obstacles that prevent them from using Web 2.0 tools in practice (Manca & Ranieri, 2016).

So while there are numerous potential benefits of using Web 2.0 technologies in education, there are a wide variety of issues that warrant consideration.

Web 2.0 Design Vignettes

From a design point of view, it is useful to not only know about different Web 2.0 technologies, uses, benefits and issues, but also to have some exemplars that engender a better understanding of what educational uses of Web 2.0 look like in practice. The following two brief use case descriptions ('vignettes') showcase the use of Web 2.0 technologies for learning and teaching purposes. The selected cases – one at school level and the other in higher education – illustrate how multiple Web 2.0 tools can be used to establish a technology-mediated learning ecology.

VIGNETTE 1 – USING WEB 2.0 TOOLS TO CREATE PERSONAL LEARNING ENVIRONMENTS FOR SCHOOL STUDENTS

In this case study conducted by (Rahimi, 2015) first-year high school students aged between 11- and 13-years old designed and built virtual travel guides over eight weeks as part of their geography studies. Although many of the 29 students were familiar with Web 2.0 tools, they had no prior experience using Web 2.0 technologies for student-centered learning in a formal school setting. The three design principles underpinning the module where providing students with appropriate resources, offering students activity spaces, and supporting learner co-construction of content. Students were required to work in teams of four or five to create the virtual travel guide, with the teacher taking on a facilitative rather than instructive role. As part of the facilitation process, the teacher suggested (but did not mandate) learning activities using Web 2.0 tools in order to activate their roles as knowledge developers, socializers and decision makers (see Table 7.2). Some of the Web 2.0 tools were introduced to the students to assist them in performing the suggested activities.

Table 7.2.   Suggested Activities and Tools to Facilitate the Personal Learning Experience of Students (Rahimi, 2015, p. 56).

Student's Role(s)	Learning Activities Derived from the Design Principles	Provided Technological Choices
Knowledge developer	Observing several web-based travel guides, conducting research about Egypt, aggregating/filtering content and web feeds, building the travel guide	Search engines, Wikipedia, Google reader YouTube, web hosting & building tools
Socialiser	Conducting group mind mapping to design the structure of travel guide, participating in digital storytelling	Email, Twitter, Hyves, Google Chat, MindMeister, Google Docs
Decision maker	Planning and timing the different steps of their project, creating personal set of web tools and resources, Expressing their progress	Google calendar, iGoogle, Blog

In order to create their travel guides, students completed a range of decision-making processes (dealing with technical problems, selecting web tools, setting up their home pages, attending to the aesthetics of their digital creations, and deciding about what to post online). To support them with their planning and decision-making, students were provided with a personal learning interface that they could customize and use to suit their needs. Figure 7.4 provides an illustration of the type of interface students used (note figures used in this section have been translated from Dutch).

Students also completed a range of social processes, including communicating with the teacher via email and blogs, posting on Twitter, as well as giving and receiving support. There were several group processes that required social interaction, for instance completing group mind mapping tasks in order to plan their digital travel guide. An illustration of this is shown in Figure 7.5.

Producing the digital travel guide also necessitated that students complete a range of knowledge development processes, such as searching the web for text, images and videos, blogging, analyzing the content of their own product as well as others. An example of a student travel guide is shown in Figure 7.6.

Students indicated that the approach had caused them to take more responsibility for their learning process, as well as broadened their technological and content choices. One student

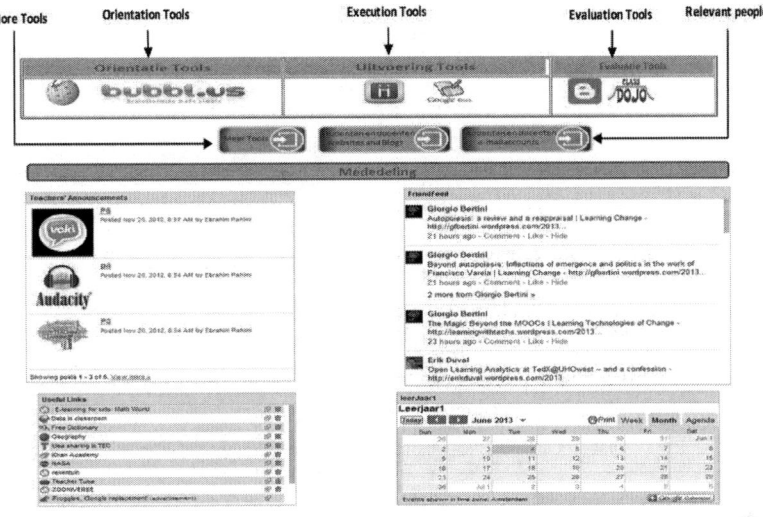

Figure 7.4. Example of the Web 2.0 Personal Learning Interface Used in the Rahimi (2015) Study, Showing Links to Tools, Teachers Announcements, Discussion Feed, and Calendar.

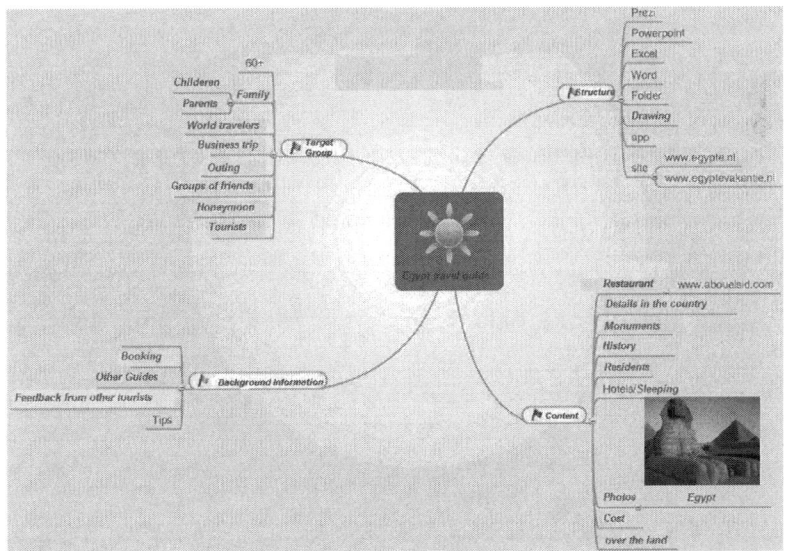

Figure 7.5. A Group's Web 2.0 Mind Map Used to Help Plan the Digital Travel Guide in the Rahimi (2015) Study.

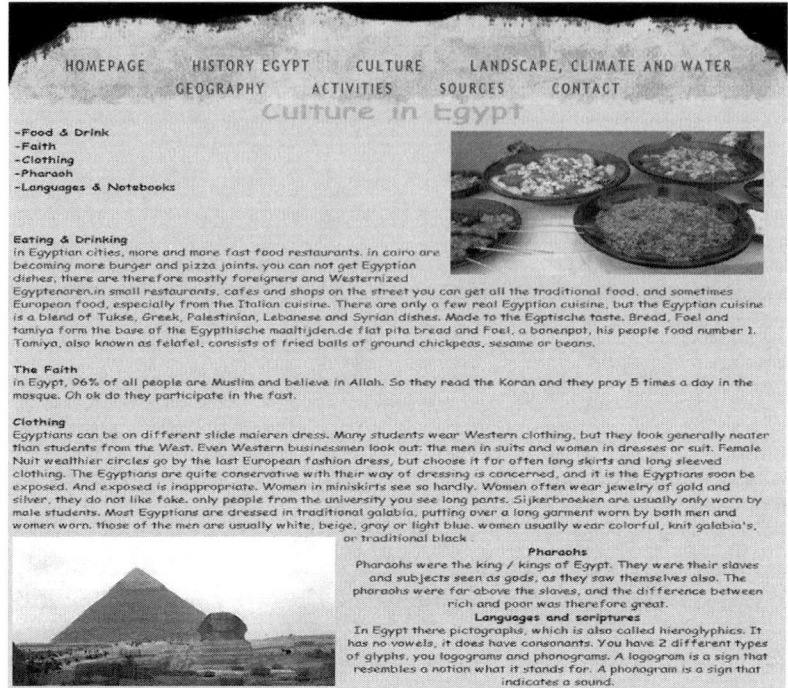

Figure 7.6.   An Example of a Student Digital Travel Guide Developed through the Web 2.0 Project from the Rahimi (2015) Study.

commented "When you are provided with more control you feel yourself more independent and responsible and as a person who owns her work" (Rahimi, 2015, p. 59). Students also indicated that they acquired valuable new digital learning skills as part of the project, as illustrated by the following quotes:

> Now, by using Google Docs we can work on a same document through our laptops in a more efficient and comfortable way. Also we can continue working on the document at home.

> You can do mind mapping in a piece of paper or on a white board but I think it is more useful when you do it in MindMeister. Because then you have it in a digital format and you can share it or put it in your blog to receive the teacher's or other students' feedback and comments on it. (Rahimi, 2015, p. 59)

Several challenges were experienced throughout the project, including technical issues (forgotten passwords, incompatibility between some web tools and the operating systems), social issues (job sharing, group coordination, team disagreements about content, and loafing) and distraction (students playing games or completing non-school related tasks). Some students indicated that time management was a problem, as was adopting a student-directed rather than teacher-driven approach. Furthermore, some students struggled to understand how the technology could best be used to support their work:

> We can quickly learn how to use and work with tools such as Google Docs or MindMeister, or iGoogle. But the purpose of using them is not clear for us. What we need is to link the functionalities of these tools to our learning needs. (Rahimi, 2015, p. 65)

By creating personal learning environments using Web 2.0 tools, the students developed a range of thinking skills, through processes such as searching, reading, brainstorming, storytelling, mind mapping, as well as analyzing, evaluating and creating digital artifacts. They were better able to collaborate and network with one another, their teacher, and people outside the class. Students also appreciated that the approach helped them to develop their awareness of digitally responsible practices, as well as their technical and web skills (Rahimi, 2015, p. 59).

VIGNETTE 2 – SUPPORTING SMALL GROUP LEARNING USING MULTIPLE WEB 2.0 TOOLS IN HIGHER EDUCATION

Laru, Näykki, and Järvelä (2012) present a case study where groups of four to five undergraduate teacher education students worked for twelve weeks on a project requiring them collaboratively construct a wiki site. The teacher issued students with all of the pre-configured Web 2.0 accounts they would need for the impending activities. Students were provided with freedom to decide what they would create and present to the class, based on the topics being covered throughout the course. The coursework consisted of several phases:

A. Ground – via lectures
B. Reflect – through discussion
C. Conceptualize – using photo taking
D. Reflect and elaborate – via blog posts

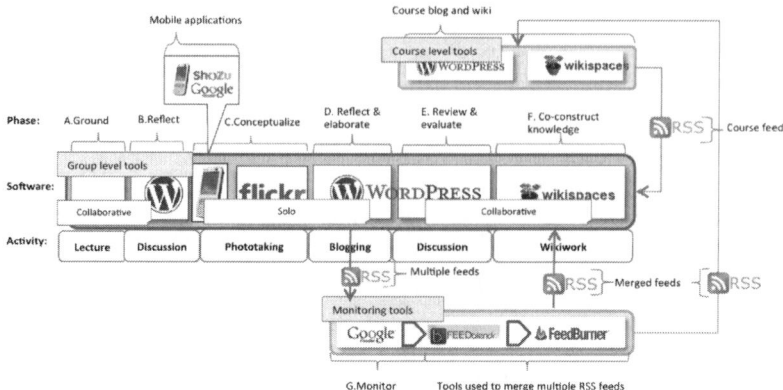

Figure 7.7.   Web 2.0 Tools Used to Support Phases of Teacher Education Group Work (Laru et al., 2012, p. 32).

E. Review and evaluate – through group analysis of blog posts
F. Co-construction of knowledge – using the wiki
G. Monitor – observing class contributions using RSS.

The tools that were used to support the various phases are shown in Figure 7.7. Specifically, Wordpress was used for individual blogs, Flickr was used to share photos, Wikispaces provided the wiki platform, Google Reader, Feedblender and Feedburner were used to create the RSS feeds (Laru et al., 2012).

Detailed examination of the relationship between Web 2.0 activities and learning revealed that editing and contributing content to wiki posts distinguished high achievers from low performers (Laru et al., 2012). As well, the students who were inserting and modifying information in the wikis were also more actively reflecting and elaborating on their blogs, as well as more actively monitoring the work of their peers. The authors conclude that more active use of Web 2.0 tools to perform multiple tasks increased student knowledge acquisition during the course (Laru et al., 2012).

Web 2.0 Learning Design Recommendations

As well as the benefits and limitations of Web 2.0 technologies, and familiarity with exemplars, the findings and insights from the research provide a crucial (perhaps the most crucial) source of design knowledge. The following findings for Web 2.0 learning design emerged from the empirical evidence and research observations contained within the Web 2.0 education literature. They have been presented as recommendations in order to facilitate expedient application.

DECIDE ON THE LEVEL OF OPENNESS THAT IS APPROPRIATE

Institutions and educators have a clear responsibility to promote safe engagement with Web 2.0 tools and the Internet in general (Crook, 2008). Consequently, one important consideration is whether to use a publicly available and open Web 2.0 platform or a closed environment that is only accessible by students (Boulos et al., 2006). Institutions, especially schools, should have policies around this (Crook & Harrison, 2008). From a design perspective, there may be an inherent trade-off between authentic use of the Internet and maintaining sufficient security and control (Crook, 2008). Also consider that publishing to a wider audience has been shown to enhance motivation and engagement (Li et al., 2012; Wheeler et al., 2008; Zorko, 2009).

UNDERSTAND AND LEVERAGE INSTITUTIONAL SUPPORT

From the outset educators need to have an understanding of the broader technological context in which they operate, as this will impact on what Web 2.0 tasks they can design. In order for Web 2.0 initiatives to be successful it is often important to have institutional support (Beckers et al., 2016), as organizational and financial assistance can have a critical impact on the success of a Web 2.0 implementation (Redecker et al., 2009). Valuable forms of support include funds, equipment, infrastructure, policy and personnel (Redecker et al., 2009). As just one example, teachers need to ensure that learners have the required access to the technologies (Harris & Rea, 2009; Redecker et al., 2009). Thus institutional support in the forms above is often a fundamental starting point.

SELECT APPROPRIATE TOOLS BASED ON REPRESENTATIONAL AND INTERACTIONAL REQUIREMENTS

In order to capitalize on Web 2.0 technologies, educators need to first appreciate the sorts of Web 2.0 tools that are available and their various potentials (Dohn, 2009; Redecker et al., 2009). Selecting appropriate Web 2.0 technologies for given tasks has been shown to influence the quality of the learning experience and outcomes achieved (Bennett et al., 2012; Naismith et al., 2011). Based on the intended learning outcomes, Web 2.0 technologies need to enable effective representation of content and the desired interactions between participants (Bower et al., 2010). The review of research evidence by Hew and Cheung (2013) validates the belief that technology should be selected according to the pedagogies and instructional strategies being used. For instance dialogic, constructionist or co-constructive pedagogy supported by instructional strategies such as questioning, peer review and self-reflection appear to increase student learning in blog and wiki tasks. Alternately, transmissive use of podcasting with review activities is appropriate for supporting recall of knowledge (Hew & Cheung, 2013).

Selecting appropriate tools is a significant undertaking, particularly with such a variety of tools that educators can choose between. Engagement with professional communities of practice such as Classroom 2.0 (http://www.classroom20.com) can provide assistance. A range of pragmatic issues also warrants consideration. For instance, Schwartz, Clark, Cossarin, and Rudolph (2004) recommend selecting wikis based on their cost, complexity, control, clarity, interoperability, and features, which are criteria that can be applied to other Web 2.0 technologies. The Web 2.0 landscape is in continual state of flux, so the stability of the technology is a critical factor to consider in order to promote reliable and sustainable implementation over time (Bower, 2016; Redecker et al., 2009).

DECIDE HOW WEB 2.0 TECHNOLOGIES WILL INTERFACE WITH OTHER TOOLS AND COURSE COMPONENTS

An important consideration is how Web 2.0 tools will integrate with other technologies. For instance, as noted above, in some instances wikis are used to provide the primary course management tool, whereas in other cases they are used to extend or supplement the functionality of the learning management system (Jones et al., 2012). Educators using learning management systems need to consider whether they will use some of the inherent Web 2.0 technologies (for instance many learning management systems include wiki and blog tools) or opt for external tools based on their additional features. Yet another consideration is the interface between Web 2.0 technologies and other elements of the course. Students often indicate that they want Web 2.0 tools to be used in conjunction with more traditional face-to-face approaches, not as a replacement of them (Karvounidis et al., 2014), so when to use face-to-face as opposed to online approaches is another important decision.

It may also be worthwhile to combine a variety of Web 2.0 tools, depending on task requirements. The interoperability and ease of use of Web 2.0 tools means students can be encouraged to integrate information from a variety of sources and of a variety of modalities (Kim, 2008). This sort of approach is often appreciated by students — high school mathematics students felt that the combination of wiki projects, personal blog reflections, lecture podcasts, sharing video resources and web-conferencing helped them to learn more and faster than traditional approaches (Köse, 2010).

DESIGN AUTHENTIC, INTEGRATED, AND STUDENT-DIRECTED TASKS TO PROMOTE PARTICIPATION

It is obviously important to design Web 2.0 tasks to promote participation. Authentic tasks should be utilized to encourage motivation and deep engagement in learning (Yang et al., 2015). For instance, allowing students to choose wiki topics that relate to their context has been observed to enhance participation (Zheng, Niiya, & Warschauer, 2015). Also in terms of participation, a review of using e-portfolios to enhance self-directed learning found that integrating e-portfolios into the educational routine of courses meant that they were better used and received (Beckers et al., 2016). On the other hand, a task offering students the option of posting material onto a wiki that could form the basis of a final examination question led to very little participation due to lack of incentive for individual contribution (Cole, 2009). Thus authentic integration of Web 2.0 tasks into the course is advisable.

CONSIDER THE PRIOR KNOWLEDGE OF STUDENTS TO DETERMINE THE RIGHT LEVEL OF CHALLENGE

It is also important to consider the prior knowledge of learners and the amount of challenge inherent in the task in order to promote contribution. Simply prescribing a Web 2.0 task does not encourage deep critical engagement, rather, the task itself needs to require and encourage higher order thinking (Elgort et al., 2008). Pre-service teachers who saw a blogging task as challenging and holding intrinsic value were significantly more likely to engage with the task (Cakir, 2013). However, the degree of challenge should be commensurate with students' prior knowledge. One study found that when wiki content had a medium level of overlap with students' prior knowledge the students were significantly more likely to add and adjust content than if there was low or high levels of overlap (Moskaliuk, Kimmerle, & Cress, 2012). As well, when there was a higher degree of difference between a student's knowledge and the knowledge on the wiki, a student was more likely to contribute (Moskaliuk et al., 2012). Thus, it appears prudent to design tasks that are pitched at a level where students have some (not too little or too much) prior knowledge, and that draw upon the unique perspectives or understanding that students possess.

The scope of the task is another important issue. For instance, student are more likely to be dissatisfied with a learning experience if tasks are disproportionally time consuming compared to their weighting in the course assessment (Snodgrass, 2011).

DESIGN FOR EFFECTIVE COLLABORATION

Tasks that genuinely require collaboration can result in greater interaction and negotiation of meaning (Lund & Smørdal, 2006). For instance, wiki tasks requiring students to co-create a single product (such as a program or explanation) resulted in more integrated responses than tasks that simply asked for points relating to a topic (Bower et al., 2006). In another case, establishing a collaborative context through the use of profile pages, homework pages, exam review pages, soapboxes and design galleries where students could showcase their work resulted in hundreds of student driven pages throughout a course and positive feedback from learners (Rick & Guzdial, 2006). The size of the group can influence participation – a wiki task that required people to track everyone's activity became too cumbersome for a class of twenty students to manage (Raman et al., 2005). A single blog for a whole class promoted more egalitarian contribution, whereas individual blogs and allocated feedback groups encouraged stronger and deeper interaction among clusters of students (Sharma & Tietjen, 2016).

CONSIDER HOW WEB 2.0 TECHNOLOGIES CAN BE USED TO BUILD COMMUNITY

Students and teachers report that Web 2.0 technologies can facilitate community building (Garcia et al., 2015; Waycott et al., 2013). For instance, blogs can be used to offer social and emotional support (Robertson, 2011). Twitter can be employed to enable students to discuss personal issues, as well as catalyze friendships (Junco et al., 2011). Thus, consider how Web 2.0 technologies can be effectively used by students to build relationships, particularly through prolonged use over the duration of a course.

ENCOURAGE REFLECTIVE THINKING

As previously noted, reflective thinking has been shown to improve learning outcomes (Meyer et al., 2010; Xie et al., 2008). Students and teachers identify how being able to review the posts and work of others helps them to learn vicariously (Churchill, 2009; Waycott et al., 2013). Thus, designing tasks that encourage students to view one another's posts and review their own posts over time may result in better learning outcomes. Group reflection can also support deeper learning, though the quantity of online contributions may not be as important as the level of critical thinking embedded within group reflection posts (Kim, Hong, Bonk, & Lim, 2011). As such, teachers can prescribe reflection tasks such as having students present their group work pages or separately documenting their individual reflections in an accessible space. Teacher prompting to think more critically about post contents has resulted in substantial increase in the degree of reflective thinking students demonstrated in their blogging tasks (Yang, 2009). Involvement of the teacher during group work reflection has been shown to improve the quality of thinking that occurs (Kim et al., 2011).

DECIDE UPON WHAT SCAFFOLDING TO PROVIDE

Different forms of scaffolding can be provided to students in Web 2.0 environments. Reflective prompts have been found to be particularly useful to students (Zheng et al., 2015), especially when the prompts closely related to the practical components of the unit (Roberts, Maor, & Herrington, 2016). Students in another study indicated that patterns or templates explaining how they should contribute would have been helpful to them

(Bower et al., 2006). Provision of past students' work as exemplars has also been found to support student understanding of task requirements (Zheng et al., 2015). Though it is worth considering the extent of structural guidance that takes place — another study found that brief templates as opposed to detailed models for wiki-based authoring tasks resulted in more diverse and creative production, as well as higher student satisfaction (Jung & Suzuki, 2015). Research relating to the use of e-portfolios has shown that teacher guidance and scaffolding makes an important contribution to the learning process generally (Beckers et al., 2016).

ESTABLISH A CLEAR MOTIVATION FOR USING WEB 2.0 TECHNOLOGIES

Not only is it important for the teacher to have a clear pedagogical goal behind using Web 2.0 technologies (Crook, 2008), it is also important that the goals behind using the technology are clear to students in order to promote motivation and relevance (Raman et al., 2005; Roberts et al., 2016). For instance, some researchers note that while students were familiar with Web 2.0 tools such as blogs, more guidance on the pedagogical aims of blogging as a self-reflexive practice may have made the exercise more user friendly, relevant and critically transformative (Farmer et al., 2008). It is useful to establish that creating a community of practice through the use of Web 2.0 technologies enables students to learn from one another and avoid individual and privatized learning (Albion, 2008). Taking such steps addresses previously noted issues relating to cultural incompatibility (Crook, 2008; Dohn, 2009; Grant, 2009; McLoughlin & Lee, 2008; Rick & Guzdial, 2006), negative student dispositions (Chou & Chen, 2008; Harris & Rea, 2009; Ruth & Houghton, 2009; Waycott et al., 2013; Yang et al., 2015), and student misuse (Boulos et al., 2006; Harris & Rea, 2009; Li et al., 2012; Rahimi et al., 2015b).

DELIBERATELY DEVELOP STUDENT DIGITAL LEARNING CAPABILITIES

Educators should not assume that students are familiar with how to use Web 2.0 technologies, because often they are not, and without adequate support this lack of skills can impede the learning process (Bennett et al., 2012; Kennedy et al., 2009). Thus, strong an explicit scaffolding may be required to develop their skills (McLoughlin & Lee, 2010). It may take an initial investment of time to learn how to use the tools effectively (Bennett et al., 2012), or in some cases may be a longer term process (Rahimi et al., 2015b), but development of required technological skills is critical so that students can make the most of the learning experience (Zorko, 2009). Initial low risk activities can be used to help develop technical skills (Zheng et al., 2015). As well, it is important that teachers help students to develop the appropriate communication, multitasking, metacognitive and higher order thinking capabilities as this will impact on their capacity to complete activities (Redecker et al., 2009; Zheng et al., 2015). Supporting the development of critical Internet literacy is also a major concern (Crook, 2008).

POSITIVELY ENGAGE IN THE LEARNING PROCESS

The teacher plays several critical roles in the use of Web 2.0 technologies for learning, including a pedagogical role in designing and supporting learning activities, a social role in establishing a positive learning community, a managerial role in terms of scheduling and administering tasks, and a technical role in so far as resolving issues and providing student technological assistance (Minocha, Schroeder, & Schneider, 2011). Through their very participation teachers can have a positive impact on the learning experience. In one study the involvement of the teacher and their active participation in blogging tasks was a key motivator for students (Churchill, 2009). Modeling a positive attitude is also important. The teacher's attitude toward the use of Web 2.0 technologies has been found to significantly correlate with the extent to which students perceive the technology as useful (Guo & Stevens, 2011).

ENCOURAGE CONTRIBUTION

There are several runtime strategies that teachers can apply in order to encourage student contribution to Web 2.0 tasks. Simply requesting or requiring students to make posts is an obvious way to promote active participation in a task (Kim, 2008). Setting ongoing deadlines for contributions is recommended in order to avert students posting all of their content at the last minute (Cole, 2009; Ladyshewsky & Gardner, 2008). Providing early feedback to students about their contributions may result in greater clarity surrounding the requirements of the task and therefore greater participation (Farmer et al., 2008). In one case, having primary school students publish to blogs anonymously meant that they felt less inhibited about writing their posts (Chen et al., 2011). Teacher prompts about how to improve a wiki-based collaborative writing piece led to significant increases in student work on the teacher-identified aspects of the text (Kump et al., 2013). Integrating posts into class discussions may mean that students see the posts as more relevant and are therefore more likely to contribute (Cole, 2009).

Some researchers believe that assessing contributions is key to encouraging participation in Web 2.0 tasks (Beckers et al., 2016; Snodgrass, 2011). In one study, only two groups out of twenty-two completed a wiki statistics task that was not assessed (Neumann & Hood, 2009). Student comfort with contributing to Web 2.0 tasks appears to improve over time (Su & Beaumont, 2010).

APPLY STRATEGIES TO SUPPORT GROUP WORK PROCESSES

As previously noted, students may be reluctant to engage in group work processes because they are uncomfortable editing the work of others or having their work edited (Dohn, 2009; Karasavvidis, 2010; Lund & Smørdal, 2006; Wheeler et al., 2008). However, it is important that work is spread among the group and that individual learners are held accountable for their contribution to the task. Collaborative authoring jointly completed by team members has been observed to result in less surface level changes, with students reporting significantly greater learning and satisfaction (Lai, Lei, & Liu, 2016). Groups that also concurrently reviewed their compositions together reported learning more about writing techniques and text organization (Lai et al., 2016).

Teachers have a critical role to play in terms of helping students learn how to collaborate using Web 2.0 technologies and encouraging a truly collaborative approach (Crook & Harrison, 2008; Grant, 2009). There are several ways that teachers can help to structure interactions in order to support group work processes. Having students assume roles within a team (such as discussion facilitator, wiki recorder, and so on) has been observed to promote effective collaboration (Engstrom & Jewett, 2005; Zheng et al., 2015). Providing students with scripts about how to collaboratively author their wiki essays (using phases of planning, drafting and reviewing) has been shown to lead to significantly greater contribution, editing of peer work, integration of multiple perspectives, as well as significantly less grammatical errors (Wichmann & Rummel, 2013). Collaborative cues, for instance about how to ask for other points of view, express agreement or disagreement, provide reasons and summarize findings have been used in primary school to support more effective collaboration (Pifarré & Staarman, 2011). Heterogeneous cultural grouping for collaborative authoring tasks has been found to lead to more widespread and egalitarian participation as well as greater diversity of topics and views (Jung & Suzuki, 2015; Zheng et al., 2015).

Configuration of the technology can also be used to support group work processes. Using Really Simple Syndication (RSS) feeds can be a useful way to keep track of the ongoing contributions to blogs and other Web 2.0 technologies all in one place (Churchill, 2009; Kim, 2008), and students indicate that using RSS is helpful to them (Huang et al., 2011). Some researchers argue that dialogic spaces are useful to support wiki collaboration in order for students to understand one another's perspectives, noting that the wiki itself may provide this through discussion pages (Pifarré & Staarman, 2011; Zheng et al., 2015).

PROVIDE STUDENTS WITH FORMATIVE FEEDBACK

Teacher formative feedback about student posts and what is expected, for instance on e-portfolios, can lead to improved quality of student posts over time (Beckers et al., 2016). Students verify that formative feedback from teachers makes a valuable contribution to their learning experience (Bower et al., 2006; Yang et al., 2015; Zorko, 2009). It is also worth considering the type of feedback that is provided. In one study, students indicated that they valued teacher feedback about their self-regulation (strategies and approaches to learning) more than any other type of feedback, including about the task or process (Chen, 2014).

ENCOURAGE HIGH-QUALITY PEER FEEDBACK

Providing peer feedback to students has been shown to improve learning outcomes and student satisfaction. Having students provide one another with formative feedback on a wiki writing task significantly improved their work over time compared to control groups (Gielen & De Wever, 2015). An e-portfolio task that integrated peer feedback led to significantly higher grades than a traditional e-portfolio task (Barbera, 2009), while in another study, blog-based peer feedback led to significantly better writing performance than traditional pen and paper peer feedback (Novakovich, 2016). Receiving feedback from peers has also been found to enhance student attitudes toward the benefit of collaborative writing (Lai et al., 2016), and the sophistication of students' design tasks (Liu et al., 2016).

The nature and quality of feedback that students provide can have a significant impact. A study of 232 primarily undergraduate students who received peer-based formative feedback on their wiki essays found that providing qualitative feedback along with ratings resulted in significantly better final performance than having students purely provide one another with formative ratings (Xiao & Lucking, 2008). Providing the additional qualitative feedback also resulted in significantly higher levels of student satisfaction with the assessment process (Xiao & Lucking, 2008). In another study, the opportunity to request peer feedback on specific parts of their individual academic writing significantly increased student satisfaction with wiki-based peer feedback (Gielen & De Wever, 2015).

If peer feedback is to be used, then there are considerations that should be kept in mind. It is important to consider whether students have the requisite skills to provide constructive rather than offensive feedback (Levy et al., 2015). It may be useful for the teacher to model appropriate feedback – in one study students were more willing to make critical comments on peer work only after the teacher had modeled this (Chou & Chen, 2008). Promisingly, another study found that the quality of student feedback significantly improves with practice over time (Gielen & De Wever, 2015). As well, it may be sensible to make peer feedback an integral part of the assessment task in order to avoid students being frustrated by lack of responses (Levy et al., 2015). Educators can also consider incorporating feedback from students outside the course – in one study having Japanese speakers from outside the course provide feedback to Japanese language learners meant that students could improve their language skills at the same time as they formed a better understand cultural perspectives (Jung & Suzuki, 2015).

LEVERAGE THE OPPORTUNITY TO UNDERTAKE NEW FORMS OF ASSESSMENT

As previously noted, Web 2.0 technologies provide teachers with new ways to assess learning (Redecker et al., 2009). Educators need to consider how they will conduct assessment in Web 2.0 environments, with pertinent issues being the extent to assess content versus participation, the validity of synthesizing existing content as opposed to creating new content, and the role of peer evaluation (Dohn, 2009). Based on a review of Web 2.0 educational assessment best practice, researchers recommend having a close match between the knowledge and skills being examined and the affordances of the Web 2.0 technologies being deployed in the tasks (Gray, Thompson, Sheard, Clerehan, & Hamilton, 2010). The teacher can also use the accessibility and functionality of Web 2.0 tools to monitor student progress on tasks (Bower et al., 2006; Zheng et al., 2015), provide formative feedback (Kabilan & Khan, 2012; Woo et al., 2011), track the collaborative process via page histories (Trentin, 2009; Woo et al., 2011), and determine the contribution made by individuals (Bower et al., 2006; Zheng et al., 2015).

The ability to facilitate technology-enabled peer assessment is another advantage of using Web 2.0 technologies (Crook & Harrison, 2008), which has been shown to increase motivation and higher order thinking (Beckers et al., 2016). Strategies to promote effective peer assessment using Web 2.0 tools include providing students with sufficient training on how to peer assess, using peer assessment groups of approximately three to seven students, incentivizing diligent execution of peer grading (for instance through attaching a grade to it), and taking measures to have peer assessment and feedback performed anonymously (Xiao & Lucking, 2008). On a pragmatic level, it may be advisable to place constraints on the number of words included in posts in order to avoid quantities of content that are unmanageable in terms of student (and teacher) review (Philip & Nicholls, 2009).

ADOPT A PROACTIVE APPROACH TO MANAGING PLAGIARISM AND STUDENT SAFETY

With the range of risks regarding student safety, privacy, trust and identity, teachers need to adopt a proactive approach (Redecker et al., 2009). This means vigilant monitoring of student activity and erring on the side of caution. Through their interactions and directions the teacher can also play an important role in managing online interaction of a class in terms of the 'netiquette' that students exercise (Waycott et al., 2013). With such ease of use and reuse of content on the Internet, educators also need to consider and account for the possibility of student plagiarism (Harris & Rea, 2009). Thus, students may need guidance about what is (and is not) appropriate in terms of intellectual property (Franklin & Van Harmelen, 2007; Harris & Rea, 2009). Students in one study had to be taught over time about writing their own work rather than copying and pasting directly from other sources (Wheeler et al., 2008). It is advisable to provide students with up-front and specific details about correct protocols regarding safe online behavior and plagiarism in order to avoid undesirable circumstances.

UTILIZE PROFESSIONAL LEARNING OPPORTUNITIES

In student-centered Web 2.0 environments, teachers typically need to shift their role from one of information deliverer to facilitator of a learning community (Garcia et al., 2015; Ladyshewsky & Gardner, 2008; Redecker et al., 2009). Access to appropriate professional learning opportunities supports teachers to make this shift toward effective Web 2.0 integration (Crook & Harrison, 2008; Meyer, 2010; Redecker et al., 2009), and lack of support can inhibit use (Manca & Ranieri, 2016). One review of e-portfolio use to promote self-directed learning found that lack of teacher training had a critical (negative) impact on the student learning experience (Beckers et al., 2016).

Providing educators with time for innovation is also proposed to be crucial in order to successfully propagate Web 2.0 adoption (Crook & Harrison, 2008). Becoming a member of a professional community of practice is seen as valuable in order for teachers to source support and resources that help them effectively apply Web 2.0 in their classes (Crook & Harrison, 2008; Redecker et al., 2009).

Concluding Comments on Web 2.0 Learning Design

An exhaustive (and perhaps exhausting!) collection of Web 2.0 design knowledge has been presented in this chapter, based on the current state of literature. There is no doubt in the future that Web 2.0 landscape will change, in terms of the variety of different tools available, the features they encompass, their ease of use and underlying intelligence. Some educators have even adopted the phrase 'Web 3.0' to denote the evolution of web technologies to be more semantically oriented (Lassila & Hendler, 2007), though this terminology has not gained as much traction or prevalence as the term 'Web 2.0.' Nevertheless, we should expect the continual evolution of Web 2.0 tools to expand out the variety of modalities and pedagogies that can be employed due to the diversity of technologies available (Grosseck, 2009). This is quite exciting for educators! But it will no doubt change the pedagogical possibilities and issues relating to Web 2.0 usage, and hence increase the need for further research.

One of the most valuable contributions of Web 2.0 technologies is that they challenge our pedagogical and epistemological assumptions. To what extent is knowledge fixed and objective as opposed to negotiated and subjective? How do people come know? The pedagogy and cultural practice of Web 2.0-based learning entails a shift in attitude to one that values the multi-perspective nature of knowledge, collaborative contribution, creativity and multiple literacies, rather than merely involving a decision to use Web 2.0 tools (Crook, 2008). According to the vision put forward by Grosseck (2009):

> [W]e must ask our students, when they use Web 2.0 technologies, to prove initiative and responsibility, curiosity and imagination, the ability to explore, creativity, to work cooperatively and constructively, to communicate and collaborate distinctly with each other, to be open towards identifying and solving problems. (p. 481)

By enabling multimodal composition and new forms of collaboration Web 2.0 technologies offer not only teachers but most importantly students with unprecedented design possibilities (Arola, 2010). Now and in the future, Web 2.0 technologies can provide educators with a valuable catalyst for learning and teaching transformation (Albion, 2008; Crook, 2008; McLoughlin & Lee, 2008).

Yet, the level of challenge for educators is high. As McLoughlin and Lee (2010) point out:

> There is a fine balance to be achieved in attempting to promote learner control, knowledge creation, agency

and autonomy by offering flexible options and choice, whilst offering guidance and structure when needed and adding value to the learning process through personalized, customized and adaptive approaches. (p. 38)

Thus, it is crucial that educators develop the underlying critical thinking skills to understand how the affordances of technologies can be effectively deployed but also the constraints to their application in practice.

In terms of research, the open nature of Web 2.0 technologies makes them eminently suitable for studying learning and teaching (Ullrich et al., 2008). To date, however, educational research has only focused on a narrow subset of the many Web 2.0 tools that are available. Even within the more extensively explored technologies only a fraction of the learning design possibilities have been investigated. The most useful research to inform Web 2.0 learning design will examine the relative effects of different pedagogical designs, rather than focusing on the technology per se. Moreover, it is important that educators critically evaluate research findings between different classes of technologies so that we can abstract general principles of technology-enhanced learning design as well as understand which effects are particular to the tools that we are using. This is a core purpose of the next three chapters on social networking, mobile learning and virtual worlds.

References

Albion, P. R. (2008). Web 2.0 in teacher education: Two imperatives for action. *Computers in the Schools*, 25(3), 181–198.

Alexander, B. (2006). Web 2.0 — A new wave of innovation for teaching and learning? Retrieved from http://www.educause.edu/ero/article/web-20-new-wave-innovation-teaching-and-learning. Accessed on November 12, 2014.

Altanopoulou, P., Tselios, N., Katsanos, C., Georgoutsou, M., & Panagiotaki, M.-A. (2015). Wiki-mediated activities in higher education: Evidence-based analysis of learning effectiveness across three studies. *Journal of Educational Technology & Society*, 18(4), 511–522.

Arola, K. L. (2010). The design of Web 2.0: The rise of the template, the fall of design. *Computers and Composition*, 27(1), 4–14.

Barbera, E. (2009). Mutual feedback in e-portfolio assessment: An approach to the netfolio system. *British Journal of Educational Technology*, 40(2), 342–357.

Beckers, J., Dolmans, D., & van Merriënboer, J. (2016). e-Portfolios enhancing students' self-directed learning: A systematic review of influencing factors. *Australasian Journal of Educational Technology*, 32(2), 2.

Beer, D., & Burrows, R. (2007). Sociology and, of and in Web 2.0: Some initial considerations. *Sociological Research Online*, 12(5), 17.

Ben-Zvi, D. (2007). Using wiki to promote collaborative learning in statistics education. *Technology Innovations in Statistics Education*, 1(1).

Bennett, S., Bishop, A., Dalgarno, B., Waycott, J., & Kennedy, G. (2012). Implementing Web 2.0 technologies in higher education: A collective case study. *Computers & Education*, 59(2), 524–534.

Biasutti, M., & El-Deghaidy, H. (2012). Using Wiki in teacher education: Impact on knowledge management processes and student satisfaction. *Computers & Education*, 59(3), 861–872.

Boulos, M. N., Maramba, I., & Wheeler, S. (2006). Wikis, blogs and podcasts: A new generation of Web-based tools for virtual collaborative clinical practice and education. *BMC medical education*, 6(1), 41.

Bower, M. (2013). An ability approach to within-class curriculum differentiation using student response systems and Web 2.0 technologies: Analysing teachers' responsiveness. *Themes in Science and Technology Education*, 5(1–2), 5–26.

Bower, M. (2015). A typology of Web 2.0 learning technologies. *EDUCAUSE digital library*. Retrieved from http://www.educause.edu/library/resources/typology-web-20-learning-technologies

Bower, M. (2016). Deriving a typology of Web 2.0 learning technologies. *British Journal of Educational Technology*, 47(4), 763–777.

Bower, M., Cavanagh, M., Moloney, R., & Diao, M. (2011). Developing communication competence using an online video reflection system: Pre-service teachers' experiences. *Asia-Pacific Journal of Teacher Education*, 39(4), 311–326.

Bower, M., Hedberg, J., & Kuswara, A. (2010). A framework for Web 2.0 learning design. *Educational Media International*, 47(3), 177–198.

Bower, M., Woo, K., Roberts, M., & Watters, P. (2006, July 10–13). Wiki pedagogy – A tale of two wikis. Paper presented at the 7th International Conference on Information Technology Based Higher Education and Training, Sydney, Australia.

Boyd, D. (2007). The significance of social software. In T. N. B. J. Schmidt (Ed.), *BlogTalks reloaded: Social software research & cases* (pp. 15–30). Norderstedt: Books on Demand.

Cakir, H. (2013). Use of blogs in pre-service teacher education to improve student engagement. *Computers & Education*, 68, 244–252.

Chandra, V., & Chalmers, C. (2010). Blogs, wikis and podcasts: Collaborative knowledge building tools in a design and technology course. *Journal of Learning Design*, 3(2), 35–49.

Chang, C.-C., Liang, C., Shu, K.-M., Tseng, K.-H., & Lin, C.-Y. (2016). Does using e-portfolios for reflective writing enhance high school students' self-regulated learning? *Technology, Pedagogy and Education*, 317–336.

Chang, C.-C., Tseng, K.-H., Liang, C., & Chen, T.-Y. (2013). Using e-portfolios to facilitate university students' knowledge management performance: E-portfolio vs. non-portfolio. *Computers & Education*, *69*, 216–224.

Chen, L., & Chen, T. L. (2012). Use of Twitter for formative evaluation: Reflections on trainer and trainees' experiences. *British Journal of Educational Technology*, *43*(2), E49–E52.

Chen, W.-C. (2014). Actual and preferred teacher feedback on student blog writing. *Australasian Journal of Educational Technology*, *30*(4), 402–414.

Chen, Y. L., Liu, E. Z. F., Shih, R. C., Wu, C. T., & Yuan, S. M. (2011). Use of peer feedback to enhance elementary students' writing through blogging. *British Journal of Educational Technology*, *42*(1), E1–E4.

Chou, P.-N., Chang, C.-C., & Lu, P.-F. (2015). Prezi versus PowerPoint: The effects of varied digital presentation tools on students' learning performance. *Computers & Education*, *91*, 73–82.

Chou, P.-N., & Chen, H.-H. (2008). Engagement in online collaborative learning: A case study using a web 2.0 tool. *Journal of Online Learning and Teaching*, *4*(4), 574–582.

Churchill, D. (2009). Educational applications of Web 2.0: Using blogs to support teaching and learning. *British Journal of Educational Technology*, *40*(1), 179–183.

Chwo, G. S. M. (2015). Empowering EIL learning with a Web 2.0 resource: An initial finding from the cross campus Storybird feedback study. *Computers & Education*, *84*, 1–7.

Cole, M. (2009). Using Wiki technology to support student engagement: Lessons from the trenches. *Computers & Education*, *52*(1), 141–146.

Conole, G., & Alevizou, P. (2010). *A literature review of the use of Web 2.0 tools in higher education*. A report commissioned by the Higher Education Academy.

Cormode, G., & Krishnamurthy, B. (2008). Key differences between Web 1.0 and Web 2.0. *First Monday*, *13*(6).

Crook, C. (2008). *Web 2.0 technologies for learning: The current landscape – Opportunities, challenges and tensions.*

Crook, C., & Harrison, C. (2008). *Web 2.0 technologies for learning at key stages 3 and 4: Summary report.*

Dabbagh, N., & Kitsantas, A. (2012). Personal learning environments, social media, and self-regulated learning: A natural formula for connecting formal and informal learning. *The Internet and Higher Education*, *15*(1), 3–8.

Deng, L., & Yuen, A. H. K. (2011). Towards a framework for educational affordances of blogs. *Computers & Education*, *56*(2), 441–451.

Divitini, M., Haugaløkken, O. K., & Morken, E. M. (2005). Blog to support learning in the field: Lessons learned from a fiasco. Paper presented at the 5th IEEE International Conference on Advanced Learning Technologies (ICALT2005), Kaohsiung, Taiwan.

Dohn, N. B. (2009). Web 2.0: Inherent tensions and evident challenges for education. *International Journal of Computer-Supported Collaborative Learning*, *4*(3), 343–363.

Ebner, M., Lienhardt, C., Rohs, M., & Meyer, I. (2010). Microblogs in higher education – A chance to facilitate informal and process-oriented learning? *Computers & Education*, 55(1), 92–100.

Elgort, I., Toland, J., & Smith, A. G. (2008). *Is wiki an effective platform for group course work?*

Engstrom, M. E., & Jewett, D. (2005). Collaborative learning the wiki way. *TechTrends*, 12–15.

Farmer, B., Yue, A., & Brooks, C. (2008). Using blogging for higher order learning in large cohort university teaching: A case study. *Australasian Journal of Educational Technology*, 24(2), 123–136.

Fitch, D., Peet, M., Reed, B. G., & Tolman, R. (2008). The use of ePortfolios in evaluating the curriculum and student learning. *Journal of Social Work Education*, 44(3), 37–54.

Franklin, T., & Van Harmelen, M. (2007). Web 2.0 for content for learning and teaching in higher education. *JISC*. http://www.jisc.ac.uk/media/documents/programmes/digitalrepositories/web2-contentlearningand-teaching.pdf

Gao, F., Luo, T., & Zhang, K. (2012). Tweeting for learning: A critical analysis of research on microblogging in education published in 2008–2011. *British Journal of Educational Technology*, 43(5), 783–801.

Garcia, E., Elbeltagi, I., Brown, M., & Dungay, K. (2015). The implications of a connectivist learning blog model and the changing role of teaching and learning. *British Journal of Educational Technology*, 46(4), 877–894.

Gielen, M., & De Wever, B. (2015). Scripting the role of assessor and assessee in peer assessment in a wiki environment: Impact on peer feedback quality and product improvement. *Computers & Education*, 88, 370–386.

Grant, L. (2009). 'I DON'T CARE DO UR OWN PAGE!' A case study of using wikis for collaborative work in a UK secondary school. *Learning, Media and Technology*, 34(2), 105–117.

Gray, K., Thompson, C., Sheard, J., Clerehan, R., & Hamilton, M. (2010). Students as Web 2.0 authors: Implications for assessment design and conduct. *Australasian Journal of Educational Technology*, 26(1), 105–122.

Greenhow, C., Robelia, B., & Hughes, J. E. (2009). Learning, teaching, and scholarship in a digital age Web 2.0 and classroom research: What path should we take now? *Educational Researcher*, 38(4), 246–259.

Grosseck, G. (2009). To use or not to use web 2.0 in higher education? Procedia – Social and Behavioral Sciences, 1(1), 478–482.

Guo, Z., & Stevens, K. J. (2011). Factors influencing perceived usefulness of wikis for group collaborative learning by first year students. *Australasian Journal of Educational Technology*, 27(2).

Haave, N. (2016). E-Portfolios rescue biology students from a poorer final exam result: Promoting student metacognition. *Bioscene: Journal of College Biology Teaching*, 42(1), 8–15.

Harris, A. L., & Rea, A. (2009). Web 2.0 and virtual world technologies: A growing impact on IS education. *Journal of Information Systems Education*, 20(2), 137.

Heinrich, E., Bhattacharya, M., & Rayudu, R. (2007). Preparation for lifelong learning using ePortfolios. *European Journal of Engineering Education, 32*(6), 653–663.

Hew, K. F., & Cheung, W. S. (2013). Use of Web 2.0 technologies in K-12 and higher education: The search for evidence-based practice. *Educational Research Review, 9,* 47–64.

Holotescu, C., & Grosseck, G. (2011). Mobile learning through microblogging. *Procedia-Social and Behavioral Sciences, 15,* 4–8.

Hourigan, T., & Murray, L. (2010). Using blogs to help language students to develop reflective learning strategies: Towards a pedagogical framework. *Australasian Journal of Educational Technology, 26*(2), 209–225.

Huang, C. D., & Behara, R. S. (2007). Outcome-driven experiential learning with Web 2.0. *Journal of Information Systems Education, 18*(3), 329–336.

Huang, T.-C., Huang, Y.-M., & Yu, F.-Y. (2011). Cooperative weblog learning in higher education: Its facilitating effects on social interaction, time lag, and cognitive load. *Educational Technology & Society, 14*(1), 95–106.

Jones, P. (2007). *When a wiki is the way: Exploring the use of a wiki in a constructively aligned learning design.*

Jones, S. A., Green, L., Hodges, C. B., Kennedy, K., Downs, E., Repman, J., & Clark, K. F. (2012). Supplementing the learning management system: Using Web 2.0 for collaboration. In D. Polly, C. Mims, & K. A. Persichitte (Eds.), *Developing technology-rich teacher education programs: Key issues* (pp. 118–134). Hershey, PA: IGI Global.

Judd, T., Kennedy, G., & Cropper, S. (2010). Using wikis for collaborative learning: Assessing collaboration through contribution. *Australasian Journal of Educational Technology, 26*(3), 341–354.

Junco, R., Heiberger, G., & Loken, E. (2011). The effect of Twitter on college student engagement and grades. *Journal of Computer Assisted Learning, 27*(2), 119–132.

Jung, I., & Suzuki, Y. (2015). Scaffolding strategies for wiki-based collaboration: Action research in a multicultural Japanese language program. *British Journal of Educational Technology, 46*(4), 829–838.

Kabilan, M. K., & Khan, M. A. (2012). Assessing pre-service English language teachers' learning using e-portfolios: Benefits, challenges and competencies gained. *Computers & Education, 58*(4), 1007–1020.

Kale, U., & Goh, D. (2014). Teaching style, ICT experience and teachers' attitudes toward teaching with Web 2.0. *Education and Information Technologies, 19*(1), 41–60.

Kam, H.-J., & Katerattanakul, P. (2014). Structural model of team-based learning using Web 2.0 collaborative software. *Computers & Education, 76,* 1–12.

Kamel Boulos, M. N., & Wheeler, S. (2007). The emerging Web 2.0 social software: An enabling suite of sociable technologies in health and health care education. *Health Information & Libraries Journal, 24*(1), 2–23.

Karasavvidis, I. (2010). Wiki uses in higher education: Exploring barriers to successful implementation. *Interactive Learning Environments, 18*(3), 219–231.

Karvounidis, T., Chimos, K., Bersimis, S., & Douligeris, C. (2014). Evaluating Web 2.0 technologies in higher education using students' perceptions and performance. *Journal of Computer Assisted Learning, 30*(6), 577–596.

Kennedy, G., Dalgarno, B., Bennett, S., Gray, K., Waycott, J., Judd, T. … Chang, R. (2009). *Educating the net generation: A handbook of findings for practice and policy.*

Kim, H. N. (2008). The phenomenon of blogs and theoretical model of blog use in educational contexts. *Computers & Education, 51*(3), 1342–1352.

Kim, P., Hong, J.-S., Bonk, C., & Lim, G. (2011). Effects of group reflection variations in project-based learning integrated in a Web 2.0 learning space. *Interactive Learning Environments, 19*(4), 333–349.

Köse, U. (2010). A blended learning model supported with Web 2.0 technologies. *Procedia-Social and Behavioral Sciences, 2*(2), 2794–2802.

Kreber, C., & Kanuka, H. (2013). The scholarship of teaching and learning and the online classroom. *Canadian Journal of University Continuing Education, 32*(2).

Kump, B., Moskaliuk, J., Dennerlein, S., & Ley, T. (2013). Tracing knowledge co-evolution in a realistic course setting: A wiki-based field experiment. *Computers & Education, 69*, 60–70.

Ladyshewsky, R. K., & Gardner, P. (2008). Peer assisted learning and blogging: A strategy to promote reflective practice during clinical fieldwork. *Australasian Journal of Educational Technology, 24*(3), 241–257.

Lai, C., Lei, C., & Liu, Y. (2016). The nature of collaboration and perceived learning in wiki-based collaborative writing. *Australasian Journal of Educational Technology, 32*(3).

Laru, J., Näykki, P., & Järvelä, S. (2012). Supporting small-group learning using multiple Web 2.0 tools: A case study in the higher education context. *The Internet and Higher Education, 15*(1), 29–38.

Larusson, J. A., & Alterman, R. (2009). Wikis to support the "collaborative" part of collaborative learning. *International Journal of Computer-Supported Collaborative Learning, 4*(4), 371–402.

Lassila, O., & Hendler, J. (2007). Embracing 'Web 3.0.' *IEEE Internet Computing, 11*(3), 90–93.

Levy, B. L., Journell, W., He, Y., & Towns, B. (2015). Students blogging about politics: A study of students' political engagement and a teacher's pedagogy during a semester-long political blog assignment. *Computers & Education, 88*, 64–71.

Li, X., Chu, S. K. W., & Ki, W. W. (2014). The effects of a wiki-based collaborative process writing pedagogy on writing ability and attitudes among upper primary school students in Mainland China. *Computers & Education, 77*, 151–169.

Li, X., Chu, S. K. W., Ki, W. W., & Woo, M. (2012). Using a wiki-based collaborative process writing pedagogy to facilitate collaborative writing among Chinese primary school students. *Australasian Journal of Educational Technology.*

Li, Y., Dong, M., & Huang, R. (2011). Designing collaborative E-Learning environments based upon semantic Wiki: From design models to application scenarios. *Educational Technology & Society, 14*(4), 49–63.

Liu, C.-C., Lu, K.-H., Wu, L. Y., & Tsai, C.-C. (2016). The impact of peer review on creative self-efficacy and learning performance in Web 2.0 learning activities. *Journal of Educational Technology & Society*, 19(2), 286–297.

Liu, S. H.-J., & Lan, Y.-J. (2016). Social constructivist approach to web-based EFL learning: Collaboration, motivation, and perception on the use of Google docs. *Journal of Educational Technology & Society*, 19(1), 171–186.

Lund, A. (2008). Wikis: A collective approach to language production. *ReCALL*, 20(01), 35–54.

Lund, A., & Smørdal, O. (2006). Is there a space for the teacher in a WIKI? Paper presented at the Proceedings of the 2006 international symposium on Wikis, Odense, Denmark.

Manca, S., & Ranieri, M. (2016). Facebook and the others. Potentials and obstacles of social media for teaching in higher education. *Computers & Education*, 95, 216–230.

McLoughlin, C., & Lee, M. J. (2007). Social software and participatory learning: Pedagogical choices with technology affordances in the Web 2.0 era. Paper presented at the ICT: Providing choices for learners and learning. Proceedings ascilite Singapore 2007.

McLoughlin, C., & Lee, M. J. (2008). Mapping the digital terrain: New media and social software as catalysts for pedagogical change. *Ascilite Melbourne*.

McLoughlin, C., & Lee, M. J. W. (2010). Personalised and self regulated learning in the Web 2.0 era: International exemplars of innovative pedagogy using social software. *Australasian Journal of Educational Technology*, 26(1), 28–43.

Meyer, E., Abrami, P. C., Wade, C. A., Aslan, O., & Deault, L. (2010). Improving literacy and metacognition with electronic portfolios: Teaching and learning with ePEARL. *Computers & Education*, 55(1), 84–91.

Meyer, K. A. (2010). A comparison of Web 2.0 tools in a doctoral course. *The Internet and Higher Education*, 13(4), 226–232.

Minocha, S., Schroeder, A., & Schneider, C. (2011). Role of the educator in social software initiatives in further and higher education: A conceptualisation and research agenda. *British Journal of Educational Technology*, 42(6), 889–903.

Miyazoe, T., & Anderson, T. (2010). Learning outcomes and students' perceptions of online writing: Simultaneous implementation of a forum, blog, and wiki in an EFL blended learning setting. *System*, 38(2), 185–199.

Moskaliuk, J., Kimmerle, J., & Cress, U. (2012). Collaborative knowledge building with wikis: The impact of redundancy and polarity. *Computers & Education*, 58(4), 1049–1057.

Naismith, L., Lee, B. Ä., & Pilkington, R. M. (2011). Collaborative learning with a wiki: Differences in perceived usefulness in two contexts of use. *Journal of Computer Assisted Learning*, 27(3), 228–242.

Neumann, D. L., & Hood, M. (2009). The effects of using a wiki on student engagement and learning of report writing skills in a university statistics course. *Australasian Journal of Educational Technology*, 25(3), 382–398.

Ng, E. M. W. (2016). Fostering pre-service teachers' self-regulated learning through self-and peer assessment of wiki projects. *Computers & Education, 98,* 180–191.

Nicolaidou, I. (2013). E-portfolios supporting primary students' writing performance and peer feedback. *Computers & Education, 68,* 404–415.

Novakovich, J. (2016). Fostering critical thinking and reflection through blog-mediated peer feedback. *Journal of Computer Assisted Learning, 32*(1), 16–30.

O'Reilly, T. (2007). What is Web 2.0 – Design patterns and business models for the next generation of software. *Communications and Strategies, 65*(1), 17–37.

Orús, C., Barlés, M. J., Belanche, D., Casaló, L., Fraj, E., & Gurrea, R. (2016). The effects of learner-generated videos for YouTube on learning outcomes and satisfaction. *Computers & Education, 95,* 254–269.

Philip, R., & Nicholls, J. (2009). Group blogs: Documenting collaborative drama processes. *Australasian Journal of Educational Technology, 25*(5), 683–699.

Pifarré, M., & Staarman, J. K. (2011). Wiki-supported collaborative learning in primary education: How a dialogic space is created for thinking together. *International Journal of Computer-Supported Collaborative Learning, 6*(2), 187–205.

Project Tomorrow. (2016). From print to pixel – The role of videos, games, animations and simulations within K-12 education. Retrieved from http://www.tomorrow.org/speakup/SU15AnnualReport.html

Rahimi, E. (2015). *A design framework for personal learning environments.* PhD. TU Delft, Delft University of Technology. Retrieved from http://repository.tudelft.nl/islandora/object/uuid:432bbd60-c6b9-4f08-aef4-615c2f2a101c

Rahimi, E., van den Berg, J., & Veen, W. (2015a). A learning model for enhancing the student's control in educational process using Web 2.0 personal learning environments. *British Journal of Educational Technology, 46*(4), 780–792.

Rahimi, E., van den Berg, J., & Veen, W. (2015b). Facilitating student-driven constructing of learning environments using Web 2.0 personal learning environments. *Computers & Education, 81,* 235–246.

Raman, M., Ryan, T., & Olfman, L. (2005). Designing knowledge management systems for teaching and learning with wiki technology. *Journal of Information Systems Education, 16*(3), 311.

Redecker, C., Ala-Mutka, K., Bacigalupo, M., Ferrari, A., & Punie, Y. (2009). *Learning 2.0: The impact of Web 2.0 innovations on education and training in Europe.* Final report. European Commission-Joint Research Center-Institute for Porspective Technological Studies, Seville.

Reich, J., Murnane, R., & Willett, J. (2012). The state of wiki usage in US k-12 schools leveraging Web 2.0 data warehouses to assess quality and equity in online learning environments. *Educational Researcher, 41*(1), 7–15.

Richardson, W. (2006). *Blogs, wikis, podcasts, and other powerful tools for classrooms.* Thousand Oaks, CA: Sage.

Rick, J., & Guzdial, M. (2006). Situating CoWeb: A scholarship of application. *International Journal of Computer-Supported Collaborative Learning*, *1*(1), 89–115.

Rienzo, T., & Han, B. (2009). Microsoft or Google Web 2.0 Tools for Course Management. *Journal of Information Systems Education*, *20*(2), 123–127.

Roberts, P., Maor, D., & Herrington, J. (2016). ePortfolio-Based learning environments: Recommendations for effective scaffolding of reflective thinking in higher education. *Journal of Educational Technology and Society*, *19*(4), 22–33.

Robertson, J. (2011). The educational affordances of blogs for self-directed learning. *Computers & Education*, *57*(2), 1628–1644.

Ruth, A., & Houghton, L. (2009). The wiki way of learning. *Australasian Journal of Educational Technology*, *25*(2).

Schneckenberg, D., Ehlers, U., & Adelsberger, H. (2011). Web 2.0 and competence-oriented design of learning – Potentials and implications for higher education. *British Journal of Educational Technology*, *42*(5), 747–762.

Schwartz, L., Clark, S., Cossarin, M., & Rudolph, J. (2004). Educational wikis: Features and selection criteria. *The International Review of Research in Open and Distributed Learning*, *5*(1).

Shah, N. A. K., Shabgahi, S. L., & Cox, A. M. (2015). Uses and risks of microblogging in organisational and educational settings. *British Journal of Educational Technology*.

Sharma, P., & Tietjen, P. (2016). Examining patterns of participation and meaning making in student blogs: A case study in higher education. *American Journal of Distance Education*, *30*(1), 2–13.

Shih, R.-C. (2010). Blended learning using video-based blogs: Public speaking for English as a second language students. *Australasian Journal of Educational Technology*, *26*(6), 883–897.

Snodgrass, S. (2011). Wiki activities in blended learning for health professional students: Enhancing critical thinking and clinical reasoning skills. *Australasian Journal of Educational Technology*, *27*(4), 563–580.

Statistica. (2017). Number of monthly active Twitter users worldwide from 1st quarter 2010 to 4th quarter 2016. Retrieved from https://www.statista.com/statistics/282087/number-of-monthly-active-twitter-users/. Accessed on February 20, 2017.

Stevenson, M., & Hedberg, J. G. (2011). Head in the clouds: A review of current and future potential for cloud-enabled pedagogies. *Educational Media International*, *48*(4), 321–333.

Su, F., & Beaumont, C. (2010). Evaluating the use of a wiki for collaborative learning. *Innovations in Education and Teaching International*, *47*(4), 417–431.

Tan, S. M., Ladyshewsky, R. K., & Gardner, P. (2010). Using blogging to promote clinical reasoning and metacognition in undergraduate physiotherapy fieldwork programs. *Australasian Journal of Educational Technology*, *26*(3), 355–368.

Trentin, G. (2009). Using a wiki to evaluate individual contribution to a collaborative learning project. *Journal of Computer Assisted Learning, 25*(1), 43−55.

Trigwell, K., Martin, E., Benjamin, J., & Prosser, M. (2000). Scholarship of teaching: A model. *Higher Education Research & Development, 19*(2), 155−168.

Tsai, W.-T., Li, W., Elston, J., & Chen, Y. (2011). Collaborative learning using wiki web sites for computer science undergraduate education: A case study. *IEEE Transactions on Education, 54*(1), 114−124.

Ullrich, C., Borau, K., Luo, H., Tan, X., Shen, L., & Shen, R. (2008). Why Web 2.0 is good for learning and for research: Principles and prototypes. Paper presented at the Proceedings of the 17th international conference on World Wide Web.

Waycott, J., Sheard, J., Thompson, C., & Clerehan, R. (2013). Making students' work visible on the social web: A blessing or a curse? *Computers & Education, 68*, 86−95.

Wheeler, S., Yeomans, P., & Wheeler, D. (2008). The good, the bad and the wiki: Evaluating student-generated content for collaborative learning. *British Journal of Educational Technology, 39*(6), 987−995.

Wichmann, A., & Rummel, N. (2013). Improving revision in wiki-based writing: Coordination pays off. *Computers & Education, 62*, 262−270.

Williams, J., & Chinn, S. J. (2009). Using Web 2.0 to support the active learning experience. *Journal of Information Systems Education, 20*(2), 165.

Woo, M., Chu, S. K.-W., Ho, A., & Li, X. (2011). Using a Wiki to scaffold primary-school students' collaborative writing. *Educational Technology & Society, 14*(1), 43−54.

Xiao, Y., & Lucking, R. (2008). The impact of two types of peer assessment on students' performance and satisfaction within a Wiki environment. *The Internet and Higher Education, 11*(3), 186−193.

Xie, Y., Ke, F., & Sharma, P. (2008). The effect of peer feedback for blogging on college students' reflective learning processes. *The Internet and Higher Education, 11*(1), 18−25.

Yang, M., Tai, M., & Lim, C. P. (2015). The role of e-portfolios in supporting productive learning. *British Journal of Educational Technology.*

Yang, S.-H. (2009). Using blogs to enhance critical reflection and community of practice. *Educational Technology & Society, 12*(2), 11−21.

Yeo, H. I., & Lee, Y. L. (2014). Exploring new potentials of blogs for learning: Can children use blogs for personal information management (PIM)? *British Journal of Educational Technology, 45*(5), 916−925.

Zhang, J. (2009). Comments on Greenhow, Robelia, and Hughes: Toward a creative social web for learners and teachers. *Educational Researcher, 38*(4), 274−279.

Zheng, B., Niiya, M., & Warschauer, M. (2015). Wikis and collaborative learning in higher education. *Technology, Pedagogy and Education, 24*(3), 357−374.

Zorko, V. (2009). Factors affecting the way students collaborate in a wiki for English language learning. *Australasian Journal of Educational Technology, 25*(5), 645−665.

8

Designing for Learning Using Social Networking

ABSTRACT

Social networking platforms such as Facebook have infiltrated the lives of many students, and as such it is natural to consider how they can be effectively used to enhance learning. This chapter provides a comprehensive review of social networking in education from a design perspective. Social networking is defined based on Boyd & Ellison's seminal definition of connected profiles, and is distinguished from social media for the purposes of investigation. Facebook, Edmodo, and other social networking platforms are briefly described, before summarizing the wide variety of social networking usage reported in the research literature. The various benefits of social networking in education are distilled from the literature, including their capacity to facilitate community building, collaboration, reflection, and expedient access to learning. Issues surrounding the educational use of social networking are also organized into themes, for instance privacy concerns, distraction, cyber-safety, and technical constraints. The implications of findings from the social networking literature are synthesized into learning design and implementation recommendations. The chapter concludes with a discussion of open questions and areas for further investigation.

Introduction to Designing for Learning Using Social Networking

This chapter unpacks what is known about designing for learning using social networking. The continued proposition is that understanding the potentials, constraints, and recommendations from the research literature provides the best basis upon which educators can make design decisions when using the technology. Educational issues surrounding the use of social networking are interesting to compare to the those raised in the previous chapter on Web 2.0 technologies, because social networking is actually a sophisticated, complex, and widely used type of Web 2.0 platform. Comparing social networking to Web 2.0 technologies enables us to start to see patterns and differences relating to how various technologies and practices might influence learning.

The same method and form of reporting is used for this analysis of social networking as was used in the previous Web 2.0 chapter. The benefits, issues, and design recommendations relating to teaching using social networking have been thematically derived from the research literature. Using the same approach in these two (and the next two) chapters enables patterns and differences to more clearly emerge. However, it is important to note that although the same approach has been adopted for the four technology review chapters, the reviews themselves were conducted as independently as possible. That is to say, the findings from one chapter were not used as a starting point for categorization in other chapters. This was done in order to allow different themes to emerge authentically, rather than being artificially influenced by the analysis of another technological platform.

In order to understand how to design for learning using social networking, it is once again important to clearly define the scope of analysis, the features of the technologies, the educational possibilities, benefits, limitations, and design implications. Let's start by defining what we mean by the term 'social networking.'

What Are Social Networking Technologies?

Social networking sites have been seminally defined as web-based services that allow individuals to:

(1) Construct a public or semi-public profile within a bounded system,
(2) Articulate a list of other users with whom they share a connection, and
(3) View and traverse their list of connections and those made by others within the system (Boyd & Ellison, 2007, para. 4).

While there are other definitions of social networking, this established definition has been quite pervasively accepted among the field.

Pertinent social networking communication channels include private messaging, public 'wall' postings, instant messaging, and status updates (Lampe, Wohn, Vitak, Ellison, & Wash, 2011). Teachers can use inbuilt social networking tools to organize classes, for instance by uploading course materials and photos (Wang, Woo, Quek, Yang, & Liu, 2012). Students can share course resources and post comments (Bowman & Akcaoglu, 2014), as well as upload videos and label or 'tag' each other as they appear in various media resources (Ractham & Firpo, 2011). Educational uses and potentials of social networking will be covered extensively in later sections.

At this point it is worth mentioning that the boundaries of what is and is not a social networking system are somewhat blurred and open to interpretation. There are platforms that provide the capacity for users to follow and connect with one another around particular areas of interest, such as LinkedIn (http://linkedin.com) for professional networking, and ResearchGate (http://researchgate.com) for academic research. These undoubtedly enable users to form social networks, but their customized focus means that they are not suitable for designing online social networking environments, for instance, that could be used in a general educational context.

Other platforms enable users to connect around media of interest, such as videos (e.g. http://youtube.com), photos (see http://instagram.com), and websites (for instance social bookmarking platforms such as http://diigo.com). Pinterest (http://pinterest.com)

enables communities to share resources around any topics of interest. Twitter (http://twitter.com) provides a microblogging platform to broadcast instantaneous thoughts and knowledge. Snapchat (http://snapchat.com) enables people to synchronously share text, image and video messages. These platforms tend to focus less on the profile of the individuals as well as apply constraints (either cultural or technical) on type of content that is posted and the way the content is structured. As such these platforms will be considered as 'social media' rather than traditional identity-focused social networking systems, and consequently will not be considered in subsequent discussion. This chapter will focus upon how to design educational environments that utilize commonly accepted social networking platforms such as Facebook, Edmodo, and Ning.

Examples of Social Networking Technologies

FACEBOOK

The most popular and well renown social networking site is Facebook (http://facebook.com), with over 1.8 billion active users each month (Statistica, 2017). Students often use Facebook in their personal lives to communicate with friends, establish a personal identity, maintain relationships, and disseminate information (Pempek, Yermolayeva, & Calvert, 2009). It has been used in several studies of social networking in higher education (as will be elaborated below).

Facebook provides the facility to create a 'page,' where a user can broadcast information via posts on their wall to any people that follow them. Facebook also enables the creation of groups, including 'open' groups that anyone can join, 'closed' groups where people can ask to join but need to be accepted, and 'secret' groups who can only see evidence of the group once they have been added (Miron & Ravid, 2015). Pages are generally more suitable for teacher-centered broadcast of information, whereas groups are more appropriate when the intention is for students to take a more active role in the learning process (Bowman & Akcaoglu, 2014). A screenshot of a closed Facebook group page is shown in Figure 8.1.

Figure 8.1. A Closed Facebook Group Page Showing a Poll Setup in the Discussion Area, with Members, Events, Photos, and Files Areas Available via Separate Tabs.

EDMODO

As an alternative to Facebook, Edmodo (http://edmodo.com) provides a freely available social network platform that has been designed specifically for education (see Figure 8.2). Edmodo has many of the features of Facebook but instead of being entirely open to the public, access to the class spaces is controlled by the teacher. This means that it can be used as a way to overcome security and privacy concerns that may exist in educational contexts, and can even be used as a training environment to develop safe Internet behavior (Holland & Muilenburg, 2011). Edmodo provides teachers with the ability to set assignments and quizzes, as well as instantaneous 'snapshot' overviews of students' performances on tasks. In one study of high school students Edmodo was the most frequently identified example of good social technology usage by teachers (Mao, 2014). In another study high school students responded favorably to the use of Edmodo in their classes, although teachers noted the disadvantages such as absence of a chat tool, and no ability to tag posts or files (Fardoun, Alghazzawi, López, Penichet, & Gallud, 2012).

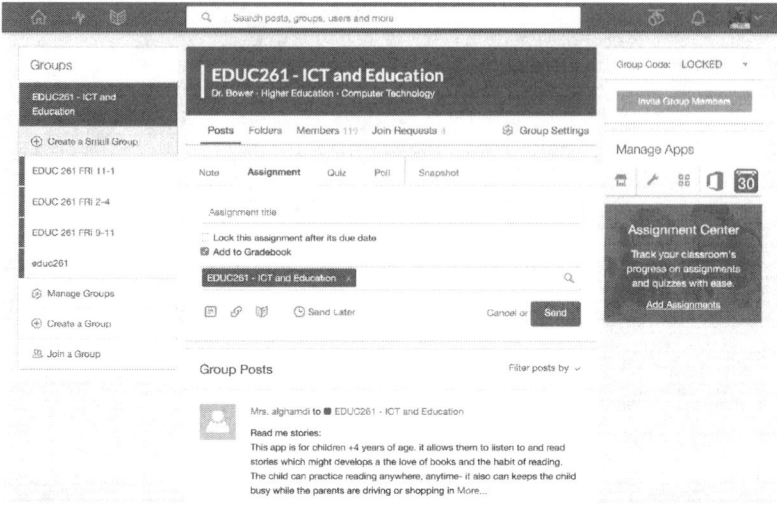

Figure 8.2. Screenshot of the Edmodo Social Networking System Showing the Capacity to Set Groups, Create Wall Posts, and Set Group Entry Codes.

OTHER SOCIAL NETWORKING SYSTEMS

Ning (http://ning.com) is another social networking site that allows educators to control who participates in the social network. Ning has been used in several studies of social networking in education (Arnold & Paulus, 2010; Barbour & Plough, 2009; Brady, Holcomb, & Smith, 2010; Callaghan & Bower, 2012; Casey & Evans, 2011; Hung & Yuen, 2010; Reich, Levinson, & Johnston, 2011; Toetenel, 2014), though it should be noted that it is now a fee-for-service platform. Google Plus (https://plus.google.com) is another commonly used and freely available general social networking platform, though has not been used in many studies of social networking. MySpace (http://myspace.com) was a previously popular social networking platform that has now been supplanted by Facebook. Elgg (http://elgg.org) provides an open source social networking platform that educational institutions can install on their own servers or have hosted, though it has had limited application compared to the other aforementioned social networking systems.

Uses of Social Networking in Education

Notwithstanding student-initiated educational uses of social networking (such as those explored by Lampe et al., 2011), there are numerous examples of educators deliberately deploying social networking within their subjects and courses to support learning. In high school, Facebook has been used in mathematics classes to disseminate information and facilitate homework discussions (Fewkes & McCabe, 2012), English classes to support out of lesson class interactions (Kio, 2015), and chemistry classes to assist student preparation for final examinations (Rap & Blonder, 2016). The 'groups' feature of Edmodo has been used to enable reciprocal teaching approaches in high school English studies classes (Holland & Muilenburg, 2011). Ning has been used to facilitate modules of work for middle school commerce students (Callaghan & Bower, 2012), as well as to develop argumentation capabilities and appreciation of alternative perspectives for senior school English students (Beach & Doerr-Stevens, 2011). On a larger scale, Ning has been used across several high school classes within a school to provide a central portal for learning (Casey & Evans, 2011).

In higher education, social networking systems have in some cases been used as a replacement for the traditional learning management system. Facebook has been used as the entire course management system in a Health Informatics course in order to facilitate a more collaborative and contribution-oriented learning environment (LaRue, 2012). It has been used as the learning management system in introduction to programming and discrete mathematics courses as a way to distribute general information, notify students of events, and offer a platform for holding discussions (Albayrak & Yildirim, 2015). It has similarly been used in an educational media course to disseminate course materials as well as have students share links and solicit feedback from their peers (Lambić, 2016). Ning has been used as the learning management system in Taiwanese undergraduate courses in order to enhance the sense of connectedness and facilitate a community of practice (Hung & Yuen, 2010).

University educators have also deployed Facebook in addition to traditional course management systems. Facebook group sites have been used in an introductory mass media course and a graduate management information systems course in order to provide supplementary class discussion spaces (Ractham & Firpo, 2011). Facebook groups have been used a first year psychology course to share relevant news articles prior to face-to-face classes so that lectures could build upon and respond to the emergent online discussions (Dyson, Vickers, Turtle, Cowan, & Tassone, 2015). They have been used in undergraduate and postgraduate teacher education courses to make announcements, share course resources, organize weekly tutorial sessions and conduct online discussions (Wang et al., 2012), undergraduate educational technology courses to post exam preparation questions and enable students to respond and discuss (O'Bannon, Beard, & Britt, 2013; O'Bannon, Britt, & Beard, 2014), and business management courses to provide announcements, facilitate faculty-led and student-led discussions, offer question and answer opportunities, conduct polls, and enable sharing resources such as websites, videos, news articles and images (Buzzetto-More, 2012). Facebook 'pages' have been used in university health care courses in addition to the traditional learning management system as a means to disseminate lecture notes, provide links to relevant media items, offer administrative updates relating to class schedules, and promote course-related discussion among students (Irwin, Ball, Desbrow, & Leveritt, 2012).

Social networking has also been used to enable external experts and mentors to guide and interact with students. Ning has been used to enable pre-service teachers to engage with a professional 'community of praxis,' blending theory and practice in a series of reflective dialogues with experienced social studies teachers (Reich et al., 2011). Facebook has been used to enable postgraduate digital media students in Australia to mentor undergraduate digital design students in the United States, as well as engage industry experts (McCarthy, 2012). Facebook has also been used to provide an ancillary informal learning environment where practicing pharmacist experts could share their perspectives with pharmacy students (Cain & Policastri, 2011).

Social networking can be used as the basis for more divergent learning designs. For instance, groups of students learning English used Facebook in combination with Skype to coordinate buying and selling activities as part of a business role-play module (Yen, Hou, & Chang, 2015). Political science students from different nations used Facebook to share images and further their understanding of different cultural perspectives on politics (Shaw, 2016). Groups of advanced oral communication students used Facebook to organize team presentations and provide one another with affective support (Magogwe, Ntereke, & Phetlhe, 2015). Language students used Facebook groups to provide one another with feedback on their written work (Wichadee, 2013). Undergraduate chemistry students used Facebook to conduct authentic role-play activities relating to unresolved social scientific issues (Geyer, 2014).

Educators have also used social networking as a platform for assessment. Facebook galleries have been used to conduct assessment tasks in architecture courses, where students have to upload photos and videos and critique each other's contributions (McCarthy, 2010). Facebook was also used as the entire course management system in a course on distance education, where students were assessed on their ability to create a library of videos, links and pictures (Baran, 2010). Peer assessment has been used within Facebook to develop English as a Second Language capabilities (Shih, 2011). Secondary school students used the blog tool within Ning to complete e-Portfolio summative assessment tasks (Callaghan & Bower, 2012).

So there is wide variety of learning designs and innovation with relation to the use of social networking in education. In order to be able to create and implement effective social networking learning designs, it is obviously critical that educators have a strong understanding of the potentials as well as the limitations of the technology.

Benefits and Potentials of Social Networking in Education

Social networking subtends several benefits and potentials to educators. While social networking can be used in a wide variety of ways (as illustrated above) the social and networked nature of the platform means that educational uses generally fall within two pedagogical paradigms – social constructivism and connectivism. The fact that social networking systems are designed for people to communicate with one another means that they are well suited to facilitating social constructivist learning (Buzzetto-More, 2012; Gunawardena et al., 2009). The ability to easily access social networking from anywhere and make contact with a wide variety of people outside the classroom means that they can also be used to facilitate connectivist learning (Greenhow & Askari, 2015; Rambe, 2012b; Salavuo, 2008).

Advantages and potentials of social networking, as distilled from the research literature, are outlined below.

ENABLING COMMUNICATION

Social networking systems can be used to enable and in many cases increase the amount of communication that transpires. Teachers can use social networking platforms such as Facebook to post announcements, share resources, organize classes, facilitate online discussions and conduct polls and solicit feedback from students (Barbour & Plough, 2009; Lambić, 2016; Miron & Ravid, 2015; Ractham & Firpo, 2011; Wang et al., 2012). Students can post contributions relating to exam revision, external links (either class related or otherwise), as well as social contributions relating to peer support or humorous anecdotes (Bowman & Akcaoglu, 2014). Students can also help each other to quickly resolve course-related administrative matters online (Bosch, 2009; Madge, Meek, Wellens, & Hooley, 2009). They can also express interest in questions and comments on walls by 'liking' the posts, and review the 'likes' from others in order to gauge relevance (Lambić, 2016). The use of social networking can increase the amount that students communicate with their peers and teacher (Albayrak & Yildirim, 2015). The amount of feedback to wall posts may well exceed the content in the initial posts – Bowman and Akcaoglu (2014) found the ratio of responsive comments to initial posts was 3.6 to 1.

Students identify communication advantages such as easier interaction with peers, ability to utilize discussion forums, and increased help with homework (Fewkes & McCabe, 2012; Greenhow & Robelia, 2009). Many students consider the ability to easily share and view videos, documents and discussions as the most valuable reason to use a social networking system such as Facebook as a course management system (Albayrak & Yildirim, 2015). In one study students felt Facebook was significantly better for distributing information between learners than a traditional learning management system (Petrovic, Jeremic, Cirovic, Radojicic, & Milenkovic, 2014). Research has also found that many students appreciate communicating with their instructor via social networking, though the extent to which the interactions are viewed positively depends upon how the teacher uses the social networking system (Mazer, Murphy, & Simonds, 2007). For instance, using Facebook to provide virtual office hours had a positive effect on student satisfaction (Li & Pitts, 2009).

FACILITATING COLLABORATION

Students generally agree that social networking systems provide an effective platform for collaboration (Lim & Richardson, 2016). Social networking can support collaborative learning by providing a means for gathering project materials, brainstorming ideas, sharing written work, and exchanging feedback (Greenhow & Robelia,

2009). Even when social networking is not prescribed as part of a course, students may use it informally to contact one another about scheduling of project group meetings, revision, and for coursework queries (Madge et al., 2009). Students who use social networking sites such as Facebook as an educational aid may learn more through the exchange and review of alternative sources of information, such as presentations, videos and books (Lambić, 2016). Cooperative learning in social networking sites has been positively correlated with student learning outcomes (Wang, Lin, Yu, Wu, & Gung, 2013). Collecting and sharing information using social networking platforms has also been shown to positively predict academic performance (Junco, 2012).

LEVERAGING A POPULAR PARADIGM THAT IS EASY TO USE

Because most students are generally familiar with the interfaces and operational paradigms utilized in social networking systems they do not need to learn new digital literacies to participate in course-related social networking activities (Salavuo, 2008). A review of Facebook use in education found that teachers almost universally agree on the benefits of using a popular system that students already know how to use (Manca & Ranieri, 2013). The Facebook interface has been well refined over time so that it is intuitive and easy for students to use (Albayrak & Yildirim, 2015; Hurt et al., 2012; McCarthy, 2012). If an alternative social networking system is being used, most students are able to easily transfer their familiarity with social networking paradigms in order to operate the new environment (Callaghan & Bower, 2012; Holland & Muilenburg, 2011). Students indicate that Facebook has a better graphical user interface and is easier to use than traditional learning management systems (Petrovic et al., 2014).

CONVENIENT ACCESS

Students appreciate that the use of social networking increases access to learning (O'Bannon et al., 2013). Using Facebook as part of courses provides students with convenience since they are 'already there' and can access it at any time (Albayrak & Yildirim, 2015; Kio, 2015; Schroeder & Greenbowe, 2009). The fact that Facebook is readily available via customized mobile applications that the students are already using means that it is more accessible and convenient for students to contribute (Hurt et al., 2012; McCarthy, 2012). People can keep more updated with course-related developments because they are checking Facebook most days anyway (Irwin et al., 2012). Many students prefer using Facebook for discussions compared to more traditional learning management systems, in part due to familiarity and convenience (Deng & Tavares, 2013; Hurt et al., 2012). And the more people use social networking, the more positive they are about using it for educational purposes (Lim & Richardson, 2016).

DEVELOPING NEW LITERACIES

Another potential advantage of using social networking for learning is that it helps students develop contemporary literacies. The fact that social networking platforms such as Facebook have been designed to facilitate sharing of images and video means that students are readily able to exchange and critique each other's digital work (McCarthy, 2010, 2012). This has led to social networking systems being used as a platform for students to collaboratively develop multimedia artifacts (Manca & Ranieri, 2013). The desire to attract positive attention in terms of visits, recognition and new connections can be an incentive for students to be creative about what they post, in a new literacies sense (Greenhow & Robelia, 2009). Participating in learning communities also helps students to cultivate the collaborative competencies that they will need for future learning and professional success (Fewkes & McCabe, 2012; Greenhow & Robelia, 2009). For instance, academically motivated students can leverage social networking systems to provide them with a personal learning network (Rambe, 2012a).

PROMOTING LEARNER AGENCY AND STUDENT-CENTERED LEARNING

Social networking platforms can provide learners with greater control over the learning environment, and thus support more student-centered learning (Salavuo, 2008). As opposed to learning management systems that are typically teacher controlled, social networking systems can encourage more egalitarian contributions by all users, allowing students to have greater influence over the topics of discussion (Asterhan & Rosenberg, 2015). Students who use social networking technologies can also become more self-directed, which meant that they can discover and create new knowledge for themselves (Hamid, Waycott, Kurnia, & Chang, 2015). A consequence of more self-directed student learning is that the teacher is able to assume a more facilitative role (Callaghan & Bower, 2012).

FACILITATING PEER LEARNING

Social networking systems can help students to learn from one another in a number of ways. At one end of the spectrum, students can benefit from simply using social networking to ask peers for help with course concepts and homework (Fewkes & McCabe, 2012). The ubiquity of social networking can mean students receive more rapid responses to their questions than if using the traditional learning management systems, because peers are more often using social networking platforms (Deng & Tavares, 2013; Irwin et al., 2012; Kio, 2015). In many cases students are able to respond to the questions posted by their peers before the teacher has even seen them, thus reducing the load on the teacher (Lambić, 2016). Students can also learn vicariously by silently observing the contributions and conversations of others (Arnold & Paulus, 2010). In one study researchers suggest the reason that fourth-year graphic design students who used Facebook outperformed those who did not was in part due to the exposure to peer progress and thinking (Güler, 2015).

MOTIVATING CONTRIBUTION AND ENGAGEMENT

Some studies propose that social networks may level the playing field for introverted students who may be shy in face-to-face settings, allowing them to become more comfortable and hence make greater contributions within their learning community (Fewkes & McCabe, 2012; McCarthy, 2012; Rambe, 2012a; Shih, 2011). Students perceive Facebook as being more self-regulated than the traditional learning management systems that are provided by educational institutions, and thus may be more willing to express themselves freely (Rambe, 2012b). For instance, students may be reticent to ask a question in a face-to-face lecture, but may be comfortable to ask in a social networking environment (Bosch, 2009). As students see other students' questions and realize that they are not the only ones experiencing problems they can become more willing to post questions of their own (Rambe, 2012b). The predominantly asynchronous and textual mode of communication is particularly beneficial for students who are not studying in their native language, as it enables them to read and respond to peer comments at their own pace (McCarthy, 2010).

The novelty, popularity and usability of using social networking systems may also lead to increased student engagement (Shih, 2011). One study found nearly four times as many posts on (optional) Facebook discussions than on the traditional (compulsory) LMS forums, as well as more in-depth peer-to-peer feedback (Schroeder & Greenbowe, 2009). Students in another study felt that they interacted more frequently with their teachers in courses that used social networking technologies than those that did not (Hamid et al., 2015). The students also felt that the heightened engagement with the content and peers in the social networking system increased the amount that they learnt (Hamid et al., 2015). Social networking systems can also provide an authentic and motivating environment for language students to develop their writing and comprehension skills (Kabilan, Ahmad, & Abidin, 2010).

ENABLING REFLECTION

Social networking systems provide students with a convenient way to reflect upon classmates responses (Brady et al., 2010). Using the discussion features of social networking systems enables students to learn from their peers through critical reflection, negotiation of meaning, and consideration of alternative perspectives (Beach & Doerr-Stevens, 2011; Manca & Ranieri, 2013). A majority of students in one study felt that social networking enhanced their critical thinking capabilities because they needed to think carefully before posting or responding in spaces that were communally accessible by their peers (Hamid et al., 2015). Students are also able to self-reflect on their learning progress by virtue of comparison with their peers (Hamid et al., 2015).

EXPANDING THE BOUNDARIES OF THE CLASSROOM

In a sense social networking can be seen as providing a bridge between formal classroom learning and informal learning in life outside the classroom (Fewkes & McCabe, 2012). Many students leverage the capacity to access social networking environment outside school hours to access learning materials and collaborate with peers (Callaghan & Bower, 2012; Fardoun et al., 2012). Students in one study agreed that social networking using Ning facilitated out-of-class communication more strongly than any other item on their evaluation survey (Brady et al., 2010).

ENGAGING A WIDER COMMUNITY

One of the benefits of social networking is that it enables students to participate more broadly in communities of practice beyond the people in their class (Salavuo, 2008). For instance, Facebook has been used to enable postgraduate students to mentor under-graduates from different continents as well as draw industry experts into the course, thus providing students with an effective means of professional networking (McCarthy, 2012). Similarly, engaging in a Ning-based professional community enabled pre-service teachers to receive expert input from existing practitioners, hence developing their motivation to engage in professional learning communities once they commenced teaching (Reich et al., 2011). Social networking has also been used to allow pharmacy students to learn about real-world business issues from discussions involving practicing experts (Cain & Policastri, 2011). Being a part of a broader community through social networking can provide students with greater access to learning support (for instance when troubleshooting problems) and enable them to share their creative outputs with a wider audience (Salavuo, 2008).

FOSTERING RELATIONSHIPS AND COMMUNITY DEVELOPMENT

The ability for people to communicate around a common domain of inquiry makes social networking systems eminently suitable for facilitating 'communities of practice' (Gunawardena et al., 2009; Ractham & Firpo, 2011). Students in courses where social networking was used have indicated high levels of support and connectedness so as to enhance their community practices (Hung & Yuen, 2010). The ability to set up personal profiles and engage in social acts is what helps to build up the sense of community (Callaghan & Bower, 2012; Hung & Yuen, 2010; Salavuo, 2008).

Students can use social networking as a means to grow and maintain their relationships with other students (for instance, Arnold & Paulus, 2010; Barbour & Plough, 2009; Greenhow & Robelia, 2009). For example, using Facebook to supplement a traditional English language course enhanced students' sense of friendship and trust (Shih, 2011). 'Friending' one another in the social networking system can even lead to people becoming friends in real life (McCarthy, 2010). Using social networking within a course can lead to student learning networks that are sustained after the semester has finished (Baran, 2010).

Students have identified social networking systems such as Facebook as being superior to learning management systems when it comes to creating a sense of community (Buzzetto-More, 2012). Students appear to feel more comfortable making social contributions to the social networking group for a course as opposed to the official learning management system (Lambić, 2016). Use of Facebook as opposed to traditional learning management system discussion forums has been shown to significantly enhance students' sense of knowing other students and being a valued participant in the class (Hurt et al., 2012).

Use of social networking can also influence the student-teacher relationship. Students can use social networking to establish stronger relationships with their teachers (Barbour & Plough, 2009). Early research indicated that a degree of teacher self-disclosure in social networking systems on average led to higher levels of student motivation, greater student satisfaction with the instructor, and a more positive classroom environment (Mazer et al., 2007). Some teachers have even deliberately used Facebook to improve their relationships with students and provide them with pedagogical support outside class time (Asterhan & Rosenberg, 2015).

PROVIDING SOCIAL SUPPORT

Students explain how social networking can provide social support, such as by "'chatting' online to mitigate school-related stress" (Greenhow & Robelia, 2009, p. 1148). Social networking systems can also support social development and reduce isolation for students who are completing studies online (Barbour & Plough, 2009). In one study, the provision of social networking for online and distance learners to supplement the traditional coursework sites led to substantially increased social interaction between students, including affective support (Barbour & Plough, 2009).

There is even some evidence to suggest that general use of social networking may even result in improved university performance by virtue of social support. A survey of 187 university students found that general use of Facebook was positively correlated with their self-rating of academic proficiency, as partially mediated by improved socialization (Yu, Tian, Vogel, & Kwok, 2010). That is to say, students who used Facebook more felt more socially connected, which in turn supported them to perform better in their studies.

FACILITATING ASSESSMENT

Social networking systems can provide an effective means to conduct assessment. Using Facebook to enable architectural students to create and peer-review photo and video galleries was observed to lead to more interaction and peer learning than traditional approaches, particularly between local and international students within the course (McCarthy, 2010). Facebook also enabled English as a Second Language students to complete peer assessment of their writing tasks (Shih, 2011). The blog tool within Ning provided a means for high school students' to demonstrate their summative understanding of employment concepts through the completion of an e-Portfolio assessment task (Callaghan & Bower, 2012).

Completing assessment tasks using social networking systems can support students in a variety of ways. Postings can provide peers with models so that they can learn vicariously about the requirements of an assignment or task (Arnold & Paulus, 2010). Alternately, students may choose to share materials collected for group assignments (Hamid et al., 2015). Peer assessment approaches in social networking systems enable students to self-examine, review, observe, compare and comment on each other's work, which in turn can enhance their learning (Shih, 2011).

One of the advantages of using social networking platforms is that they allow the teacher to track online discussions and collaboration, which is not possible when using traditional face-to-face approaches (Holland & Muilenburg, 2011). Tracking enables analysis of the way that knowledge and learning have been achieved, rather than mere examination of the final product (Roblyer, McDaniel, Webb, Herman, & Witty, 2010).

Issues and Limitations of Social Networking in Education

As with the use of any technology for educational purposes, there are a variety of issues or constraints that can impact on the learning process when using social networking. Issues and limitations relating to educational use of social networking that arose from the literature are summarized below.

TECHNICAL CONSTRAINTS

Social networking systems place constraints on the way that information is organized and presented, which can impact on the learning process. Limitations of using Facebook as an alternative to an LMS include lack of support for upload of some file formats, and the purely chronological (unthreaded) structure of discussion contributions (Wang et al., 2012). The unthreaded nature of wall posts can mean that it is difficult to follow the narrative of a conversation (DeSchryver, Mishra, Koehler, & Francis, 2009). The descending chronological order of posts means that users need to read from the bottom up (LaRue, 2012). Only the first part of substantive textual contributions is revealed and users need to constantly click the 'see more' link to read the entire post (LaRue, 2012).

The design of social networking systems can often mean that related information is distributed across many people's profiles or 'walls,' resulting in ineffective representation of content and concepts for learning purposes (Zhang, 2009). Posts, comments and chats are not treated as 'objects' meaning that it is not immediately possible to index, search, reference, reorganize and thus integrate discourse into more meaningful higher level knowledge structures (Zhang, 2009). Some consider that social networking systems place lamentable constraints on the visual design and layout of information within their pages (Arola, 2010). Another issue has been that the lack of audio and video communication capabilities in social networking systems may have constrained the development of social relationships (Wang et al., 2012), though Facebook has more recently addressed this through their Messenger system. Technical constraints have led some researchers to conclude that either third party applications are required in order for Facebook to be used as a learning management system, or that social networking should only be used as a supplement to course management systems (Wang et al., 2012).

NEGATIVE STUDENT DISPOSITIONS

It is possible that while some students clearly favor social networking, others simply have an intrinsic preference against it. For instance, in studies examining the use of social networking in distance education many students expressed a preference for face-to-face interaction (Baran, 2010; Brady et al., 2010). Students may object to the increase in notifications traffic caused by other people's postings (O'Bannon et al., 2013). However, student preferences do not appear consistent across studies and cohorts. For instance one early study found that high school students were generally comfortable with the idea of conducting classes using

Facebook (DeSchryver et al., 2009). Students' general familiarity with social networking appears to influence their preferences – as Lim and Richardson (2016) pointed out, students who use social networking more frequently were more positive about using social networking technologies for educational purposes. Another study found that younger students appear more receptive to the idea of using a Facebook group as an LMS (Wang et al., 2012). On other occasions students may not have a resistance to social networking per se, but may be generally reluctant to fully engage in tasks and provide feedback to peers (Shaw, 2016).

OVERLAP WITH OTHER PLATFORMS

If a social networking system is to be used in conjunction with a traditional course website or learning management system, then integration of the two systems can be problematic in terms of clearly demarcating when students should use each (Salavuo, 2008). For instance, using Facebook as well as a traditional learning management system can create unnecessary duplication if the two sites are merely disseminating the same information (Irwin et al., 2012). Poor use of social networking and learning management systems side-by-side can divide student attention surrounding a topic of conversation (DeSchryver et al., 2009). Unless discerningly implemented, the use of two systems can merely create yet another communication channel that students need to monitor (Irwin et al., 2012).

DISTRACTION

Social networking may also have a negative impact on learning by distracting students from the learning tasks at hand. High school students acknowledge that Facebook can be a significant distraction in classes (Fewkes & McCabe, 2012; Mao, 2014). One reason that university students indicate a reluctance to use social networking (Facebook) in their courses was because they felt they would be too easily distracted from their studies (Madge et al., 2009; Ophus & Abbitt, 2009). Students in one study found it significantly more distracting to use Facebook as their online platform as compared to the Moodle learning management system (Petrovic et al., 2014). An examination of 451 students found that the tendency to task-switch between formal study and social networking contributed toward the explanation of why students who used social networking while studying tended to score lower grades (Karpinski, Kirschner, Ozer, Mellott, & Ochwo, 2013). Other research has shown a negative relationship between the frequency with which students check Facebook and academic grades (Junco, 2012).

PRIVACY ISSUES

Using social networking systems in education, particularly Facebook, involves a set of highly complex issues in terms of intertwining formal learning with students' informal personal lives (Manca & Ranieri, 2013). Some students express concern about their peers and teachers being able to see their personal social network profiles as compared to traditional learning management systems (Miron & Ravid, 2015; Ophus & Abbitt, 2009; Petrovic et al., 2014). The presence of learning interactions within the students' personal profile can be seen as an unwelcome intrusion into their private world (Wang et al., 2012). This leads to many students wanting to keep their study and personal networks separate (Grosseck, Bran, & Tiru, 2011; Madge et al., 2009).

Another concern for some students is the potential for teachers to act inappropriately via social networking, where the appropriateness of actions is based on the teacher's intentions (Malesky & Peters, 2012). In one study 37% of students surveyed found high levels of teacher self-disclosure in social networking systems to be inappropriate or highly inappropriate (Mazer et al., 2007). However, other research found that the large majority of students felt it was appropriate for teachers to use Facebook for both educational and social purposes (Baran, 2010).

Perceptions of whether privacy is an important concern can also vary widely between people within a cohort. For instance one study found that approximately 19% of university students only wanted education-related social networking contact with their teachers, whereas approximately 13% of the same cohort felt they only wanted non-educational social networking contact with their teachers (Malesky & Peters, 2012). In another study 46% of students agreed that their privacy would be invaded if their courses and social networking system usage overlapped, whereas 28% disagreed (Lim & Richardson, 2016).

Teachers also indicate that protecting their privacy can be an issue when using social networking with their students (Asterhan & Rosenberg, 2015). Teachers who use social networking to interact with students have experienced boundary issues, for instance in defining the boundary between authority and friendship, or the boundary between availability and responsibility (Asterhan & Rosenberg, 2015).

One of the reasons that users of social networking systems such as Facebook often feel that their privacy is compromised is because they do not feel that they have adequate control over how their information is shared with others (Fox & Moreland, 2015). One study found that students who use Facebook more often and feel more confident about how to use Facebook privacy settings were more likely to engage in positive learning collaboration (Lampe et al., 2011).

It should be noted that social networking platform providers are aware of the privacy concerns held by many users and in recent years have taken steps to increase the control that users can exercise over access to their content (BBC, 2012). Teachers can use privacy settings to manage privacy issues, for instance by changing the class social networking group to private in the case of unwanted contributions by external parties (Buzzetto-More, 2012).

CYBERBULLYING AND CYBERSAFETY

Related to privacy, cyberbullying is another concern when using social networking systems for educational purposes, particularly when younger learners are involved. Cyberbullying can be defined as "using electronic means to cause the victim harm which may occur repeatedly, or result in repeated harm by continued exposure" (DeSmet et al., 2015, p. 192). One study found that cyber-safety and security were the most prevalent concerns held among high school students when using social media (Mao, 2014). Extensive use of social networking sites has been associated with poor psychological functioning in high school children (Sampasa-Kanyinga & Lewis, 2015), although it may be that adolescents with poor psychological functioning resort to social networking as a form of support.

In one study of over sixteen-hundred Singaporean high school students, almost 60% of those who used Facebook had experienced some form of Facebook cyberbullying in the previous 12 months (Kwan & Skoric, 2013). However, the same study showed that 85% of students had experienced some form of face-to-face school bullying, and that being victimized on Facebook is positively correlated with being victimized in school. To this extent Facebook bullying can be seen as a manifestation of a deeper problem, namely bullying behavior more generally (Kwan & Skoric, 2013).

There are a raft of other safety and ownership concerns that educators need to manage, including issues surrounding identity theft, misuse of information for unsavory purposes, stalking, and intellectual property rights (Willems & Bateman, 2011). As well, students may inadvertently leave a 'digital footprint' that is difficult or impossible to remove and that may adversely affect their reputation and opportunities (O'Keeffe & Clarke-Pearson, 2011). Students themselves identify hacking, viruses, bullying and stalking as concerns (Mao, 2014). While addressing each of these in detail is beyond the scope of this section and chapter, Cluett (2010) notes that some of the most extreme risks (such as libel, abuse, bullying and spam) that can arise when using social networking with students are in turn the most straight-forward to manage because page/group administrators have the capacity to block users who post inappropriate content.

ASSESSMENT ISSUES

Assessment can be problematic when social networking is being used because the sharing culture of social networking systems runs in opposition to traditional approaches to evaluating student work (Salavuo, 2008). Plagiarism and the general integrity of online submissions may present as issues that the teacher needs to address (Moran, Seaman, & Tinti-Kane, 2011; Salavuo, 2008). Also, if peer feedback and assessment is being used then it is possible that students may provide incorrect or inaccurate feedback to one another (Shih, 2011).

TECHNICAL SKILLS OF STUDENTS AND TEACHERS

Sometimes student and teacher technical skills can present as problems in social networking environments. Not everyone is familiar with how to use all of the features of social networking, and technical difficulties may occur (Hung & Yuen, 2010). Subtle differences in technical setup can impact upon the learner experience. For instance, if a teacher uses a Facebook page rather than a group to disseminate course-related information it may mean that students do not receive notifications of updates, and this may impact on the administration of the course (Irwin et al., 2012). Thus it is imperative that educators as well as students have a comprehensive understanding of how the social networking platform works before it is used for learning purposes.

NEGATIVE TEACHER DISPOSITIONS

Some research has indicated that academics are generally less likely to use Facebook than their students (Roblyer et al., 2010). A 2011 study of nearly two-thousand university faculty in the United States found that perceived barriers to using social media included privacy concerns, time expended, lack of training, lack of confidence, lack of integration with institutional learning and teaching technologies, lack of institutional support, and issues relating to integrity of online contributions (Moran et al., 2011). Increased teacher workload in terms of examining, evaluating, correcting and responding to students' comments, feedback and assessments can also be a concern (Shih, 2011).

INAPPROPRIATE TASK DESIGN

Just because teachers setup a social networking space for students is no guarantee that students will actually use it (Barbour & Plough, 2009). It can be challenging for teachers to design meaningful activities and encourage students to fully engage with them (Salavuo, 2008). Attempts to inject social networking into classes can appear forced and thus constrain the amount and depth of interaction (Arnold & Paulus, 2010; Wang et al., 2012). Students identify that it very easy for teachers to use social networking technologies poorly, in a way that renders activities pointless (Mao, 2014).

INSTITUTIONAL ISSUES

Another issue, particularly in schools, is that institutions may not support the use of open social networking systems such as Facebook at a cultural or policy level. Students indicate that they would prefer greater use of social networking, and believe that prohibiting or blocking the use of social networking in classes is unnecessary (Mao, 2014). Students also note that many staff have a negative attitude toward the use of social networking in education (Fewkes & McCabe, 2012). Accordingly, there are cultural barriers that may need to be overcome for successful integration of social networking within educational institutions.

Thus, using social networking to form learning communities affords several advantages for educators, but also raises a raft of issues that warrant consideration.

Social Networking Design Vignettes

In order to provide more detailed insight into design issues and potentials relating to the use of social networking in education, two studies are presented as vignettes. The first vignette relates to the use of Ning as a platform for middle school students to learn business studies, and the second vignette investigates the use of Facebook to support second language learners develop their reading and writing skills.

VIGNETTE 1 – USING SOCIAL NETWORKING IN HIGH SCHOOL BUSINESS STUDIES

In one study by Callaghan and Bower (2012) the Ning social networking platform was used to teach business studies concepts to two Year 10 commerce classes. The module, run over five in-class lessons, required students to complete a series of prescribed tasks relating to the topic of 'employment.' A visually appealing interface was designed in order to motivate students and provide them with direct access to all of the learning tasks and instructions (see Figure 8.3). The tasks involved using the chat tools, forum discussions (13 in total), and the blog tool to create an e-portfolio. Students could also add resources to their video and photo albums, and create a profile page. The tools that students were supposed to use were generally prescribed within each task description. The fact that social networking was used to house all module activities meant that students could (and often did) logon to collaborate and complete activities outside class time.

Supported by different types of tools, the learning tasks enabled students to demonstrate different levels of thinking. For instance, students were able to demonstrate factual understanding of definitions by posting their responses on the discussion forums. The e-portfolio task (using the blog tool) enabled students demonstrate higher order thinking skills of synthesis, evaluation and creativity. Figure 8.4 shows an example of how students evaluated and selected information from across the site in order to create their e-portfolio responses.

Figure 8.3.   Front Page for a Year 10 Commerce Module on 'Employment' (Callaghan & Bower, 2012).

A key finding of the study was how the teacher could critically influence student activity and learning outcomes. Across two equal ability classes the teacher who logged into the social networking environment, spent substantial periods of time discussing class content and interacted with students in one-on-one consultations was able to establish a view of the social networking environment as a learning site. Students in this class were able to demonstrate higher order thinking skills by virtue of completing the e-Portfolio task, and used the chat and forums to help one another and troubleshoot learning problems. This teacher also made deliberate efforts to establish a trusting relationship with peers, for instance by asking for students' permission to share their work with other students.

In contrast, in the other class the teacher did not log onto Ning and rarely interacted with students in a face-to-face manner. Students in this class primarily saw the online platform as a social site, and spent the majority of time engaging in solely social activities (social chat, profile creation, gift giving). Because students were somewhat distracted by social interactions, it was difficult for them to develop or demonstrate higher order thinking skills. Thus, use of social networking systems in education

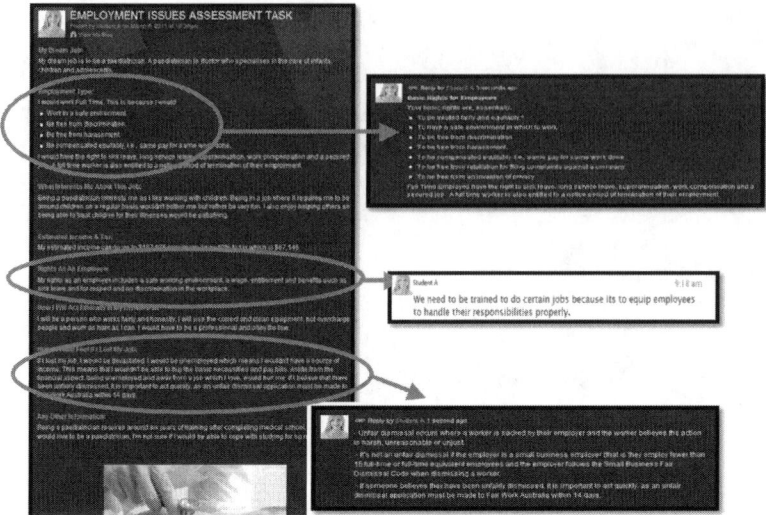

Figure 8.4. Synthesis of Information in an E-Portfolio by Drawing from Contributions across the Social Networking Site (Callaghan & Bower, 2012).

may lead to very different outcomes in different classes depending on how the social networking system is used by the teacher (Callaghan & Bower, 2012).

VIGNETTE 2 – USING SOCIAL NETWORKING TO ENHANCE SECOND LANGUAGE LEARNING

In a study by Shih (2011) Facebook was used to support development of university students' English as a Second Language abilities. Students were divided into writing groups of three or four members and required to post their weekly writing assignments on Facebook. Students then assessed the work of their teammates and provided them with written feedback. They also reviewed and comment on other group members' feedback. Students were able to use emoticons to indicate their tone or show empathy in their posts. An example of one team's Facebook page is shown in Figure 8.5.

According to pre- and post-testing all groups registered significant improvements in the English language ability of their members, with the groups that provided more peer feedback registering greater improvement than groups that provided less. In responses to a 'blended English writing course satisfaction' questionnaire, students indicated that using Facebook to facilitate peer feedback was an effective way for students to develop their English grammar,

Figure 8.5.   An Example of One Team's Facebook English Writing Page (Shih, 2011).

vocabulary, spelling, structure, and content, as well as their learning organization. On a more affective level, student feedback also showed that the approach improved their friendship, trust, interaction, active learning, and learning attitudes (Shih, 2011).

Interviews with students revealed that their motivation to learn English was most influenced by the instructor's teaching techniques, enthusiasm and sense of humor (Shih, 2011). Using Facebook to facilitate peer assessment of their writing tasks was seen as an effective way for them to learn English writing through negotiation of meaning. It enabled them to learn English by not only by applying English in social context, but through finding and receiving corrections. One limitation of using Facebook for learning English was at times their writing became more social, in which case the correctness of their writing could become lax. It was also possible for students to provide one another with incorrect feedback. The teacher reflected that the overall success of the Facebook peer assessment design was dependent on their proactive approach to engaging with students' comments and feedback (Shih, 2011).

Social Networking Learning Design Recommendations

So what design and implementation principles should we adopt to effectively use social networking for education? Research and researchers offer a variety of recommendations for designing learning environments using social networking. As was the case with the previous chapter, some of the recommendations are based on evidence (ranging from large sample quantitative surveys through to individual student perceptions), while other recommendations are based on researcher observations according to their proximity to the data and insights into the educational processes taking place. A synthesis of recommendations from these sources is outlined below.

DECIDE WHETHER SOCIAL NETWORKING SYSTEMS WILL BE USED AS THE PRIMARY MEANS OF ONLINE COMMUNICATION OR AS A SUPPLEMENT

When considering the use of a social networking system one of the first decisions to make is whether it will serve as the main course website or as an adjunct site (for instance when supplementing a learning management system). If the social networking system is being used in conjunction with another course website then it is important to avoid unnecessary duplication of information so that students do not need to spend time disambiguating material coming from the two different sources (Irwin et al., 2012). It is also important to clarify where different forms of student contribution should take place so that student attention is not divided between overlapping conversations in the two online platforms (DeSchryver et al., 2009).

CONSIDER HOW THE ENVIRONMENT WILL UPHOLD PRIVACY

Some students may not feel comfortable about their private life and educational life infiltrating one another through the use of social networking (Grosseck et al., 2011; Madge et al., 2009; Ophus & Abbitt, 2009; Wang et al., 2012). In cases where privacy and safety are a primary concern, for instance in schools and due to institutional policies, then it may be important to use a closed social networking platform such as Edmodo or Ning (Holland & Muilenburg, 2011). If Facebook is going to be utilized, then using a private group can avoid unwanted contributions by external parties (Buzzetto-More, 2012). When using groups to facilitate class interaction, teachers almost always choose to setup a closed group for privacy and security reasons (Manca & Ranieri, 2013). Additionally, individuals can adjust their settings so that the details on their personal profile are not automatically visible to other group members (Miron & Ravid, 2015).

THINK CAREFULLY ABOUT SOCIAL NETWORKING TOOL SELECTION WITH RELATION TO REQUIRED LEARNING TASKS

Selecting appropriate social networking tools for a learning task means that students can more easily contribute and share their thinking. Social networking can be used for students to engage in a wide range of learning processes, for instance participate in discourse, reorganize knowledge, and undertake collaborative actions to complete goal-oriented tasks (Gunawardena et al., 2009). Consequently it is important to consider how different tools might be used to support different types of learning. Practical examples include using wall posts to develop English writing skills (Kabilan et al., 2010; Shih, 2011), or using image galleries for architectural students to create design portfolios (McCarthy, 2010). Sometimes the social networking system may not incorporate all of the features that are required (for instance, a wiki), in which case it may be necessary for educators to draw upon third party applications (Arnold & Paulus, 2010).

LEVERAGE THE COMMUNICATION POTENTIALS OF SOCIAL NETWORKING TO ENABLE STUDENT-CENTERED AND INTERACTIVE LEARNING

The ability to make posts, provide feedback, chat, conduct polls, upload files, organize events as well as share images and videos provides a range of communication potentials for educators and students alike. Leveraging these communication modes can facilitate knowledge sharing and consequently improve learning outcomes (Eid & Al-Jabri, 2016). Encouraging student questioning and peer responses can result in lively subject-matter discussion that enables students to learn through debate and negotiation of meaning (Manca & Ranieri, 2013). It may be useful to reward and re-enforce critical and creative use of social networking systems in order to catalyze constructive knowledge generating practices (Rambe, 2012a).

CONSIDER THE LEVEL OF STRUCTURE AND AUTHORITY THAT WILL BE EXERCISED

Students value being able to use social networking systems to hold discussions, collaborate in groups, organize resources, sharing useful links, source help with homework, schedule events, provide feedback and so on (Albayrak & Yildirim, 2015; Fewkes & McCabe, 2012; Greenhow & Robelia, 2009;

Lambić, 2016). One advantage that the educator can capitalize upon is that students tend to see Facebook as being more self-regulated than institutionally controlled, and thus may be more willing to express their true thoughts and feelings (Rambe, 2012b). An advantage of relinquishing the amount of teacher control is that students are more likely to respond to one another, receiving more rapid responses to their inquiries and reducing the load on the teacher (Lambić, 2016). Students can also help monitor class contributions for inappropriate content (Barbour & Plough, 2009).

UTILIZE AUTHENTIC AND MEANINGFUL TASKS

It can be challenging to set authentic and meaningful learning tasks in social networking environments (Arnold & Paulus, 2010; Salavuo, 2008; Wang et al., 2012). Unauthentic tasks can lead to students feeling that activities are pointless (Mao, 2014). Authentic tasks that relate to student issues and are enhanced through the interactive features of the social networking system are proposed to encourage greater intellectual engagement and contribution (Beach & Doerr-Stevens, 2011). Forging links between the social networking activities and any face-to-face activities – for instance by continuing online discussions in tutorial classes – is one way to promote relevance and extended knowledge building (McCarthy, 2010). Consider that more structured tasks in social networking systems may actually reduce the level of perceived authenticity of social networking usage and thus constrain contributions (Arnold & Paulus, 2010).

BUILD REFLECTION INTO THE LEARNING PROCESS

Social networking technologies enable reflection-on-action as well as "socially mediated metacognition" whereby the learning community reviews how understanding was developed (Gunawardena et al., 2009). Because communication in social networking environments is both open and persistent (recorded) it enables students to reflect on the contributions of others (Brady et al., 2010) as well as their own. Educators can capitalize on this by incorporating reflection and feedback into the prescribed learning tasks (for instance, Shih, 2011). Group reflection has been shown to promote higher levels of learning than individual reflection in socially networked learning contexts (Kim, Hong, Bonk, & Lim, 2011).

MONITOR PLAGIARISM

Because of the openness of social networking systems and easy transfer of information freely sourced from the Internet, plagiarism can occur in social networks. In some cases this is because students do not have a clear understanding of what is (and is not) appropriate sharing of information with relation to assessment tasks (Salavuo, 2008). If contributions to the social networking systems are going to be assessed then identity verification can also become an issue because students are using accounts that are not institutionally controlled and login details can easily be shared between people (Moran et al., 2011; Salavuo, 2008).

OPTIMIZE ASSESSMENT PROCESSES

Using peer feedback within assessment tasks can enhance student learning, but the teacher needs to be involved because in some instances students may provide incorrect or inaccurate feedback to each other (Shih, 2011). Educators also need to consider what will, and will not be assessed – greater participation in social networking has been found to occur when contributions were assessed (Albayrak & Yildirim, 2015). Validity of assessment is also important to consider, with analysis in one study revealing that the amount of contribution being less relevant that the degree of collective reflection in terms of determining the amount of learning that took place (Kim et al., 2011). Expectations also require consideration – if expectations are set too low then the quality of student engagement may suffer (O'Bannon et al., 2014).

CONSIDER ENGAGING A WIDE RANGE OF STAKEHOLDERS

Social networking systems can be used to draw in external parties in order to enhance the learning process (Manca & Ranieri, 2013). Possibilities include collaborations between students located in different continents (McCarthy, 2012), seconding external experts to participate in course discussions (Cain & Policastri, 2011; McCarthy, 2012), engaging in professional learning communities (Reich et al., 2011), and having students at different levels form mentoring partnerships (McCarthy, 2012). There are obviously many more possibilities involving parents, multiple teachers, subject-based communities and the like – in each case potentially providing students with greater learning support and a more motivating learning environment.

TAKE STEPS TO CREATE A POSITIVE LEARNING COMMUNITY

Social networking can be used to facilitate a constructive learning community (Callaghan & Bower, 2012; Gunawardena et al., 2009; Hung & Yuen, 2010; Ractham & Firpo, 2011; Salavuo, 2008). However, simply using social networking systems is no guarantee that a positive learning environment will be established (Bowman & Akcaoglu, 2014; Callaghan & Bower, 2012; Irwin et al., 2012). Thus teachers may choose to apply deliberate strategies in order to create a positive learning community, for example by using ice-breaker tasks to promote class rapport (Munoz & Towner, 2009). Other strategies can be applied in order to encourage ongoing social networking usage by students, including rewards for best responses to questions, teacher uploads of supporting links and guidance, and early moderation of negative comments (Kio, 2015).

CREATE SPACE FOR SOCIAL CONTRIBUTIONS

Students often make more informal and social contributions in social networking systems as opposed to course management systems (Deng & Tavares, 2013). One of the benefits of social networking systems is that they enable students to provide one another with social support (Barbour & Plough, 2009; Greenhow & Robelia, 2009; Yu et al., 2010). However, there is also the possibility that excessive social discussion may interfere with the learning process (Callaghan & Bower, 2012). Depending on the circumstances, the teacher may encourage social conversation, but also establish ground rules around when, where and how it occurs.

INVITE STUDENT INPUT INTO COURSE DESIGN AND IMPLEMENTATION

Because social networking systems are often seen as more egalitarian and less formal (Rambe, 2012b), they can provide an environment conducive to soliciting genuine input from students. Examples include asking students about the topics that they might want to cover, or the groups in which they would like to be placed (Barbour & Plough, 2009). There are undoubtedly a variety of other possibilities in terms of soliciting feedback from students about course design.

CONSIDER STRATEGIES FOR MANAGING GROUP WORK PROCESSES

The ability for students to gather project materials, brainstorm ideas, share written work and provide one another with feedback makes social networking systems a natural platform for group work collaboration (Greenhow & Robelia, 2009; Hamid et al., 2015; Lim & Richardson, 2016). However, students may not be able to self-determine the most effective way to collaborate in teams, in which case the teacher may decide to provide explicit directions about how people should go about their group work projects. For instance, appointing team leaders may enhance the quality of collaboration (Shih, 2011).

VIGILANTLY MONITOR AND MANAGE THE CYBERSAFETY OF PARTICIPANTS

Upholding the health and safety of students is a serious responsibility for teachers. Pre-emptive education by teachers can play a critical role in maintaining the cybersafety of students (DeSmet et al., 2015). While the effectiveness of educator strategies to address cyberbullying have not been extensively substantiated by research, secondary school teachers suggest providing supportive advice to victims, enlisting the support of professionals, involving parents, and talking with the pupils involved (DeSmet et al., 2015). Research has found that parental involvement in cybersafety programs significantly increases students' knowledge of online safety and also the propensity to engage in safe online behaviors (Vanderhoven, Schellens, & Valcke, 2016). In cases of particularly inappropriate behavior it may be necessary to block the offending user (Cluett, 2010).

BE MINDFUL OF MAINTAINING PROFESSIONAL BOUNDARIES BETWEEN STUDENTS AND TEACHERS

Many students feel that large amounts of self-disclosure by teachers is inappropriate (Malesky & Peters, 2012; Mazer et al., 2007). However, some self-disclosure is often well received by students (Baran, 2010; Mazer et al., 2007). At the same time, it may transpire that students do not appropriately respect the privacy of their teachers, for instance in terms of authority versus friendship and availability versus responsibility (Asterhan & Rosenberg, 2015). There are a wide variety of preferences and dispositions within each student cohort (as established above), so maintaining professional boundaries at all times can reduce the likelihood of teacher-student problems arising (Mazer et al., 2007; Munoz & Towner, 2009; Ophus & Abbitt, 2009). Strategies to maintain professional boundaries with students include creating and utilizing a professional user account that is separate from their personal account (Asterhan & Rosenberg, 2015; Munoz & Towner, 2009), not 'friending' students (Munoz & Towner, 2009; Wang et al., 2012), and refraining from initiating personal interactions with students (Teclehaimanot & Hickman, 2011). Also, crucially, learning occurs in a context, and consequently educators must be mindful of their institutional policies surrounding the use of social networking.

CREATE OPPORTUNITIES FOR PROFESSIONAL LEARNING

Teaching in social networking sites is complex because educators not only need to understand how the technological platform operates but also how it can be effectively used to promote learning (Rap & Blonder, 2016). The learning experience may be compromised if teachers do not fully understand or utilize the capabilities of the social networking system (Brady et al., 2010). For instance, the precise ways that the environment is configured can have a large impact on learning outcomes – in one instance using a Facebook group as opposed to a page influenced student participation (Irwin et al., 2012). As such, it may be useful for educators to undertake ongoing professional learning so as to be able to fully leverage social networking system potentials (Brady et al., 2010).

BE ACTIVELY INVOLVED IN THE SOCIAL NETWORKING ENVIRONMENT

Bowman and Akcaoglu (2014) argue that simply creating a social networking page for a course is not enough – the teacher needs to monitor and contribute to the Facebook group if they hope that students will do the same. Teachers also often play a crucial role in soliciting initial involvement, providing learning support and encouraging ongoing contribution (Rap & Blonder, 2016). Teacher participation and contribution in the social networking environment has been shown to lead to greater student propensity to use the social networking system for collaboration (Lampe et al., 2008), increased levels of higher order thinking (Callaghan & Bower, 2012), greater student satisfaction with courses (Çoklar, 2012; Shih, 2011) and better performance on tasks (Kim et al., 2011). Teacher participation can take many forms – for instance, Irwin et al. (2012) recommend that teachers respond to student posts even if students have already provided their opinions, just to promote confidence in the answers.

Concluding Comments on Social Networking Learning Design

Based on the analysis above, it is clear that social networking systems offer great potential for students and teachers alike in terms of supplementing or supplanting the traditional learning management system, but there is also a complex set of issues that educators need to consider when using social networking for learning purposes. As Dyson et al. (2015) conclude, the success of designs appears to depend upon "complex interactions between a number of factors including the timing of content delivery, the integration of social media content with course assessment and the students' own perspectives" (p. 303).

The amount of empirical research into the deliberate use of social networking systems in education is quite limited (Tess, 2013). Based on the current analysis it was apparent that the majority of substantive empirical research related to whether and how students use social networking generally in their lives and its relation to education, rather than how different designs might influence the learning process. While there are several case studies that report on applications of social networking in classes, there is remarkably little work analyzing the effectiveness of design patterns in terms of improving learning outcomes. There are even fewer studies that examine the relative impact of applying different design features within social networking environments.

There is express need for further qualitative analysis of information-sharing and learning patterns within social networking environments (Hung & Yuen, 2010). Greenhow and Robelia (2009) contend that:

> understanding better how … learning occurs in the social and technical contexts young people currently inhabit – e.g., how and with whom expressions are crafted, displayed and utilized, and ideas evolved and distributed through interaction and negotiation – might suggest improvements to instructional designs in formal education (p. 1136).

We simply have not examined in sufficient detail the different ways learning occurs in social networking environments, which constrains the ability of educators to make design decisions from an informed perspective.

There are several questions that beg investigation. What are the optimal ways to blend social networking into face-to-face and distance courses (Arnold & Paulus, 2010)? What factors should be prioritized when making decisions about social networking system integration (Tess, 2013)? How important are the design and functionality of the social networking system in relation to different types of curricular activities (Tess, 2013)? How can the collaborative and cooperative potentials of social networking enhance learning outcomes (Irwin et al., 2012)? What is the role of the instructor in community building and supporting learning (Arnold & Paulus, 2010)? How can cutting edge technologies and social networking applications be used together to further student outcomes and best practice (Greenhow & Askari, 2015)?

There is also scope to investigate how the attributes of the learner may influence activity and how that should be accounted for during environment design. For instance, one study found that participants in a women's study course significantly increased their preferences for online discussion after having used Facebook for course discussions, with no significant change for students in a philosophy course (Hurt et al., 2012). How should the characteristics of the cohort being taught influence our learning designs? Further, how might the nature of different discipline areas (for instance law as opposed to physics) impact upon the way we design for learning using social networking?

Given the rapid pace of technological change, it is difficult to know what might lie ahead for social networking systems. With the current shift toward high bandwidth multimedia communication and immersive environments it is possible that social networking systems may end up appearing more like 3D virtual worlds than static web pages. How this and other changes might impact upon the nature of learning and design is yet to be seen. Ultimately, however, it is unlikely that we will ever be able to merely rely on the use of social networking incarnations to improve learning outcomes — we can expect that it will be the principled design and implementation decisions of educators that will have a significant influence on learning.

References

Albayrak, D., & Yildirim, Z. (2015). Using social networking sites for teaching and learning students' involvement in and acceptance of Facebook® as a course management system. *Journal of Educational Computing Research*, 52(2), 155–179.

Arnold, N., & Paulus, T. (2010). Using a social networking site for experiential learning: Appropriating, lurking, modeling and community building. *The Internet and Higher Education*, 13(4), 188–196.

Arola, K. L. (2010). The design of Web 2.0: The rise of the template, the fall of design. *Computers and Composition*, 27(1), 4–14.

Asterhan, C. S. C., & Rosenberg, H. (2015). The promise, reality and dilemmas of secondary school teacher–student interactions in Facebook: The teacher perspective. *Computers & Education*, 85, 134–148.

Baran, B. (2010). Facebook as a formal instructional environment. *British Journal of Educational Technology*, 41(6), E146–E149.

Barbour, M., & Plough, C. (2009). Helping to make online learning less isolating. *TechTrends*, 53(4), 57.

BBC. (2012). *Facebook changes privacy control*. Retrieved from http://www.bbc.com/news/technology-20693203. Accessed on July 1, 2016.

Beach, R., & Doerr-Stevens, C. (2011). Using social networking for online role-plays to develop students' argumentative strategies. *Journal of Educational Computing Research*, 45(2), 165–181.

Bosch, T. E. (2009). Using online social networking for teaching and learning: Facebook use at the University of Cape Town. *Communicatio: South African Journal for Communication Theory and Research*, 35(2), 185–200.

Bowman, N. D., & Akcaoglu, M. (2014). "I see smart people!": Using Facebook to supplement cognitive and affective learning in the university mass lecture. *The Internet and Higher Education*, 23, 1–8.

Boyd, D. M., & Ellison, N. B. (2007). Social network sites: Definition, history, and scholarship. *Journal of Computer-Mediated Communication*, 13(1), 210–230.

Brady, K. P., Holcomb, L. B., & Smith, B. V. (2010). The use of alternative social networking sites in higher educational settings: A case study of the e-learning benefits of Ning in education. *Journal of Interactive Online Learning*, 9(2), 151–170.

Buzzetto-More, N. A. (2012). Social networking in undergraduate education. *Interdisciplinary Journal of Information, Knowledge, and Management*, 7(1), 63–90.

Cain, J., & Policastri, A. (2011). Using Facebook as an informal learning environment. *American Journal of Pharmaceutical Education*, 75(10), 1.

Callaghan, N., & Bower, M. (2012). Learning through social networking sites – The critical role of the teacher. *Educational Media International*, 49(1), 1–17.

Casey, G., & Evans, T. (2011). Designing for learning: Online social networks as a classroom environment. *The International Review of Research in Open and Distributed Learning*, 12(7), 1–26.

Cluett, L. (2010). *Online social networking for outreach, engagement and community: The UWA Students' Facebook page.*

Çoklar, A. N. (2012). Evaluations of students on Facebook as an educational environment. *Online Submission, 3*(2), 42–53.

Deng, L., & Tavares, N. J. (2013). From Moodle to Facebook: Exploring students' motivation and experiences in online communities. *Computers & Education, 68,* 167–176.

DeSchryver, M., Mishra, P., Koehler, M., & Francis, A. (2009). Moodle vs. Facebook: Does using Facebook for discussions in an online course enhance perceived social presence and student interaction? Paper presented at the Society for Information Technology & Teacher Education International Conference.

DeSmet, A., Aelterman, N., Bastiaensens, S., Van Cleemput, K., Poels, K., Vandebosch, H., ... De Bourdeaudhuij, I. (2015). Secondary school educators' perceptions and practices in handling cyberbullying among adolescents: A cluster analysis. *Computers & Education, 88,* 192–201.

Dyson, B., Vickers, K., Turtle, J., Cowan, S., & Tassone, A. (2015). Evaluating the use of Facebook to increase student engagement and understanding in lecture-based classes. *Higher Education, 69*(2), 303–313.

Eid, M. I. M., & Al-Jabri, I. M. (2016). Social networking, knowledge sharing, and student learning: The case of university students. *Computers & Education, 99,* 14–27.

Fardoun, H. M., Alghazzawi, D. M., López, S. R., Penichet, V. M., & Gallud, J. A. (2012). Online social networks impact in secondary education. Paper presented at the International Workshop on Evidence-Based Technology Enhanced Learning.

Fewkes, A. M., & McCabe, M. (2012). Facebook: Learning tool or distraction? *Journal of Digital Learning in Teacher Education, 28*(3), 92–98.

Fox, J., & Moreland, J. J. (2015). The dark side of social networking sites: An exploration of the relational and psychological stressors associated with Facebook use and affordances. *Computers in Human Behavior, 45,* 168–176.

Geyer, A. M. (2014). Social networking as a platform for role-playing scientific case studies. *Journal of Chemical Education, 91*(3), 364–367.

Greenhow, C., & Askari, E. (2015). Learning and teaching with social network sites: A decade of research in K-12 related education. *Education and Information Technologies,* 1–23.

Greenhow, C., & Robelia, B. (2009). Old communication, new literacies: Social network sites as social learning resources. *Journal of Computer-Mediated Communication, 14*(4), 1130–1161.

Grosseck, G., Bran, R., & Tiru, L. (2011). Dear teacher, what should I write on my wall? A case study on academic uses of Facebook. *Procedia-Social and Behavioral Sciences, 15,* 1425–1430.

Güler, K. (2015). Social media-based learning in the design studio: A comparative study. *Computers & Education, 87,* 192–203.

Gunawardena, C. N., Hermans, M. B., Sanchez, D., Richmond, C., Bohley, M., & Tuttle, R. (2009). A theoretical framework for building online communities of practice with social networking tools. *Educational Media International, 46*(1), 3–16.

Hamid, S., Waycott, J., Kurnia, S., & Chang, S. (2015). Understanding students' perceptions of the benefits of online social networking use for teaching and learning. *The Internet and higher education, 26,* 1–9.

Holland, C., & Muilenburg, L. (2011). Supporting student collaboration: Edmodo in the classroom. Paper presented at the Society for Information Technology & Teacher Education International Conference.

Hung, H.-T., & Yuen, S. C.-Y. (2010). Educational use of social networking technology in higher education. *Teaching in higher education, 15*(6), 703–714.

Hurt, N. E., Moss, G. S., Bradley, C. L., Larson, L. R., Lovelace, M., Prevost, L. B., … Camus, M. S. (2012). The 'Facebook' effect: College students' perceptions of online discussions in the age of social networking. *International Journal for the Scholarship of Teaching and Learning, 6*(2), 10.

Irwin, C., Ball, L., Desbrow, B., & Leveritt, M. (2012). Students' perceptions of using Facebook as an interactive learning resource at university. *Australasian Journal of Educational Technology, 28*(7), 1221–1232.

Junco, R. (2012). Too much face and not enough books: The relationship between multiple indices of Facebook use and academic performance. *Computers in Human Behavior, 28*(1), 187–198.

Kabilan, M. K., Ahmad, N., & Abidin, M. J. Z. (2010). Facebook: An online environment for learning of English in institutions of higher education? *The Internet and Higher Education, 13*(4), 179–187.

Karpinski, A. C., Kirschner, P. A., Ozer, I., Mellott, J. A., & Ochwo, P. (2013). An exploration of social networking site use, multitasking, and academic performance among United States and European university students. *Computers in Human Behavior, 29*(3), 1182–1192.

Kim, P., Hong, J.-S., Bonk, C., & Lim, G. (2011). Effects of group reflection variations in project-based learning integrated in a Web 2.0 learning space. *Interactive Learning Environments, 19*(4), 333–349.

Kio, S. I. (2015). Feedback theory through the lens of social networking. *Issues in Educational Research, 25*(2), 135–152.

Kwan, G. C. E., & Skoric, M. M. (2013). Facebook bullying: An extension of battles in school. *Computers in human behavior, 29*(1), 16–25.

Lambić, D. (2016). Correlation between Facebook use for educational purposes and academic performance of students. *Computers in Human Behavior, 61,* 313–320.

Lampe, C., Wohn, D. Y., Vitak, J., Ellison, N. B., & Wash, R. (2011). Student use of Facebook for organizing collaborative classroom activities. *International Journal of Computer-Supported Collaborative Learning, 6*(3), 329–347.

LaRue, E. M. (2012). Using Facebook as course management software: A case study. *Teaching and Learning in Nursing, 7*(1), 17–22.

Li, L., & Pitts, J. P. (2009). Does it really matter? Using virtual office hours to enhance student-faculty interaction. *Journal of Information Systems Education, 20*(2), 175–185.

Lim, J., & Richardson, J. C. (2016). Exploring the effects of students' social networking experience on social presence and perceptions of using SNSs for educational purposes. *The Internet and higher education, 29,* 31–39.

Madge, C., Meek, J., Wellens, J., & Hooley, T. (2009). Facebook, social integration and informal learning at university: 'It is more for socialising and talking to friends about work than for actually doing work.' *Learning, Media and Technology, 34*(2), 141–155.

Magogwe, J. M., Ntereke, B., & Phetlhe, K. R. (2015). Facebook and classroom group work: A trial study involving University of Botswana Advanced Oral Presentation students. *British Journal of Educational Technology, 46*(6), 1312–1323.

Malesky, L. A., & Peters, C. (2012). Defining appropriate professional behavior for faculty and university students on social networking websites. *Higher Education, 63*(1), 135–151.

Manca, S., & Ranieri, M. (2013). Is it a tool suitable for learning? A critical review of the literature on Facebook as a technology-enhanced learning environment. *Journal of Computer Assisted Learning, 29*(6), 487–504.

Mao, J. (2014). Social media for learning: A mixed methods study on high school students' technology affordances and perspectives. *Computers in Human Behavior, 33*, 213–223.

Mazer, J. P., Murphy, R. E., & Simonds, C. J. (2007). I'll see you on "Facebook": The effects of computer-mediated teacher self-disclosure on student motivation, affective learning, and classroom climate. *Communication Education, 56*(1), 1–17.

McCarthy, J. (2010). Blended learning environments: Using social networking sites to enhance the first year experience. *Australasian Journal of Educational Technology, 26*(6), 729–740.

McCarthy, J. (2012). International design collaboration and mentoring for tertiary students through Facebook. *Australasian Journal of Educational Technology, 28*(5).

Miron, E., & Ravid, G. (2015). Facebook groups as an academic teaching aid: Case study and recommendations for educators. *Journal of Educational Technology and Society, 18*(4), 371–384.

Moran, M., Seaman, J., & Tinti-Kane, H. (2011). *Teaching, learning, and sharing: How today's higher education faculty use social media.* Babson Survey Research Group.

Munoz, C., & Towner, T. (2009). Opening Facebook: How to use Facebook in the college classroom. Paper presented at the Society for Information Technology & Teacher Education International Conference.

O'Bannon, B., Britt, V., & Beard, J. (2014). The writing on the wall: Using a Facebook group to promote student achievement. *Journal of Educational Multimedia and Hypermedia, 23*(1), 29–54.

O'Keeffe, G. S., & Clarke-Pearson, K. (2011). The impact of social media on children, adolescents, and families. *Pediatrics, 127*(4), 800–804.

O'Bannon, B. W., Beard, J. L., & Britt, V. G. (2013). Using a Facebook group as an educational tool: Effects on student achievement. *Computers in the Schools, 30*(3), 229–247.

Ophus, J. D., & Abbitt, J. T. (2009). Exploring the potential and perceptions of social networking systems in university courses. *Journal of Online Learning and Teaching, 5*(4), 639.

Pempek, T. A., Yermolayeva, Y. A., & Calvert, S. L. (2009). College students' social networking experiences on Facebook. *Journal of Applied Developmental Psychology*, *30*(3), 227–238.

Petrovic, N., Jeremic, V., Cirovic, M., Radojicic, Z., & Milenkovic, N. (2014). Facebook versus Moodle in practice. *American Journal of Distance Education*, *28*(2), 117–125.

Ractham, P., & Firpo, D. (2011). Using social networking technology to enhance learning in higher education: A case study using Facebook. Paper presented at the 44th International Conference on System Sciences, Hawaii.

Rambe, P. (2012a). Activity theory and technology mediated interaction: Cognitive scaffolding using question-based consultation on "Facebook". *Australasian Journal of Educational Technology*, *28*(8), 1333–1361.

Rambe, P. (2012b). Critical discourse analysis of collaborative engagement in Facebook postings. *Australasian Journal of Educational Technology*, *28*(2), 295–314.

Rap, S., & Blonder, R. (2016). Let's Face (book) it: Analyzing interactions in social network groups for chemistry learning. *Journal of Science Education and Technology*, *25*(1), 62–76.

Reich, J., Levinson, M., & Johnston, W. (2011). Using online social networks to foster preservice teachers' membership in a networked community of praxis. *Contemporary Issues in Technology and Teacher Education*, *11*(4), 382–397.

Roblyer, M., McDaniel, M., Webb, M., Herman, J., & Witty, J. V. (2010). Findings on Facebook in higher education: A comparison of college faculty and student uses and perceptions of social networking sites. *The Internet and Higher Education*, *13*(3), 134–140.

Salavuo, M. (2008). Social media as an opportunity for pedagogical change in music education. *Journal of Music, Technology & Education*, *1*(2–3), 121–136.

Sampasa-Kanyinga, H., & Lewis, R. F. (2015). Frequent use of social networking sites is associated with poor psychological functioning among children and adolescents. *Cyberpsychology, Behavior, and Social Networking*, *18*(7), 380–385.

Schroeder, J., & Greenbowe, T. J. (2009). The chemistry of Facebook: Using social networking to create an online community for the organic chemistry laboratory. *Innovate: Journal of Online Education*, *5*(4), 1–7.

Shaw, C. M. (2016). Connecting students cross-nationally through Facebook. *Journal of Political Science Education*, 1–16.

Shih, R.-C. (2011). Can Web 2.0 technology assist college students in learning English writing? Integrating Facebook and peer assessment with blended learning. *Australasian Journal of Educational Technology*, *27*(5), 829–845.

Statistica. (2017). Number of monthly active Facebook users worldwide. Retrieved from http://www.statista.com/statistics/264810/number-of-monthly-active-facebook-users-worldwide/. Accessed on February 22, 2017.

Teclehaimanot, B., & Hickman, T. (2011). Student-teacher interaction on Facebook: What students find appropriate. *TechTrends*, *55*(3), 19–30.

Tess, P. A. (2013). The role of social media in higher education classes (real and virtual) – A literature review. *Computers in Human Behavior*, *29*(5), A60–A68.

Toetenel, L. (2014). Social networking: A collaborative open educational resource. *Computer Assisted Language Learning*, *27*(2), 149–162.

Vanderhoven, E., Schellens, T., & Valcke, M. (2016). Decreasing risky behavior on social network sites: The impact of parental involvement in secondary education interventions. *The Journal of Primary Prevention*, *37*(3), 247–261.

Wang, J., Lin, C.-F. C., Yu, W.-C. W., Wu, E., & Gung, C. (2013). Meaningful engagement in Facebook learning environments: Merging social and academic lives. *Turkish Online Journal of Distance Education*, *14*(1), 302–322.

Wang, Q., Woo, H. L., Quek, C. L., Yang, Y., & Liu, M. (2012). Using the Facebook group as a learning management system: An exploratory study. *British Journal of Educational Technology*, *43*(3), 428–438.

Wichadee, S. (2013). Peer feedback on Facebook: The use of social networking websites to develop writing ability of undergraduate students. *Turkish Online Journal of Distance Education*, *14*(4), 260–270.

Willems, J., & Bateman, D. (2011, December). *The potentials and pitfalls of social networking sites such as Facebook in higher education contexts*.

Yen, Y.-C., Hou, H.-T., & Chang, K. E. (2015). Applying role-playing strategy to enhance learners' writing and speaking skills in EFL courses using Facebook and Skype as learning tools: A case study in Taiwan. *Computer Assisted Language Learning*, *28*(5), 383–406.

Yu, A. Y., Tian, S. W., Vogel, D., & Kwok, R. C.-W. (2010). Can learning be virtually boosted? An investigation of online social networking impacts. *Computers & Education*, *55*(4), 1494–1503.

Zhang, J. (2009). Comments on Greenhow, Robelia, and Hughes: Toward a creative social web for learners and teachers. *Educational Researcher*, *38*(4), 274–279.

9 Designing for Mobile Learning

ABSTRACT

Mobile devices, through their capacity to enable anytime-anywhere learning as well as capture, annotate and share multimedia, offer entirely new ways for students to learn. This chapter provides review of mobile learning with a particular focus on learning design. First various definitions and characteristics of mobile learning are examined in order to establish a common understanding of its boundaries and meaning. Example uses of mobile learning in schools and higher education are described as a way to provide a more concrete understanding of design possibilities. Benefits of mobile learning are unpacked, as distilled from the literature, including the ability to provide flexible, accessible, authentic, personalized, ubiquitous and seamless learning. Mobile learning issues are also examined, including technical problems, cognitive load issues, distraction, equity and safety. A primary school science and a university pre-service teacher education vignette are described so as to offer a more in-depth illustration of what mobile learning can look like and achieve in practice. Finally, mobile learning research findings and observations are synthesized into recommendations, to inform and guide evidence-based mobile learning design practices. Opportunities for future research and investigation are also discussed.

Introduction to Designing for Mobile Learning

This chapter provides a comprehensive review of mobile learning design, based on the continuing premise that technology-enhanced learning design principles should be founded upon an in in-depth understanding of the research evidence of the field. Mobile learning constitutes quite a contrast to education using Web 2.0 and social networking technologies in so far as the attributes of the devices being used to undertake activities.[5] If we see common patterns of benefits, issues and design implications emerging across Web 2.0, social networking and mobile learning then we can start to have more confidence that the themes are generalizable. Alternately, understand how mobile learning might be quite different in nature to education using other technologies can inform our learning design thinking.

The chapter will adopt a similar structure to the previous chapters, in order to facilitate ongoing comparison. That is to say, we will start by defining mobile learning and the sorts of technologies involved, followed by an examination of research literature relating to mobile learning uses, benefits, limitations, and design implications. Let's start by exploring the definition of mobile learning.

What Is Mobile Learning?

Mobile learning (or 'm-learning') has been simply defined as "the use of mobile or wireless devices for the purpose of learning while on the move" (Park, 2011, p. 79). The United Nations Educational, Scientific and Cultural Organization (UNESCO) elaborates:

> Mobile learning involves the use of mobile technology, either alone or in combination with other information and communication technology (ICT), to enable learning

---

[5]While mobile learning is different to education using Web 2.0 and social networking technologies because by definition it uses mobile devices, it should be noted that mobile learning activities can use Web 2.0 and social networking apps. This overlap will be explored later in the chapter.

anytime anywhere. Learning can unfold in a variety of ways: people can use mobile devices to access educational resources, connect with others, or create content, both inside and outside the classroom. (UNESCO, 2013)

The 'mobile' aspect of mobile learning at the same time refers to the mobility of the technology, people's mobility in physical space, conceptual mobility between topics of interest, social mobility in how people connect with each other, and learning dispersed over time across formal and informal contexts (Sharples, Arnedillo-Sánchez, Milrad, & Vavoula, 2009). Mobile devices support 'ubiquitous learning,' which is learning anywhere at any time (Shih, Chu, & Hwang, 2011).

Definitions and descriptions of mobile learning (or 'm-learning') within the literature variously emphasize mobility, accessibility, immediacy, situativity, ubiquity, convenience and contextuality (Baran, 2014). In early theoretical thinking about the rise of mobile learning Sharples, Taylor, and Vavoula (2005) identify how emerging views of education as personalized, learner centered, situated, collaborative, ubiquitous and lifelong, can be actualized through mobile technologies which are personal, user-centered, mobile, networked, ubiquitous and durable. In a similar vein Traxler (2007) describes mobile learning as often being personal, spontaneous, opportunistic, informal, pervasive, situated, private, context-aware, bite-sized, and portable. Mobile learning enables educators to push and pull information to and from students wherever they are located, to enable more personalized content and collaborative learning (Motiwalla, 2007). Ozdamli and Cavus (2011) define the core characteristics of mobile learning as being ubiquitous, portable, blended, private, interactive, collaborative and instantaneous, enabling anywhere anytime learning.

Based on a review of several mobile learning models and iterative feedback from academics Kearney, Schuck, Burden, and Aubusson (2012) identify the three key pedagogical features of mobile learning as being personalization, authenticity and collaboration. Each of these three features is in turn underpinned by two sub-constructs, whereby personalization is comprised of agency and customization, authenticity is constituted by situatedness and contextualization, and collaboration is underpinned by conversation and data sharing (see Figure 9.1). According to Kearney et al., it is these features of m-learning designs that enable teachers and students to overcome traditional time and space barriers in order to enhance learning.

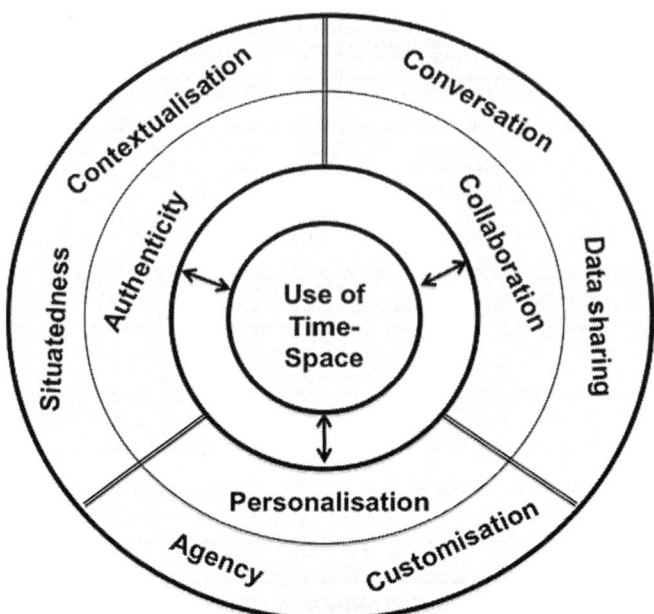

Figure 9.1.   Features of Mobile Learning According to Kearney et al. (2012).

Mobile devices create intriguing opportunities for new types of learning design because they "change the nature of the physical relations between teachers, learners, and the objects of learning" (Laurillard, 2007, p. 153). Traxler (2007) defines various categories of learning enabled by mobile devices, including:

- *Technology-driven mobile learning* that investigates the efficacy of new applications
- *Miniature but portable e-Learning* that enable access to conventional e-Learning from mobile devices
- *Connected classroom learning* that uses mobile technologies in classroom settings to support collaborative learning
- *Informal, personalized, situated mobile learning* where additional functionality of mobile devices such as location awareness or video capture is used to enhance educational experiences
- *Mobile training and performance support* where mobile devices provide just-in-time contextually relevant information to practitioners

- *Remote and rural mobile learning* where mobile technologies are used to address environmental and infrastructure challenges to enable education.

Wong and Looi (2011) identify dimensions of closely related construct, 'seamless' learning, that characterize mobile and ubiquitous learning. Seamless learning is seen as encompassing formal and informal learning, incorporating personalized and social learning, occurring across time and location, involving ubiquitous knowledge access, encompassing physical and digital worlds, possibly combining the use of multiple devices, promoting ease of switching between learning tasks, and potentially encompassing a multitude of pedagogical models. Looi et al. (2010) identify how with mobile technologies:

> the learning space is no longer defined by the 'class' but by 'learning' unconstrained by scheduled class hours or specific locations. With the mobile technologies at hand, students can learn seamlessly — both in classroom and out of classroom, both in school time and after school time. While learning can be facilitated or scaffolded by teachers or peers, at other times it could be student-initiated, impromptu and emergent. (pp. 156–157)

Thus, seamless learning can be characterized in terms of crossing boundaries between in and out of class, as well as between planned and emergent learning (Toh, So, Seow, Chen, & Looi, 2013). Seamless learning can be seen as a subset of ubiquitous learning (learning anytime, anywhere), which in turn can be seen as a subset of mobile learning (learning using mobile devices). This chapter will focus on mobile learning more broadly, on occasions noting how mobile learning supports ubiquitous and seamless learning.

Mobile Learning Technologies

Mobile technologies are constantly evolving and the boundaries between different devices are becoming more blurred, making it difficult to create a definitive list of mobile devices (UNESCO, 2013). Early incarnations of mobile learning devices included personal digital assistants and mobile phones without Internet connectivity, though more recent instances of mobile learning utilize smartphones and tablet devices. Smartphones supersede earlier incarnations of mobile devices by offering the ability to access the Internet, as well as a range of additional capabilities such as touch screens, camera for image and video capture, microphone for audio recording, multimedia playback, location awareness through Global Positioning System (GPS) and compass, and also motion detection through a gyroscope and accelerometer. Samsung distributes the majority of mobile phones globally (25% of the market), followed by Apple iPhone with 15% of the market (IDC, 2016). The different hardware vendors means that there is a range of operating systems used on mobile devices, including Android, iOS, Windows Phone, Chrome OS and variants of Linux.

Tablet devices have become increasingly popular in education, with the additional screen size supporting greater display and interaction with content at any one time. While Apple's share of overall tablet market has reduced in the last five years, the iPad is still the most popular tablet device with 26% of the market in the first quarter of 2016 (Statistica, 2016). Apple iPads are also by far the most popular tablet device used in education (as detailed later in this chapter).

While laptop computers can also be considered 'mobile,' their less portable nature means that they do not lend themselves as well to the transient and spontaneous nature often encapsulated by m-learning, and as such they will not be a focus of this chapter. E-readers and portable audio players can also fall under the banner of mobile technologies (UNESCO, 2013), however, the features and uses of these devices constitute a subset of phone and tablet devices, and so will not be considered as a separate category for the purposes of the following discussions.

Several authors have attempted to define the key educational affordances of mobile technologies. In early work Churchill and Churchill (2008) define the educational affordances of personal digital assistants (early incarnations of smartphones) to be multimedia access, connectivity, multimedia capture, knowledge representation, and information analysis. Looi et al. (2009) argue that the four affordances of mobile technology that enable differentiated instruction and personalized learning are its ability to (i) support multiple entry points and learning paths, (ii) enable multimodal viewing and creation, (iii) facilitate in-situ improvisation, and (iv) allow creation and sharing of artifacts on the move. Melhuish and Falloon (2010) claim that the five unique affordances of m-learning that set it aside from e-learning are: (i) portability (ii) affordable and ubiquitous access, (iii) situated, just-in-time learning opportunities, (iv) connection and convergence, and (v) individualized and personalized experiences. More recently Churchill and Wang (2014) divide the uses of tablet devices into those of (i) a resource tool, (ii) a connectivity tool, (iii) a collaborative tool, (iv) a capture tool, (v) an analytic tool, (vi) a representational tool, and (vii) an administration tool. Thus, there is no universal consensus on the affordances of mobile devices, yet when taken together the various definitions provide a sense of the potentials that mobile devices offer.

Example Uses of Mobile Learning

There is an extensive literature base relating to educational applications of mobile learning. For instance, a review of articles appearing in six high-quality learning technology journals between 2008 and 2012 found that there were over 200 studies relating to applications of mobile learning across a range of subject areas including languages, environmental studies, engineering, and history and culture (Hwang & Wu, 2014). Obviously it is not possible to detail all applications of mobile learning in this section, so a selection have been chosen in order to illustrate the range of possibilities across a variety of education levels, discipline areas, devices, and contexts.

In selecting examples for this section, more contemporary applications have been preferenced (those reported from 2010 onwards) because early instances of mobile learning and associated devices were radically different to those of today. For instance, many of the early applications of mobile learning related to SMS-based activities (Levy & Kennedy, 2005), or pure delivery of information using podcasts (Evans, 2008), which do not showcase the educational potential of contemporary mobile devices and learning designs. Preferencing examples from 2010 onwards also corresponds to an inflection point when the amount of mobile learning research increased sharply (Hwang & Tsai, 2011; M. Liu et al., 2014; Wu et al., 2012) and GPS functionality began to be utilized in applications (Wu et al., 2012).

MOBILE LEARNING IN SCHOOLS

A sizeable proportion of the school level applications of mobile learning occurs at elementary school level. In one review of K-12 mobile learning, the majority of studies (55%) related to primary education (Liu et al., 2014). Mobile devices have been used in primary education to enable students to take field notes, search for information, be provided with scaffolding, and form an embodied understanding of place during historic site visits (Price, Jewitt, & Sakr, 2016; Shih, Chuang, & Hwang, 2010). Interactive mindmapping tools on mobile devices have been used to enable primary school students to learn field-based animal classification within the natural sciences (Hwang, Wu, & Ke, 2011). Primary school students have used mobile devices to capture and annotate photos in order to demonstrate their understanding of English idioms in context (Wong, Chin, Tan, & Liu, 2010). Posting the photos and sentences from their mobile devices to a wiki enabled students to correct each other's grammar and negotiate the meaning of idiom usage (Wong et al., 2010).

Apart from field-based applications, mobile devices are also often used within classrooms to enhance learning. In particular, the iPad tablet device has proven to be a popular tool for in-class learning, and has consequently been the focus of several multi-school investigations (Burden, Hopkins, Male, Martin, & Trala, 2012; Domingo & Garganté, 2016; Goodwin, 2012; Pegrum, Oakley, & Faulkner, 2013; Queensland Department of Education Training and Employment, 2012). Students can use iPads to research on the Internet, complete written work, take photos, shoot videos, as well as create animations, books, or audio recordings (Burden et al., 2012). The type of apps available on mobile phone and tablet devices can vary greatly, from more instructive apps, to apps that allow some manipulation, to constructive apps the enable more open-ended creation (Goodwin, 2012). In their study of iPads in 12 Spanish schools Domingo and Garganté (2016) classify the use of 20 primary school iPad apps as either learning skills tools (e.g., reading, writing, speaking, applying mathematics and literacy, drawing), information management tools (e.g., searching, understanding, analyzing, synthesizing, mapping), or content learning tools (e.g., new vocabulary, mathematics knowledge, phonetics). Through the various apps, the teacher can craft a comprehensive curriculum that increases engagement, autonomy, collaboration and access to information (Domingo & Garganté, 2016).

Popular iPad apps in primary school include Pages, Keynote, iMovie, Brushes, Minecraft, Art Rage, Book Creator, whereas in secondary school students were more likely to use apps like Office HD, Notes, iMovie, Keynote and Calculator (Burden et al., 2012). In another study primary teachers additionally valued Comic Life and Puppet Pals, whereas middle and upper level teachers additionally utilized Garageband and Numbers (Pegrum et al., 2013). There are a host of practice-based sites that provide curations of iPad apps as well as further supporting information. For instance, see:

- Kathy Schrock's iPads4Teaching website: http://www. ipads4teaching.net/ipads-in-the-classroom.html
- The TechChef website: https://techchef4u.com
- The Victorian Government iPads For Learning website: http://www.ipadsforeducation.vic.edu.au

MOBILE LEARNING IN HIGHER EDUCATION

In higher education there is an equally vibrant variety of mobile learning examples. Mobile devices have been used to create web-based trails with extra information for undergraduate museum visitors (Reynolds, Walker, & Speight, 2010). Alternatively, students can record field-based video or voice memos and then upload them for discussion by the class (Gikas & Grant, 2013). Mobile devices have also been used to enable remote students to watch and participate in live lecture classes via interactive streaming services (Wang, Shen, Novak, & Pan, 2009).

Web 2.0 tools are often used in conjunction with mobile devices to support ubiquitous collaboration and sharing. Use of mobile Web 2.0 apps means students can take advantage of connectivity, mobility, geolocation, social networking, personal podcasting and vodcasting while they are on the move (Cochrane & Bateman, 2010). For instance, students were able to perform mobile blogging (including video blogging) in a product design courses to document their thinking as it was inspired by their surroundings (Cochrane, 2010). Mobile devices have been used in conjunction with Facebook to support virtual professional networks and informal learning for medical students in developing countries (Pimmer, Linxen, & Gröhbiel, 2012). Students can use apps such as Storify to curate and critique articles and events using social media (Cochrane, Narayan, & Oldfield, 2013). Alternatively, tools such as Dropbox and Google Docs can be used for people to quickly share files while they are away from their computer (Cochrane et al., 2013). Cochrane (2014) illustrates how Web 2.0 in conjunction with mobile devices can form an overall ecology of collaboration (see Figure 9.2).

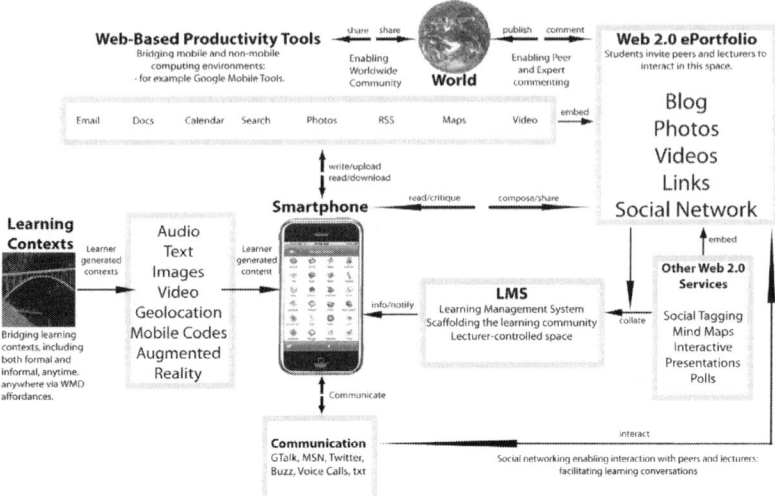

Figure 9.2.   A Mobile Web 2.0 Framework (Cochrane, 2014, p. 71).

Web 2.0 tools can also promote greater in-class interaction. PollEverywhere can be used on mobile devices to create a student response system (Cochrane et al., 2013). An advantage of using voting tools like PollEverywhere and Quickpolls is that students can respond from their mobile phone, potentially anonymously, and this information can then be used to inform the teacher about class perceptions as well as act as a catalyst for discussions (Gikas & Grant, 2013). Alternatively, Twitter via mobile devices provides a simple means of creating a backchannel in class where students can exchange ideas about a lecture (Gikas & Grant, 2013). In classes teachers can use remote presentation devices such as AppleTVs over the wi-fi network to enable mobile presentation using web tools such as Prezi and Slideshare (Cochrane et al., 2013).

A case study of university teachers' iPad usage by Churchill and Wang (2014) provides an indication of popular apps in higher education. They found teachers were often using apps to access content (e.g., iBooks, YouTube, iTunes), facilitate teaching instruction (e.g., TeacherPal, Prezi Viewer, Slides Shark), enable document editing and creation (e.g., iAnnotate, Docs2PDF, Office2HD), communicate with others (e.g., Facebook, Skype, FaceTime), save documents to the cloud (e.g., Dropbox, ZumoDrive, AirDisk), enable blogging (e.g., Wordpress and Blogsy), and record ideas (e.g., AudioNote, Draw Free, Penultimate). Curations of apps can also be found for higher education. For instance, see:

- The University of Vermont Centre for Learning and Teaching: http://blog.uvm.edu/ctl/2010/09/14/ipads-for-scholars-whats-on-your-ipad
- 20 Apps for Academics in Higher Education: http://www.themarketingprof.com/higher-education-marketing/20-apps-academics-higher-education

QR CODES

Mobile devices can also be used to provide rapid access to content by means of Quick Response codes ('QR codes'). Two QR codes are shown in Figure 9.3 below. Free QR code readers can be downloaded from the app store associated with the particular mobile device, and when users scan the QR code with their QR reader their device will be immediately redirected to other content. Content commonly includes static text information or links to websites, but there are a number of other dynamic and multimedia content options. Teachers can create QR codes using QR generator websites such as http://www.qr-code-generator.com. The resultant images can be downloaded and printed, or placed in electronic resources.

Examples of QR code usage include embedding them into science books to provide quick access to online mindmapping via mobile devices (Yang, Hwang, Hung, & Tseng, 2013) or placing them out in the field for situated access to relevant web-based information (Lai, Chang, Wen-Shiane, Fan, & Wu, 2013).

Figure 9.3. Two QR Codes (Daring Readers Might Like to Try Them).

MOBILE GAMES AND AUGMENTED REALITY

There is a vast and varied ecology of other ways mobile devices can and have been used in education, with two notable possibilities including games-based mobile learning and augmented reality. Games-based mobile learning has been widely documented and investigated. They have been used across a range of subject areas, for instance to teach earth sciences (Furió, Juan, Seguí, & Vivó, 2015), languages (Hwang, Shih, Ma, Shadiev, & Chen, 2016), as well as English and mathematics (Goodwin, 2012). Games may variously apply cooperation (Lee et al., 2016) or competition (Hwang & Chang, 2016), but critically should involve some form of feedback (Goodwin, 2012). For a more detailed explication of mobile games see the games-based learning subsection below.

Mobile devices can also be used to create 'augmented reality' learning experiences whereby an information layer is superimposed on the world around us (Bower, Howe, McCredie, Robinson, & Grover, 2014). Augmented reality enables educators to provide students with perfectly situated scaffolding and transcend physical and temporal boundaries (Bower et al., 2014). It can also be used to create situated field-based games (Klopfer & Squire, 2008), classroom-based games (Furió et al., 2015) or even to have students become designers of augmented reality experiences (Bower et al., 2014). Note that augmented reality constitutes a large area of investigation so will not be covered further in this chapter, but for more information about the potential of augmented reality the aforementioned resources offer a starting point.

Benefits and Potentials of Mobile Learning

Mobile devices incorporate increasingly powerful multimedia, communication and geolocation capabilities, which provides numerous opportunities to educators (Kearney et al., 2012). Teachers often have students use mobile devices to access a range of constructive applications such as eBook creation apps, video production apps such as iMovie, audio production apps such as Garageband, and mindmapping apps (Kearney, Burden, & Rai, 2015). The communication features provided by mobile learning devices enables educators to apply social-constructivist pedagogies

(Cochrane, 2010). Various potentials and benefits of mobile learning are outlined below.

PROVIDING FLEXIBLE AND CONVENIENT ACCESS TO LEARNING

By enabling people to access information and collaborate from wherever they are whenever they have access to the Internet, mobile devices enable "malleable spatial-temporal contexts for learning" (Kearney et al., 2012, p. 4). With mobile devices students can access information from any location, for instance downloading notes and viewing websites while on the move (Ozdamli & Cavus, 2011). Students can use mobile devices such as tablets to access information via the Internet, through the institutional portal, or on digital textbooks (Project Tomorrow, 2015). Anytime access can individualize learning by enabling students to work at their own pace, monitor their progress, and access additional help from outside the classroom (Liu et al., 2014). Because mobile devices such as iPads are lightweight and can be kept with students, school teachers can spontaneously integrate them into the classroom learning on demand (Hutchison, Beschorner, & Schmidt-Crawford, 2012).

Fourth grade language students in one study indicated that their immediate and situated access to vocabulary information was a fundamental reason for their significantly better learning as compared to a control group that learnt by traditional means (Huang, Yang, Chiang, & Su, 2016). A study involving over 100 teachers from 12 schools found that highest rated perceived benefits of learning via tablet devices was the access to information that it provided (Domingo & Garganté, 2016). The capacity and convenience of being able to access files and multimedia information while on the move, as well as communicate with anyone, anywhere, anytime, is also highly valued by university students (Gikas & Grant, 2013; Rossing, Miller, Cecil, & Stamper, 2012).

ENABLING COMMUNICATION

Mobile devices are powerful enablers of communication. Teachers can broadcast instructional content such as videos of scientific processes so that students can refer to them as many times as they like at the time and place of need (Ekanayake & Wishart, 2014). Students frequently communicate via their mobile device using email (Project Tomorrow, 2015), or for a larger audience and more rapid response while on the move students can choose to connect via Twitter (Gikas & Grant, 2013; Hsu & Ching, 2012). A review of mobile learning research in K-12 education found the ability to communicate with peers and teachers at any time as well as download content were critical benefits of learning through mobile devices (Liu et al., 2014).

FACILITATING SITUATED AND AUTHENTIC LEARNING

Mobile technologies constitute a shift from user-generated content to learner-generated contexts (Laurillard, 2007). They support the investigation of location-specific phenomena and completion of in-situ field lessons (Liu et al., 2014). There are many wonderful examples of this. For instance, mobile devices have been used to provide students with context specific guidance when learning about the features of local vegetation (Shih et al., 2011). Global Positioning System (GPS) technology have been used to create location aware mobile learning games (Lee et al., 2016). Access to cloud based note taking software (such as Evernote) via mobile devices has allowed people to more spontaneously capture and organize emergent ideas (Schepman, Rodway, Beattie, & Lambert, 2012). Students can photograph and annotate images from personally meaningful user-generated contexts (Kearney & Maher, 2013). Video capture via mobile devices can be used to bring the outside world into the classroom, making use of authentic contexts and promoting learning that is personally relevant (Ekanayake & Wishart, 2014). Similarly, the audio recording capabilities of mobile devices can be used to document thinking wherever it might occur (Wang, Wiesemes, & Gibbons, 2012). Students can then share data, for instance through a blog, immediately as they come across it in their everyday lives (Gikas & Grant, 2013).

A situated approach to learning language whereby primary students took photos of their everyday environment and wrote about them led to significantly better post-test writing performance as compared to a traditional in-class approach (Hwang, Chen, Shadiev, Huang, & Chen, 2014). Adopting a situated outdoor 'web-quest' approach in upper primary school resulted in significantly superior learning results when compared to a classroom-based web-quest (Chang, Chen, & Hsu, 2011b).

MOTIVATING AND ENGAGING LEARNERS

A meta-analysis of 44 studies of mobile learning found that in the large majority of cases (82%) students expressed a significantly greater learning interest as compared to traditional instruction (Hwang & Wu, 2014). For example, a mobile-based inquiry learning module during a cultural site visit led to significantly greater interest and enjoyment than a standard human guide and worksheet approach (Hwang, Wu, Zhuang, & Huang, 2013). Using a gamification approach with mobile devices has been shown to significantly increase attitude positivity toward learning (Hwang & Chang, 2016).

Fourth grade students who learnt language vocabulary via mobile devices as opposed to traditional methods reported significantly higher attention and satisfaction (Huang et al., 2016). The different forms of production enabled by mobile devices can lead to greater participation by typically shy students (Ng & Nicholas, 2013). Large-scale studies of iPad usage in schools are also unanimous about the positive effects on student motivation and engagement (Burden et al., 2012; Domingo & Garganté, 2016; Goodwin, 2012; Pegrum et al., 2013; Queensland Department of Education Training & Employment, 2012).

Increased motivation and engagement can lead to other positive educational effects. Using a student-centered mobile learning approach to help fifth graders learn about botany was shown to significantly increase their subject matter interest (Shih et al., 2011). Teachers also report greater student focus and less time off-task using the student-centered botanical mobile learning activities (Shih et al., 2011). In the iPad Scotland trial over 90% of students surveyed (n = 257) report increases in interest and understanding when using the iPads (Burden et al., 2012). Additionally, 75% of parents felt that the iPad intervention had led to their child being more willing to complete homework (Burden et al., 2012). Higher student motivation to learn with mobile devices has been shown to lead to more time spent learning and therefore superior learning outcomes (Sandberg, Maris, & de Geus, 2011).

PROMOTING PERSONALIZED STUDENT-CENTERED LEARNING

Traxler (2007) argues that mobile learning supports personalized learning because it "recognizes the context and history of each individual learner and delivers learning to the learner when and where they want" (p. 7). There are often multiple entry and exit points for tasks, for instance those that require documentation and analysis in the field (Looi et al., 2009). The large array of apps available and the number of apps that can be used to facilitate open-ended tasks means that teachers are more able to cater to different ability levels (Goodwin, 2012).

Another advantage of mobile learning is that it can facilitate more student-centered learning. When fifth-grade students used a self-directed mobile learning approach to learn botany, they reported feeling not only more liberated but also feeling that they had learned significantly more than they would have through a teacher-led instruction approach (Shih et al., 2011). Using mobile devices to enable first year university students to learn language at their own pace led to significantly better learning performance than in class collaborative group learning (Oberg & Daniels, 2013). Large-scale studies of iPad usage in schools report greater student autonomy and student-centered learning as key benefits (Burden et al., 2012; Domingo & Garganté, 2016).

ENABLING UBIQUITOUS AND SEAMLESS ACCESS

Mobile devices enable ubiquitous learning (learning anywhere, anytime, Shih et al., 2011), and seamless learning (continuity of learning experience across different environments, Chan et al., 2006). For instance, students can take learning out of the classroom, to continue learning in the playground or at home (Pegrum et al., 2013). Using file-sharing apps such as Evernote and Dropbox means that information is also accessible across a range of devices, e.g., laptop, tablet or smartphone (Kearney & Maher, 2013). As previously noted, providing students with access to mobile devices at home as well as school can lead to greater time spent on tasks, which in turn can lead to improved learning outcomes (Sandberg et al., 2011).

ENABLING COLLABORATIVE AND COOPERATIVE LEARNING

A review of mobile learning journal articles published between 2008 and 2012 found that 28% related to cases where students learnt in groups (Hwang & Wu, 2014). Collaborative learning using mobile devices has been shown to result in improved learning outcomes across a range of disciplines including natural science (Liu, Tan, & Chu, 2009), mathematics (Roschelle et al., 2010), languages (Hwang et al., 2014), business (Lee et al., 2016), and computing (Lan, Tsai, Yang, & Hung, 2012; C. C. Liu, Tao, & Nee, 2008).

Mobile devices can be used to provide students with access to a shared workspace where they collate data, post reflections, provide feedback to one another, and negotiate meaning as part of a community of learners (Chen, Tan, Looi, Zhang, & Seow, 2008). One study found that using mobile devices to facilitate online asynchronous problem solving discussions resulted in significantly more sharing and comparing of information between university students, which in turn led to better performance on a group-based project task (Lan et al., 2012). Posting of useful comments on peers' work using mobile devices was found to be highly correlated with primary school students' post-test language writing performance (Hwang et al., 2014).

Well-designed mobile learning tasks can require students to collaborate in order to derive the solutions (Boticki, Looi, & Wong, 2011). For instance, using handheld technology to facilitate cooperative learning of mathematics resulted in primary school classes learning significantly more about fractions than when an individualized computer-based approach was used (Roschelle et al., 2010). The positive interdependence of the approach encouraged students to question, explain, and discuss disagreements, which in turn supported their conceptual development (Roschelle et al., 2010). Using cooperative mobile learning designs where students needed to exchange and discuss information at different stations has been shown to lead to higher levels of critical thinking (Lee et al., 2016).

Alternatively, much of the mobile learning collaboration that occurs has been found to be *at* the device, in terms of pairs or groups working with a single device, rather than *through* the device by means of online communication (Kearney et al., 2015). For instance, technical features of iPads such as screen rotation, a wide viewing angle, multi-user touch input, good audio quality and portability have been shown to support effective collaboration around the device for school children in classes (Falloon, 2015). The portable, tactile and intuitive nature of iPads was also found to support more effective collaborative engagement in undergraduate business mathematics classes, as compared to laptops (Fisher, Lucas, & Galstyan, 2013). As well as through structured tasks, iPads have been found to foster spontaneous collaboration as students help one another use the technology (Burden et al., 2012). Collaboration may also be between students and teachers who work together as part of an authentic learning community (Burden et al., 2012). Students and teachers agree that iPads in the classroom supports collaborative learning (Domingo & Garganté, 2016; Rossing et al., 2012).

ENCOURAGING MEDIA LITERACIES AND DIGITAL CREATIVITY

Mobile devices provide a comprehensive range of tools for image and video creation, editing and sharing, as well as audio recording and editing (Cochrane et al., 2013). Teachers identify access to a camera, voice recorder, the Internet and multimedia through a lightweight touch screen interface as providing excellent opportunities for developing creativity (Goodwin, 2012). For instance, students are able to film, produce and share videos through one app instead of as multi-software project (Burden et al., 2012). The touch screen interface also makes mobile devices such as iPads easier for infants with evolving motor skills and hand eye coordination to operate as compared to a traditional keyboard and mouse (Neumann & Neumann, 2014). This enables students from quite young ages to use iPads to make professional looking digital artifacts with comparative ease (Goodwin, 2012). Additionally, the touch screen can be a particularly useful mode of input to support young children to develop their writing capabilities (Lu, Meng, & Tam, 2014).

CATERING TO SPECIAL NEEDS

Mobile technologies can be particularly useful for students with special needs because the usability, adaptability and portability of the devices enables learning designers to better cater to their cognitive, sensorial or mobility impairments (Fernández-López, Rodríguez-Fórtiz, Rodríguez-Almendros, & MartíNez-Segura, 2013). Text-enlargement, voice transcription, location aware and text-to-speech technologies mean that mobile devices can dramatically improve the learning of students with physical disabilities (UNESCO, 2013).

There is qualitative evidence to suggest that the use of mobile devices such as iPads by students with intellectual disabilities facilitates higher levels of learning than traditional notebooks, in part because the multimodal input options (audio recording and drawing as well as text) provides them with alternative forms of representation (Miller, Krockover, & Doughty, 2013). The multimodal representation possible through mobile devices can also lead to more accurate assessment of understanding by teachers (Miller et al., 2013).

CAPTURING IN-SITU REFLECTIONS

The fact that students carry mobile devices with them most of the time can lead to them being more systematic in terms of documenting their reflections (Kearney & Maher, 2013). For instance and as previously mentioned students can use the audio recording capabilities of mobile devices to capture their reflections wherever they might occur (Wang et al., 2012). Sharing their reflections via the Internet, for instance via blogs or Twitter, enables other students to benefit from these in-situ reflections.

PROMOTING NEW FORMS OF ASSESSMENT

Mobile devices can be used to implement formative assessment during field-work activities, which in turn can improve student learning outcomes (Hwang & Chang, 2011). Having students record and annotate their learning process using photos and videos enables teachers to formatively and summatively diagnose misconceptions (Ekanayake & Wishart, 2014). In the iPad Scotland study the presence of devices encouraged many teachers to explore alternative forms of assessment for learning (Burden et al., 2012). Teachers in the iPad Scotland trial also felt that devices enabled them to provide better feedback to students about their learning (Burden et al., 2012).

PROVIDING MORE EQUITABLE ACCESS TO EDUCATION

One of the greatest benefits of mobile learning is its capacity to expand the reach and equity of education (UNESCO, 2013). The cost of mobile devices is generally far less than for desktop computers, meaning that students and people in developing nations are more likely to be able to afford them (Elias, 2011). As examples, the BridgeIT initiative in Latin America and Asia has brought up-to-date content to geographically isolated schools via mobile networks, and the government of Columbia has provided inexpensive mobile devices to a quarter of a million people in an effort to eradicate illiteracy (UNESCO, 2013).

FACILITATING GAMES-BASED LEARNING

Games-based learning has been utilized in many mobile learning studies (Liu et al., 2014). Custom build mobile games have been used to enhance learning outside the classroom. For instance, using a competition-based mobile learning task during social studies field trip was shown to significantly improve learning interest, learning attitude, and sense of local cultural identity for primary students as compared to the conventional mobile learning approach (Hwang & Chang, 2016). As previously mentioned, a field-based mobile learning game design incorporating reciprocal cooperation led to higher levels of critical thinking (Lee et al., 2016). A mobile language learning game involving students utilizing authentic data from the world around them led to significantly greater speaking performance scores than a traditional classroom approach (Hwang et al., 2016). Gains were attributed to more frequent practice, greater reflection, and the more authentic context that promoted accuracy and confidence over time (Hwang et al., 2016).

In terms of promoting learning in class using publically available applications, teachers generally agree that game-based apps on the iPad can be useful for aspects of the curriculum that demand rote memorization of facts such as spelling and multiplication (Goodwin, 2012). Critical motivating elements of game apps are the instant feedback, different progress levels and competition aspects (Goodwin, 2012).

In sum, offering learning that is more situated, personalized, flexible and so on constitute powerful motivators to consider using mobile learning designs.

Issues and Limitations of Mobile Learning

As well as understanding the benefits and potentials of mobile learning, it is equally important to understand the issues and limitations so as to avoid unnecessary problems in lessons. Mobile learning studies often do not report on the difficulties of conducting mobile learning activities, and if they do it is usually in a brief and superficial manner (Hwang & Tsai, 2011). However, there is a collection of research that highlights the potential pitfalls when using mobile learning designs. Issues and limitations collected from across the research literature are summarized below.

TECHNICAL ISSUES

Designing learning experiences for mobile devices can involve several technical challenges including the variability in the devices used, potentially limited access to the Internet, smaller screen sizes in the case of mobile phones, and depending on the device, there may be limited processing power or memory available as compared to desktop computers (Elias, 2011). Sometimes the small screen and input mechanisms of some mobile devices can make information retrieval and contribution quite difficult (Huang, Lin, & Cheng, 2010; Pegrum et al., 2013). For example, it may be more difficult to input textual information into a mobile device, for instance due to the lack of external keyboard (Elias, 2011; Gikas & Grant, 2013; Rossing et al., 2012). Apps on mobile devices often have a reduced feature set as compared to desktop computers, for instance word processing applications, which can constrain productivity (Hutchison et al., 2012). At times, collaboration around a mobile device such as iPad can be difficult because of the relatively smaller screen size compared to many desktop machines (Rossing et al., 2012). Wireless connectivity (including access to content through institutional firewalls) can constrain the ability to utilize mobile learning in the classroom (Burden et al., 2012; Pegrum et al., 2013).

COGNITIVE OVERLOAD DURING FIELDWORK

For field-based mobile learning the combination of the real-world environment with information represented on mobile devices has the potential to cause cognitive overload. In one study, students who learnt about an art exhibition via mobile devices learnt less than students who completed the learning module component of the lesson back in the computer lab (Martin & Ertzberger, 2013). The researchers posit whether students using mobile devices may have been distracted by their peers or the novelty of the situation during the field-based art appreciation lesson, or whether the students learning by mobile phones may have experienced cognitive overload by viewing the in-situ exhibition at the same time as the mobile learning content (Martin & Ertzberger, 2013). Another study found that requiring students to process text and pictures inside a mobile app as well as real objects outside an app during a mobile learning lesson on leaf morphology led to lower performance than just having text and pictures or text and real objects (Liu, Lin, Tsai, & Paas, 2012). This latter result in direct accordance with the redundancy effect (Kalyuga & Sweller, 2014).

ASSESSMENT ISSUES

Using mobile learning for assessment can also be problematic. Traditional forms of assessment may not accord with more transient and collaborative forms of assessment using mobile devices (Melhuish & Falloon, 2010; Traxler, 2010). For instance, school teachers may be reluctant to employ mobile learning assessment when it is so different in nature to traditional summative examinations (Pegrum et al., 2013). Another consideration is whether devices have the required functionality for students to complete the intended assessment tasks (Hwang et al., 2016).

DISTRACTION AND MISUSE

In the 2015 Undergraduate Students and IT survey, students acknowledged that in-class use of mobile devices could be distracting for them (41% agreement), for other students (49% agreement) or for the teacher (54% agreement) (Dahlstrom, Brooks, Grajek, & Reeves, 2015). Fifty-five percent of U.S. academics believe that students typically use smartphones in their classes for non-class activities (Dahlstrom et al., 2015). Students concede that the small and portability nature of mobile devices makes it easier to hide when engaging in distractions such as social networking, email and games (Rossing et al., 2012). Sometimes the distraction may not be related to off-task behavior, but rather that students find it hard to focus on the teacher's explanations because they are exploring a relevant app or device (Rossing et al., 2012). A minority of parents in the iPads Scotland trial felt that the use of iPads distracted their children from learning, for instance because of the games they could access (Burden et al., 2012). In one study issues such as forgetting their devices, not caring for them, or being distracted by games were the most prevalent type of student issues relating to mobile learning implementation (Ng & Nicholas, 2013).

INTELLECTUAL PROPERTY AND COPYRIGHT

If students and teachers are to utilize the productive and creative capacities of mobile devices to produce videos, share annotated images and the like, then stakeholders (students, teachers, principals, policy makers) need a clear understanding of issues relating to intellectual property and copyright to avoid moral and legal complications (Goodwin, 2012; Traxler, 2010).

STUDENT SAFETY

Particularly in schools and as part of school curricula, students need to be educated about safe, ethical and responsible usage of mobile devices (Traxler, 2010). This may extend from unambiguous concerns such as protecting themselves from contact by strangers and not using devices while driving, to more subjective issues like not using devices while someone is speaking (Traxler, 2010). Some schools insist that devices are not used for audio or video recording without permission from teachers or other students (Pegrum et al., 2013). There is an identified need to conduct student and parent sessions covering issues such as digital safety and cyberbullying (Pegrum et al., 2013).

EQUITY ISSUES

Equity issues may exist when some students do not have access to mobile devices, or have access to lower quality mobile devices (Traxler, 2010). One study found that the introduction of tablet devices into a school led to greatest improvement by students with the worst academic record and benefited historically disadvantaged students, thus contributing to socio-educational equity (Ferrer, Belvís, & Pàmies, 2011).

TECHNICAL SKILLS OF TEACHERS AND STUDENTS

Meta-analysis of research findings have shown that the technical competence of students undertaking mobile learning activities can have a critical impact on the quality of the learning experience (Alrasheedi & Capretz, 2015). Teachers (and students) are typically high-end consumers when it comes to using mobile technologies but very few are producers, meaning that technological and pedagogical support is often required for mobile learning initiatives to be successful (Cochrane, 2014). For instance, teachers may lack the confidence and competence to fix technical problems as they occur (Ng & Nicholas, 2013).

LACK OF PEDAGOGICAL AND TECHNICAL SUPPORT

Half of university faculty that took part in one large U.S. survey indicate that they would like to have more training to help them effectively incorporate mobile devices into their courses (Dahlstrom et al., 2015). School teachers identify lack of resources and expert advice as constraining their endeavors (Ng & Nicholas, 2013). Educators in one study (n = 213) initially identified the need for mobile learning professional development that focused on technology integration and pedagogical coaching, but over time this shifted to an expressed need for more ongoing support and relief time (Crompton, Olszewski, & Bielefeldt, 2015). Support from the institution in terms of technical and administrative support can also critically effect the success of mobile learning endeavors (Alrasheedi & Capretz, 2015).

TIME

Time for professional learning can have a critical impact on the success of mobile learning initiatives (Looi et al., 2014). Pedagogical sustainability of mobile learning depends on teachers' knowledge of the capabilities and limitations of the mobile devices (Ng & Nicholas, 2013). A study of over 100 teachers across 12 schools provided evidence for the rather obvious conclusion that teachers actually need time to use apps in order to understand their potential learning impact (Domingo & Garganté, 2016). School teachers have identified time as an issue when it comes to the extra work required to plan and prepare for mobile learning lessons (Ng & Nicholas, 2013).

INSTITUTIONAL ISSUES

The coordinated support of executive leaders within the institution to foster a positive culture of innovation can make a critical difference to the success of mobile learning initiatives (Ng & Nicholas, 2013). As a starting point, the use of mobile devices in class can in many cases run against the learning policies of the institution, particularly in schools (Liu et al., 2014). Even when institutional policy doesn't prohibit the use of mobile phones in class, some teachers find the use of mobile devices in their lessons to be offensive (Gikas & Grant, 2013). In many classes the use of mobile devices is actively discouraged or banned (Dahlstrom et al., 2015).

Thus, issues relating to mobile learning design span from the instantaneous (such as cognitive load, distraction and technical problems) to the systemic (safety, support and institutional issues).

Mobile Learning Design Vignettes

In order to illustrate some of the potentials and issues of mobile learning, two vignettes are presented. The first vignette showcases the use of mobile pedagogies to enhance the primary school science curriculum, and the second looks at the use of iPads to support pre-service teacher reflection on mathematics teaching.

VIGNETTE 1 – A MOBILIZED 5E SCIENCE CURRICULUM

Looi and colleagues (Looi et al., 2014; Looi, Sun, & Xie, 2015; Sun, Looi, Wu, & Xie, 2016) report on a multi-phase Mobilized 5E Science Curriculum (M5ESC) project in a Singaporean primary school. The approach involved transforming the science curriculum into one with an inquiry-based orientation by leveraging the affordances of mobile technologies. Smartphones were used to support the five phases of inquiry used in their pedagogical model, namely, engagement, exploration, explanation, elaboration and evaluation (the 5 'E's). The approach was based on the epistemological beliefs that science learning should draw connections between ideas and be connected to peoples' everyday lives across multiple formal and informal settings.

The MyDesk application was used, which enabled teachers to set tasks integrating text, graphics, spreadsheets, animations and other multimedia elements, and students to then login, complete and submit the tasks (Looi et al., 2014). For instance, as part of a module of work on Fungi, students used Sketchbook (drawing and annotation), MapIT (concept mapping), Recorder (audio recording), Notepad (data recording), KWL (self-reflection documenter) and Blurb (open-ended questioning) tools, with each activity mapping to one or more components of the 5Es. On other occasions teachers could choose between alternative tools (blogging, forums, video camera, search engines) depending on the requirements of the activity and the components of the 5E model that were being addressed. The system also allowed teachers to provide feedback on students' work. Figure 9.4 illustrates the learning process and the sorts of activities that students undertook.

Using the M5ESC approach, students were able to take greater ownership over their learning by using the mobile devices to complete learning activities (Looi et al., 2014; Looi et al., 2015; Sun et al., 2016). They were able to better relate science to the world around them through seamless capture of data from

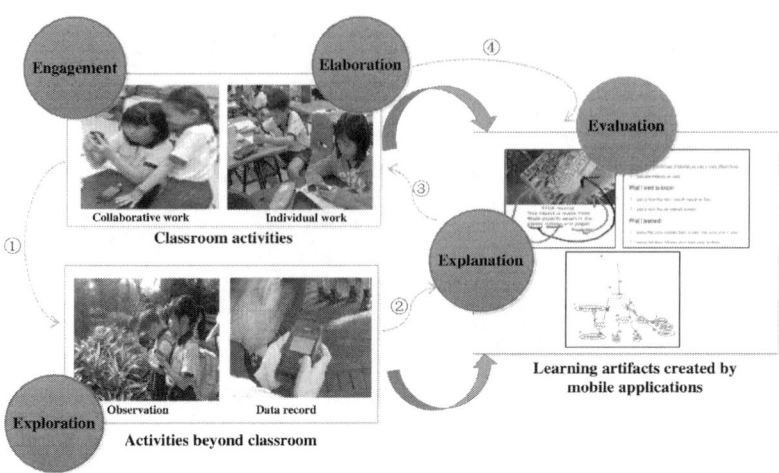

Figure 9.4. Student Annotated Photos to Demonstrate Understanding of Materials and Their Properties (Sun et al., 2016).

their real-life experiences. A constructivist approach was encouraged as learners undertook student-centered inquiry-based activities rather than learning through direct instruction from the teacher. Having students annotate and post findings via their mobile devices from any location meant teachers were more able to focus on students' evolving understanding rather than just summative assessment task results. The classroom culture changed from one of teacher direction to learner autonomy, where students were more likely to work with each other to form an understanding and became more confident completing tasks by themselves. The approach led to significantly higher student performance in test scores, with strongest gains on open-ended questions (Looi et al., 2014; Looi et al., 2015; Sun et al., 2016).

Critical to up-scaling the initiative year-on-year was to ensure that school leadership fully supported the project, teachers were prepared for the change to pedagogy, students were provided with the requisite technology and training, and that a robust technological infrastructure underpinned activities (Looi et al., 2014). Time for professional development and regular meetings between teachers enabled them to shift toward a more constructivist orientation involving inquiry questions, reflection upon phenomena, and a primary focus upon student thinking. The mobile learning initiative has had long term impact because of the transformation in teacher pedagogy that took place (Looi et al., 2014).

VIGNETTE 2 — USING IPADS TO SUPPORT PRE-SERVICE TEACHER REFLECTION

Kearney and Maher (2013) report on how iPads supported pre-service teachers to become more aware of mathematics in the everyday environment and helped to prepare them for teaching authentic technology-mediated mathematics in their future classrooms. The pre-service teachers captured and annotated images from within their user-generated contexts, which in turn formed the basis of reflective discussions with peers and teaching staff in class about how technology and real-world contexts could be used to make mathematics more meaningful. For instance, one pre-service teacher took photos of geometrical shapes in the urban landscape, which she was able to annotate on the train home and then discuss with her peers and teacher in class (see Figure 9.5 left). Another teacher created examples of how fractions could be illustrated using real-world situations (see Figure 9.5 right), noting in her journal that having students create a gallery of such work would cater to different ability levels and interests (Kearney & Maher, 2013).

The iPad enabled instant capture of pre-service teacher field-based experiences and thinking in written, visual, and auditory form (Kearney & Maher, 2013). They could also spontaneously take photos or notes in class so that they follow up later or share with absent peers. File-sharing apps such as Evernote and Dropbox enabled them to synchronize their work across devices. They were also able to utilize the iPads to enhance their teaching practices during their practicum, for instance by using the ShowMe app so that children could reflect upon their explanatory capabilities (Kearney & Maher, 2013).

Across various mobile learning use cases the pre-service teachers displayed different levels of personalization, authenticity

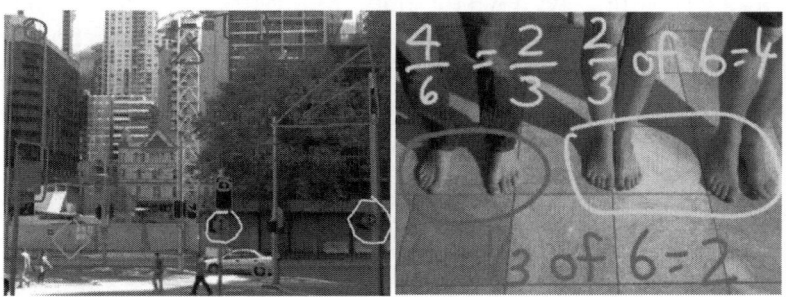

Figure 9.5. Annotated Photos Showing How Geometry (Left) and Fractions (Right) Can Be Found in the Everyday Environment (Kearney & Maher, 2013).

and collaboration (Kearney & Maher, 2013). This is in accordance with the three key dimensions of the mobile learning pedagogical framework proposed by Kearney et al. (2012). High levels of personalization were evidenced through the agency and customization that students exercised, with higher levels of collaboration potentially possible through greater use of Web 2.0 tools to support data sharing and conversation (Kearney & Maher, 2013). Pre-service teachers expressed how the use of the mobile technology had enhanced their capacity to find inspiration from their surroundings so as to make learning more relevant, meaningful and fun for their students (Kearney & Maher, 2013).

Mobile Learning Design and Implementation Recommendations

Having examined educational uses of mobile learning, and come to understand the benefits and issues associated with it, we now examine the research findings and observations that inform mobile learning design and implementation. These findings, as distilled from the research literature and organized into recommendations, are outlined below.

DETERMINE THE PEDAGOGIES THAT WILL UNDERPIN THE MOBILE LEARNING DESIGN

A review of mobile and ubiquitous learning in higher education found that the most prevalent form of pedagogy was an 'instructionist' approach (Pimmer, Mateescu, & Gröhbiel, 2016). While distribution of direct instruction can be convenient and informative for students, we have the opportunity to also utilize mobile learning technologies to take advantage of more constructionist, collaborative, hybridized and situated approaches (Pimmer et al., 2016). This accords with Low and O'Connell (2006), who recommend designing mobile learning environments that emphasize learning rather than technology, and that use situated, networked, distributed and social-constructivist principles.

Several noteworthy mobile learning initiatives are founded upon an underlying pedagogical model and utilize mobile technologies to enact the approach. For instance, Chen et al. (2008) use mobile devices to provide cognitive and collaborative scaffolding in order to help primary students' develop their environmental awareness as part of a Challenge-Experience-Reflect-Plan-Apply model. As we have already seen Looi et al. (2014) determine that the ability to successfully scale a mobile learning science curricula was primarily due to the shift in teachers' pedagogical toward more inquiry-based and constructivist learning based on an Engagement-Exploration-Explanation-Elaboration-Evaluation (5E) model.

UNDERSTAND THE CONSTRAINTS OF THE TECHNOLOGICAL ENVIRONMENT AND ENLIST SUPPORT WHERE REQUIRED

The technological infrastructure that underpins mobile learning can have a critical impact upon the success of any initiative (Looi et al., 2014). Poor wireless connectivity and access to the Internet via the firewall can cause a mobile learning design to fail (Burden et al., 2012; Pegrum et al., 2013). As well, mobile devices can be problematic and time consuming to manage in terms of bulk maintenance and upgrading (Burden et al., 2012; Pegrum et al., 2013; Traxler, 2010). Technological advice and support can be crucial in order for mobile learning initiatives to be successful (Alrasheedi & Capretz, 2015; Cochrane, 2014).

CONSIDER THE SORT OF MOBILE DEVICES THAT WILL BE USED

The nature of the technology — the extent to which it is available, accessible, affordable, cross-platform compatible, and Internet connected — can have a crucial influence on the success of mobile learning initiatives (Alrasheedi & Capretz, 2015; Cochrane, 2010, 2014). Thus, if institutions are purchasing equipment it is important to weigh up the relative advantages and disadvantages of different devices. Alternatively, if a Bring Your Own Device (BYOD) policy is being exercised, students need to be aware of the minimum capabilities that will be required to engage in the mobile learning curriculum.

OPT FOR A BYOD POLICY IF POSSIBLE

Meta-analysis of several mobile learning studies revealed that using students' own mobile devices could have a significant impact on the quality of learning experience (Alrasheedi & Capretz, 2015). Use of own devices has been associated with greater amounts of online learning conversations and more authentic use of mobile devices at school level (Kearney et al.,

2015). Findings from the iPad Scotland trial indicated that device ownership was the most critical element for successful application of iPads in the classroom (Burden et al., 2012).

SELECT THE TYPE OF MOBILE LEARNING APPLICATIONS ACCORDING TO PEDAGOGICAL OBJECTIVES

Appropriate selection of apps according to the underlying pedagogical objectives of the mobile learning design can have a critical impact on student learning (Cochrane, 2010). For instance, teachers in one trial generally agreed that more instructive games-based apps were appropriate for rote learning of facts, whereas productivity apps were better for developing higher order thinking (Goodwin, 2012). Also consider the type of interaction that will be appropriate for the desired outcomes – content creation apps are seen to be more useful for encouraging collaborative learning (Goodwin, 2012).

EVALUATE THE QUALITY OF APPS BEING CONSIDERED FOR USE

While teachers may have a general idea of which type of apps may be more or less suitable for their lessons, there can be great variety in the quality of apps of a particular type. There are several frameworks that have been developed to guide evaluation of apps aimed to help students learning specific knowledge and skills (as opposed to more generic and open-ended productivity apps). Green, Hechter, Tysinger, and Chassereau (2014) recommend considering accuracy, relevance, sharability, feedback, navigation, and inquiry practices of the discipline. As part of a design review of 80 mathematics apps Cayton-Hodges, Feng, and Pan (2015) recommend assessing educational apps on the bases of quality of subject matter content, feedback and scaffolding, richness of interactions, and adaptability of applications. When attempting to select apps that will encourage thoughtful engagement and productive learning Falloon (2013) recommends looking for apps that: i) clearly communicate learning objectives, ii) provide smooth and distraction-free learning pathways, iii) include accessible and understandable instructions and teaching elements, iv) incorporate corrective formative feedback, v) combine an appropriate blend of game, practice and learning components, and vi) provide restrictions on how the target students can interact with the app in order to reduce guessing and unproductive playing. Combinations of elements from these frameworks may be appropriate for different contexts.

GUIDE STUDENTS TO DEVELOP THE PREREQUISITE LEARNING SKILLS

As previously mentioned, the technical competence of students can have a critical impact on the quality of their learning experience (Alrasheedi & Capretz, 2015; Looi et al., 2014). While the intuitive nature of most mobile devices has been noted (Burden et al., 2012; Goodwin, 2012; Pegrum et al., 2013), and students may be able to transfer some of their familiarity with operating mobile devices into learning contexts (Hutchison et al., 2012), the success of a mobile learning initiative may depend on teachers modeling the educational use of the tools to students (Cochrane, 2010, 2014).

PROMOTE SAFE AND RESPONSIBLE USE OF MOBILE TECHNOLOGY

Teachers, particularly in schools, have a duty of care to educate students about the safe, ethical and responsible use of mobile devices (Traxler, 2010). Students may also need directions about how they should care for their devices, particularly if they are owned by the institution (Ng & Nicholas, 2013). Students at all levels will most likely need guidance to understand how copyright, privacy and ethics influence the use and publication of online resources (Goodwin, 2012; Traxler, 2010).

UTILIZE PRODUCTIVE AND OPEN-ENDED MOBILE LEARNING TASKS

Teachers identify the importance of using mobile devices for production rather than just consumption (Pegrum et al., 2013). Evidence suggests that more constructive and productive use of mobile devices can lead to superior learning results. For instance, using an active learning approach where students annotated photos and to-be-learnt content was found to correlate with higher performance in language learning tasks than traditional approaches (Shadiev, Hwang, Huang, & Liu, 2015). The study of iPad integration in 12 Spanish schools found that the greatest learning benefits were derived from using apps that related more to learning processes as opposed to content learning or information management (Domingo & Garganté, 2016). An analysis of pre-school children's exploratory talk and types of engagement when using iPad apps conclude that apps which support easily accessible open-ended content accomplishments had a more positive educational impact than those which did not (Kucirkova, Messer, Sheehy, & Panadero, 2014). Apps that enabled more open-ended creativity (as opposed to those that contained particular content) were also found to be the most popular in the iPad Scotland trial (Burden et al., 2012).

DESIGN FOR EFFECTIVE COLLABORATION AND COOPERATION

Well-designed collaborative and cooperative mobile learning tasks can lead to more effective learning (Hwang et al., 2014; Lan et al., 2012; Lee et al., 2016; C. C. Liu et al., 2008; Liu et al., 2009; Roschelle et al., 2010). Roschelle et al. (2010) found that it was the integrated design involving social participation in questioning, explaining and discussing disagreements that led to greater learning of mathematical concepts, not purely the use of mobile devices or the provision of feedback. Using cooperative mobile learning designs where students needed to exchange and discuss information at different stations was shown to lead to higher levels of critical thinking (Lee et al., 2016). Boticki et al. (2011) conclude that mobile devices can serve as a form of 'technological scaffolding' for collaborative activities in order to provide the structure that increases the effectiveness of peer-based learning approaches.

DESIGN FOR USER-FRIENDLY CONTENT BASED ON MULTIMEDIA LEARNING EFFECTS

Unsurprisingly, a meta-analysis of mobile learning studies revealed that the user friendliness of mobile content can have a significant impact upon the quality of the learning experience (Alrasheedi & Capretz, 2015). Elias (2011) proposes recommendations for inclusive m-learning based on Universal Instructional Design (UID) principles, namely, that educators should design for equitable and flexible use, make interfaces simple and intuitive, provide situated scaffolding, aim for low physical and technical effort, promote interaction with a community of learners, and regularly push and pull information to and from learners. Use of multimedia as opposed to one modality has been show to result in superior learning outcomes on mobile devices (Chang, Tseng, & Tseng, 2011a). Additionally, attention to cognitive load (such as the split-attention effect, modality effect, and redundancy effect) in the design of online resources is proposed to increase cognitive efficiency especially for small-screen devices (Shih et al., 2010). Recall that lower performance by students completing a field-based leaf morphology lesson was attributed to cognitive overload (Liu et al., 2012).

TAKE ADVANTAGE OF AUTHENTIC CONTEXTS TO ENHANCE LEARNING

A review of comparative studies of mobile learning in K-12 education found positive learning gains when students learned academic content in real-world contexts (Liu et al., 2014). In particular, approaches to learning that utilize situated data capture and annotation have been shown to lead to superior learning outcomes (Chang et al., 2011b; Hwang et al., 2014). Students can use mobile devices to capture and annotate their real-world experiences, including through images (Kearney & Maher, 2013), sound (Wang et al., 2012), and video (Ekanayake & Wishart, 2014). Web 2.0 technologies accessible via mobile devices can be used for students to organize and refine their thinking (Cochrane, 2010; Gikas & Grant, 2013).

TAKE AN ACTIVE ROLE IN THE LEARNING EXPERIENCE

Teachers play a fundamentally critical role in determining the success of lessons that utilize mobile devices, not only through design but also implementation (Goodwin, 2012). A meta-analysis of mobile learning research revealed the critical impact of the teacher upon the success of mobile learning designs in terms of their ability to create a positive learning community, their technical competence, and (of course) their pedagogical capacity to integrate mobile learning into the curriculum (Alrasheedi & Capretz, 2015). Falloon and Khoo's (2014) examination of the quality of student discourse when collaborating on iPad tasks found that the teacher plays a crucial role in shifting students toward more exploratory collaboration and thinking (as opposed to disputational interaction or always agreeing with each other).

PROVIDE REGULAR FEEDBACK TO STUDENTS

In order for more authentic activities and assessment approaches to be successful, it may be necessary for teachers to provide regular formative feedback (Cochrane, 2010). Using mobile devices to provide instant feedback to students completing fieldwork has been shown to increase learning achievement and learning attitudes (Huang et al., 2016; Hwang et al., 2011).

BE OPEN TO PEDAGOGICAL SHIFT

The idea of using of mobile devices in class may initially run against institutional policy (Liu et al., 2014) and teacher views of acceptable behavior (Gikas & Grant, 2013). Teaching with mobile devices can require a different sort of pedagogical approach, which involves relinquishing some control and being more flexible (Ng & Nicholas, 2013). Distraction caused by mobile devices can be an issue, but Merchant (2012) argues that "if ways of accessing, sharing and building knowledge are changing then a more principled consideration of how educational institutions relate to these changes is needed" (p. 770). Mifsud and Mørch (2010) recommend avoiding closed mindedness about so called 'off-task behavior' — at times when students are not working on the prescribed learning activities they may be learning about the functionality of their mobile devices or exploring apps that add to their education. An increased acceptance for the use of mobile phones in class may be complemented by student guidance on acceptable practices (Traxler, 2010).

LEVERAGE TEACHER PROFESSIONAL LEARNING SUPPORT AND COMMUNITIES

The quality of staff professional development and support can influence the success of mobile learning initiatives (Cochrane, 2014; Ng & Nicholas, 2013). Teachers identify the need for pedagogically grounded and adequately contextualized professional development to successfully implement mobile learning (Pegrum et al., 2013). Particular professional learning issues for teachers were finding designated time, maintain a focus on pedagogy ahead of technology, and receiving support that was relevant to their teaching circumstances (Pegrum et al., 2013). However, studies relating to the use of iPads found that the devices themselves were reasonably intuitive to use so that extensive professional development about the technology was not required, and could even be counterproductive (Burden et al., 2012; Goodwin, 2012; Pegrum et al., 2013). In any case, creation of a professional learning community around the application of mobile learning is seen as extremely useful for teachers (Burden et al., 2012; Cochrane, 2014; Goodwin, 2012; Pegrum et al., 2013).

Concluding Comments on Mobile Learning Design

By enabling capture of context, annotation of media and sharing data anytime-anywhere, mobile learning undoubtedly offers entirely new ways for students to learn. While these potentials constitute exciting design possibilities for educators, they also come with responsibilities. For instance, as Pegrum et al. (2013) points out, we need to aim to authentically embed mobile learning within the curriculum as part of an 'ecology of learning' as opposed to mere tokenistic uses of mobile devices that replicate pen-and-paper approaches and demotivate students.

Capitalizing on the benefits of mobile learning takes time and commitment on the part of teachers in order to understand the design and implementation implications of mobile technologies within their specific learning contexts (Domingo & Garganté, 2016; Ng & Nicholas, 2013). Additional time is subsequently required in order to actually plan and create the mobile learning designs. For a teacher with a full portfolio, commencing on mobile learning design may be overwhelming and potentially even seem burdensome. But when viewed from a positive perspective, new technology can be a catalyst for teachers to advance their pedagogical thinking and approaches (Goodwin, 2012). The ability to facilitate more authentic learning, encourage multimedia creativity, cater to special needs, orchestrate new types of learning, and perhaps most of all heighten the motivation and engagement of students, provide teachers and institutions with appealing incentives for teachers to undertake pedagogical shift.

In terms of future research, a review of mobile computer supported collaborative learning (mCSCL) research between 2004 and 2011 found that all experimental and quasi-experimental studies related to the use of Palm or Windows OS rather than the currently more popular iOS and Android OS mobile platforms (Hsu & Ching, 2013). Similarly in K-12 education studies of mobile learning tended to evaluate custom built apps rather than "off-the-shelf" apps from online marketplaces such as Apple's App Store or Google Play (Liu et al., 2014). There is a need for further research on use of contemporary social media and Web 2.0 mobile applications to support regular teachers to design and implement effective computer supported collaborative learning (Hsu & Ching, 2013; M. Liu et al., 2014).

There is a wide variety of possible mobile learning applications, ranging from drill and practice learning, to student-centered constructivist approaches, to field-based inquiry learning, all across a wide range of discipline areas (Liu et al., 2014). Typically reviews of mobile learning do not focus upon the different forms, theoretical underpinnings, and practices being applied, yet these attributes of the underlying activities are likely to result in quite different educational effects (Pimmer et al., 2016). With such difference between mobile learning instantiations, there is opportunity to no longer consider mobile learning as one phenomenon for comparative purposes, but rather start comparing research within particular pedagogical and disciplinary contexts. That is to say, we can afford to stop talking about mobile learning as one general phenomenon and start to interrogate different subsets of mobile learning that might share a particular disciplinary or pedagogical approach, so as to understand the nuanced impact of different strategies.

No research was found that actually reported on results of systematically analyzing the transactions between student mobile devices, and apart from work by Falloon and Khoo (2014), no studies analyzed student discussion and behaviors while conducting mobile learning in any structured way (for instance using some sort of qualitative coding scheme). Thus, there is an opportunity to perform more extensive and detailed analysis of the activity that occurs within and around mobile devices in order to better understand how different tasks, technologies and environments might influence learning.

We can anticipate that in the future the sorts of applications available on mobile devices will be more powerful in terms of their creative and communicative capabilities. Evolutions of augmented reality and mobile games are but two examples, with the additional possibility of new types of applications that haven't yet been imagined. As well, the very nature of mobile devices themselves may be radically different in the future. The rise of wearable devices and immersive virtual reality headsets may mean that situated and authentic nature of mobile learning may be simulated as well as in-situ.

Despite advances in technology, we can expect that educators will still need to make decisions about which mobile technologies to use, the sorts of pedagogies that are most suitable for the context, how to promote collaboration and creativity, how to most effectively target and differentiate learning activities based on learner needs, and so on. We know that these sorts of decisions by teachers have a critical impact on the learning experience (Alrasheedi & Capretz, 2015; Goodwin, 2012). Consequently, it is crucial that educators develop flexible learning design capabilities so that they are able to adapt to their particular technological, temporal, social and pedagogical context. The critical mobile learning design factors according to current research have been outlined in this chapter, as a basis for developing more flexible and generalizable design thinking. In the next chapter we examine learning in virtual worlds, to assist in further developing principles for technology-enhanced learning design.

References

Alrasheedi, M., & Capretz, L. F. (2015). Determination of critical success factors affecting mobile learning: A meta-analysis approach. *TOJET: The Turkish Online Journal of Educational Technology, 14*(2).

Baran, E. (2014). A review of research on mobile learning in teacher education. *Educational Technology & Society, 17*(4), 17–32.

Boticki, I., Looi, C.-K., & Wong, L.-H. (2011). Supporting mobile collaborative activities through scaffolded flexible grouping. *Educational Technology & Society, 14*(3), 190–202.

Bower, M., Howe, C., McCredie, N., Robinson, A., & Grover, D. (2014). Augmented reality in education – Cases, places and potentials. *Educational Media International, 51*(1), 1–15.

Burden, K., Hopkins, P., Male, T., Martin, S., & Trala, C. (2012). *iPad Scotland evaluation*. Retrieved from http://www.janhylen.se/wp-content/uploads/2013/01/Skottland.pdf

Cayton-Hodges, G. A., Feng, G., & Pan, X. (2015). Tablet-based math assessment: What can we learn from math apps? *Educational Technology & Society, 18*(2), 3–20.

Chan, T.-W., Roschelle, J., Hsi, S., Kinshuk, Sharples, M., Brown, T., … Norris, C. (2006). One-to-one technology-enhanced learning: An opportunity for global research collaboration. *Research and Practice in Technology Enhanced Learning, 1*(01), 3–29.

Chang, C.-C., Tseng, K.-H., & Tseng, J.-S. (2011a). Is single or dual channel with different English proficiencies better for English listening comprehension, cognitive load and attitude in ubiquitous learning environment? *Computers & Education, 57*(4), 2313–2321.

Chang, C.-S., Chen, T.-S., & Hsu, W.-H. (2011b). The study on integrating WebQuest with mobile learning for environmental education. *Computers & Education, 57*(1), 1228–1239.

Chen, W., Tan, N. Y. L., Looi, C.-K., Zhang, B., & Seow, P. S. K. (2008). Handheld computers as cognitive tools: Technology-enhanced environmental learning. *Research and Practice in Technology Enhanced Learning*, 3(03), 231–252.

Churchill, D., & Churchill, N. (2008). Educational affordances of PDAs: A study of a teacher's exploration of this technology. *Computers & Education*, 50(4), 1439–1450.

Churchill, D., & Wang, T. (2014). Teacher's use of iPads in higher education. *Educational Media International*, 51(3), 214–225.

Cochrane, T. D. (2010). Exploring mobile learning success factors. *Research in Learning Technology*, 18(2).

Cochrane, T. D. (2014). Critical success factors for transforming pedagogy with mobile Web 2.0. *British Journal of Educational Technology*, 45(1), 65–82.

Cochrane, T. D., & Bateman, R. (2010). Smartphones give you wings: Pedagogical affordances of mobile Web 2.0. *Australasian Journal of Educational Technology*, 26(1), 1–14.

Cochrane, T. D., Narayan, V., & Oldfield, J. (2013). iPadagogy: Appropriating the iPad within pedagogical contexts. *International Journal of Mobile Learning and Organisation*, 7(1), 48–65.

Crompton, H., Olszewski, B., & Bielefeldt, T. (2015). The mobile learning training needs of educators in technology-enabled environments. *Professional Development in Education*, 1–20.

Dahlstrom, E., Brooks, D. C., Grajek, S., & Reeves, J. (2015). ECAR study of students and information technology: 2015.

Domingo, M. G., & Garganté, A. B. (2016). Exploring the use of educational technology in primary education: Teachers' perception of mobile technology learning impacts and applications' use in the classroom. *Computers in human behavior*, 56, 21–28.

Ekanayake, S. Y., & Wishart, J. (2014). Mobile phone images and video in science teaching and learning. *Learning, Media and Technology*, 39(2), 229–249.

Elias, T. (2011). Universal instructional design principles for mobile learning. *The International Review of Research in Open and Distributed Learning*, 12(2), 143–156.

Evans, C. (2008). The effectiveness of m-learning in the form of podcast revision lectures in higher education. *Computers & Education*, 50(2), 491–498.

Falloon, G. (2013). Young students using iPads: App design and content influences on their learning pathways. *Computers & Education*, 68, 505–521.

Falloon, G. (2015). What's the difference? Learning collaboratively using iPads in conventional classrooms. *Computers & Education*, 84, 62–77.

Falloon, G., & Khoo, E. (2014). Exploring young students' talk in iPad-supported collaborative learning environments. *Computers & Education*, 77, 13–28.

Fernández-López, Á., Rodríguez-Fórtiz, M. J., Rodríguez-Almendros, M. L., & MartíNez-Segura, M. J. (2013). Mobile learning technology based on iOS devices to support students with special education needs. *Computers & Education*, 61, 77–90.

Ferrer, F., Belvís, E., & Pàmies, J. (2011). Tablet PCs, academic results and educational inequalities. *Computers & Education, 56*(1), 280–288.

Fisher, B., Lucas, T., & Galstyan, A. (2013). The role of iPads in constructing collaborative learning spaces. *Technology, Knowledge and Learning, 18*(3), 165–178.

Furió, D., Juan, M. C., Seguí, I., & Vivó, R. (2015). Mobile learning vs. traditional classroom lessons: A comparative study. *Journal of Computer Assisted Learning, 31*(3), 189–201.

Gikas, J., & Grant, M. M. (2013). Mobile computing devices in higher education: Student perspectives on learning with cellphones, smartphones & social media. *The Internet and higher education, 19,* 18–26.

Goodwin, K. (2012). *Use of tablet technology in the classroom.* NSW Department of Education and Communities. Retrieved from http://clic.det.nsw.edu.au/clic/documents/iPad_Evaluation_Sydney_Region_exec_summary.pdf

Green, L. S., Hechter, R. P., Tysinger, P. D., & Chassereau, K. D. (2014). Mobile app selection for 5th through 12th grade science: The development of the MASS rubric. *Computers & Education, 75,* 65–71.

Hsu, Y.-C., & Ching, Y.-H. (2012). Mobile microblogging: Using Twitter and mobile devices in an online course to promote learning in authentic contexts. *The International Review of Research in Open and Distributed Learning, 13*(4), 211–227.

Hsu, Y.-C., & Ching, Y.-H. (2013). Mobile computer-supported collaborative learning: A review of experimental research. *British Journal of Educational Technology, 44*(5), E111–E114.

Huang, C. S., Yang, S. J., Chiang, T. H., & Su, A. Y. (2016). Effects of situated mobile learning approach on learning motivation and performance of EFL students. *Journal of Educational Technology & Society, 19*(1).

Huang, Y.-M., Lin, Y.-T., & Cheng, S.-C. (2010). Effectiveness of a mobile plant learning system in a science curriculum in Taiwanese elementary education. *Computers & Education, 54*(1), 47–58.

Hutchison, A., Beschorner, B., & Schmidt-Crawford, D. (2012). Exploring the use of the iPad for literacy learning. *The Reading Teacher, 66*(1), 15–23.

Hwang, G.-J., & Chang, H.-F. (2011). A formative assessment-based mobile learning approach to improving the learning attitudes and achievements of students. *Computers & Education, 56*(4), 1023–1031.

Hwang, G.-J., & Chang, S.-C. (2016). Effects of a peer competition-based mobile learning approach on students' affective domain exhibition in social studies courses. *British Journal of Educational Technology, 47*(6), 1217–1231.

Hwang, G.-J., & Tsai, C.-C. (2011). Research trends in mobile and ubiquitous learning: A review of publications in selected journals from 2001 to 2010. *British Journal of Educational Technology, 42*(4), E65–E70.

Hwang, G.-J., & Wu, P.-H. (2014). Applications, impacts and trends of mobile technology-enhanced learning: A review of 2008–2012 publications in selected SSCI journals. *International Journal of Mobile Learning and Organisation, 8*(2), 83–95.

Hwang, G.-J., Wu, P.-H., & Ke, H.-R. (2011). An interactive concept map approach to supporting mobile learning activities for natural science courses. *Computers & Education, 57*(4), 2272–2280.

Hwang, G.-J., Wu, P. H., Zhuang, Y. Y., & Huang, Y. M. (2013). Effects of the inquiry-based mobile learning model on the cognitive load and learning achievement of students. *Interactive Learning Environments*, 21(4), 338–354.

Hwang, W.-Y., Chen, H. S. L., Shadiev, R., Huang, R. Y.-M., & Chen, C.-Y. (2014). Improving English as a foreign language writing in elementary schools using mobile devices in familiar situational contexts. *Computer Assisted Language Learning*, 27(5), 359–378.

Hwang, W.-Y., Shih, T. K., Ma, Z.-H., Shadiev, R., & Chen, S.-Y. (2016). Evaluating listening and speaking skills in a mobile game-based learning environment with situational contexts. *Computer Assisted Language Learning*, 29(4), 639–657.

IDC. (2016). Worldwide smartphone growth goes flat in the first quarter as Chinese vendors churn the top 5 vendor list, according to IDC. Retrieved from http://www.idc.com/getdoc.jsp?containerId=prUS41216716. Accessed on July 25, 2016.

Kalyuga, S., & Sweller, J. (2014). The redundancy principle in multimedia learning. In R. E. Mayer (Ed.), *The Cambridge handbook of multimedia learning* (pp. 247–262). New York, NY: Cambridge University Press.

Kearney, M., Burden, K., & Rai, T. (2015). Investigating teachers' adoption of signature mobile pedagogies. *Computers & Education*, 80, 48–57.

Kearney, M., & Maher, D. (2013). Mobile learning in maths teacher education: Using iPads to support pre-service teachers' professional development. *Australian Educational Computing*, 27(3), 76–84.

Kearney, M., Schuck, S., Burden, K., & Aubusson, P. (2012). Viewing mobile learning from a pedagogical perspective. *Research in Learning Technology*, 20, 1–17.

Klopfer, E., & Squire, K. (2008). Environmental Detectives – The development of an augmented reality platform for environmental simulations. *Educational Technology Research and Development*, 56(2), 203–228.

Kucirkova, N., Messer, D., Sheehy, K., & Panadero, C. F. (2014). Children's engagement with educational iPad apps: Insights from a Spanish classroom. *Computers & Education*, 71, 175–184.

Lai, H.-C., Chang, C.-Y., Wen-Shiane, L., Fan, Y.-L., & Wu, Y.-T. (2013). The implementation of mobile learning in outdoor education: Application of QR codes. *British Journal of Educational Technology*, 44(2), E57–E62.

Lan, Y.-F., Tsai, P.-W., Yang, S.-H., & Hung, C.-L. (2012). Comparing the social knowledge construction behavioral patterns of problem-based online asynchronous discussion in e/m-learning environments. *Computers & Education*, 59(4), 1122–1135.

Laurillard, D. (2007). Pedagogical forms of mobile learning: Framing research questions. In N. Pachler (Ed.), *Mobile learning: Towards a research agenda* (pp. 153–175). London: WLE Centre, IoE.

Lee, H., Parsons, D., Kwon, G., Kim, J., Petrova, K., Jeong, E., & Ryu, H. (2016). Cooperation begins: Encouraging critical thinking skills through cooperative reciprocity using a mobile learning game. *Computers & Education*, 97, 97–115.

Levy, M., & Kennedy, C. (2005). Learning Italian via mobile SMS. *Mobile learning: A handbook for educators and trainers* (pp. 76–83).

Liu, C. C., Tao, S. Y., & Nee, J. N. (2008). Bridging the gap between students and computers: Supporting activity awareness for network collaborative learning with GSM network. *Behaviour & Information Technology, 27*(2), 127–137.

Liu, M., Scordino, R., Geurtz, R., Navarrete, C., Ko, Y., & Lim, M. (2014). A look at research on mobile learning in K−12 education from 2007 to the present. *Journal of Research on Technology in Education, 46*(4), 325–372.

Liu, T.-C., Lin, Y.-C., Tsai, M.-J., & Paas, F. (2012). Split-attention and redundancy effects on mobile learning in physical environments. *Computers & Education, 58*(1), 172–180.

Liu, T.-Y., Tan, T.-H., & Chu, Y.-L. (2009). Outdoor natural science learning with an RFID-supported immersive ubiquitous learning environment. *Educational Technology & Society, 12*(4), 161–175.

Looi, C.-K., Seow, P., Zhang, B., So, H. J., Chen, W., & Wong, L. H. (2010). Leveraging mobile technology for sustainable seamless learning: A research agenda. *British Journal of Educational Technology, 41*(2), 154–169.

Looi, C.-K., Sun, D., Wu, L., Seow, P., Chia, G., Wong, L.-H., … Norris, C. (2014). Implementing mobile learning curricula in a grade level: Empirical study of learning effectiveness at scale. *Computers & Education, 77*, 101–115.

Looi, C.-K., Sun, D., & Xie, W. (2015). Exploring students' progression in an inquiry science curriculum enabled by mobile learning. *IEEE Transactions on Learning Technologies, 8*(1), 43–54.

Looi, C.-K., Wong, L.-H., So, H.-J., Seow, P., Toh, Y., Chen, W., … Soloway, E. (2009). Anatomy of a mobilized lesson: Learning my way. *Computers & Education, 53*(4), 1120–1132.

Low, L., & O'Connell, M. (2006). Learner-centric design of digital mobile learning. In *Proceedings of the OLT Conference* (pp. 71–82).

Lu, J., Meng, S., & Tam, V. (2014). Learning Chinese characters via mobile technology in a primary school classroom. *Educational Media International, 51*(3), 166–184.

Martin, F., & Ertzberger, J. (2013). Here and now mobile learning: An experimental study on the use of mobile technology. *Computers & Education, 68*, 76–85.

Melhuish, K., & Falloon, G. (2010). Looking to the future: M-learning with the iPad.

Merchant, G. (2012). Mobile practices in everyday life: Popular digital technologies and schooling revisited. *British Journal of Educational Technology, 43*(5), 770–782.

Mifsud, L., & Mørch, A. I. (2010). Reconsidering off-task: A comparative study of PDA-mediated activities in four classrooms. *Journal of Computer Assisted Learning, 26*(3), 190–201.

Miller, B. T., Krockover, G. H., & Doughty, T. (2013). Using iPads to teach inquiry science to students with a moderate to severe intellectual disability: A pilot study. *Journal of Research in Science Teaching, 50*(8), 887–911.

Motiwalla, L. F. (2007). Mobile learning: A framework and evaluation. *Computers & Education, 49*(3), 581–596.

Neumann, M. M., & Neumann, D. L. (2014). Touch screen tablets and emergent literacy. *Early Childhood Education Journal, 42*(4), 231–239.

Ng, W., & Nicholas, H. (2013). A framework for sustainable mobile learning in schools. *British Journal of Educational Technology, 44*(5), 695–715.

Oberg, A., & Daniels, P. (2013). Analysis of the effect a student-centred mobile learning instructional method has on language acquisition. *Computer Assisted Language Learning, 26*(2), 177–196.

Ozdamli, F., & Cavus, N. (2011). Basic elements and characteristics of mobile learning. *Procedia-Social and Behavioral Sciences, 28*, 937–942.

Park, Y. (2011). A pedagogical framework for mobile learning: Categorizing educational applications of mobile technologies into four types. *The International Review of Research in Open and Distributed Learning, 12*(2), 78–102.

Pegrum, M., Oakley, G., & Faulkner, R. (2013). Schools going mobile: A study of the adoption of mobile handheld technologies in Western Australian independent schools. *Australasian Journal of Educational Technology, 29*(1), 66–81.

Pimmer, C., Linxen, S., & Gröhbiel, U. (2012). Facebook as a learning tool? A case study on the appropriation of social network sites from mobile phones in developing countries. *British Journal of Educational Technology, 43*(5), 726–738.

Pimmer, C., Mateescu, M., & Gröhbiel, U. (2016). Mobile and ubiquitous learning in higher education settings. A systematic review of empirical studies. *Computers in Human Behavior, 63*, 490–501.

Price, S., Jewitt, C., & Sakr, M. (2016). Embodied experiences of place: A study of history learning with mobile technologies. *Journal of Computer Assisted Learning, 32*(4), 345–359.

Project Tomorrow. (2015). *Digital learning 24/7 – Understanding technology-enhanced learning in the lives of today's students.* Retrieved from http://www.tomorrow.org/speakup/SU14DigitalLearning24-7_StudentReport.html

Queensland Department of Education Training and Employment. (2012). *iPad trial report.* Retrieved from http://education.qld.gov.au/smartclassrooms/documents/enterprise-platform/pdf/ipad-trial-report.pdf

Reynolds, R., Walker, K., & Speight, C. (2010). Web-based museum trails on PDAs for university-level design students: Design and evaluation. *Computers & Education, 55*(3), 994–1003.

Roschelle, J., Rafanan, K., Bhanot, R., Estrella, G., Penuel, B., Nussbaum, M., & Claro, S. (2010). Scaffolding group explanation and feedback with handheld technology: Impact on students' mathematics learning. *Educational Technology Research and Development, 58*(4), 399–419.

Rossing, J. P., Miller, W. M., Cecil, A. K., & Stamper, S. E. (2012). iLearning: The future of higher education? Student perceptions on learning with mobile tablets. *Journal of the Scholarship of Teaching and Learning, 12*(2), 1–26.

Sandberg, J., Maris, M., & de Geus, K. (2011). Mobile English learning: An evidence-based study with fifth graders. *Computers & Education*, *57*(1), 1334–1347.

Schepman, A., Rodway, P., Beattie, C., & Lambert, J. (2012). An observational study of undergraduate students' adoption of (mobile) note-taking software. *Computers in Human Behavior*, *28*(2), 308–317.

Shadiev, R., Hwang, W.-Y., Huang, Y.-M., & Liu, T.-Y. (2015). The impact of supported and annotated mobile learning on achievement and cognitive load. *Journal of Educational Technology & Society*, *18*(4), 53–69.

Sharples, M., Arnedillo-Sánchez, I., Milrad, M., & Vavoula, G. (2009). Mobile learning. *Technology-Enhanced Learning* (pp. 233–249). Springer.

Sharples, M., Taylor, J., & Vavoula, G. (2005). Towards a theory of mobile learning. Paper presented at the Proceedings of mLearn.

Shih, J.-L., Chu, H.-C., & Hwang, G.-J. (2011). An investigation of attitudes of students and teachers about participating in a context-aware ubiquitous learning activity. *British Journal of Educational Technology*, *42*(3), 373–394.

Shih, J.-L., Chuang, C.-W., & Hwang, G.-J. (2010). An inquiry-based mobile learning approach to enhancing social science learning effectiveness. *Educational Technology & Society*, *13*(4), 50–62.

Statistica. (2016). Global market share held by tablet vendors from 2nd quarter 2011 to 2nd quarter 2016. Retrieved from http://www.statista.com/statistics/276635/market-share-held-by-tablet-vendors/. Accessed on February 25, 2017.

Sun, D., Looi, C.-K., Wu, L., & Xie, W. (2016). The innovative immersion of mobile learning into a science curriculum in Singapore: An exploratory study. *Research in Science Education*, *46*(4), 547–573.

Toh, Y., So, H.-J., Seow, P., Chen, W., & Looi, C.-K. (2013). Seamless learning in the mobile age: A theoretical and methodological discussion on using cooperative inquiry to study digital kids on-the-move. *Learning, Media and Technology*, *38*(3), 301–318.

Traxler, J. (2007). Defining, discussing and evaluating mobile learning: The moving finger writes and having writ.... . *The International Review of Research in Open and Distributed Learning*, *8*(2).

Traxler, J. (2010). Will student devices deliver innovation, inclusion, and transformation? *Journal of the Research Center for Educational Technology*, *6*(1), 3–15.

UNESCO. (2013). *Policy guidelines for mobile learning*. Retrieved from http://unesdoc.unesco.org/images/0021/002196/219641E.pdf

Wang, M., Shen, R., Novak, D., & Pan, X. (2009). The impact of mobile learning on students' learning behaviours and performance: Report from a large blended classroom. *British Journal of Educational Technology*, *40*(4), 673–695.

Wang, R., Wiesemes, R., & Gibbons, C. (2012). Developing digital fluency through ubiquitous mobile devices: Findings from a small-scale study. *Computers & Education*, *58*(1), 570–578.

Wong, L.-H., Chin, C.-K., Tan, C.-L., & Liu, M. (2010). Students' personal and social meaning making in a Chinese idiom mobile learning environment. *Educational Technology & Society*, *13*(4), 15–26.

Wong, L.-H., & Looi, C.-K. (2011). What seams do we remove in mobile-assisted seamless learning? A critical review of the literature. *Computers & Education*, *57*(4), 2364–2381.

Wu, W.-H., Wu, Y.-C. J., Chen, C.-Y., Kao, H.-Y., Lin, C.-H., & Huang, S.-H. (2012). Review of trends from mobile learning studies: A meta-analysis. *Computers & Education*, *59*(2), 817–827.

Yang, C.-C., Hwang, G.-J., Hung, C.-M., & Tseng, S.-S. (2013). An evaluation of the learning effectiveness of concept map-based science book reading via mobile devices. *Educational Technology & Society*, *16*(3), 167–178.

10 Designing for Learning Using Virtual Worlds

ABSTRACT

The ability for learners to interact online via their avatars in a 3-D simulation space means that virtual worlds afford a host of educational opportunities not offered by other learning technology platforms, but their use also raises several pertinent issues that warrant consideration. This chapter reviews the educational use of virtual worlds from a design perspective. Virtual-world definitions are explored, along with their key educational characteristics. Different virtual-world environments are briefly contrasted, including Second Life, Active Worlds, Open Sim, and Minecraft. A wide variety of virtual-world uses in schools and universities are examined so as to understand their versatility. Key educational benefits of virtual worlds are distilled from the literature, such as the ability to facilitate 3-D simulations, role-plays, construction tasks, and immersive learning. Emergent issues surrounding the use of virtual worlds are also analyzed, including cognitive load, safety, and representational fidelity. One higher education and one school level vignette are provided in order to offer more detailed insight into the use of virtual worlds in practice. Recommendations for learning design and implementation are presented, based on the thematic analysis of contemporary virtual-worlds research.

Introduction to Designing for Learning Using Virtual Worlds

This chapter is the final of the four chapters to review research relating to the educational use of a technology platform, this time virtual worlds. Virtual worlds are quite different in nature to Web 2.0, social networking and mobile technologies, which make them a particularly interesting and useful point of contrast. If patterns in the benefits, issues and design recommendations extend out to virtual worlds, then we can start to conclude that the themes are reasonably generalizable across learning technology platforms.

Once again, a similar format to previous chapters will be adopted to facilitate comparison. That is to say, first we will examine the definitions and characteristics of virtual worlds, followed by educational uses, benefits, issues, and design recommendations arising from the literature. Let's start by exploring what exactly is meant by the term 'virtual worlds.'

What Are Virtual Worlds?

Virtual worlds have been defined as "A synchronous, persistent network of people, represented as avatars, facilitated by networked computers" (Bell, 2008, p. 2). In early work Dickey (2005a) defined the three main components of three-dimensional (3-D) worlds as "the illusion of 3-D space, avatars that serve as the visual representation of users, and an interactive chat environment for users to communicate with one another" (p. 121). Warburton (2009) suggests that there are four different types of virtual worlds: *flexible narrative worlds* where games play out (for instance, World of Warcraft), *social worlds* that have a primary purpose of enabling people to interact (such as Second Life), *simulation worlds* that emulate the real world (e.g., Google Earth) and *workspaces* that are designed to facilitate collaborative work (e.g., Project Wonderland).

Users typically participate in virtual worlds via an 'avatar,' which is a "visual representation of his or her real or surrogate identity and appearance" (Dalgarno & Lee, 2010, p. 15). Avatars are typically moved around a virtual world using a computer mouse and the arrow keys on the keyboard (Antonacci & Modaress, 2008). In some virtual worlds, users can also use the arrow keys to fly, or 'teleport' to different locations in the virtual world (Antonacci & Modaress, 2008). Thus, avatars afford the capacity for the user to change their point-of-view within the virtual world, so they can observe objects and phenomena from multiple perspectives (Dickey, 2003). A screenshot of the Second Life virtual world is shown in Figure 10.1.

Because virtual worlds incorporate synchronous chat tools, participants are able to verbally interact with one another, provide each other with feedback, and hence socially negotiate meaning (Dickey, 2003). Users can also use their avatars to gesture, smile, dance and use body language in other ways to express themselves (McKerlich & Anderson, 2007).

Virtual worlds can also include 'agents' or 'non-player characters,' which are programmed characters within the environment that can be used to support learning (Lin, Wang, Grant, Chien, & Lan, 2014). For instance, in a virtual-world problem-based learning task agents were used to prompt fifth grade students to generate more in-depth explanations about the causes of virtual river pollution (Holmes, 2007).

Multi-User Virtual Environments are a construct that is closely related to virtual worlds (Mennecke et al., 2008). Multi-User Virtual Environments (MUVEs) have been defined as "online three-dimensional virtual environments that allow many

Figure 10.1. Screenshot of Second Life Orientation Island.

users to simultaneously log into them, to communicate and interact with each other and with the environment, being represented by avatars" (Papachristos, Vrellis, Natsis, & Mikropoulos, 2014, p. 636). A virtual world need not enable interaction between multiple participants like a MUVE, though contemporary virtual worlds usually do. In this chapter we will use the more familiar term 'virtual worlds' to describe 3-D platforms that enable avatars to interact. Although purists might argue that MUVEs is a technically more accurate description of our focus, even among the research literature the term 'virtual worlds' is used more frequently than MUVEs.

Massively Multiplayer Online Games are another construct that is related to virtual worlds (Mennecke et al., 2008). Massively multiplayer online games (MMOGs) are "highly graphical 2-D or 3-D videogames played online, allowing individuals, through their self-created digital characters or 'avatars' to interact not only with the gaming software… but with other players' avatars as well" (Steinkuehler, 2004, p. 521). Virtual worlds need not have any objectives or game dynamics like a MMOG, though 'gamified' tasks can be prescribed within virtual worlds. Because they are a specialized (and often commercial) application of virtual worlds and can even be two-dimensional, MMOGs will not be a primary focus throughout this chapter.

Based on an in-depth review of literature, Dalgarno and Lee (2010) propose that the distinguishing characteristics of 3-D virtual environments can be divided into those that promote representational fidelity and those than allow learner interaction. Representational fidelity characteristics include the realistic display of the environment, smooth display of view changes and object motion, consistency of object behavior, user representation, spatial audio, as well as kinesthetic and tactile force feedback. Learner interaction characteristics include embodied actions, embodied verbal and non-verbal communications, control of environment attributes and behavior, as well as construction and scripting of objects and behaviors. These characteristics can combine to provide users with a sense of identity construction, presence and co-presence. Taken together, the characteristics of virtual worlds and the user experience can afford learning tasks which result in representation of spatial knowledge, experiential learning, engagement, contextual learning, and collaborative learning (Dalgarno & Lee, 2010). The relationship between these elements is represented in Figure 10.2.

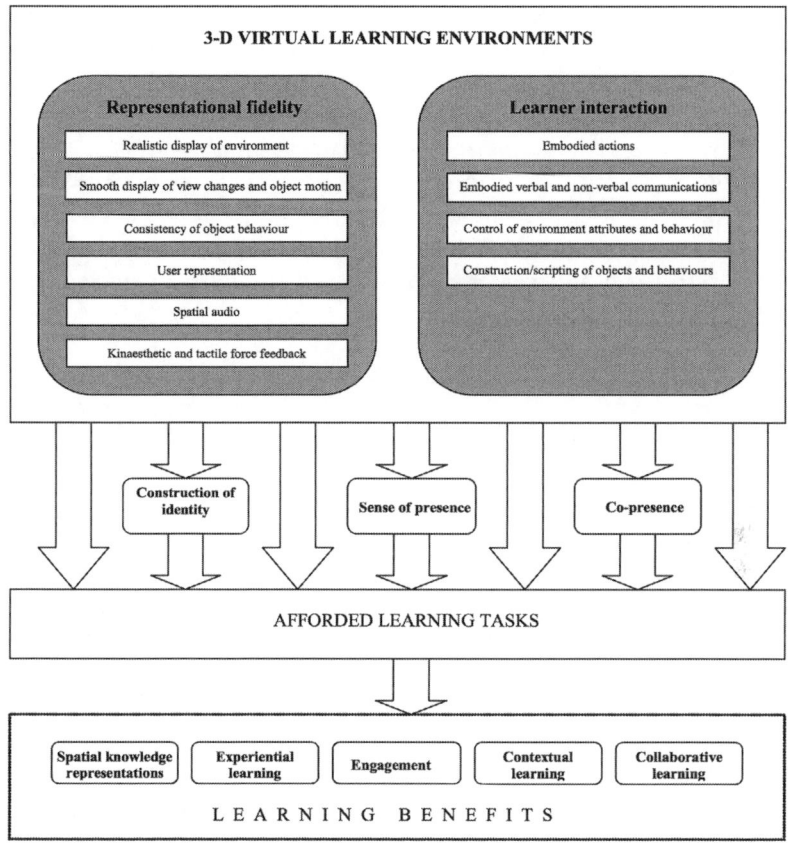

Figure 10.2. Unique Characteristics and Learning Affordances of 3-D Virtual Learning Environments (Dalgarno & Lee, p. 24).

There have been several other attempts to define characteristics and affordances of virtual worlds. Gamage, Tretiakov, and Crump (2011) propose the learning affordances of virtual worlds to be 3-D experiential learning, flow, role projection, awareness and co-presence, and emotional connection. They observe that educators with and without experience in virtual-worlds teaching generally perceive these affordances (Gamage et al., 2011). Based on an analysis of virtual worlds for language learning Henderson, Huang, Grant, and Henderson (2012) define the pertinent affordances as being the reduction of learner apprehension, persistence of the learning environment over time, physical as well as linguistic co-presence, autonomy of learners via their avatars, text as well as audio communication, mediation of content to meet learner needs, contextualized interaction, and body language. Mikropoulos and Natsis (2011) define the features of virtual worlds that contribute to learning as being "free navigation, first-person point of view, first-order experiences, natural semantics, size, transduction, reification, autonomy and presence" (p. 771). While there are some different elements and ontological positions represented among all of these definitions, taken together they all help to form an overall impression of the nature and features of virtual worlds.

Examples of Virtual-World Technologies

There are dozens of live and open virtual-world platforms (KZero, 2014). Based on the review detailed in the following sections, the most frequently used virtual worlds in education are Active Worlds, Open Simulator (OpenSim) and Second Life, with the latter being by far the most frequently used. Creative and technically advanced educators can also establish their own virtual-world instances by installing and serving open-source systems such as OpenSimulator, Open Wonderland, and Open Cobalt (Potkonjak et al., 2016). Other virtual-world platforms being used by educators include Croquet and realXtend (Lorenzo, Sicilia, & Sánchez, 2012), Kitely, ReactionGrid and Jibe (Gregory et al., 2014). The relatively new iSee platform offers an interesting virtual-world communication alternative by allowing people's avatars to be represented by their webcam videos (Lee et al., 2016). The Lego-like Minecraft virtual world is another emergent virtual world that is popular among school children (Schifter & Cipollone, 2013).

Four virtual worlds are described in more detail here: the most used virtual world, Second Life; the long established Active Worlds; an open source and thus highly customizable virtual world, OpenSim; and the more recent and noteworthy virtual world for school children, Minecraft.

SECOND LIFE

Visually, Second Life is a 3-D emulation of the real world, complete with islands, oceans, buildings, gardens and so on (Duncan, Miller, & Jiang, 2012). New avatars start on Second Life's Orientation Island where they can learn how to modify their avatar appearance, communicate with others, navigate by walking running or flying, or teleport themselves to other locations (Richardson, Hazzard, Challman, Morgenstein, & Brueckner, 2011). Users can communicate with each other using text chat or voice (Baker, Wentz, & Woods, 2009). A screenshot of Orientation Island was shown in Figure 10.1 above.

A defining characteristic of Second Life is that it enables content creation by users, while also including libraries of objects for people to utilize (Duncan et al., 2012). Objects in the virtual world can be programmed or 'scripted' using Linden Scripting Language (LSL), for instance to provide audio scaffolding when clicked (Lin et al., 2014). One of the most remarkable features of Second Life is its in-world economy founded on user-generated content and 'Linden dollars' that can in turn be 'cashed in' for real-world money (Bell, 2009).

While recent figures are difficult to source, one account indicates that there are approximately 14 million virtual community users of Second Life with an average of half a million residents logging in on a weekly basis (Faiola, Newlon, Pfaff, & Smyslova, 2013). Historically, a Second Life and Moodle learning management system integration (called 'SLOODLE') was developed that enabled students to access components of Moodle from within Second Life, for instance assignment dropboxes, blogs, calendars, text chat and quizzes (Kemp, Livingstone, & Bloomfield, 2009; Livingstone, Kemp, & Edgar, 2008), though SLOODLE has not been developed for more recent versions of the Moodle platform (see https://www.sloodle.org/download).

It should be noted that Second Life is a single instance hosted environment, meaning that it is open to all people across the world and institutional versions cannot be setup. The implications of this are discussed in later sections. For more information about Second Life see:

- Second Life website: http://secondlife.com
- Second Life Education home page: http://wiki.secondlife.com/wiki/Second_Life_Education
- Second Life Education forum: http://wiki.secondlife.com/wiki/SLED

ACTIVE WORLDS

Active Worlds has been in existence for over 20 years, and runs in both served and downloadable form (http://activeworlds.com).

As with most other 3-D virtual worlds it supports actions such as walking, running, flying, and non-verbal communication such as waving (Peterson, 2006). The virtual-world server is free to download so that people can setup their own 'world', and there are a range of (paid) hosting services available if institutional hosting is not feasible (Active Worlds, 2016). The free Active Worlds browser software also supports voice chat, media streaming and web searching (Active Worlds, 2016). Active Worlds has been used in several studies of 3-D virtual environments in education, particularly in earlier work (Bouta, Retalis, & Paraskeva, 2012; Dickey, 2003, 2005a, 2005b; Merchant, 2009, 2010; Peterson, 2006).

For further information about Active Worlds, see:

- The Active Worlds website: http://activeworlds.com
- The Active Worlds wiki: http://wiki.activeworlds.com

OPENSIMULATOR (OPENSIM)

OpenSim is an open-source, multi-user virtual-world platform that enables users to form private virtual worlds (Coban, Karakus, Gunay, & Goktas, 2015). An advantage of Open Sim is that (like ActiveWorlds) educators can download and install it on their own server so that students are not exposed to the risk of taking part in a global community (Childs, Schnieders, & Williams, 2012). OpenSim allows users to run their own 'island' on their computer, or it can be run as a virtual-world network in 'grid' mode (Lorenzo et al., 2012). The fact that OpenSim is open source means that users with sufficient technical skills can customize the virtual world however they like to suit their needs (OpenSimulator, 2014). It should be noted that there are only a small number of uses documented throughout the educational literature (e.g., Coban et al., 2015; Garrido-Iñigo & Rodríguez-Moreno, 2015). There is also a 'Sim-on-a-Stick' version of OpenSim that can be run directly from a USB stick (subQuark, 2016).

For more information about OpenSim and to download the software, see:

- The Open Simulator home page: http://opensimulator.org
- The Sim-on-a-Stick home page: http://simonastick.com

MINECRAFT

Minecraft can be considered as a form of 3-D virtual Lego where students can build and interact with a virtual world (Bos, Wilder, Cook, & O'Donnell, 2014; Overby & Jones, 2015). Minecraft requires users to logon to a dedicated server rather than to an open-to-the-world platform, which makes it safer for use by school children (Schifter & Cipollone, 2013). The environment has two main modes – creative mode and survival mode (Bos et al., 2014). Survival mode is a game mode that requires users to collect materials (food, minerals, ore, and so on) to build tools and survive being killed by 'hostile' characters in the game (List & Bryant, 2014). In creative mode there are no hostile characters and users have unlimited access to materials, so that they can utilize it as a design and building environment (Bos et al., 2014). The ability to construct in three dimensions with unlimited materials makes creative mode the most suitable for educational purposes (Overby & Jones, 2015). Some early educational uses of Minecraft in schools have been documented, including for geography (List & Bryant, 2014), mathematics (Bos et al., 2014), and English (Schifter & Cipollone, 2013). See Figure 10.3 for an example of the Minecraft environment.

For more information about Minecraft, see:

- The Minecraft website: https://minecraft.net
- The Minecraft Education edition: http://education.minecraft.net

Figure 10.3. The Minecraft Virtual World as an Educational Environment.

- The Minecraft wiki: http://minecraft.gamepedia.com/Minecraft_Wiki
- Examples from Coffs Harbour Public School: http://coffsharbourpublicschool.edublogs.org/minecraft

Uses of Virtual Worlds in Education

There is a wonderful variety of ways in which virtual worlds have been used in education. Based on a review by Duncan et al. (2012), virtual worlds have been used to facilitate simulations, collaborative construction, games-based learning, role-play activities, virtual quests, virtual field work, virtual laboratories, and even traditional lectures and classes. A scoping study of Australian and New Zealander tertiary educators concurs and adds to this list place exploration, concept exploration, task practice, scripting, and straight communication instruction (Dalgarno & Lee, 2012). A survey of the active Virtual Worlds Working Group agrees and identifies other uses such as virtual tours, research, and creation of 'machinima' (virtual-world screen recordings) (Gregory et al., 2015a). Virtual worlds have also been used for group work (including group projects) and community building (Inman, Wright, & Hartman, 2010). Using virtual worlds for discussions and meetings is another popular usage (Ghanbarzadeh & Ghapanchi, 2016).

Brief descriptions of virtual world uses emerging from the research literature are provided below to illustrate the wide range of possibilities. In order to constrain the complexity of discussion and promote relevance, the examples primarily focus upon learning designs using readily available virtual worlds that could conceivably be achieved by educators, rather than professionally or commercially developed virtual-world packages or games. Most uses relate to Second Life, unless otherwise stated.

SCHOOL LEVEL USES OF VIRTUAL WORLDS

Virtual worlds have been used in high school geography classes to simulate landscapes and environments. Groups of early high school geography students created landscapes of drainage basins so that they could learn about hydrological processes and demonstrate their evolving geomorphological understandings from the perspective of being a geographer (Hung, Lee, & Lim, 2012). High school geography students have also completed group-based topographical mapping exercises using virtual-world landscapes (Cho & Lim, 2015). Minecraft has been used in early high school geography classes to teach navigation, colonization, animal husbandry, building construction, and a range of other concepts relating to societal development (List & Bryant, 2014).

In English, virtual worlds have been used to enable situated learning. Active Worlds has been deployed to create a mysteriously abandoned town where primary school students could develop their literacy skills by collect evidence from a variety of media and textual forms in order to work out the reason for the desertion (Merchant, 2009, 2010). As another example, Minecraft has been used in English to help students understand 'point of view' and 'characterization' by building environments that allowed students to role-play a narrative (Schifter & Cipollone, 2013). At primary school level, Second Life has been used for students to learn English as a second language through situated vocabulary activities (Lan, 2015), and OpenSim has been used to help students learn the Irish language via games-based tasks such as treasure hunts (Dalton & Devitt, 2016).

There are also instances of virtual worlds being used to help school students learn history. Virtual worlds have been used to help children learn about ancient civilizations throughout history by reconstructing the architecture of those times and hence creating a high degree of involvement through presence (Mikropoulos, 2006). Similarly, virtual worlds have been used to make artefacts from archeological sites accessible to learners in order to promote interest in cultural heritage (Bertacchini & Tavernise, 2016).

Virtual worlds have also been used to provide a situated and creative environment for learning mathematics and science in schools. For instance, Active Worlds has been used to enable groups of primary school students to collaboratively learn about fractions through a series of situated simulation tasks, such as determining quantities of pizza being sold (Bouta et al., 2012). Creative mode of Minecraft has been used to help third-grade children explore measurement concepts in mathematics, for instance by building towns with objects of certain area and perimeter specifications (Bos et al., 2014). Additionally, Second Life has been used to enable senior high school students to conduct chemistry experiments as though they were in a physical laboratory (Winkelmann, Scott, & Wong, 2014).

There have been several educational virtual-worlds projects that have created purpose-built virtual worlds in order for students to meet learning outcomes in specific domains. For instance, River City (http://muve.gse.harvard.edu/rivercityproject) is a virtual world in which students behave as scientists to collaboratively identify scientific problems, hypothesize, test and reach evidence-based conclusions about why people in a 19th-century city are falling ill (Dede, 2009). Quest Atlantis (http://atlantisremixed.org) provides a role-play environment where primary school students can collaboratively perform curriculum related quests against a mythical backdrop of Atlantis in order to make learning more fun and meaningful (Barab, Thomas, Dodge, Carteaux, & Tuzun, 2005). While this chapter principally focuses on uses of virtual worlds that teachers could design themselves, developments such as the two aforementioned projects are valuable reference points and those interested are encouraged to explore them.

VIRTUAL WORLDS IN HIGHER EDUCATION

One common way that virtual worlds have been used in higher education is to replicate face-to-face classes (Ghanbarzadeh & Ghapanchi, 2016). For instance, Second life has been used as an instructive tool in a university visual communication course to allow students to attend virtual lectures (Lester & King, 2009). It has also been used to simulate traditional university buildings and classrooms providing an online campus, for instance, where nursing students can enter a building and teachers can deliver a presentation (Johnson, Vorderstrasse, & Shaw, 2009). Virtual-world classes need not always take a transmissive approach; for instance, Second life lectures for doctors have incorporated avatars acting as patients in scenario-based learning sessions (Wiecha, Heyden, Sternthal, & Merialdi, 2010).

Virtual worlds have also been used in higher education to enable international communication and collaboration. Second Life has been used for undergraduate students in Finland, The Netherlands, United States and India to complete global virtual collaboration projects where they were required to work together in groups to solve authentic management problems (Keskitalo, Pyykkö, & Ruokamo, 2011). In a language learning context, Second Life has been used to enable Swedish students to be paired with American students to develop their English speaking capabilities (Petrakou, 2010), and to enable undergraduate Mandarin students in Australia to be taught by instructors in Taiwan (Lin et al., 2014).

Still on the topic of language learning, virtual worlds have been used to create contextualized, student-centered and authentic environments for practicing language skills. As a simple example, Active Worlds and Second Life have been used to promote language learning using the text chat facility (Peterson, 2006, 2010). A virtual airport and other installations created in OpenSim have enable French language students to develop and practice their communication skills (Garrido-Iñigo & Rodríguez-Moreno, 2015). Using audio as well as text via their avatars in Mandarin classes students could develop their negotiation skills by going to a virtual restaurant and discussing the best dishes to suit the table members (Henderson et al., 2012). Task-based language teaching activities (such as a maze navigation task) in Second Life provided students with multiple opportunities for input, language production and feedback (Lin et al., 2014).

Second Life has also been used in several instances as a collaborative simulation environment in medical education contexts. For example, in one case, undergraduate nursing students from different locations could watch an in-world video briefing about a virtual patient's condition, then take the patient's blood pressure, oxygen saturation levels, and breathing rate in order to diagnose appropriate treatment (Rogers, 2011). Virtual wards and video training have been created in Second Life for nursing students to learn 'Rapid Sequence Intubation' so that they could safely manage patient airways during an emergency (Chow, Herold, Choo, & Chan, 2012). In health sciences, Second Life has been used to construct a virtual anatomy laboratory for medical students to learn about the human body (Richardson et al., 2011), as elaborated later in this chapter.

In other instances, virtual worlds are used to provide an environment for conducting authentic projects. For instance, Second life was used for business students to practice their marketing skills, including product development, promotion and sales (Noteborn, Dailey-Hebert, Carbonell, & Gijselaers, 2014). Students created video advertisement, flyers, posters, and social network communities in order to promote their product, and a fair was held where students used Linden Dollars (online virtual money) to buy products created by peers (Noteborn et al., 2014). As another example, Second Life was used to enable students to undertake all aspects of a supply chain management system development project, including problem analysis, modeling of components, and project management (Dreher, Reiners, Dreher, & Dreher, 2009).

Virtual worlds have also been used in several universities to enable pre-service teachers to undertake role-play simulations in order to develop their classroom management skills. In one case, this meant pre-service teachers were able to meet from any location and take turns to be the 'teacher', building up their classroom confidence (Cheong, 2010). Recording their practice sessions allowed the pre-service teachers to undertake collaborative and individual reflection (Cheong, 2010). Some cases of pre-service teacher practice sessions even incorporate artificial intelligence 'agents' to act as children in the classroom alongside role-playing peers (Gregory et al., 2011b; Mahon, Bryant, Brown, & Kim, 2010).

In other cases, virtual worlds have been used in face-to-face courses as a catalyst for developing students' interpretive and human skills. In media studies avatars were used as a provocation for in-class discussion of identity issues, Chinese areas in Second Life were used to catalyze critical reflection on cultural symbols, and corporate installations were used as a focus for interpreting how value systems can be represented through media (Herold, 2010). Second Life has also been used as a context to teach ethics, both by having students find examples of ethical behavior from the cultural viewpoints being discussed in class, and by considering the ethicalness of different actions that occurred within the virtual world (Houser et al., 2011). Virtual-world activities were used to help psychology students learn about issues relating to workplace behavior, counseling practice, and entrepreneurial thinking (Ward et al., 2015).

Educators have used virtual worlds (Second Life) to create models that help students visualize and experience phenomena. For instance, one installation allowed archaeology students to explore social structures and spaces of traditional cultures, such as a Saami tent and a Kalasha village (Edirisingha, Nie, Pluciennik, & Young, 2009). In another development, undergraduate chemistry students learnt about molecular structures, as well as respond to assessment tasks (Merchant et al., 2012). Architectural design students were able to explore the interior of a proposed building from a first-person viewpoint in order to help improve their understanding of user navigation behaviors (Memikoğlu, 2014).

Virtual worlds have also been used as environments for students to create, design and plan physical spaces. Second Life has been used to have art students create a virtual exhibition of their work, hence developing their ability to individually and collaboratively explore, experiment, research, improvise, reflect, discuss, critique and evaluate their digitally manipulated artworks (Grenfell, 2013). Undergraduate information technology and business management students were required to design a meeting space in Second Life including posters and presentations (Sutcliffe & Alrayes, 2012). Film students have used virtual worlds to plan their camera angles on a set reconstruction and perform risk assessments (Foss, 2009).

Computing teachers have deployed virtual worlds to develop students' programming skills. For instance, Second Life has been used to provide a virtual campus where computing students could learn about function-based shape modeling and web visualization (Sourin, Sourina, & Prasolova-Førland, 2006). In another case students were set tasks to develop programming scripts for objects such as dogs, robots and cars, within Second Life using the integrated Linden Scripting Language (Esteves, Fonseca, Morgado, & Martins, 2011). Having programming activity occur in the virtual world meant the teacher could meet with students in-world from a remote location to examine their programming products and resolve any issues that students were experiencing (Esteves et al., 2011).

So we can see that there are a tremendous variety of ways virtual worlds can be used to facilitate learning.

Benefits and Potentials of Virtual Worlds in Education

One interesting and valuable attribute of virtual worlds is that they can be used to apply a range of pedagogies. The graphically rich 3-D environment, the capacity to view from multiple perspectives, the ability to manipulate objects, the possibility of discovering new information, and the ability to actively experimenting mean that virtual worlds are well suited for facilitating constructivist learning (Coffman & Klinger, 2007; Dickey, 2003, 2005b; Gregory et al., 2011b; Mahon et al., 2010; Mikropoulos & Natsis, 2011; Wang & Burton, 2013). At the same time, the combination of communication tools, immersive environment and opportunities for collaboration make virtual worlds particularly appropriate for application of social constructivist pedagogies (Bronack, Riedl, & Tashner, 2006; Girvan & Savage, 2010). On top of this, by allowing people to build objects and environments together, virtual worlds also support constructionist learning (Dreher et al., 2009; Girvan, Tangney, & Savage, 2013). Across the literature, a range of pedagogical approaches have been noted including collaborative learning, situated learning, experiential learning, authentic learning, project-based learning, inquiry-based learning and problem-based learning (Mikropoulos & Natsis, 2011; Wang & Burton, 2013).

Based on a review of the research literature, the educational benefits and potentials of virtual worlds are outlined below.

ENABLING AND ENCOURAGING COMMUNICATION

Virtual worlds are often deployed as communication spaces where people can interact with one another verbally (for instance using text chat) or non-verbally using avatar appearance and gestures (Hew & Cheung, 2010). One of the distinct characteristics of communication in virtual worlds is its immediacy (Choi & Baek, 2011). Participants can choose between public text-chat, private text-chat, and potentially voice, depending on what is most appropriate for the intended communication (Petrakou, 2010). Virtual worlds also enable users to simultaneously hold many-to-many conversations (Kim, Lee, & Thomas, 2012), utilizing the capacity to move around in order to talk to whoever they want (Gregory et al., 2016). Because participants can use virtual worlds such as Second Life to interact using text and audio channels, language learners can develop their reading, writing listening and speaking skills in the one environment (Sarac, 2014).

Communication in virtual worlds can be richer than in purely text-based platforms because users have the opportunity to align the body language of their avatar with what they are saying (Lee, 2009). Virtual worlds enable people to project their feelings through their avatar expressions, potentially overcoming a sense of psychological alienation (Van der Land, Schouten, van den Hooff, & Feldberg, 2011). Educators have also observed that in virtual-worlds students "state emotional content more readily because they can't share it with a facial expression" (Gamage et al., 2011, p. 2411).

Students who are reluctant to comment or ask questions in face-to-face classes may be more willing to communicate via their avatar (Baker et al., 2009; Gamage et al., 2011; Sierra, Gutiérrez, & Garzón-Castro, 2012). As a student in one study articulated, "I may not brave enough to ask many questions, and talk with other students freely, but in Second Life we can share our views, opinions freely" (Herold, 2009, p. 14). Psychology students suggested that participating in virtual-world role-play scenarios was less confronting than having to complete face-to-face simulation activities (Ward et al., 2015). Medical students in a virtual laboratory appeared more comfortable answering questions from teachers and peers than in the traditional face-to-face setting (Richardson et al., 2011).

FACILITATING COLLABORATIVE LEARNING

Many propose that virtual worlds have the potential to facilitate effective collaborative learning (Duncan et al., 2012; Gregory et al., 2015b). Because most virtual worlds are online, the collaboration can be cross-disciplinary, cross-institutional and cross-border (Gregory et al., 2011a). Different locations within a virtual world can be used to provide private synchronous group work spaces within a single online environment (Andreas, Tsiatsos, Terzidou, & Pomportsis, 2010; Bower, Lee, & Dalgarno, 2017). It is conjectured that the realism, presence and avatar-based interaction of virtual worlds can be leveraged to support information processing and communication, which is the reason that effective team collaboration can arise (Van der Land et al., 2011). In order to support a full range of collaborative processes, virtual worlds may be complemented by a suite of other productive tools such as Moodle, G Suite, Skype, and Wordpress (Olteanu, Bîzoi, Gorghiu, & Suduc, 2014).

PROVIDING ACCESS TO LEARNING

Another benefit of using virtual worlds in education is they can provide access to learning. Disparately located people can hold group meetings, obviating the financial, environmental and temporal cost of needing to travel (Foss, 2009). Students who may not have the opportunity to attend sites or participate in activities due to location, distance, disability, cost and so on can have equitable access to somewhat equivalent learning experiences via virtual worlds (Childs et al., 2012). Instructors can hold office hours or arrange to meet with students who would not otherwise be able to meet face-to-face (Baker et al., 2009). For tasks requiring student construction teachers can meet in the virtual world to provide feedback and advice (Esteves et al., 2011). By streaming face-to-face classroom activity into a virtual world and projecting virtual-world activity into the face-to-face class 'blended reality' environments have been created where remote students can engage in live on-campus classes (Bower et al., 2017; Dreher et al., 2009).

Students appreciate the convenience of being able to participate online and from any location (Sierra et al., 2012). The immediacy of Second Life has been observed to reduce the sense of remoteness for distance learners (Edirisingha et al., 2009).

EMBODIMENT AND IDENTITY CONSTRUCTION

Contemporary virtual worlds enable users, through their avatars, to "engage in embodied verbal communication through text and voice, as well as embodied non-verbal communication in the form of gestures and facial expressions" (Dalgarno & Lee, 2010, p. 17). The combination of 3-D representational affordances of virtual worlds and interactions via avatars is what helps people to construct a sense of identity within the environment (Dalgarno & Lee, 2010). Free navigation through the virtual world and first person point of view lead to first-order experiences as opposed to learning from second hand accounts or descriptions (Mikropoulos & Natsis, 2011). In turn, this can be used to provide learners with a more visceral appreciation of a situation than if it were depicted via other means (Gregory et al., 2014).

Qualitative feedback from students suggests that the use of avatars can provoke them to self-reflect upon their own identity, the perspectives they hold, and their approach to communication (Jarmon, Traphagan, Mayrath, & Trivedi, 2009). In one study, contextualized virtual-world role-playing activities on the topic of euthanasia enabled students to develop a more embodied understanding of issues relating to ethics, morality and religion, as well as a better appreciation for the perspectives of others (Jamaludin, San Chee, & Ho, 2009).

REPRESENTATION OF 3-DIMENSIONAL (3-D) ENVIRONMENTS

Contemporary virtual worlds can provide convincing representations of real-world environments. The representational fidelity is supported through realistic display of the environment, the depiction of users via their avatars, smooth view changes and object motion, consistency of object behavior, as well as kinesthetic and tactile force feedback (Dalgarno & Lee, 2010). In virtual worlds, natural semantics can be used (e.g., visual objects such as molecules or plant organelles) in order to avoid confusion or mis-conceptions that might occur with symbolic representations such as words or equations (Mikropoulos & Natsis, 2011). Virtual worlds can also include 'spatial audio' (Dalgarno & Lee, 2010), whereby the volume of sounds will depend on their proximity from the point of observation in the virtual world. The ability to move around virtual worlds, view them from any position, and manipulate objects within them affords learners the capac-ity to develop spatial knowledge of the environment in a way that is not possible in non 3-D alternatives (Dalgarno & Lee, 2010).

Teachers generally agree that virtual worlds can provide important assistance for learners to develop familiarity with a place and objects within it (Gregory et al., 2015b). Creating buildings and artifacts in virtual worlds is unlimited by financial, spatial, material or physical constraints of the real world (Papachristos et al., 2014). Virtual worlds can also be adapted and scaled over time to meet changes in learning needs (Antonacci & Modaress, 2008). The persistence of the environ-ment enables students to share learning artifacts between sessions and build on one another's learning (Antonacci & Modaress, 2008; Girvan & Savage, 2010). Depending on the virtual world, users may even be able to control the attributes and behavior of the environment, for instance, altering time or gravity, which provides additional possibilities for learning design (Dalgarno & Lee, 2010).

The use of 3-D representations in virtual worlds can lead to superior learning outcomes. Having students learn spatial and analogic reasoning in 3-D environments resulted in more effective learning than using 2-D representations (Passig, Tzuriel, & Eshel-Kedmi, 2016). The realism and interactivity of 3-D virtual worlds contributed to learners' abilities to evaluate architectural plans compared to when 2-D plans or 3-D static models were used (Van Der Land, Schouten, Feldberg, Van Den Hooff, & Huysman, 2013). Conducting a virtual campus orientation tour led to significantly greater general learning and recollection of spatial route details than an on-campus orientation, with signifi-cantly lower levels of perceived complexity noted (Tüzün & Özdinç, 2016). The accuracy with which virtual worlds can rep-resent 3-D environments (i.e. their 'representational fidelity') has also been shown to contribute to primary school students' sense of 'flow' (Choi & Baek, 2011).

ENABLING SIMULATION

Virtual worlds are often used as simulation spaces (Hew & Cheung, 2010; Kim et al., 2012). They enable simulation of phenomena (for instance, physics experiments, astronaut training, historical events) that are impractical, dangerous or impossible to undertake in the real world (Dalgarno & Lee, 2010; Twining, 2009; Warburton, 2009). The ability for objects in virtual worlds to programmed via scripting languages provides a powerful platform for creating automated and dynamic simulation environments (Dreher et al., 2009). Virtual-world simulations can also free-up time on equipment by having students engage with replicas of apparatus or spaces (Foss, 2009). For instance, virtual worlds have often been used to create virtual laboratories that provide 24 hour access to students and are less expensive and risk laden than physical laboratories (Ghanbarzadeh & Ghapanchi, 2016). Several studies have shown that using virtual worlds to provide students with remote access to laboratories for subjects such as physics, chemistry and engineering can match learning outcomes achieved in real-world laboratories (Heradio et al., 2016).

Numerous examples of how virtual-world simulations could be used to support otherwise difficult or infeasible learning were provided in the previous section, for instance, replicating historical villages for learning archaeology (Edirisingha et al., 2009), modeling molecular interactions for chemistry learning (Merchant et al., 2012), and even simulation of traditional classroom spaces to provide immersive remote instruction (Wiecha et al., 2010). Another less common but interesting way to use virtual world simulations is as a teaching tool to promote collaborative observation. When a high school teacher modeled geography phenomena using the virtual world and then had students hold classroom discussions about what they observed, higher knowledge gains resulted than when students collaboratively solved problems in the virtual world or when traditional classroom instruction was used (Cho & Lim, 2015).

ALLOWING STUDENT CONSTRUCTION AND MODELING

With adequate permissions, learners in virtual worlds can also construct their own virtual places and objects (Dalgarno & Lee, 2010). Virtual worlds often contain libraries of objects that builders can draw upon, which can expedite their building progress and promote a consistent look and feel (Gül, Gu, & Williams, 2008). Some virtual-worlds (for instance, Second Life) support parametric design where the geometry of objects can be adjusted by manipulating parameters (Gül et al., 2008). The open potential for construction afforded by virtual worlds means they can stimulate creativity and playfulness (Twining, 2009). Examples of student construction and modeling in virtual worlds from the previous section included creating landscapes of drainage basins (Hung et al., 2012), building function-based objects (Sourin et al., 2006), and student-developed virtual art exhibitions (Grenfell, 2013).

The benefits of construction and modeling for students is showcased in one project conducted by Dreher et al. (2009) where information systems students used Linden Scripting Language in Second Life to simulate supply chain processes. Students not only developed the skills to model in Second Life, but also gained valuable experience in systems development processes, from analysis of the problem through to implementation and refinement. While they were developing systems students could also learn project management skills including teamwork. Furthermore, modeling supply chain management systems in Second Life allowed students to test their designs immediately (Dreher et al., 2009).

ENABLING ROLE-PLAY

One common application of 3-D virtual environments is to have students conduct role-play activities (Gregory et al., 2016; Gregory et al., 2015a). Examples include creating a restaurant scenario for students to practice language learning (Henderson et al., 2012), recreating a hospital ward situation for nursing students to practice diagnosis skills (Rogers, 2011), and enabling pre-service teachers to practice their classroom management skills (Cheong, 2010). In virtual-world role-plays students can utilize a variety of avatars, enabling them to appreciate multiple perspectives and develop empathy (Gregory et al., 2014).

Students in some studies indicate the benefits of role-play. Psychology students who completed a virtual-world supermarket role-play activity designed to develop their understanding of workplace psychology indicated significantly greater task satisfaction than students who completed the corresponding face-to-face activity (Ward et al., 2015). Nursing students taking part in a virtual-world simulation observed that the environment encouraged collaboration and peer learning (Rogers, 2011). Marketing students who were required to design, promote and sell products in Second Life noted how the project enabled them to practice the skills that they were learning in class (Noteborn et al., 2014).

FACILITATING SITUATED AND EXPERIENTIAL LEARNING

Educators generally agree experiential learning is one of the important benefits of virtual worlds (Gregory et al., 2015b). Offering realistic situated learning environments has traditionally been difficult for teachers, but virtual worlds can be used to create life-like settings for problem-based learning (Dede, 2009). Learners can be placed in an environment with authentic content and culture (Warburton, 2009). Thus, virtual worlds are often used as student-centered experiential spaces, where people can learn by doing and observe the outcomes of their actions (Hew & Cheung, 2010). Gamification can be used to provide motivation and promote learning in experiential virtual-worlds tasks (Ghanbarzadeh & Ghapanchi, 2016; Gregory et al., 2016).

Teachers can provide students with situated learning tasks in an attempt to promote transfer of knowledge and skills to real-world scenarios (Dalgarno & Lee, 2010). It is proposed that learning in an immersive environment that replicates the real world can promote such transfer of virtual-world skills into everyday life (Coffman & Klinger, 2007; Dede, 2009). Several students who participated in an interdisciplinary communication course through Second Life indicated that experiential learning in virtual worlds helped them to better appreciate how they could apply their new-formed understanding in real-life contexts (Jarmon et al., 2009).

FOSTERING PRESENCE, CO-PRESENCE, AND IMMERSION

The 3-D representation and interaction that virtual worlds enable can lead to a sense of presence and co-presence (Dalgarno & Lee, 2010). Whereas presence is the sense of 'being there', co-presence can be considered the sense of 'being there together' (Dalgarno & Lee, 2010). The degree of realism used in virtual worlds has been shown to impact on students' sense of presence (Chen, Warden, Tai, Chen, & Chao, 2011). The use of avatars in the environment is seen as key to creating the sense of student presence in virtual worlds (Peterson, 2006). Media richness has also been observed to contribute to presence (Edirisingha et al., 2009).

User characteristics such as computing self-efficacy, perceived usefulness and ease of use of virtual worlds, and the subjective perceptions of others have also been shown to influence the perceived sense of presence (Chow, 2016).

By providing space, locality and 'dynamic conditionality' with other users virtual worlds can also create a sense of immersion (Van der Land et al., 2011). Immersion can be distinguished from presence as being the more objective and measurable properties of the system and how it is rendered that lead to the psychological sense of being present in the environment (Dalgarno & Lee, 2010).

The enhanced sense of presence and virtual embodiment induced via avatars is proposed to potentially increase the affective, empathic and motivational impact of learning experiences (Warburton, 2009). Students completing lectures in Second Life reported a high sense of social presence (Papachristos et al., 2014). Presence has been found to positively correlate with student satisfaction in virtual-world learning environments (Bulu, 2012). The sense of presence that virtual worlds can engender has been positively correlated with a sense of 'flow' (enjoyable psychological immersion) (Faiola et al., 2013). However, when it comes to learning outcomes it should be noted that presence was not shown to influence students' tactics in a virtual-world business English negotiation activity (Chen et al., 2011), and in another study, presence was not found to have any significant impact on the learning of molecular concepts in a virtual world (Merchant et al., 2012). Yet, in a more recently reported study presence was positively correlated with knowledge retention (Wilkes, 2016).

MOTIVATING AND ENGAGING LEARNERS

One frequently reported benefit of virtual worlds is high levels of learner engagement (Gregory et al., 2016). The interactivity that 3-D virtual worlds provide was found to contribute to primary school students' sense of 'flow' (Choi & Baek, 2011). Undergraduates who completed a global virtual team project using Second Life generally indicated that it was motivating and fun (Keskitalo et al., 2011). Students completing language learning in Second Life indicated high levels of interest and enjoyment (Peterson, 2010). Some students participating in psychology simulations commented that the novelty and immersive nature of the virtual world was appealing, which motivated them to want the approach used in other subjects (Ward et al., 2015).

There are some studies that report improved motivation when using virtual worlds as opposed to traditional face-to-face approaches. For instance, upper primary school students report significantly higher engagement and motivation when learning about the ecological issues of the Mediterranean Sea using a virtual world than their counterparts who learnt via traditional instructional approaches (Wrzesien & Raya, 2010). Using virtual worlds to teach school students geography concepts resulted in greater intrinsic motivation of students than when traditional direct instruction approaches were used (Cho & Lim, 2015). School students participating in the River City 3-D science simulation activities were more engaged than counterparts who completed tasks in pen and paper form (Dede, 2009). A study of agro-industrial engineering students suggest that motivation and engagement was enhanced in virtual-world classes (Sierra et al., 2012). Wehner, Gump, and Downey (2011) conclude that students who completed a Spanish course using Second Life demonstrated higher levels of motivation on several measures compared to students who completed the same course using traditional face-to-face classes (though it should be noted in this last case that there were no statistical adjustments for the large number of measures tested).

FACILITATING ASSESSMENT

There are several potential benefits of conducting assessment in virtual worlds. For instance, virtual worlds can be used to facilitate assessment across disparate geographical locations (Gregory et al., 2011a). They may also enable physical barriers (such as a mobility disability) to be overcome (Gregory et al., 2011a). Virtual worlds can be used to conduct otherwise difficult to conduct role-play activities that can potentially be used for assessment (Gregory et al., 2011b; Ward et al., 2015). Because assessment submissions are in digital form, with sufficient know-how the marking of tasks can be automated (Gregory et al., 2011a).

Setting tasks that require students to be constructive in the virtual world has the additional benefit of allowing the teacher to conduct formative and informal assessment. For instance, having school students create virtual-world landscapes of drainage basins in geography enabled teachers to detect and treat hydrological misconceptions that most likely would not have been identified if pen-and-paper approaches were used (Hung et al., 2012).

COMMUNITY BUILDING

Another frequently cited educational benefit of virtual worlds is their ability to help foster community building (Gregory et al., 2016). Students from different countries who completed a global virtual collaboration project in Second Life indicated a strong sense of team membership as a result of the process (Keskitalo et al., 2011). Learners who completed collaborative evaluation tasks in a virtual world were found to interact more completely as a community, as compared to students using a traditional learning management system who tended to have more individual interactions (Lorenzo et al., 2012). Researchers note that students appear more comfortable interacting with teachers and other students in virtual worlds due to the less formal nature, and that this carried over to cause a stronger sense of community within face-to-face classes (Baker et al., 2009). Qualitative observations of a small sample of students found that use of Second Life contributed to a sense of connectedness and triggered real-world networking between them (Edirisingha et al., 2009).

ENGAGING A WIDER COMMUNITY

Using virtual worlds also enables people from outside a course to contribute to the learning activities. Guest lecturers from around the world can be invited to present without having to travel to a real-world location (Herold, 2009). Second Life enabled the global teams of undergraduate engineering and business students from different countries to hold ongoing meetings so that they complete their global virtual collaboration projects together (Keskitalo et al., 2011). Conducting an architectural design project in a Second Life meant people from beyond the classroom and around the world could become a part of the development initiative (Jarmon, Traphagan, & Mayrath, 2008).

So we can see that simulating a 3-D space that affords communication, navigation and construction subtends a range of design possibilities for educators.

Issues and Limitations of Virtual Worlds in Education

As for with the other learning technology platforms, there are also a variety of issues and limitations that warrant consideration when designing virtual-world learning tasks. These issues and limitations, as distilled from the research literature, are outlined below.

TECHNICAL CONSTRAINTS

Virtual worlds require greater computing power than other forms of contemporary online technologies. The large amounts of graphics data involved in virtual-world visualization means that the computers being used need to have reasonably high level specifications (Herold, 2009; Sarac, 2014). Specifically, users typically require computers with high graphics card and RAM specifications (Duncan et al., 2012). Whether students at home or on campus, if they do not have sufficient computing power or bandwidth then it can impact upon the quality of experience and in some cases render the environment unusable (Dalgarno, Lee, Carlson, Gregory, & Tynan, 2011a; De Freitas, Rebolledo-Mendez, Liarokapis, Magoulas, & Poulovassilis, 2010; Herold, 2009; Sierra et al., 2012; Zhang, 2013). The variability of Internet access for distance students can prevent teachers from making virtual-world activities compulsory (Gregory et al., 2015a). These factors may lead to virtual worlds being less frequently adopted than other technologies (Gregory et al., 2015b).

The high-end hardware demands and relatively emergent nature of virtual worlds means users can experience technical problems. The virtual world itself may have technical issues or 'bugs' due to erroneous software builds (Childs et al., 2012). Server issues are frequently cited as problems (Garrido-Iñigo & Rodríguez-Moreno, 2015). Bandwidth or other issues can lead to voice communications dropping out (Dalgarno et al., 2011a; Papachristos et al., 2014).

A time delay or 'lag' is often experienced in virtual worlds, for instance when many people (upwards of 30) are present in the one virtual space (Gregory et al., 2011a; Gregory et al., 2016). Alternately, some users may simply have difficulty configuring the virtual-world viewer to run on their computer (Dalgarno et al., 2011a). Institutional firewalls can also be an issue if they block access to the virtual world being used (Dalgarno et al., 2011a; Gregory et al., 2011a; Winkelmann et al., 2014).

FIDELITY

If a process or experiment is being represented in the virtual world then limits to the authenticity of representation may cause information loss or misunderstanding (Dalgarno, Lee, Carlson, Gregory, & Tynan, 2011b). For instance, scripted 'avatar chat-bots' in psychology simulations used text-chat to communicate and did not understand some phrases entered by students, which detract from the realism of the experience (Ward et al., 2015). Pre-service teachers who were practicing student management skills in a virtual classroom simulation noticed that the behaviors of the programmed student-avatars were in some ways unrealistic, which diminished the educational value (Mahon et al., 2010). Film and television students struggled to replicate the building materials, lighting, ambient noise, weather patterns and so on that would influence real-world cinematographic capture, thus compromising their ability to authentically plan their shoot (Foss, 2009). A high school virtual world chemistry experiment could not reproduce some of the detailed instrumentation and processes of a real-world experiment (Winkelmann et al., 2014).

STUDENT TECHNICAL SKILLS

Students may struggle with a variety of technical skills that are required when using virtual worlds for learning. To start with, people accessing the virtual world from their own equipment will need to download the appropriate viewer software, which may be seen as problematic (Gregory et al., 2011a). People may also struggle to setup their audio/headset to enable voice communication (Petrakou, 2010). Once in the virtual-world students who are unfamiliar with the environment may find it difficult to navigate (Petrakou, 2010). Students may also initially struggle with basic operations such as picking up objects and using the chat interface (Herold, 2009). Acquisition of these skills is not optional — if students do not have the technical competencies to operate specific functions of the virtual world then they cannot participate in the learning activities (Lim, Nonis, & Hedberg, 2006). Finally, creating and programming objects in virtual worlds that allow it (such as Second Life, Active Worlds and Open Sim) demands an even higher level of technical competencies (Girvan et al., 2013). Learning the technical skills required to operate in the virtual world imposes a time overhead for students before they can use the technology for learning (Childs et al., 2012).

People with lower technology skills and confidence appear at a greater disadvantage when it comes to learning in virtual worlds. Students with lower technical skills have been observed to customize their avatars and the environment less, subsequently feeling less connected with the virtual world and hence participating less (deNoyelles & Seo, 2012). In one experiment, female students indicated significantly greater difficulty operating virtual worlds, potentially because they have less experience in first-person 'shooter' style games (Lin, Tutwiler, & Chang, 2012). Similarly teachers indicate that they find it more difficult to use virtual worlds initially because they are unfamiliar with 3-D games use (Gregory et al., 2014). Structural equation modeling has shown that if people lack computing self-efficacy then it can negatively influence their perceptions about virtual-world usability, which in turn can reduce intentions to use virtual-world environments in the future (Chow et al., 2012; Shen & Eder, 2009).

COGNITIVE OVERLOAD

The increased representational complexity of virtual worlds can add to cognitive load, which in turn can negatively impact on the amount of learning that occurs. A study of educational computer games found that that increased representational complexity that contributes to immersion in 3-D virtual worlds led to significantly lower levels of learning as a result of increased cognitive load (Schrader & Bastiaens, 2012). An examination of learning gains for biology students using 2-D versus 3-D models found that the 2-D model delivered better learning outcomes (Richards & Taylor, 2015). Coming to group consensus about selecting an apartment was less effective using a 3-D virtual world as compared to three-dimensional static diagrams, with people in the virtual world experiencing higher cognitive load and taking longer to reach their decisions (Van Der Land et al., 2013).

COMMUNICATION AND COLLABORATION CONSTRAINTS

Communicating through avatars can cause communication difficulties. It can be difficult to identify people in the class from their avatar, particularly if they are using a pseudonym (Dalgarno et al., 2011b). It can also be difficult for students to find other people within the geography of the virtual world, which is made more complicated by the fact that unlike social media their identity is only present when they are logged in (Warburton, 2009).

Moreover, communicating through avatars can lead to loss of face-to-face meanings and cues (Dalgarno et al., 2011b). While avatar gestures can be manually specified by virtual-world users, it is not possible to see peoples' actual facial expressions and body language so it can be difficult for teachers to know when and what type of feedback might be required (Lin et al., 2014). This lack of visual cues can make it more difficult to coordinate discussion and form a shared understanding (Dickey, 2003; Gül et al., 2008). For instance, people may find it difficult to know the appropriate time to comment, which can cause people to accidently talk over the top of one another and cause confusion (Baker et al., 2009; Petrakou, 2010; Zhang, 2013). It can also be difficult to control an avatar to signify desired meaning, for instance pointing to an object to draw attention to it (Dickey, 2003).

Issues can also arise with the use of audio and text for communication. As previously mentioned audio communication can be unreliable, but at the same time text-chat among multiple participants can be difficult to follow because it takes time to type out comments and the conversations are not threaded (Hew & Cheung, 2010; Keskitalo et al., 2011). The spatial nature of sound can be difficult to manage, with avatars not hearing one another if they are located too far apart (Petrakou, 2010). Taken together, all of these issues lead to many participants finding traditional methods of communication easier and more direct than using virtual worlds (though less interesting) (Andreas et al., 2010).

Virtual worlds are generally limited or cumbersome when it comes to semantic representation, for instance with no support for document creation or representing symbols such as equations (Sierra et al., 2012). To this extent, external tools are often utilized to facilitate effective collaboration, such as blogs and wikis (Warburton, 2009) and social networking systems (Lumkin, Cram, Eade, Buck, & Evans, 2011).

NEGATIVE STUDENT DISPOSITIONS

Some students have negative perceptions of virtual worlds and online games, which may need to be overcome in order for successful learning to take place (Gamage et al., 2011; Herold, 2009). For instance, women may be less familiar with operating 3-D virtual worlds due to less gaming experience, and this can influence their learning behaviors and attitudes (deNoyelles & Seo, 2012). In one study, several of the female non-gamers tended to find the virtual world as 'fake', which affected their propensity to engage in the environment (deNoyelles & Seo, 2012). The game-like look and feel of the virtual world may also cause students not to take it seriously, thus limiting their focus and constraining the degree of transfer to real-world applications (Childs et al., 2012). As an example, primary school students completing literacy activities in Active Worlds were observed to initially treat the environment as a game, attempting to collect items and seeing if they could escape the confines of the learning space (Merchant, 2009). Depending on the virtual-world environment and the background of the students, there may also be cultural norms in virtual worlds that are unfamiliar and disconcerting to newcomers (Warburton, 2009).

DISTRACTION

The 3-D environment and the freedom to explore virtual worlds can result in students not focusing on learning (Lim et al., 2006). It is easy for people to become distracted by the presence of other avatars in the environment and engage in off-task conversation (Omale, Hung, Luetkehans, & Cooke-Plagwitz, 2009). For instance, students attempting to conduct a virtual debate in Second Life were often distracted by activity occurring elsewhere in the virtual world, and this may explain why they exhibited lower levels of cognitive presence than learners who completed the debate using a plain text-chat tool (Traphagan et al., 2010). Students can also be easily distracted by elements outside the virtual world, for instance social networking sites that may be running on the same computer, or family members if working from home (Sierra et al., 2012). Higher levels of perceived distraction have been shown to correlate with lower levels of conceptual learning (Tüzün & Özdinç, 2016).

SAFETY

In many cases virtual worlds are open, anonymous and uncontrolled, which means that people may not feel accountable for their actions (Warburton, 2009) and engage in deliberate misconduct or 'griefing' of others (Bell, 2009). Thus student well-being is a major concern, particularly for school teachers using open virtual worlds like Second Life where adult content or influence are a possibility (Dickey, 2011). Using open virtual worlds such as Second Life with students exposes them to the risk of deception, deliberate offense, lewd behavior, or sexually offensive imagery (Childs et al., 2012). In any case, the age restrictions for some virtual worlds (e.g., Second Life) need to be taken into consideration before utilization in classes (Dalgarno et al., 2011a). Concerns for student safety extend through to higher education – in one study a sizeable proportion (18%) of university educators who used virtual world for reasons other than teaching did not want to use virtual worlds for teaching because they did not want to expose their students to inappropriate content (Gregory et al., 2015a).

ASSESSMENT

Depending on the type of assessment that is to be conducted in virtual worlds, it may be difficult to capture, attribute and analyze performance data. If assessment is to be conducted in the virtual world then confirming the identity of the remote student operating an avatar can be an issue (Childs et al., 2012). If group work tasks are prescribed in the virtual world it can be difficult to determine the contribution of individual group members (Noteborn et al., 2014). Some proposed models of assessment involving machinima and virtual-world log files (such as those by Chodos, Stroulia, King, & Carbonaro, 2014) may not practicable for everyday teaching use. The technical problems that can occur in virtual worlds also make them high risk environments for conducting compulsory tasks or assessments (Childs et al., 2012). Although plagiarism was rarely mentioned across the literature, it is possible for students to pass each other login details, for instance in order to complete Second Life programming assignments (Dreher et al., 2009).

TEACHER TECHNICAL SKILLS

Educators may also struggle with the technical skills required to teach in virtual worlds. The teacher is ultimately responsible for managing activity and providing support for students in the virtual world, which can be challenging when students are new to the environment or the technology is causing problems

(Petrakou, 2010). Assisting students who are experiencing technical difficulties can be particularly challenging if they are located off campus (Gregory et al., 2015a). It takes skill to be able to monitor and manage students in virtual worlds, particularly if group work activities are being utilized (Zhang, 2013). Adapting and importing externally sourced virtual-worlds resources also requires a certain level of technical expertise (Gregory et al., 2015a). To this extent, S. Gregory et al. (2015b) found that 20% of educators surveyed who were not using virtual worlds felt that they lacked the computing skills to use virtual worlds in their teaching.

NEGATIVE EDUCATOR DISPOSITIONS

Risk of technical problems can deter teachers from attempting to use virtual worlds in their classes (Childs et al., 2012). There is also a (perhaps naïve) perception among many educators that virtual worlds were a fad and are no longer a worthwhile platform for designing and conducting learning activities (Gregory et al., 2014; Gregory et al., 2015a; Gregory et al., 2015b).

TIME

It can be immensely time-consuming to design, construct and test a virtual-world environment (Warburton, 2009). Time is required to download and install software, create avatars, and learn how to communicate and navigate in the virtual world (Baker et al., 2009; Zhang, 2013). It can also be time-consuming to research the right environment or locations within a virtual world for students to explore or experience (Zhang, 2013). It takes time to designing and developing appropriate scaffolding and instruction within the virtual world (Zhang, 2013). It also takes instructors time to assist learners with how use the virtual world, both before and during activities (Zhang, 2013).

The time factor is often exacerbated if educators start from scratch with virtual worlds rather than building on the work of others (Gregory et al., 2014). On the other hand, while there is a plethora of virtual-world environments and resources readily available for educational use, sourcing the right resources can take a considerable amount of time (Gregory et al., 2015a). In a study by S. Gregory et al. (2015b), 29% of educators who were not using virtual worlds cited time as a prohibiting factor.

COST

Using virtual worlds often carries a cost, so if funding is not available it can be difficult for teachers to adopt virtual worlds in their courses (Dalgarno et al., 2011a; Gregory et al., 2015a). The two basic choices for using virtual-world platforms are downloading and installing software on an in-house server or using a virtual world hosted by an external party (Warburton, 2009), with both options potentially involving a cost. Creating an in-house installation of a virtual-worlds server can be time consuming and is prone to configuration problems (Coban et al., 2015). On the other hand purchasing space on open servers so that teachers and students can undertake design projects can involve a complicated and time-consuming purchase process (Coban et al., 2015). For instance, in Second Life, purchasing land, uploading images, buying useful in-world tools, and employing building and scripting expertise all cost money (Warburton, 2009). In one project it cost £29,000 to develop three role-play scenarios for psychology students (Ward et al., 2015). Members of the Virtual Worlds Working Group report cost of purchasing and developing 3-D virtual worlds as a major challenge (Gregory et al., 2015a).

INSTITUTIONAL SUPPORT

University teachers identify funding, technical support and teaching support as institutional factors that inhibit their use of virtual worlds for teaching (Gregory et al., 2015b). Support from management within the institution may be required but lacking (Dalgarno et al., 2011a). Virtual-worlds software is continually being developed and hence updated, so in-house installations may need substantial amounts of maintenance by technical staff to avoid becoming unreliable (Gregory et al., 2015b). Sustainability over time can also be an issue, as information technology and teaching staff change (Dalgarno et al., 2011b). Then there is the important question of pedagogical support and awareness raising – teachers without any experience in virtual worlds are less likely to understand how virtual worlds can be effectively used in their discipline area (Gregory et al., 2015b).

In summary, while the 3-D simulation environment provided by virtual worlds provides a range of extra opportunities to educators, there are also additional risks and issues to consider.

Virtual-World Design Vignettes

As with previously considered platforms, it is not only important to know the potentials and constraints of teaching using the technology, but it is also critical to have a more in-depth and concrete understanding of how they can be applied in practice. Two vignettes are presented below to exemplify how virtual worlds can be used for learning and teaching, one involving medical education at university and the other relating to architectural design education for school students.

VIGNETTE 1 – USING SECOND LIFE TO TEACH MEDICAL STUDENTS ABOUT HUMAN ANATOMY

The College of Medicine at the University of Kentucky created a virtual laboratory in Second Life for medical students to learn anatomy (Richardson et al., 2011). The anatomy laboratory contains several stations and features including areas focusing on cadavers (see Figure 10.4), a guided tour through cross-sectional anatomy, video tutorials and group quizzes. Students click on the station heading to receive a note-card in their inventory that contains an explanation of anatomical structure under consideration as well as associated questions (see Figure 10.5). The questions aimed to provide triggers that the instructor can use to promote group discussion. Students were able to watch video tutorials within the virtual world, for instance of cadaver dissections. Students were also required to wear appropriate attire (i.e. laboratory coat) at all times in order to teach them appropriate behavior that can transfer into real-world settings (Richardson et al., 2011).

Access to the virtual laboratory was much greater than to traditional laboratories that were only accessible at certain times and on campus (Richardson et al., 2011). Students were able to interact with each other while viewing the same material, despite the physical distance between them. Having medical professionals visit the laboratory enables students to form and maintain a network via distance (Richardson et al., 2011).

Using the virtual-world laboratory also involved far lower risks and expense than running a real-world laboratory, and is much more sustainable over time. Constructing difficult anatomical models within the virtual world enables more thorough illustration of anatomical intricacies, as students can use their avatar

Figure 10.4. The Virtual Anatomy Laboratory Showing Cadaver and Students Reviewing Explanatory Slides (Richardson et al., 2011, p. 40).

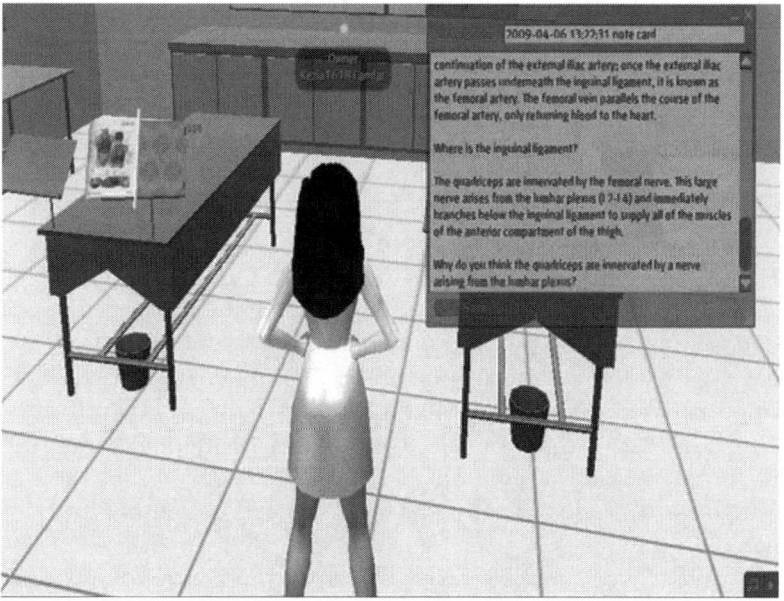

Figure 10.5. Notecard Issued to Student Inventory Containing Explanatory Information and Questions (Richardson et al., 2011, p. 41).

to fly or maneuver in and out of the model components (Richardson et al., 2011).

Anecdotal feedback from students suggests that the 'pseudo-anonymity' afforded by avatars helped them feel more comfortable answering questions in group discussions (Richardson et al., 2011). Students also appeared more comfortable to respond to questions by the teacher in the virtual-world environment.

VIGNETTE 2 – USING OPENSIM AS AN ARCHITECTURAL DESIGN ENVIRONMENT FOR SCHOOL STUDENTS

This vignette is based upon the Macquarie ICT Innovations Centre 3-D Virtual Worlds Project 3.0 (Lumkin et al., 2011). The goal of the project was to evaluate how design and construction activities within virtual worlds could support school students to develop skills relating to independent enquiry, creative thinking, reflective learning and collaboration. In particular, visual arts students were required to design cities of the future that incorporated ideas of sustainability, aesthetic appeal and functionality. The task was purposefully designed to involve students in an authentic and meaningful context that required analytical rather than reproductive thinking.

A closed OpenSim virtual-world installation was used to protect children from adverse external influence. A private instance of an Edmodo social networking group was used for students to post their ongoing reflections and for teachers to provide constructive feedback. A code of conduct was outlined that encouraged students to interact respectfully and support one another.

Students initially learnt about architectural history and concepts, followed by two days training on the use of the technologies. Virtual-world training started with highly structured tasks, gradually shifting to ill-structured activities that allowed for creative expression. Online training videos were made available as support material for students and teachers. Students then formed groups of two or three people to draft and create their designs in the virtual world. Having all the designing occur within the one virtual-world region meant that even though students had their own design space they could learn vicariously from others.

Student work was assessed based on the aesthetics, sustainability, technological skills, research and documentation that students completed. Student work later formed part of a public exhibition entitled WHEN2050, resulting in overwhelmingly positive community acclaim. Screenshots of example designs are provided in Figure 10.6 and Figure 10.7 below.

Throughout the project teachers observed high levels of student confidence, engagement and enthusiasm. Teachers also noted the way that virtual worlds enable students to actualize their creative visions in a way that would not otherwise be possible:

> In effect it is as if students are given free rein in a magical world where their imaginations can run freely ... and actually have their ideas 'materialize'! (Lumkin et al., 2011, p. 16)

Students observed how modeling their designs made them realize complexities that they would not otherwise have considered, and learn about global issues that they would not have otherwise broached:

> When using the virtual world many complications occur and so your ideas have to change to suit the world .... Also working on a project where we had to think about sustainability was very important. I learnt how to come up with new ideas that would be environmentally friendly. (Lumkin et al., 2011, p. 17)

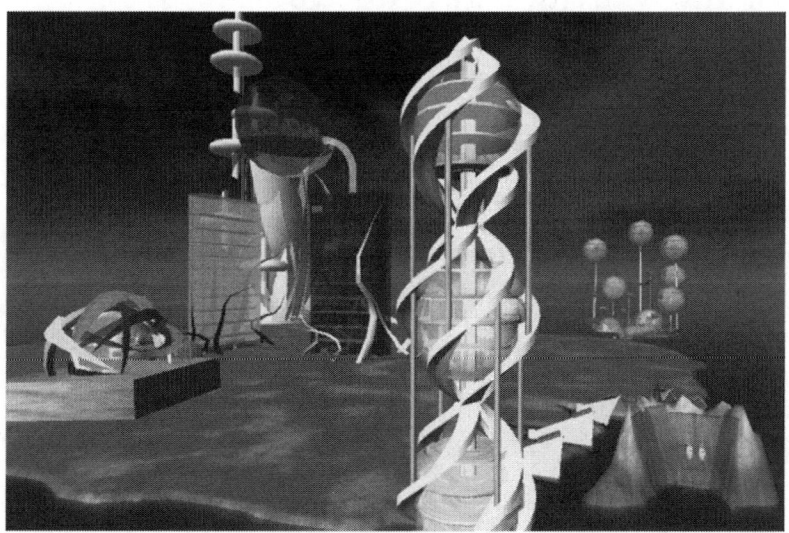

Figure 10.6. School Students' Futuristic Virtual-World Building Designs (Lumkin et al., 2011, p. 44).

Figure 10.7.   Close-Up View of Futuristic Building Designs Showing Interior Architecture (Lumkin et al., 2011, p. 44).

The quote illustrates how the use of virtual worlds in this vignette targeted more critical and higher order thinking, which is in contrast to the previous example. This once again showcases how the type of thinking that is encouraged is very much dependent on the tasks that educators design rather than the technology that is used.

Virtual-World Learning Design Recommendations

Once again, understanding the potentials and issues of a technology and seeing how it can be used in practice is only part of the picture. It is important to know the how research findings and observations can and should inform learning design efforts. Recommendations for the design and implementation of virtual-worlds learning tasks and environments, as emergent from international virtual-worlds literature, are outlined below.

HAVE A GOOD REASON TO USE VIRTUAL WORLDS

It is important that virtual worlds are used in order to capitalize on their affordances, rather than merely being used for their own sake (Gregory et al., 2014). Whether to simulate scenarios, build objects, or remotely facilitate role-play activities, there are many useful applications of virtual worlds in education. Lim (2009) proposes that there are six fundamental forms of learning that take place in virtual worlds, namely, learning by exploring, learning by collaborating, learning by being, learning by building objects and/or scripting them, learning by championing, and learning by transferring into the real world. Situated, experiential and spatially oriented learning experiences leverage the 3-D and interactive affordances of virtual worlds outlined by Dalgarno and Lee (2010). If virtual worlds are used in a way that doesn't capitalize on their potentials it can result in sub-optimal learning experiences (Van Der Land et al., 2013).

ASSESS THE TECHNOLOGICAL LANDSCAPE AND SUPPORT AVAILABLE

Given that virtual worlds require reasonably high-end computing power and bandwidth in order to run (Herold, 2009; Sarac, 2014), there are a variety of technical problems that can occur including software bugs (Childs et al., 2012), server glitches (Garrido-Iñigo & Rodríguez-Moreno, 2015) or firewall or bandwidth issues (Dalgarno et al., 2011a). Access to institutional support can be a critical factor affecting the success of virtual-worlds projects (Dalgarno et al., 2011a; Gregory et al., 2015b). Making a case for improved infrastructure and enlisting institutional support are often necessary for virtual-world projects to be successful (Dalgarno et al., 2011b). Exploring whether there are other virtual-world projects that you may be able to work with or build upon could be a way of saving time and resources (Gregory et al., 2015a).

CONSIDER HOW STUDENT SAFETY AND RIGHTS WILL BE MAINTAINED

Student wellbeing and cybersafety are important concerns when using technology, which is amplified if open virtual-world platforms such as Second Life are being used (Dickey, 2011). Exposing students to the risk of untoward behavior or sexually explicit imagery is not an option, particularly for school children. If an open virtual world is being used, access controls (such as password protection) may be necessary in order to prevent unauthorized people from entering the learning space (Minocha & Reeves, 2010; Zhang, 2013). If student safety is paramount, then a closed virtual world such as Open Sim may be preferable to an open world such as Second Life (Childs et al., 2012). Intellectual property rights, object permissions and accessibility all require consideration (Warburton, 2009).

SELECT THE VIRTUAL WORLD BASED ON STUDENT, TASK, AND INSTITUTIONAL REQUIREMENTS

Different virtual worlds have different affordances and constraints, so finding an appropriate virtual world depends on the students being taught, what needs to happen in the virtual world, and what is feasible within the institution. It is important to establish that students have access to computers with sufficient processing and Internet bandwidth in order to be able to operate the virtual world, especially if the intention is that they work from home (Coban et al., 2015; Herold, 2009). Different virtual-world platforms will allow users to build, share and script objects more easily than others (Gül et al., 2008) so it is important to check that the virtual world being considered will functionally enable completion of the intended tasks. On a financial and institutional level, the costs involved in downloading and self-managing a virtual-world server need to be weighed up against the cost of purchasing space and resources on a proprietary virtual-world platform (Coban et al., 2015).

DETERMINE HOW VIRTUAL WORLDS WILL BE USED WITHIN THE BROADER SCOPE OF THE CURRICULUM

Educators should decide whether the virtual world will be used for the entire learning cycle or part of it. Virtual worlds are often used for distance education, in order for teachers to conduct classes and remotely located participants to communicate and work with one another (Inman et al., 2010; Kim et al., 2012). On the other hand, virtual worlds are often used in blended mode, where the instructor teaches students in a face-to-face classroom but has students participate in the virtual world via computers for parts of the lesson (Kim et al., 2012). Thus, virtual worlds may form a small or major part of the overall curriculum, and clearly delineating the phases of learning for which virtual worlds will be utilized enables targeted design to occur.

Using virtual-world simulations to practice skills and concepts learnt outside the 3-D virtual environment has been shown to be more effective than using the virtual environment for the whole learning sequence (Merchant, Goetz, Cifuentes, Keeney-Kennicutt, & Davis, 2014). Recall that modeling geography phenomena using a virtual world and then having high school students hold classroom discussions about what they observed resulted in higher knowledge gains than when the students collaboratively solved problems in the virtual world or when traditional classroom instruction was used (Cho & Lim, 2015).

CONSIDER STUDENT BACKGROUND AND INTERESTS

Different cohorts of students may have markedly different enthusiasm for using virtual worlds and technological competencies, so understanding the dispositions and skills of the student cohort can help teachers to better cater to their needs (Herold, 2009). Research has shown that students enjoy and are less bored by virtual-world tasks that they value, and task enjoyment has been correlated with better academic performance (Noteborn, Carbonell, Dailey-Hebert, & Gijselaers, 2012). Educators may also consider what students might enjoy about using virtual worlds. A synthesis of several studies by Hew and Cheung (2010) concluded that reasons students tend to like using virtual worlds include the ability to fly and move around freely in 3-D space, the ability to socialize and meet new people, the ability to participate in virtual field trips and simulated experiences.

LEVERAGE THE OPPORTUNITY TO USE VIRTUAL WORLDS TO FACILITATE SITUATED AND EXPERIENTIAL LEARNING

One of the key benefits of virtual worlds is that they can be used to provide students with situated and experiential learning activities (Dede, 2009; Gregory et al., 2015b; Hew & Cheung, 2010; Warburton, 2009). Virtual-world role-play activities can be used to help students develop contextualized skills, appreciate multiple perspectives and develop empathy (Gregory et al., 2014). Examples include restaurant scenarios for language learning (Henderson et al., 2012), medical wards for diagnosis skills (Rogers, 2011), navigation spaces to support development of directional communication (Lin et al., 2014), and classrooms to help teachers learn behavior management (Cheong, 2010). Students across studies have indicated an appreciation of the practice (Noteborn et al., 2014) and collaboration (Rogers, 2011) that virtual-world role-plays can provide, as well as high levels of task satisfaction (Ward et al., 2015). Use of situated and experiential learning tasks in virtual worlds may also help students transfer their learning to real-life contexts (Coffman & Klinger, 2007; Dede, 2009; Jarmon et al., 2009).

CONSIDER UTILIZING VIRTUAL WORLDS TO DEVELOP SPATIAL KNOWLEDGE

Virtual worlds can be used to support the development of spatial knowledge. The use of 3-D virtual environments have been shown to be more effective than 2-D environments for facilitating spatial reasoning and evaluation (Passig et al., 2016; Van der Land et al., 2011), and can also support better spatial knowledge acquisition than real-world experiences by removing unnecessary distractions and simplifying the complexity of the subject matter (Tüzün & Özdinç, 2016). Thus, if an intended learning outcome relates to spatial understanding or interpretation then virtual worlds may offer a superior environment than 2-D or real-world experiences.

TAKE ADVANTAGE OF THE ABILITY TO TRANSCEND PHYSICALITY

Virtual worlds offer the ability to transcend time and space, simulating phenomena that are otherwise too impractical, dangerous or impossible to undertake in the real world (Dalgarno & Lee, 2010; Twining, 2009; Warburton, 2009). Historical villages can be replicated (Edirisingha et al., 2009) and molecular reactions can be modeled (Merchant et al., 2012). Educators can seize the opportunity for them and their students to defy gravity, build the impossible, and simulate life in other times and places.

CONSIDER THE DEGREE OF FIDELITY THAT IS REQUIRED

Inaccurate representation of objects or processes in a virtual world may cause information loss or misunderstanding (Dalgarno et al., 2011b). Visual realism is considered important when the objects are directly related to what students are supposed to learn, such as the architecture of Mayan buildings or the arrangement of a computer motherboard (Minocha & Reeves, 2010). Unrealistic representation may diminish the quality of student experience, as indicated when scripted avatar characters lacked the sophistication to behave like human characters (Mahon et al., 2010; Ward et al., 2015) or when a virtual film set did not full replicate the details of a real-world location (Foss, 2009).

CONSIDER THE COGNITIVE LOAD IMPLICATIONS OF LEARNING VIRTUAL WORLDS

Evidence suggests that increased representational complexity of virtual worlds can contribute to cognitive load thus negatively impacting upon learning (Richards & Taylor, 2015; Schrader & Bastiaens, 2012; Van Der Land et al., 2013). Of critical importance appears to be whether the 3-D affordances of virtual worlds contribute to conceptual understanding and whether or not the interactive affordances enhance communication. For instance, using virtual worlds for group consensus building was found to impose a higher cognitive load and increase time taken to make group decisions than less interactive and less realistic approaches (Van Der Land et al., 2013).

DESIGN THE VIRTUAL SPACE ACCORDING TO INTENDED ACTIVITY AND PEDAGOGY

Minocha and Reeves (2010) provide a comprehensive analysis of space design in virtual worlds, recommending that intended activity and pedagogy should be the key drivers. In their qualitative study students and teachers indicated that the design of the environment influenced how people act and engage in the learning tasks. For instance, the placement of pathways, signposts, or even whether the space is indoors versus outdoors can all provide students with clues about how to act. Even the positioning of the teacher (for instance on a podium) was suggested to impact upon the social dynamics in the environment. Social and informal spaces added to the environment were seen to encourage community building. Attention to aesthetics and providing variety in the virtual world were also suggested to positively impact upon interest and engagement (Minocha & Reeves, 2010).

The virtual-world space can be specifically designed to facilitate collaboration, for instance setting up team spaces for groups of students to work (Esteves et al., 2011). Space design can be tailored to support distinctive modes of collaboration, such as large group circular seating in some rooms and small group team spaces on other floors (Andreas et al., 2010). Other semiotics can be used to facilitate group work processes — for instance, the color of armchairs can be used to denote the team membership of students during 'jigsaw' activities (Andreas et al., 2010).

USE NAVIGATIONAL AIDS TO SUPPORT WAYFINDING

One way that virtual worlds are different to other online technologies is that the user needs to spatially navigate through the 3-D environment to arrive at the desired location. If virtual spaces don't resemble real-world spaces, navigational aids are difficult to locate, and areas are difficult to find, then students may become frustrated, abandon the learning activity or take longer completing activities than necessary (Minocha & Hardy, 2016). Well-designed navigational aids such as directional signs, maps, architectural landmarks and teleport stations can all be used to support quick transitions between places (Minocha & Hardy, 2016). Strategies that support navigation and wayfinding include making navigational information easy to locate and interpret, using color and formatting to highlight navigational aids and code elements within them, and using objects and metaphors that resemble the real world (Minocha & Hardy, 2016). Pathways can be used to represent the recommended learning sequence (Dickey, 2005b).

CONSIDER WHAT SORTS OF SCAFFOLDING AND TASK INSTRUCTIONS WILL BE PROVIDED

Because virtual worlds will be an unfamiliar environment for many students and there is a lot of information for newcomers to process, it is important that appropriate scaffolding and task instructions are provided. The deployment of persistent scaffolding, signals and resources within the virtual worlds means that students are able to practice more independently (Inman et al., 2010; Minocha & Reeves, 2010). Step-by-step written instructions have been observed to assist in clarifying the goals and components of the learning tasks (Lin et al., 2014) and to encourage on-task behavior (Omale et al., 2009). To achieve this, in-world bulletin boards can be used to provide students with clear and situated task instructions (Andreas et al., 2010). Alternately, course websites external to the virtual world may also be used to provide students with clear instructions and resources that they will need to perform tasks (Petrakou, 2010). Scaffolding can also take the form of scripted avatars that demonstrate activities for students (Lan, 2015).

ESTABLISH A CLEAR RATIONALE FOR USING VIRTUAL WORLDS

Many students are unfamiliar with virtual worlds and they may have negative dispositions toward using them. Consequently, there is a possibility that students may be unclear about why they are using virtual worlds (Herold, 2009). To address this, teachers can establish a clear connection between course objectives and activities undertaken in the virtual world in order to encourage participants to remain on task (Baker et al., 2009; Inman et al., 2010).

PROVIDE VIRTUAL-WORLD TRAINING

Training sessions prior to learning activities enable students to familiarize themselves with how to operate the virtual-world environment (Childs et al., 2012; Gül et al., 2008; Omale et al., 2009). Allowing students to explore the functionalities of the virtual world and modeling the execution of activities is important because it can reduce their cognitive load during learning tasks so that they can focus on the to-be-learnt subject matter (Lim et al., 2006). People who are more experienced in virtual-world usage have been shown to interact significantly more deeply with virtual worlds, for instance in the way they interact with objects, use multimedia, control their avatar, and adjust their perspective (Yilmaz, Baydas, Karakus, & Goktas, 2015).

Providing open access to computers and the virtual-world environment enables students to practice their virtual-world skills outside of class time (Dalgarno et al., 2011b). Activities such as 'scavenger hunts' have also been used as a fun way to help students build up their virtual-world operational skills (Bower et al., 2017; Yilmaz et al., 2015). It has been noted that students' virtual world technical skills do naturally improve over time (deNoyelles & Seo, 2012).

ENCOURAGE USE OF APPROPRIATE COMMUNICATION MODES

Students and teachers should choose the virtual-world communication mode that best supports the communication goals of the activity. For instance, private chat can be used to communicate between two people anywhere in the virtual world, whereas public chat can be used to broadcast information to anyone within the vicinity (20 meters in Second Life) (Esteves et al., 2011). While text messaging can be useful for providing a persistent record of conversations, audio has been noted as effective for dialogue and discussion (Sutcliffe & Alrayes, 2012). Students may not naturally think of using avatar gestures so in order for them to take advantage of this mode of communication it may be necessary to draw their attention to the array of possible gestures and associated underlying messages that they imply (Rappa, Yip, & Baey, 2009).

APPLY TACTICS TO SUPPORT EFFECTIVE INTERACTION

As a new environment for learning, students need to be introduced to the appropriate social norms and rules of virtual worlds so that they can interact effectively (Petrakou, 2010). Sutcliffe and Alrayes (2012) recommend enforcing explicit identity (rather than anonymous use of avatars) in order to promote linkages through to real-world participants and also greater accountability within the virtual world. It may be useful to formulate protocols for managing group and class discussions in the virtual world, in order to structure conversations and avoid multiple overlapping conversations (Baker et al., 2009). Strategies to overcome the absence of non-verbal cues include facilitator orchestration of discussion or appointing participants to moderate group work conversations (Zhang, 2013). Because it is not possible to see learners' facial expressions and body language, teachers can compensate by explicitly asking whether people have any questions or are experiencing difficulties (Lin et al., 2014).

In one study of collaboration in Second Life by Andreas et al. (2010), several features of the technology were deliberately deployed in order to enhance collaboration. This included having avatars put on different colored shirts depending on the 'jigsaw' collaboration group to which they had been assigned, having students raise their hand when they wanted permission to speak, and assigning moderator hats to the team member in charge of facilitating discussion. Several custom-built tools were also used to support interaction, including a sign and microphone over the designated speaker's head, a queue system to support discussion turn taking, and the ability to place symbols above avatars to denote questions or ideas (Andreas et al., 2010).

In terms of text chat, a range of strategies can be applied to enhance interaction, including addressing people by their avatar name to signify the intended message recipient, using common abbreviations in order to save time, and splitting content between messages in order to provide additional information without delaying the conversation (Peterson, 2010).

APPLY PEDAGOGICAL STRATEGIES TO SUPPORT COLLABORATION

Group dynamics can have a substantial impact on the productivity of virtual groups (Girvan & Savage, 2010). It can be useful to assign students to pairs or groups so that they can help each other in the virtual world or form mentoring relationships if one person is more experienced (Baker et al., 2009; Grenfell, 2013).

On the other hand, the ability to pick online communication partners supports socialization and relationship building (Petrakou, 2010). Allocating roles to students within a team may also support group work processes (Rappa et al., 2009).

Undergraduate students completing a global virtual project using Second Life identified the following underpinnings of effective collaboration: "careful planning and establishing of the goals and roles clearly and early enough; motivation finishing the tasks; group problem-solving; regular, well-planned meetings and intense participation; and respect and appreciation from team members among others" (Keskitalo et al., 2011, p. 22). Thus, any strategies that the teacher can apply to create these conditions may contribute to effective group work. Gül et al. (2008) point out that it may also be valuable to nurture the underlying teamwork skills required for effective collaboration in virtual worlds, including leadership, coordination, feedback, trust development, and interpersonal skills. A discourse analysis of collaborative work in a virtual world showed that the teacher can have a critical impact on activity through their guidance of the group work process (Hämäläinen & Oksanen, 2012). Specifically, the presence and guidance of the teacher encouraged students to explain their activities and refrain from off-task behavior (Hämäläinen & Oksanen, 2012).

The design of the group work tasks may also impact on collaboration. Strategies for encouraging collaboration include requiring students to collect data from each other, provide information to peers, or complete tasks together (Yilmaz et al., 2015). Esteves et al. (2011) recommends that if group projects are being prescribed then they should involve a visual element and be complex enough that all members of the group are required to complete them. In one study of English as a Foreign Language students found greater negation of meaning (using the text chat) for tasks requiring decision making as opposed to 'jigsaw' or opinion-exchange tasks (Peterson, 2006).

UTILIZE THE SPATIAL NATURE OF THE ENVIRONMENT TO ENHANCE LEARNING AND TEACHING

There are several ways that the spatial features of the environment can be used to enhance learning and teaching. First, students can move around the environment to hold paired discussions, for instance about objects in the world (Petrakou, 2010). Second, the affordances of virtual worlds enable new ways of managing classes, for example, a teacher can fly over groups so as not to interrupt them while monitoring their discussion (Petrakou, 2010). Third, the spatial nature of the environment can enhance interactivity, for instance avatar actions can enable the teacher to determine when students have misunderstood instructions (Petrakou, 2010). Finally, remote participants can be asked to move to particular locations in the virtual-world classroom based on their preferences, which is not possible in other synchronous collaboration platforms (Bower et al., 2017).

APPLY GENERAL PEDAGOGICAL PRINCIPLES

When teaching in virtual worlds, the teacher still needs to perform functions that they would in a face-to-face environment, such as preparing instruction, set up the learning space, provide instruction, respond to student problems, and facilitate discussion (Esteves et al., 2011). While virtual worlds constitute a different learning environment for many educators, a wide range of pedagogical knowledge and capabilities can be directly transferred into the virtual-world environment. For instance, just like for regular teaching, it can be invaluable to have a backup plan in case of system failure (Dalgarno et al., 2011b).

PROMOTE AND LEVERAGE PRESENCE

Bronack et al. (2008) recommend a 'presence pedagogy' approach for teaching in virtual worlds that is based upon asking questions and correct misperceptions, stimulating background knowledge and expertise, capitalizing on the presence of others, facilitating interactions and encouraging community, supporting distributed cognition, sharing tools and resources, encouraging exploration and discovery, providing and delineating context and goals, and fostering reflective practice. These positive teaching strategies, aimed at fostering a strong sense of presence, were shown to lead to a positive learning community (Bronack et al., 2008).

LEVERAGE STUDENTS AS DESIGNERS

Virtual worlds offer an exciting platform in which students can build and create (Twining, 2009). Students may even be enlisted as co-designers of spaces, providing them with a sense of connectedness and fostering their creativity (Minocha & Reeves, 2010).

Girvan and Savage (2010) advocate a 'communal constructivism' approach whereby learning artifacts created by one group of learners are fed back into subsequent iterations of the learning task, thus benefiting the experience of future learners. Involving students in the learning design process and soliciting their feedback about tasks can provide invaluable information for refinements and future iterations (Baker et al., 2009). Having students write scripts to extend the behavior of objects can further enhance the creative potential of virtual worlds (Esteves et al., 2011). It is obviously important to provide students with correct permissions to conduct the required activities (e.g., upload 3-D objects) in order for them to build within the environment (Dickey, 2003).

INTEGRATE OTHER TOOLS

Virtual worlds do not support easy document processing or exchange, so another platform (for instance, learning management system) may be useful for facilitating the sharing of resources (Esteves et al., 2011). Others go as far as to claim that virtual worlds *should* be used in combination with other tools in order to provide clearer and more direct access to information without the distraction of the graphically rich and socially dynamic virtual world (Petrakou, 2010). Other tools that may be used to compliment the functionality of virtual worlds to support productivity include Moodle, G Suite, Skype, blogs, wikis and social networking systems (Lumkin et al., 2011; Olteanu et al., 2014; Warburton, 2009).

MANAGE ONGOING TECHNICAL SUPPORT

Technical support is not generally provided by the virtual-world vendors meaning that there needs to be some sort of class or institution arrangement for offering student and teacher technical assistance (Herold, 2009). Typical technical support includes installing and configuring software, resolving firewall issues, and developing spaces within the virtual world (Dalgarno et al., 2011a). Students can be an excellent source of technical support for other students that the teacher can utilize in their classes (Lin et al., 2014). Having students form buddy pairs during class means that they can help each other with learning or technical problems, and also notify the teacher if someone is experiencing communication difficulties (Lin et al., 2014). Other strategies for providing technical support include having a virtual-world helpdesk, and providing a website with manuals, guidelines and video tutorials for using the virtual world (Noteborn et al., 2014).

ACTIVELY PURSUE PROFESSIONAL LEARNING OPPORTUNITIES

It is advisable that teachers become confident with the virtual worlds by practicing in advance, to avoid situations where they do not know how to perform standard operations while teaching a class (Baker et al., 2009). Teachers need to prepare for the fact that their students often want them to provide help on how to use virtual worlds (Noteborn et al., 2014). Professional development is recommended for staff in order to cultivate their virtual-world skills and help them learn how they can make best use of virtual-world features (Dalgarno et al., 2011a; Lumkin et al., 2011). Gregory et al. (2015b) recommend establishing a community of practice within each institution to foster sustainability of virtual-worlds initiatives. The virtual-world community can be a great source of technical and pedagogical support. For instance teachers may choose to sign up to the Second Life Education forum and listserve at http://wiki.secondlife.com/wiki/SLED (Baker et al., 2009). Having an expert virtual worlds educator present to assist with technical issues during initial attempts to use virtual worlds can mean that novice teachers are able to better concentrate on the pedagogical aspects of the lessons (Lin et al., 2014).

Concluding Comments on Virtual-World Learning Design

In conclusion, there are quite evidently numerous possible benefits of using virtual worlds, though several pertinent constraints and issues need to be managed. Once again, realizing the potentials and circumventing the constraints depends on careful planning, resourcing and appropriate supports (Gregory et al., 2015b). While virtual worlds constitute a more unorthodox and potentially higher risk environment for designing learning tasks, Childs et al. (2012) point out that educators have a professional obligation to experiment and develop. As well, by having students use virtual worlds we are also helping them to develop skills that they may need for the future, for instance, conducting a job interview via virtual-world environment or hosting a virtual tour themselves (Childs et al., 2012).

We can expect in the future that a variety of new input and output devices such as haptic gloves and Virtual Reality (VR) glasses will transform the virtual-world experience (Duncan et al., 2012). Consumer-level motion sensing and gesture-recognition controllers will conceivably enable more naturalistic interaction between people and with objects in the virtual world (Bower et al., 2017). We should also expect convergence of virtual worlds with other technologies such as augmented reality, augmented virtuality and 3-D printing (Gregory et al., 2014).

In terms of research, although much of the early research relating to 3-D virtual worlds in education tended to be opinion pieces or non-empirical descriptive papers about virtual-world implementations (Hew & Cheung, 2010), more recent work is starting to be more experimentally oriented (Kim et al., 2012). Nevertheless, Gregory et al. (2015b) note that most of the research into virtual worlds is still descriptive in nature. The field would ultimately benefit from experimental research that examines the impact of different virtual-world learning designs on educational outcomes (Hew & Cheung, 2010). Moving beyond studies that report novel designs or general positive feedback may provide substantive evidence that convinces educators and institutions to invest time, energy and resources into designing and utilizing virtual-world environments (Gregory et al., 2015b). There is also an opportunity to conduct research that extends beyond the typically short-term (one semester) time frame to measure longitudinal impact (Ghanbarzadeh & Ghapanchi, 2016).

References

Active Worlds. (2016). Active worlds wiki main page. Retrieved from http://wiki.activeworlds.com. Accessed on February 21, 2017.

Andreas, K., Tsiatsos, T., Terzidou, T., & Pomportsis, A. (2010). Fostering collaborative learning in Second Life: Metaphors and affordances. *Computers & Education*, 55(2), 603–615.

Antonacci, D. M., & Modaress, N. (2008). Envisioning the educational possibilities of user-created virtual worlds. *AACE Journal*, 16(2), 115–126.

Baker, S. C., Wentz, R. K., & Woods, M. M. (2009). Using virtual worlds in education: Second Life® as an educational tool. *Teaching of Psychology*, 36(1), 59–64.

Barab, S., Thomas, M., Dodge, T., Carteaux, R., & Tuzun, H. (2005). Making learning fun: Quest Atlantis, a game without guns. *Educational Technology Research and Development*, *53*(1), 86−107.

Bell, D. (2009). Learning from second life. *British Journal of Educational Technology*, *40*(3), 515−525.

Bell, M. W. (2008). Toward a definition of virtual worlds. *Journal of Virtual Worlds Research*, *1*(1), 1−5.

Bertacchini, F., & Tavernise, A. (2016). NetConnect virtual worlds − Results of a learning experience. In S. Gregory, M. J. W. Lee, B. Dalgarno, & B. Tynan (Eds.), *Learning in Virtual Worlds: Research and Applications* (pp. 227−240). Athabasca: Athabasca University Press.

Bos, B., Wilder, L., Cook, M., & O'Donnell, R. (2014). Learning mathematics through Minecraft. *Teaching Children Mathematics*, *21*(1), 56−59.

Bouta, H., Retalis, S., & Paraskeva, F. (2012). Utilising a collaborative macro-script to enhance student engagement: A mixed method study in a 3D virtual environment. *Computers & Education*, *58*(1), 501−517.

Bower, M., Lee, M. J. W., & Dalgarno, B. (2017). Collaborative learning across physical and virtual worlds: Factors supporting and constraining learners in a blended reality environment. *British Journal of Educational Technology*, *48*(2), 407−430.

Bronack, S., Riedl, R., & Tashner, J. (2006). Learning in the zone: A social constructivist framework for distance education in a 3-dimensional virtual world. *Interactive Learning Environments*, *14*(3), 219−232.

Bronack, S., Sanders, R., Cheney, A., Riedl, R., Tashner, J., & Matzen, N. (2008). Presence pedagogy: Teaching and learning in a 3D virtual immersive world. *International Journal of Teaching and Learning in Higher Education*, *20*(1), 59−69.

Bulu, S. T. (2012). Place presence, social presence, co-presence, and satisfaction in virtual worlds. *Computers & Education*, *58*(1), 154−161.

Chen, J. F., Warden, C. A., Tai, D. W.-S., Chen, F.-S., & Chao, C.-Y. (2011). Level of abstraction and feelings of presence in virtual space: Business English negotiation in Open Wonderland. *Computers & Education*, *57*(3), 2126−2134.

Cheong, D. (2010). The effects of practice teaching sessions in second life on the change in pre-service teachers' teaching efficacy. *Computers & Education*, *55*(2), 868−880.

Childs, M., Schnieders, H. L., & Williams, G. (2012). "This above all: To thine own self be true": Ethical considerations and risks in conducting higher education learning activities in the virtual world Second Life™. *Interactive Learning Environments*, *20*(3), 253−269.

Cho, Y. H., & Lim, K. Y. T. (2015). Effectiveness of collaborative learning with 3D virtual worlds. *British Journal of Educational Technology*.

Chodos, D., Stroulia, E., King, S., & Carbonaro, M. (2014). A framework for monitoring instructional environments in a virtual world. *British Journal of Educational Technology*, *45*(1), 24−35.

Choi, B., & Baek, Y. (2011). Exploring factors of media characteristic influencing flow in learning through virtual worlds. *Computers & Education*, *57*(4), 2382−2394.

Chow, M. (2016). Determinants of presence in 3D virtual worlds: A structural equation modelling analysis. *Australasian Journal of Educational Technology*, 32(1).

Chow, M., Herold, D. K., Choo, T.-M., & Chan, K. (2012). Extending the technology acceptance model to explore the intention to use Second Life for enhancing healthcare education. *Computers & Education*, 59(4), 1136–1144.

Coban, M., Karakus, T., Gunay, F., & Goktas, Y. (2015). Technical problems experienced in the transformation of virtual worlds into an education environment and coping strategies. *Educational Technology & Society*, 18(1), 37–49.

Coffman, T., & Klinger, M. B. (2007). Utilizing virtual worlds in education: The implications for practice. *International Journal of Social Sciences*, 2(1), 29–33.

Dalgarno, B., & Lee, M. J. W. (2010). What are the learning affordances of 3-D virtual environments? *British Journal of Educational Technology*, 40(6), 10–32.

Dalgarno, B., & Lee, M. J. W. (2012). Exploring the relationship between afforded learning tasks and learning benefits in 3D virtual learning environments.

Dalgarno, B., Lee, M. J. W., Carlson, L., Gregory, S., & Tynan, B. (2011a). Institutional support for and barriers to the use of 3D immersive virtual worlds in higher education. Paper presented at the 28th Annual Conference of the Australasian Society for Computers in Learning in Tertiary Education: Changing Demands, Changing Directions.

Dalgarno, B., Lee, M. J. W., Carlson, L., Gregory, S., & Tynan, B. (2011b). Institutional support for and barriers to the use of 3D immersive virtual worlds in higher education. Paper presented at the Changing demands, changing directions Proceedings ascilite Hobart 2011, Hobart, Tasmania.

Dalton, G., & Devitt, A. (2016). Irish in a 3D world – Engaging primary school childrenEN. *Language Learning & Technology*, 20(1), 21–33.

De Freitas, S., Rebolledo-Mendez, G., Liarokapis, F., Magoulas, G., & Poulovassilis, A. (2010). Learning as immersive experiences: Using the four-dimensional framework for designing and evaluating immersive learning experiences in a virtual world. *British Journal of Educational Technology*, 41(1), 69–85.

Dede, C. (2009). Immersive interfaces for engagement and learning. *Science*, 323(5910), 66–69.

deNoyelles, A., & Seo, K. K.-J. (2012). Inspiring equal contribution and opportunity in a 3D multi-user virtual environment: Bringing together men gamers and women non-gamers in Second Life®. *Computers & Education*, 58(1), 21–29.

Dickey, M. D. (2003). Teaching in 3D: Pedagogical affordances and constraints of 3D virtual worlds for synchronous distance learning. *Distance Education*, 24(1), 105–121.

Dickey, M. D. (2005a). Brave new (interactive) worlds: A review of the design affordances and constraints of two 3D virtual worlds as interactive learning environments. *Interactive Learning Environments*, 13(1-2), 121–137.

Dickey, M. D. (2005b). Three-dimensional virtual worlds and distance learning: Two case studies of Active Worlds as a medium for distance education. *British Journal of Educational Technology*, 36(3), 439–451.

Dickey, M. D. (2011). The pragmatics of virtual worlds for K-12 educators: Investigating the affordances and constraints of Active Worlds and Second Life with K-12 in-service teachers. *Educational Technology Research and Development*, 59(1), 1−20.

Dreher, C., Reiners, T., Dreher, N., & Dreher, H. (2009). Virtual worlds as a context suited for information systems education: Discussion of pedagogical experience and curriculum design with reference to Second Life. *Journal of Information Systems Education*, 20(2), 211.

Duncan, I., Miller, A., & Jiang, S. (2012). A taxonomy of virtual worlds usage in education. *British Journal of Educational Technology*, 43(6), 949−964.

Edirisingha, P., Nie, M., Pluciennik, M., & Young, R. (2009). Socialisation for learning at a distance in a 3-D multi-user virtual environment. *British Journal of Educational Technology*, 40(3), 458−479.

Esteves, M., Fonseca, B., Morgado, L., & Martins, P. (2011). Improving teaching and learning of computer programming through the use of the Second Life virtual world. *British Journal of Educational Technology*, 42(4), 624−637.

Faiola, A., Newlon, C., Pfaff, M., & Smyslova, O. (2013). Correlating the effects of flow and telepresence in virtual worlds: Enhancing our understanding of user behavior in game-based learning. *Computers in human behavior*, 29(3), 1113−1121.

Foss, J. (2009). Lessons from learning in virtual environments. *British Journal of Educational Technology*, 40(3), 556−560.

Gamage, V., Tretiakov, A., & Crump, B. (2011). Teacher perceptions of learning affordances of multi-user virtual environments. *Computers & Education*, 57(4), 2406−2413.

Garrido-Iñigo, P., & Rodríguez-Moreno, F. (2015). The reality of virtual worlds: Pros and cons of their application to foreign language teaching. *Interactive Learning Environments*, 23(4), 453−470.

Ghanbarzadeh, R., & Ghapanchi, A. H. (2016). Investigating various application areas of three-dimensional virtual worlds for higher education. *British Journal of Educational Technology*.

Girvan, C., & Savage, T. (2010). Identifying an appropriate pedagogy for virtual worlds: A communal constructivism case study. *Computers & Education*, 55(1), 342−349.

Girvan, C., Tangney, B., & Savage, T. (2013). SLurtles: Supporting constructionist learning in second life. *Computers & Education*, 61, 115−132.

Gregory, B., Gregory, S., Wood, D., Masters, Y., Hillier, M., Stokes-Thompson, F., … Jegathesan, J. J. (2011a, 2011). How are Australian higher education institutions contributing to change through innovative teaching and learning in virtual worlds? Hobart.

Gregory, S., Dalgarno, B., Campbell, M., Reiners, T., Knox, V., & Masters, Y. (2011b). Changing directions through VirtualPREX: Engaging pre-service teachers in virtual professional experience.

Gregory, S., Gregory, B., Grant, S., McDonald, M., Nikolic, S., Farley, H., … Irving, L. (2016). Exploring virtual world innovations and design through learner voices. Paper presented at the Show Me The Learning. Proceedings ASCILITE 2016, Adelaide.

Gregory, S., Gregory, B., Wood, D., Butler, D., Pasfield-Neofitou, S., Hearns, M., ... Jacka, L. (2014). Rhetoric and reality: Critical perspectives on education in a 3D virtual world. Paper presented at the Ascilite 2014 Annual Conference, Auckland.

Gregory, S., Gregory, B., Wood, D., O'Connell, J., Grant, S., Hillier, M., ... McDonald, M. (2015a). New applications, new global audiences: Educators repurposing and reusing 3D virtual and immersive learning resources. Paper presented at the Ascilite 2015 annual conference, Adelaide.

Gregory, S., Scutter, S., Jacka, L., McDonald, M., Farley, H., & Newman, C. (2015b). Barriers and enablers to the use of virtual worlds in higher education: An exploration of educator perceptions, attitudes and experiences. *Educational Technology & Society*, *18*(1), 3−12.

Grenfell, J. (2013). Immersive interfaces for art education teaching and learning in virtual and real world learning environments. *Procedia-Social and Behavioral Sciences*, *93*, 1198−1211.

Gül, L. F., Gu, N., & Williams, A. (2008). Virtual worlds as a constructivist learning platform: Evaluations of 3D virtual worlds on design teaching and learning: ITcon.

Hämäläinen, R., & Oksanen, K. (2012). Challenge of supporting vocational learning: Empowering collaboration in a scripted 3D game − How does teachers' real-time orchestration make a difference? *Computers & Education*, *59*(2), 281−293.

Henderson, M., Huang, H., Grant, S., & Henderson, L. (2012). The impact of Chinese language lessons in a virtual world on university students' self-efficacy beliefs. *Australasian Journal of Educational Technology*, *28*, 400−419.

Heradio, R., de la Torre, L., Galan, D., Cabrerizo, F. J., Herrera-Viedma, E., & Dormido, S. (2016). Virtual and remote labs in education: A bibliometric analysis. *Computers & Education*, *98*, 14−38.

Herold, D. K. (2009). Virtual education: Teaching media studies in Second Life. *Journal of Virtual Worlds Research*, *2*(1).

Herold, D. K. (2010). Mediating media studies − Stimulating critical awareness in a virtual environment. *Computers & Education*, *54*(3), 791−798.

Hew, K. F., & Cheung, W. S. (2010). Use of three-dimensional (3-D) immersive virtual worlds in K-12 and higher education settings: A review of the research. *British Journal of Educational Technology*, *41*(1), 33−55.

Holmes, J. (2007). Designing agents to support learning by explaining. *Computers & Education*, *48*(4), 523−547.

Houser, R., Thoma, S., Coppock, A., Mazer, M., Midkiff, L., Younanian, M., & Young, S. (2011). Learning ethics through virtual fieldtrips: Teaching ethical theories through virtual experiences. *International Journal of Teaching and Learning in Higher Education*, *23*(2), 260−268.

Hung, D., Lee, S.-S., & Lim, K. Y. T. (2012). Authenticity in learning for the twenty-first century: Bridging the formal and the informal. *Educational Technology Research and Development*, *60*(6), 1071−1091.

Inman, C., Wright, V. H., & Hartman, J. A. (2010). Use of Second Life in K-12 and higher education: A review of research. *Journal of Interactive Online Learning*, *9*(1), 44−63.

Jamaludin, A., San Chee, Y., & Ho, C. M. L. (2009). Fostering argumentative knowledge construction through enactive role play in Second Life. *Computers & Education, 53*(2), 317–329.

Jarmon, L., Traphagan, T., & Mayrath, M. (2008). Understanding project-based learning in Second Life with a pedagogy, training, and assessment trio. *Educational Media International, 45*(3), 157–176.

Jarmon, L., Traphagan, T., Mayrath, M., & Trivedi, A. (2009). Virtual world teaching, experiential learning, and assessment: An interdisciplinary communication course in Second Life. *Computers & Education, 53*(1), 169–182.

Johnson, C. M., Vorderstrasse, A. A., & Shaw, R. (2009). Virtual worlds in health care higher education. *Journal of Virtual Worlds Research, 2*(2).

Kemp, J. W., Livingstone, D., & Bloomfield, P. R. (2009). SLOODLE: Connecting VLE tools with emergent teaching practice in Second Life. *British Journal of Educational Technology, 40*(3), 551–555.

Keskitalo, T., Pyykkö, E., & Ruokamo, H. (2011). Exploring the meaningful learning of students in second life. *Educational Technology & Society, 14*(1), 16–26.

Kim, S. H., Lee, J. L., & Thomas, M. K. (2012). Between purpose and method: A review of educational research on 3D virtual worlds. *Journal of Virtual Worlds Research, 5*(1).

KZero. (2014). Virtual worlds and MMOs by genre – The Q2 2014 radar chart. Retrieved from http://www.kzero.co.uk/blog/virtual-worlds-and-mmos-by-genre-the-q2-2014-radar-chart/. Accessed on January 25, 2017.

Lan, Y.-J. (2015). Contextual EFL learning in a 3D virtual environment. *Language Learning and Technology, 19*(2), 16–31.

Lee, M. J. W. (2009). How can 3D virtual worlds be used to support collaborative learning? An analysis of cases from the literature. *Journal of e-Learning and Knowledge Society, 5*(1).

Lee, M. J. W., Nikolic, S., Vial, P. J., Ritz, C. H., Li, W., & Goldfinch, T. (2016). Enhancing project-based learning through student and industry engagement in a video-augmented 3-D virtual trade fair. *IEEE Transactions on Education, 59*(4).

Lester, P. M., & King, C. M. (2009). Analog vs. digital instruction and learning: Teaching within first and second life environments. *Journal of Computer-Mediated Communication, 14*(3), 457–483.

Lim, C. P., Nonis, D., & Hedberg, J. (2006). Gaming in a 3D multiuser virtual environment: Engaging students in science lessons. *British Journal of Educational Technology, 37*(2), 211–231.

Lim, K. Y. T. (2009). The six learnings of Second Life: A framework for designing curricular interventions in-world. *Journal of Virtual Worlds Research, 2*(1).

Lin, M. C., Tutwiler, M. S., & Chang, C. Y. (2012). Gender bias in virtual learning environments: An exploratory study. *British Journal of Educational Technology, 43*(2), E59–E63.

Lin, T.-J., Wang, S.-Y., Grant, S., Chien, C.-L., & Lan, Y.-J. (2014). Task-based teaching approaches of Chinese as a foreign language in Second Life through teachers' perspectives. *Procedia Technology, 13*, 16–22.

List, J., & Bryant, B. (2014, March). Using Minecraft to encourage critical engagement of geography concepts. Paper presented at the Society for Information Technology & Teacher Education International Conference.

Livingstone, D., Kemp, J., & Edgar, E. (2008). From multi-user virtual environment to 3D virtual learning environment. *ALT-J: Research in Learning Technology*, *16*(3), 139−150.

Lorenzo, C.-M., Sicilia, M. Á., & Sánchez, S. (2012). Studying the effectiveness of multi-user immersive environments for collaborative evaluation tasks. *Computers & Education*, *59*(4), 1361−1376.

Lumkin, K., Cram, C., Eade, J., Buck, R., & Evans, D. (2011). *3D virtual worlds project report 2011*. Retrieved from http://www.macict.edu.au/projects/virtual-worlds-project/

Mahon, J., Bryant, B., Brown, B., & Kim, M. (2010). Using second life to enhance classroom management practice in teacher education. *Educational Media International*, *47*(2), 121−134.

McKerlich, R., & Anderson, T. (2007). Community of inquiry and learning in immersive environments. *Journal of Asynchronous Learning Networks*, *11*(4), 35−52.

Memikoğlu, İ. (2014). Utilization of Second Life as a tool for spatial learning in interior architecture. *Procedia-Social and Behavioral Sciences*, *116*, 1288−1292.

Mennecke, B., Roche, E. M., Bray, D. A., Konsynski, B., Lester, J., Rowe, M., & Townsend, A. M. (2008). Second Life and other virtual worlds: A roadmap for research. *Communications of the Association for Information Systems*, *22*, 371−388.

Merchant, G. (2009). Literacy in virtual worlds. *Journal of Research in Reading*, *32*(1), 38−56.

Merchant, G. (2010). 3D virtual worlds as environments for literacy learning. *Educational Research*, *52*(2), 135−150.

Merchant, Z., Goetz, E. T., Cifuentes, L., Keeney-Kennicutt, W., & Davis, T. J. (2014). Effectiveness of virtual reality-based instruction on students' learning outcomes in K-12 and higher education: A meta-analysis. *Computers & Education*, *70*, 29−40.

Merchant, Z., Goetz, E. T., Keeney-Kennicutt, W., Kwok, O.-M., Cifuentes, L., & Davis, T. J. (2012). The learner characteristics, features of desktop 3D virtual reality environments, and college chemistry instruction: A structural equation modeling analysis. *Computers & Education*, *59*(2), 551−568.

Mikropoulos, T. A. (2006). Presence: A unique characteristic in educational virtual environments. *Virtual Reality*, *10*, 197−206.

Mikropoulos, T. A., & Natsis, A. (2011). Educational virtual environments: A ten-year review of empirical research (1999−2009). *Computers & Education*, *56*(3), 769−780.

Minocha, S., & Hardy, C. (2016). Navigation and wayfinding in learning spaces in 3D virtual worlds. In S. Gregory, M. J. W. Lee, B. Dalgarno, & B. Tynan (Eds.), *Learning in Virtual Worlds: Research and Applications* (pp. 3−41). Athabasca: Athabasca University Press.

Minocha, S., & Reeves, A. J. (2010). Design of learning spaces in 3D virtual worlds: an empirical investigation of Second Life. *Learning, Media and Technology*, *35*(2), 111–137.

Noteborn, G., Carbonell, K. B., Dailey-Hebert, A., & Gijselaers, W. (2012). The role of emotions and task significance in Virtual Education. *The Internet and Higher Education*, *15*(3), 176–183.

Noteborn, G., Dailey-Hebert, A., Carbonell, K. B., & Gijselaers, W. (2014). Essential knowledge for academic performance: Educating in the virtual world to promote active learning. *Teaching and Teacher Education*, *37*, 217–234.

Olteanu, R. L., Bîzoi, M., Gorghiu, G., & Suduc, A.-M. (2014). Working in the Second Life environment – A way for enhancing students' collaboration. *Procedia-Social and Behavioral Sciences*, *141*, 1089–1094.

Omale, N., Hung, W.-C., Luetkehans, L., & Cooke-Plagwitz, J. (2009). Learning in 3-D multiuser virtual environments: Exploring the use of unique 3-D attributes for online problem-based learning. *British Journal of Educational Technology*, *40*(3), 480–495.

OpenSimulator. (2014). Open simulator main page. Retrieved from http://opensimulator.org. Accessed on January 25, 2017.

Overby, A., & Jones, B. L. (2015). Virtual Legos: Incorporating Minecraft into the art education curriculum. *Art Education*, *68*(1), 21–27.

Papachristos, N. M., Vrellis, I., Natsis, A., & Mikropoulos, T. A. (2014). The role of environment design in an educational multi-user virtual environment. *British Journal of Educational Technology*, *45*(4), 636–646.

Passig, D., Tzuriel, D., & Eshel-Kedmi, G. (2016). Improving children's cognitive modifiability by dynamic assessment in 3D immersive virtual reality environments. *Computers & Education*, *95*, 296–308.

Peterson, M. (2006). Learner interaction management in an avatar and chat-based virtual world. *Computer Assisted Language Learning*, *19*(1), 79–103.

Peterson, M. (2010). Learner participation patterns and strategy use in Second Life: An exploratory case study. *ReCALL*, *22*(03), 273–292.

Petrakou, A. (2010). Interacting through avatars: Virtual worlds as a context for online education. *Computers & Education*, *54*(4), 1020–1027.

Potkonjak, V., Gardner, M., Callaghan, V., Mattila, P., Guetl, C., Petrović, V. M., & Jovanović, K. (2016). Virtual laboratories for education in science, technology, and engineering: A review. *Computers & Education*, *95*, 309–327.

Rappa, N. A., Yip, D. K. H., & Baey, S. C. (2009). The role of teacher, student and ICT in enhancing student engagement in multiuser virtual environments. *British Journal of Educational Technology*, *40*(1), 61–69.

Richards, D., & Taylor, M. (2015). A Comparison of learning gains when using a 2D simulation tool versus a 3D virtual world: An experiment to find the right representation involving the Marginal Value Theorem. *Computers & Education*, *86*, 157–171.

Richardson, A., Hazzard, M., Challman, S. D., Morgenstein, A. M., & Brueckner, J. K. (2011). A "Second Life" for gross anatomy: Applications for multiuser virtual environments in teaching the anatomical sciences. *Anatomical Sciences Education*, *4*(1), 39–43.

Rogers, L. (2011). Developing simulations in multi-user virtual environments to enhance healthcare education. *British Journal of Educational Technology, 42*(4), 608−615.

Sarac, H. S. (2014). Benefits and challenges of using Second Life in English teaching: Experts' opinions. *Procedia-Social and Behavioral Sciences, 158,* 326−330.

Schifter, C., & Cipollone, M. (2013). Minecraft as a teaching tool: One case study. Paper presented at the Society for Information Technology and Teacher Education International Conference.

Schrader, C., & Bastiaens, T. J. (2012). The influence of virtual presence: Effects on experienced cognitive load and learning outcomes in educational computer games. *Computers in Human Behavior, 28*(2), 648−658.

Shen, J., & Eder, L. B. (2009). Intentions to use virtual worlds for education. *Journal of Information Systems Education, 20*(2), 225.

Sierra, L. M. B., Gutiérrez, R. S., & Garzón-Castro, C. L. (2012). Second Life as a support element for learning electronic related subjects: A real case. *Computers & Education, 58*(1), 291−302.

Sourin, A., Sourina, O., & Prasolova-Førland, E. (2006). Cyber-learning in cyberworlds. *Journal of Cases on Information Technology (JCIT), 8*(4), 55−70.

Steinkuehler, C. A. (2004). Learning in massively multiplayer online games. Paper presented at the Proceedings of the 6th International Conference on Learning Sciences, Los Angeles, California.

subQuark. (2016). Sim-on-a-Stick. Retrieved from http://simonastick.com. Accessed on January 25, 2017.

Sutcliffe, A., & Alrayes, A. (2012). Investigating user experience in Second Life for collaborative learning. *International Journal of Human-Computer Studies, 70*(7), 508−525.

Traphagan, T. W., Chiang, Y.-h. V., Chang, H. M., Wattanawaha, B., Lee, H., Mayrath, M. C., … Resta, P. E. (2010). Cognitive, social and teaching presence in a virtual world and a text chat. *Computers & Education, 55*(3), 923−936.

Tüzün, H., & Özdinç, F. (2016). The effects of 3D multi-user virtual environments on freshmen university students' conceptual and spatial learning and presence in departmental orientation. *Computers & Education, 94,* 228−240.

Twining, P. (2009). Exploring the educational potential of virtual worlds – Some reflections from the SPP. *British Journal of Educational Technology, 40*(3), 496−514.

Van Der Land, S., Schouten, A. P., Feldberg, F., Van Den Hooff, B., & Huysman, M. (2013). Lost in space? Cognitive fit and cognitive load in 3D virtual environments. *Computers in Human Behavior, 29*(3), 1054−1064.

Van der Land, S., Schouten, A. P., van den Hooff, B., & Feldberg, F. (2011). Modeling the metaverse: A theoretical model of effective team collaboration in 3D virtual environments. *Journal of Virtual Worlds Research, 4*(3).

Wang, F., & Burton, J. K. (2013). Second Life in education: A review of publications from its launch to 2011. *British Journal of Educational Technology, 44*(3), 357−371.

Warburton, S. (2009). Second Life in higher education: Assessing the potential for and the barriers to deploying virtual worlds in learning and teaching. *British Journal of Educational Technology, 40*(3), 414–426.

Ward, T., Falconer, L., Frutos-Perez, M., Williams, B., Johns, J., & Harold, S. (2015). Using virtual online simulations in Second Life® to engage undergraduate psychology students with employability issues. *British Journal of Educational Technology*.

Wehner, A. K., Gump, A. W., & Downey, S. (2011). The effects of Second Life on the motivation of undergraduate students learning a foreign language. *Computer Assisted Language Learning, 24*(3), 277–289.

Wiecha, J., Heyden, R., Sternthal, E., & Merialdi, M. (2010). Learning in a virtual world: Experience with using second life for medical education. *Journal of Medical Internet Research, 12*(1), e1.

Wilkes, S. F. (2016). Communication modality, learning, and Second Life. In S. Gregory, M. J. W. Lee, B. Dalgarno, & B. Tynan (Eds.), *Learning in Virtual Worlds: Research and Applications* (pp. 43–65). Athabasca: Athabasca University Press.

Winkelmann, K., Scott, M., & Wong, D. (2014). A study of high school students' performance of a chemistry experiment within the virtual world of Second Life. *Journal of Chemical Education, 91*(9), 1432–1438.

Wrzesien, M., & Raya, M. A. (2010). Learning in serious virtual worlds: Evaluation of learning effectiveness and appeal to students in the E-Junior project. *Computers & Education, 55*(1), 178–187.

Yilmaz, R. M., Baydas, O., Karakus, T., & Goktas, Y. (2015). An examination of interactions in a three-dimensional virtual world. *Computers & Education, 88*, 256–267.

Zhang, H. (2013). Pedagogical challenges of spoken English learning in the Second Life virtual world: A case study. *British Journal of Educational Technology, 44*(2), 243–254.

11 Abstracting Technology-Enhanced Learning Design Principles

ABSTRACT

This chapter synthesizes findings from the reviews of education using Web 2.0, social networking, mobile learning, and virtual worlds, in light of the earlier chapters on context, technology, pedagogy, content, and design. Benefits and issues associated technology-enhanced learning are generalized, with an important finding being the quite different ways that different technologies contribute to each. Twenty technology-enhanced learning design principles are derived from abstracting the Web 2.0, social networking, mobile learning, and virtual worlds literature. The benefits, issues, and technology-enhanced learning design principles are then related to one another by virtue of 13 clusters of concerns, namely pedagogy, access, communication, content representation, collaboration, motivation and engagement, vicarious learning and reflection, digital learning capabilities, assessment and feedback, student-centered learning, learning communities, protecting students, and teacher support. The analysis enables the general learning technology literature to be linked to concrete examples and evidential sources, so that educators and researchers can construct a deep and connected understanding of technology-enhanced learning design.

What Is Abstraction and Why Is It Important?

Abstraction involves generalizing from the specific contexts of everyday practice through the recognition of patterns (Winters, Mor, & Pratt, 2010). As we identified in Chapter 3, abstraction is an important part of learning because the act of transforming episodic aspects of a learning experience into more semantic and conceptual forms means that knowledge can be transferred to future problem solving scenarios (Sylwester, 1995). While abstraction is essential for students in order for them to develop versatile problem solving capabilities, it is also crucial for educators so that they can respond to a wide variety of design challenges. Stated another way, unless educators can abstract their design knowledge then they are inextricably bound to the particular situations that they have learnt about. In our fast changing world, abstracting design thinking means that educators can work more confidently across unfamiliar technologies, content areas, pedagogies, and contexts.

The purpose of this chapter is not only to abstract design principles, but also to establish deep and nuanced understanding of digital learning design. After all that we have considered to date, it would be naïve to assume that technology-enhanced learning design could be entirely reduced to a numbered list of prescriptions. This is exactly the sort of mechanistic and predictive thinking that runs counter to true design, and as such we have been trying to avoid it! What we may be able to do, however, is to find within the body of technology-enhanced learning literature some emergent and recurring themes, and aim to understand how those themes may subtly vary according to the contexts and technologies.

First we will consider the benefits and limitations of technology-enhanced learning, as distilled from the analysis of Web 2.0, social networking, mobile learning and virtual worlds. This will be followed with an examination of recommendations for technology-enhanced learning design as derived from the literature. Once again, the themes presented below are necessarily a simplification, and the devil is most definitely in the detail contained in the previous four chapters. References have not been included in order to promote readability and interpretability, however, readers interested in the details of any claims made below can most certainly refer to the previous four chapters for evidence and substantiation.

Technology-Enhanced Learning Benefits and Potentials ·

The following benefits and potentials of technology-enhanced learning have been directly derived from the review of Web 2.0, social networking, mobile and virtual worlds in the proceeding chapters. Commonalities in benefits have been merged into themes, with descriptions highlighting how the different technologies contribute to each. The themes, if you like, are the 'super results'. An important point to note is that the themes below relate to how technologies can be used for learning and teaching, rather than being intrinsic qualities of the technologies themselves. The themes as distilled from the literature are as follows.

FLEXIBLE TECHNOLOGIES ENABLE EDUCATORS TO APPLY A RANGE OF PEDAGOGIES

While some technologies may tend to be used in certain pedagogical ways, flexible environments such as Web 2.0 technologies, social networking systems, mobile learning environments and virtual worlds can be used to enact a variety of pedagogies. In the previous chapters, we saw how Web 2.0 technologies could be used to promote constructivist, social constructivist, and connectivist learning. Social networking was typically used to facilitate social constructivist and connectivist learning. Mobile learning enabled constructivist and social constructivist learning. Virtual worlds were used to apply constructivist and social constructivist learning, along with collaborative, situated, project-based, inquiry-based, and problem-based learning.

So while some technologies tend to be more strongly aligned with particular pedagogies (for instance that social networking tends to be used to be used for social constructivist or connectivist learning), the actual pedagogy used depends on the design decisions of the educator. This is in accordance with the finding from Chapter 5 where individual technologies could be used to support a wide variety of thinking processes and knowledge representations. While it is important to note that there is a difference between planned pedagogy and enacted pedagogy because students themselves have the capacity to steer the lesson according to their inclinations (Conole & Jones, 2010; Goodyear & Retalis, 2010), the pedagogies adopted in flexible virtual learning environments can be strongly influenced by the educational designer. Two important implications of this pedagogical agency are that educators shouldn't select technologies based purely on the pedagogy to be applied, and educators need to take responsibility for the sort of learning that takes place in the digital environments they design.

TECHNOLOGIES CAN BE USED TO PROVIDE ACCESS TO LEARNING

A fundamental benefit of using online technologies for learning is that they can provide access to education. Web 2.0 technologies enable anytime-anywhere access to learning via online tools, enabling students to review information and contribute to blogs, wikis and a host of other productive technologies from outside the classroom. Social networking provides access to learning through familiar interfaces that students are often utilizing as part of their daily lives. Mobile devices enable students to access information and contribute to learning while they are on the move, and also make education more accessible by providing low-cost computing power to people with less financial resources. Virtual worlds enable remote participation in simulated 3-D environments, which is particularly useful for people who may not be otherwise able to take part in learning activities due to location, distance, disability, cost, risk, and so on. So different technologies offer access to learning in different ways, in combination providing a powerful suite of design potentials that educators can use to apply Universal Design Principles (Rose, Harbour, Johnston, Daley, & Abarbanell, 2006).

ONLINE TECHNOLOGIES CAN FACILITATE COMMUNICATION

Technologies such as Web 2.0, social networking, mobile environments and virtual worlds enable communication and discussion in wide variety of ways. Web 2.0 technologies typically enable discussion through text comments relating to artifacts of interest, but also sometimes using audio and video, depending on the type of Web 2.0 tools being used. Social networking systems enable users to post announcements, share resources (such as files, videos, links to websites), organize classes, participate in online discussions and conduct polls, often receiving responses more rapidly than through other communication means. Mobile learning enables communication and discussion to occur while in the field or in transit. In virtual worlds, participants can typically communicate using public text-chat, private text-chat and voice, but also through nonverbal communication such as avatar gestures and appearance. Thus, while online technology platforms enable multimodal communication, the forms that those communication channels take are markedly different across technologies and platforms.

TECHNOLOGIES CAN ENHANCE COLLABORATION

Web 2.0 technologies, social networking, mobile learning environments and virtual worlds can all be used to facilitate and enhance collaboration. Web 2.0 technologies, notably through wikis and blogs but also using other tools, enable students to collaboratively produce knowledge bases and jointly publish information. Social networking can be used to support collaborative work by helping teams to gather project materials, brainstorm ideas, share written work, schedule meetings and exchange feedback. Mobile learning enables group members in disparate locations to connect with one another and share data from the field through common repositories. Virtual worlds can support synchronous collaboration through the provision of separate team spaces, a range of in-built communication channels, and emulation of face-to-face meeting environments. The different collaborative potentials of different technologies mean that decisions need to be made about which platform will best suit the task at hand.

TECHNOLOGIES CAN FOSTER IDENTITY, PRESENCE, AND CO-PRESENCE

Technologies include features and functions that can be used to cultivate a sense of identity, presence, and co-presence. Web 2.0 tools will often have profiles corresponding to user accounts, but quite often the primary focus is upon the information being co-constructed and shared. On the other hand, social networks are based around the sharing of participant information and thus intrinsically support identity formation and building a sense of connectedness. Mobile devices may or may not be used in a way that leverages identity and a sense of co-presence, depending on the applications being utilized and how they are used. Through the navigation and interaction of avatars in a 3D space, virtual worlds support the construction of identity, presence, and co-presence, in order to create a visceral and somewhat realistic online experience. Different levels of identity, presence, and co-presence may be suitable for different educational circumstances.

TECHNOLOGIES ENABLE REPRESENTATION AND SHARING OF CONTENT

Web 2.0, social networking, mobile learning, and virtual worlds all enable different representational possibilities. Among the variety of Web 2.0 technologies there are a myriad of content representation potentials using different combinations of modalities such as text, audio, images and video. Social networking is a particularly convenient way to share content once developed, but is generally limited in terms of the ability to manipulate and create content. With mobile devices students can create content taking advantage of features such as cloud-based note taking software, photo annotation, audio and video recording, to capture and annotate data that can then be shared through Web 2.0 tools such as blogs. Virtual worlds enable 3-D environments to be realistically represented, viewed, traversed, manipulated, and even scripted, making them appropriate for the development of spatial understanding and procedural knowledge. Thus, technologies can represent content in powerful but different ways, which in turn may make them more or less suitable for different learning tasks. This is in accordance with content representation concepts discussed in Chapter 5.

TECHNOLOGIES INCREASINGLY SUPPORT EASY CONTRIBUTION

Technologies are increasingly being designed with the end user in mind, although they do differ quite substantially in usability and familiarity to users. Web 2.0 technologies mean that people can create and contribute to websites without needing to know HTML or other web-based languages required in early incarnations of the Internet. Social networking technologies are generally acknowledged as having well-designed interfaces that are familiar to most people, which means that in most cases students can readily deploy them for learning purposes. Similarly, students are usually familiar with the use of mobile devices, and can also take advantage of touch-screen input to complete educational tasks. While the use of virtual worlds can be difficult to master initially, transferring skills from 3D gaming environments can be of assistance. It should be noted, however, that although students may have or be able to acquire the technical skills they need for a particular technology, they may not know how to leverage technology for learning purposes.

THE USE OF CONTEMPORARY TECHNOLOGIES CAN ENHANCE MOTIVATION AND ENGAGEMENT

Across the research literature the use of Web 2.0 technologies, social networking, mobile learning and virtual worlds have generally been found to enhance motivation and engagement. Higher levels of engagement were observed, for instance, when Twitter was used for communication in undergraduate classes, wikis were utilized to complete statistics reports, and when G Suite was used for collaborative language learning, with the ability to publish Web 2.0 content to a wide audience consistently noted as a motivating factor. Social networking can enhance engagement by providing space for more informal contributions and catering to the preferences of people who may be intimidated by face-to-face communication (e.g., if they are shy or from a different language background). The majority of mobile learning studies report significantly greater learning interest as compared to traditional instruction, often by virtue of personalized and situated learning. High levels of learner engagement are also a frequently reported benefit of using virtual worlds in education. An important caveat is that when contemporary technologies are used poorly they can detract from motivation and engagement.

TECHNOLOGIES CAN FACILITATE VICARIOUS LEARNING AND REFLECTION

Another advantage of using technology in education is that the process of documenting, recording and sharing makes thinking visible so that students can learn through observation and reflection. For instance, when blogs and wikis are used students can examine the contributions of their peers in order to better understand the task, reflect on the thinking put forward by others, learn from more capable students, track the evolution of their own thinking and monitor their progress with respect to the class. Using the discussion features of social networking systems enables students to learn from their peers through critical reflection, negotiation of meaning and consideration of alternative

perspectives, often enhanced by a sense of needing to think carefully before presenting ideas in a communal space. Because students carry their mobile devices with them they can be more
systematic about the way they document their reflections, capturing and sharing them as they spontaneously occur. Through
experiential and role-play activities in virtual worlds students can
be encouraged to reflect upon their own actions, identity and perspectives, as well as those of others.

USE OF TECHNOLOGIES PROVIDES LEARNERS WITH OPPORTUNITIES TO DEVELOP THEIR DIGITAL CAPABILITIES AND CREATIVITY

As emphasized in Chapter 1, an important rationale for integrating technology into learning activities is so that students can
develop the digital capabilities that will help them to thrive in an
increasingly technological global society. Web 2.0 technologies
provide a platform for individual creativity through the production of posts, websites, audio recordings, images, videos and so
on. Social networking systems provide a suitable means for students to share and critique each other's digital creations, to organize the development of multimedia work, and to cultivate their
collaborative competencies for instance by establishing personalized learning networks. Mobile devices, and notably the iPad,
provide a comprehensive yet agile range of touch-based tools
for image, audio and video creation, editing and sharing. In
virtual worlds students can use text, audio and body language to
develop their digital communication capabilities, the object-
building features to develop their design capabilities, and scripting features to develop their programming capabilities.

TECHNOLOGIES CAN BE USED TO FACILITATE ACTIVE AND STUDENT-CENTERED LEARNING

A consequence of pedagogical agency residing with educators
rather than being inherent attributes of technologies is that teachers can choose to apply more active and student-centered
learning approaches. Example Web 2.0 tasks for students include
using blogs to create self-directed e-portfolios, using Twitter to
relate course material to their own experiences, or following
differentiated learning pathways using wikis. Social networking
systems can encourage student-directed and egalitarian contributions by providing students with the freedom to post content of

their choosing and influence the topic of discussion. Mobile devices can support active and student-centered learning through the large variety of apps available (including games-based apps), field-based activities and open-ended tasks that enable participation by students of different ability levels. The capacity to assume an identity and navigate within virtual worlds as part of situated and experiential learning tasks intrinsically lends itself to active and student-centered learning. The ability to self-direct and self-pace learning has been shown to improve learning performance, interest, and attitude across the different technology platforms.

TECHNOLOGIES CAN ENHANCE ASSESSMENT AND FEEDBACK

Digital technologies offer a host of new ways to assess student work and provide feedback. Web 2.0 technologies enable students to complete productive tasks involving multimedia, teachers to formatively track student progress including the contributions of individuals to group work, and peers to provide one another with feedback or evaluations. Social networking can be used as a platform to facilitate peer assessment of writing or multimedia galleries, again in a way that enables the teacher to assess the learning process rather than just the final product. Mobile devices allow students to record and annotate their in-situ learning processes so that teachers can formatively and summatively diagnose misconceptions. Virtual worlds can be used as a platform for 3-D building and simulation tasks as well as otherwise difficult to conduct role-play exercises.

TECHNOLOGY CAN SUPPORT THE DEVELOPMENT OF LEARNING COMMUNITIES

As a consequence of their ability to facilitate communication and represent identity, Web 2.0, social networking, mobile devices and virtual worlds can all be used to support the development of learning communities. Web 2.0 activities such as collaborative blogging and communication via Twitter can be used to cultivate a sense of learning community. Social networking technologies can provide a powerful means of building community through the establishment of personal profiles and engaging in social interactions that reduce isolation and strengthen relationships. Social networking can also be used to expand the learning community beyond the people in a class to include industry experts

and practicing professionals so that students can receive mentorship, advice and learning support. While community building
was not emphasized in the mobile learning literature (perhaps
because tasks tend to be shorter and more personalized) development of community can still occur within classes through
ongoing collaboration. Virtual worlds, through avatar-based
interactions, enable online community development by people in
disparate locations, for instance transnational student groups.
One of the benefits of developing learning communities generally
is that the relationships formed can often continue after the
course has finished.

REFLECTIONS ON TECHNOLOGY-ENHANCED LEARNING BENEFITS AND POTENTIALS

At the risk of oversimplification, Table 11.1 very briefly summarizes the ways in which the various benefits and potentials
manifest themselves in Web 2.0, social networking, mobile and
virtual world environments, as according to the research literature. Table 11.1 does not intend to imply that these are the only
benefits of each technology or that they need necessarily apply.
As we have established, the benefits of any technology-enhanced
learning task very much depend on the design, the context, and
the actual activity of students. The intention of Table 11.1 is to
illustrate the very different ways that Web 2.0, social networking,
mobile learning and virtual worlds can contribute to learning,
through the essence of points raised within the literature.

The striking difference in the ways that technologies contribute to the themes highlights the critical importance of educators
deeply understanding different technologies and their affordance
implications in order to be effective designers. While there is a
temptation to over-simplify learning technology usage by assuming once you know one technology you know them all, the above
analysis underscores that technologies can contribute to the
learning experience in very different ways.

A positive consequence of the variety of ways that technologies can be used to contribute to learning is that knowledgeable
educators can select between them depending on the requirements of the intended tasks. Moreover, while the technological
platforms have in the most part been considered separately in the
previous chapters for the purposes of analysis, they are obviously
complimentary and can be used in combination. For instance,
throughout a term or semester a teacher could choose to use

Table 11.1.   Benefits and Potentials Relating to Teaching Using Web 2.0, Social Networking, Mobile Technologies, and Virtual Worlds.

	Web 2.0	Social Networking	Mobile	Virtual Worlds
Pedagogical flexibility	Constructivist Social constructivist Connectivist	Social constructivist Connectivist	Constructivist Social constructivist	Constructivist Social constructivist
Provide access	Online tools	Familiar platform	Convenient device	3-D simulation
Facilitate communication	Typically around artifacts	Networked discussion posts	From any location	Text, audio, gesture
Enhance collaboration	Joint production of artifacts	Sharing resources and organization	Share data from the field	Synchronous group meeting spaces
Identity & presence	Transient accounts	User profiles	Usage dependent	Avatars in 3-D space
Represent and share content	Variety of modalities	Sharing rather than production	Capture & annotate in context	3-D environments
Easy contribution	Publish to web	Familiar tools	Touch screen	Similar to 3-D games
Enhance motivation & engagement	Joint production and broad publication	Informal and unintimidating contributions	Personalized & contextualized learning	Immersive & experiential learning
Vicarious learning & reflection	Review peer & own posts	Critique discussions	Collect & share thoughts from field	Observing others & role-play tasks
Develop digital capabilities	Producing web-pages & multimedia	Coordinating, sharing, networking	Data capture & multimedia production	Communicating, designing, programming
Active & student-centered learning	e-portfolios & learning pathways	Student-directed discussions	Interactive apps & field activities	3-D world situated & experiential tasks
Assessment & Feedback	Open collaborative production & feedback	Peer assessment & writing tasks	Capture in-situ learning processes & teacher feedback	3-D building, simulation and role-play
Learning communities	Blogging & microblogging	Sharing in identity-based network	By virtue of collaboration	Avatar-based activities

Web 2.0 tools for collaborative knowledge building, social networking to facilitate sharing and community building, mobile learning for capturing field data, and virtual worlds for emulation of 3-D scenarios.

Technology-Enhanced Learning Issues and Limitations

There were also several themes relating to technology-enhanced learning issues and limitations that emerged from the review of the Web 2.0, social networking, mobile and virtual worlds educational literature. Interestingly, the themes were less consistent across platforms than for the benefits and potentials. However, themes that were only represented in some areas of the literature could almost always be generalized (abstracted) to the other technological contexts. The issues and limitations of technology-enhanced learning, as distilled from the literature, are as follows.

TECHNICAL ISSUES

Technical issues are consistently reported across learning technology studies, though the issues vary in nature and prevalence depending on the technologies and how they are being used. Web 2.0 problems tend to relate to accessing user accounts, sub-optimal interfaces, multi-user editing conflicts, and sustainability of Web 2.0 technologies over time. Technical issues with social networking generally relate to how information is structured and organized, for instance the unthreaded nature of discussions, the reverse chronological order of posts, hidden content for more extensive posts, fragmentation of knowledge across many peoples' profiles, and difficulties searching and cross referencing. For mobile learning technical issues tend to concern the nature of the physical devices, including small screen size, limited processing power, reduced feature set, and variable access to the Internet. With virtual worlds technical issues relate to the large amounts of computing power and bandwidth required, for instance insufficiency of graphics cards, RAM, processors, network speed and server performance impacting upon the smoothness and latency of 3-D rendering and voice communications. If the aim is to replicate real world experiences in the virtual world then fidelity can also be an issue, depending on functionality of the particular platform. Problems with Internet access, firewalls, and student access to computing devices were commonly reported across all technological platforms, though less frequently for social networking.

INADEQUATE STUDENT DIGITAL CAPABILITIES

Another common issue with technology-enhanced learning is that students may lack the digital capabilities to effectively participate in activities. When using Web 2.0 tools it cannot be assumed that students will have more complex or even basic web and multimedia skills, let alone know how to use them for learning purposes. While students are generally familiar with how to use social networking and can transfer those skills into learning contexts, familiarity is not universal. Most people are familiar with how to use mobile devices for consumption purposes, but may not know how to use them productively. Using virtual worlds can propose problems for students who may not initially know how to download appropriate software, setup audio communication, navigate through the world, interact with objects, use gestures, or construct objects. If students lack the digital competencies to operate any technology it can impact upon their confidence, attitude, experience and learning outcomes.

COGNITIVE LOAD ISSUES

Cognitive load is another consideration when using technology for learning, which again manifests quite differently across platforms. Cognitive load is rarely reported as an issue when using Web 2.0 tools, perhaps because they are often used asynchronously or focus on the use of a subset of modalities. For social networking, unnecessary cognitive load may result from information being spread between the social networking system and the learning management system (LMS), with duplication and lack of clarity surrounding where different activities or resources are to be held. Cognitive load is often reported as an issue in mobile learning field-work, where students are attempting to process and interrelate information from their environment and on their device. Cognitive load is also a commonly reported issue in virtual world activities due to the representational complexity of the environment, the inclusion of redundant information in the environment, and extra operational steps that may not be relevant to the learning outcomes (such as navigating an avatar).

COLLABORATION PROBLEMS

There are several issues that can arise when using technology to collaborate. With Web 2.0 technologies students sometimes feel uncomfortable editing the work of others, become disgruntled if others edit their work, choose to divide work between people rather than truly collaborate, let one person complete the majority of the work, or leave their contribution until the last moment making team interaction difficult. Interestingly, collaboration issues are rarely reported when using social networking, perhaps because tools such as Facebook are generally only used by project teams to share resources rather than create them. Similarly, issues relating to collaboration in itself are not often reported in mobile learning tasks, notwithstanding the technical issues noted above and potential mitigation due to people collaborating 'at' rather than 'through' devices. Collaborative issues in virtual worlds include not being able to identify people via their avatars, difficulty signifying meaning using avatars, finding people within the geography of the virtual world, needing to be logged in at the same time to collaborate, lack of native productivity and word processing tools, as well as communication problems caused by multiple people trying to simultaneously use text-chat and spatial sound. Selecting cohesive groups is an issue across any learning technology platform.

NEGATIVE STUDENT DISPOSITIONS

Some students indicate negative dispositions toward using technology for learning, though more so for some platforms and for a variety of different reasons. With Web 2.0 technologies students may be reluctant to undertake more student-directed approaches, to share their work publicly, or to participate in tasks if they are not mandatory. With social networking students may object to the increased email notifications traffic, or the blurred boundary between their personal and educational lives (this latter point is elaborated in another subsection to follow). There seems to be little objection to mobile learning from students, apparently because of the extra convenience it affords them. Students may have a negative disposition toward learning in virtual worlds because they are unfamiliar with how to operate them, they are perceived as fake or too game-like, or the cultural norms of virtual worlds seem foreign. In all cases, students may simply have a preference for learning via other modes, for instance, face-to-face.

ASSESSMENT AND FEEDBACK CHALLENGES

Use of technology for assessment and feedback purposes involves intrinsic challenges. For some Web 2.0 tasks students may become more focused on aesthetics than content, and crowd-rating measures may inadvertently become proxies for correctness or quality. In social networking environments the sharing culture may run in opposition to more individualized traditions of student assessment, and the possible inaccuracy of student generated content needs to be taken into account when peer feedback is being used. Similarly, the different nature of assessment using mobile devices might be quite a cultural leap for educators who are used to more static assessment procedures, and care needs to be exercised to ensure that the mobile devices have the required functionality for the assessment tasks. Virtual world assessment can be problematic in terms of attributing performance to individuals, capturing synchronous processes, and the technical issues that may occur. No matter what learning technologies are being used, students may be uncomfortable with conducting peer assessment, it may be difficult to establish the individual contributions to group tasks, and teachers need to consider whether participation or content will be assessed. Plagiarism is also a major issue, as outlined in the following section.

PLAGIARISM

Another problem that was most commonly reported in the Web 2.0 literature was the inappropriate use of material composed by others. Students may copy-paste chunks of material from the Internet without critically engaging with the concepts or correctly acknowledging sources. This can extend to copying the work of peers. In its worst form using the material of others can constitute serious cases of plagiarism, noting that in some instances students may sincerely believe that copying and pasting is educationally appropriate based on their social uses of technology. Because students (and teachers) use technology to remix and publish digital content they need to have a clear understanding of issues relating to intellectual property and copyright. Similarly, plagiarism needs to be monitored in social networking environments because it is so easy to upload content sourced from the Internet. Plagiarism was not commonly mentioned in the mobile learning literature, perhaps because quite often students are capturing their own contextually related data using their devices or using apps to complete individualized tasks. Plagiarism was also rarely mentioned across the virtual worlds literature, though it was noted that students could easily pass each other login details to complete each other's assignments. All students and teachers need to understand the intellectual property rights issues associated with the reuse and publication of digital materials.

UNDESIRABLE STUDENT BEHAVIOR (MISUSE AND DISTRACTION)

There are many different ways that a student may misuse a technology during learning tasks. With open and collaborative Web 2.0 tasks it is possible for students to accidentally or intentionally destroy the work of their peers. If social networking is being used, the mix of personal and educational space make inappropriate conduct such as cyberbullying a possibility. When students are borrowing mobile devices to complete tasks then there is the risk that they will not adequately care for them. In virtual worlds it is easy for students to engage in unnoticed off-task conversations with others in the environment.

There are also a variety of ways that a student may become distracted while using the technology. Because they are online, students may choose to play games or undertake other noneducational activities using social media and the like. While reported for Web 2.0 tools, the risk of this is particularly high when either social networking or mobile devices are being used because educational interactions and resources occur in the same digital space as personal and social exchanges. With virtual worlds the source of distraction is often the world itself, with its fantastic landscape, objects, functions and characters. Sometimes distraction is not devious, for instance it may be that students are using mobile devices to focus on a part of the lesson that is different to that being covered by the teacher, which adversely affects their learning.

SAFETY, PRIVACY, AND EQUITY

There are several issues relating to duty of care that need to be considered when using technology for learning, particularly with younger students. Because students will have access to the Internet when using Web 2.0 technologies, they are exposed to the risk of predatory behavior by external parties or seeing inappropriate explicit content. As previously mentioned, cyberbullying is another concern when using online technologies, particularly social networking. Hacking, viruses, stalking and identity theft are other safety issues that need to be managed when using social networking environments. For mobile devices, it is once again important that students protect themselves from contact by strangers and explicit content, but also only use their devices in safe ways (for instance not while driving). With virtual worlds there is a risk of inappropriate conduct by avatars including forceful behavior or presenting offensive content.

In terms of privacy, students may be reluctant to undertake educational activities using personal Web 2.0 accounts (e.g., Twitter) because they may not want to reveal their contact details or out-of-class lives to their classmates or teacher. The same is true even more so for social networking, with many students (and teachers) not wanting educational content to infiltrate their personal spaces and some students not feeling comfortable with more informal and direct communication from teachers. Because mobile technology is often used to capture and images, audio and video as part of learning activities, there is a risk that students may capture or publish personal data that is against another individual's wishes. Privacy is not a commonly reported issue for virtual worlds, perhaps because individuals assume an avatar identity that enables them to keep personal information hidden.

Unfortunately technology access is influenced by socio-economic factors, so that the people who could derive the greatest educational benefit from technology have the least access, and often lower quality tools and resources. The mobile learning literature in particular emphasizes the importance of vigorous and continual efforts to increase access to technology for people from regional, poorer and developing areas, as a matter of social justice.

UNDERDEVELOPED TEACHER DIGITAL SKILLS

Teachers need to have the digital skills to design and manage technology-enhanced learning. For instance, when using Web 2.0 environments teachers need to know how to manage knowledge building that is dispersed and organize it in a way that promotes learning. In social networking environments educators need to understand the functionality and settings of different tools in order to optimize task designs and uphold the privacy of students. With mobile learning, teachers need to understand the devices and software being used so that they can troubleshoot issues that arise. Using virtual worlds involves teacher skills such as being able to monitor and manage students via their avatar, constructing a landscape and environment to support learning (including importing and adapting external resources), and troubleshoot student issues in real-time from a remote location. If teachers do not have the required digital teaching skills then student learning outcomes and quality of experience may suffer.

NEGATIVE EDUCATOR DISPOSITIONS

Just as students may have an intrinsic aversion to learning using technology, educators may also be reluctant to integrate technology into their teaching. For instance, educators may feel that Web 2.0 technologies are inferior to face-to-face teaching or that traditional learning management systems (LMSs) constitute a more reliable and secure means of facilitating online activities. With social networking many educators express concerns over issues such as privacy, integrity of student contributions, as well as lack of confidence and know-how. Educators generally have a positive attitude toward mobile learning, but cite time, knowledge and lack of support as constraining their practice (as elaborated in a following subsection). Unfamiliarity, the risk of technical problems and financial costs often inhibit educators from using virtual worlds in their classes.

INAPPROPRIATE DESIGN

As previously emphasized, simply using technology by no means guarantees a successful lesson, and there are many ways in which tasks may be inappropriately designed for the outcomes, students, technology and context in question. Sometimes Web 2.0 technologies are used to simply replicate existing digital or face-to-face approaches, for instance using private e-portfolios as an alternative form of assignment submission thereby adding nothing of pedagogical value to the learning experience. As well, tasks may be overwhelming in scope, or unclearly specified in terms of purpose and activity. If social networking tasks are forced and lacking in authenticity, student participation can wane. As previously mentioned, using mobile learning devices in the field can result in cognitive overload if not appropriately designed. Similarly, virtual world tasks that do not fully leverage the features of the environment can lead to less efficient learning.

TEACHER SUPPORT ISSUES (TIME, PROFESSIONAL LEARNING, INSTITUTIONAL ISSUES)

The amount and quality of teacher support is another significant issue that can impact upon technology-enhanced learning design and outcomes. Teachers at all levels and across all platforms indicate that time is a major constraint that impacts on their ability to design and utilize technology-enhanced learning. When utilizing Web 2.0 teachers need time to familiarize themselves with the tools and design their lessons. For social networking educators need to understand how to best setup permissions and then spend time seeding interactions and providing feedback. For mobile learning design educators need to come to terms with the features of the devices, the possible apps they could use, and then actually plan and develop their lessons. With virtual worlds it can be immensely time consuming to decide on the best platform, setup and test the virtual world, learn to use its functionality, design the tasks, and then build the virtual world environment that will scaffold the learning activities. Lack of time often prevents teachers from using technologies in their classes.

Professional learning for educators emerged as an important issue. Educators attempting to utilize Web 2.0 technologies may benefit from professional learning opportunities to help them make the pedagogical shift from face-to-face information delivery to facilitating distributed collaborative learning. Professional learning was seen as less of an issue for social networking, perhaps because educators could transfer operational skills acquired through their personal usage. In the case of mobile learning, teachers express a desire for pedagogical advice from experts and tailored professional learning that helps them to integrate the technology into their classes. For virtual worlds, professional development needs to target awareness raising in the first instance, and then guidance on technical and pedagogical levels. Lack of professional development was seen as a hindrance to effective usage across all four bodies of literature.

A number of institutional issues warrant consideration. When using Web 2.0 technologies cultural issues may need to be overcome, especially if institutions or disciplines are not receptive to collaborative, distributed, and nonlinear educational approaches. Institutional policy or culture may be opposed to the use of social networking in classes. Similarly, institutions and teachers may be against the use of mobile phones in classes, either prohibiting them or finding their use offensive. For virtual worlds institutional support is often lacking in terms of providing the requisite technical assistance and funding.

REFLECTIONS ON TECHNOLOGY-ENHANCED LEARNING ISSUES AND LIMITATIONS

Table 11.2 briefly summarizes the educational issues and limitations of using Web 2.0, social networking, mobile learning and virtual worlds that emerged from the literature. The emergent themes were not quite as commonly represented across the literature, for instance with cognitive load mainly being an issue for mobile learning and virtual worlds, and plagiarism mainly being raised for Web 2.0 and social networking. Yet, overall, the themes combine to span the technology-enhanced learning problem space and map out potential issues that warrant consideration in any technology-enhanced learning environment.

Table 11.2.   Issues and Limitations Relating to Teaching Using Web 2.0, Social Networking, Mobile, and Virtual World Technologies.

	Web 2.0	Social Networking	Mobile	Virtual Worlds
Technical issues	Account access, interfaces, editing conflicts, ustainability	Unthreaded discussions, fragmented knowledge	Small screens, limited power & functionality, network access	Lack of computing power impacting communication and rendering of scene
Student digital capabilities	May not know web & multimedia skills for learning	Generally familiar but potentially not for learning	Generally familiar for consumption but not production	Many unfamiliar with basic operation
Cognitive load issues	Generally not raised as an issue	Information spread, overlap with LMS	Problems with small screens and data from environment	Complexity of environment and operation
Collaboration problems	Uncomfortable editing each other's work, poor distribution of labor	Generally not raised as an issue	Generally not raised as an issue other than technical problems	Identifying and finding people, no cues, overlapping communication

Table 11.2. (*Continued*)

	Web 2.0	Social Networking	Mobile	Virtual Worlds
Negative student dispositions	Reluctant to share and work publicly	Dislike blurring private & study life	Generally positive due to convenience	Unfamiliar or too game-like
Assessment & feedback issues	Inappropriate focus on aesthetics & ratings	Feedback inaccuracy & unfamiliar with sharing culture	Functionality of devices, cultural leap for teachers	Confirming identity, capturing processes, technical issues
Plagiarism	Inappropriate reuse from Internet	Inappropriate reuse from Internet	Not commonly reported	Not commonly reported
Undesirable student behavior	Destroying other's work, off-task	Cyberbullying, off-task	Device mistreatment	Alternate conversations
Safety, privacy & equity	Predatory behavior, explicit content, privacy for personal accounts	Bullying, hacking, identity theft, education infiltrates personal life	Protecting from predatory behavior & explicit content, equitable access	Inappropriate treatment by avatars, explicit content
Teacher digital skills	Managing online collaboration	System settings for privacy, interaction	Troubleshooting devices & apps	Build landscapes, manage avatars
Negative educator dispositions	Prefer LMS or face-to-face	Own privacy, lack of confidence	Generally positive but cite time issues	Unfamiliarity, cost, technical problems
Inappropriate design	Replicating existing approaches	Lacking authenticity	Cognitive overload	Environment not suited to task
Teacher support	Time, professional learning, institutional shift	Time, acceptance by institution	Time, professional learning, acceptance by institution	Time, professional learning, institutional support

Technology-Enhanced Learning Design Principles

Based on the review of the Web 2.0, social networking, mobile learning and virtual worlds it is also possible to abstract key themes relating to technology-enhanced learning design.

Interestingly and once again, the way in which the themes are actualized can vary greatly depending on the technology. This highlights the importance of not only having an abstract understanding of technology-enhanced learning design principles but also deep and nuanced understanding of technologies in order to select and design appropriately.

The various principles have been loosely sequenced according to when they might occur as part of a design process, from early design and planning to run-time implementation. However, the temptation to categorize them according to a particular phase has been resisted because many of them recur throughout design and implementation. As previously established, design is not mechanical or linear, and there are multiple interdependencies that cannot be sequenced in lock-step. As well, once something has been designed it does not mean it can be subsequently ignored or neglected – it often requires ongoing attention in order to achieve the best outcomes. The technology-enhanced learning design principles, as distilled from the research literature, are as follows.

ESTABLISH CLEAR PEDAGOGICAL MOTIVATIONS FOR USING TECHNOLOGY

A key theme that came through from the literature was the importance of having a clear pedagogical motivation for using technologies. For instance, if situated, distributed and social constructivist learning is intended then mobile learning can be used to facilitate in-situ inquiry-based approaches. If experiential or constructionist pedagogies such as role-play activities or object building are fundamental to achieving learning outcomes then perhaps virtual worlds will offer a suitable platform. This is not to say specific technologies can only be used for certain pedagogies; we have already seen that learning technologies can be used to engage a range of pedagogies, depending largely on how the educator chooses to use them. The point is that pedagogical motivations that account for how students will best achieve the learning outcomes should drive technology selection and usage, rather than arbitrarily selecting technology or letting technology drive pedagogy. Consequently, it is important that educators start with a firm grasp of different pedagogical orientations and possibilities, as outlined in Chapter 3.

UNDERSTAND AND CATER TO STUDENTS

Another emergent theme from the literature was the importance of understanding and catering to the needs and preferences of students. The right level of challenge, depending on students' prior knowledge, has been observed to significantly increase engagement in Web 2.0 tasks. Understanding the dispositions and skills of students with relation to virtual worlds enables educators to design tasks that students value and enjoy. One more innovative idea from the social networking literature is to let in-course student input and feedback inspire course design and adaptation. In a similar vein, having students contribute to the design of virtual world learning spaces means that their interests and needs can automatically infiltrate into the course. The need to understand and cater to students was also raised as a high-level design concern in Chapter 6, with considerations including students' skills, experiences, motivations, expectations, preferences, digital literacies, and how to accordingly provide tailored learning pathways.

UPHOLD STUDENT SAFETY AND PRIVACY

Safety and privacy emerged as important concerns, no matter which technology is being used. The ability to publicly publish content using Web 2.0 technologies can be motivating to students, but the risk of harmful behavior by others needs to be managed by educators. For mobile learning tasks students may need guidance on the safe and responsible activity, for instance with relation to privacy and ethics when taking and publishing photos and videos. Using open and public virtual world platforms exposes students to the risk of untoward behavior and explicit imagery, so either precautions need to be applied or a closed (private) virtual world should be used.

For younger students closed social networks such as Ning or Edmodo are recommended in order to uphold their safety as well as align with institutional and legal requirements. On the other hand, adult learners may feel uncomfortable about their personal details becoming available to the broader public or to peers and teachers in a course, so closed or hidden groups may be used in conjunction with advice about how individuals can adjust their profile settings to avoid revealing their personal information. Strategies that teachers can use to uphold appropriate professional boundaries with students include using a work rather than personal social networking account, refraining from 'friending' students, and not initiating personal interactions. If cyber-bullying or other cybersafety incidents do occur in social networking environments then remedial action can take the form of blocking the access of the offender, providing advice to victims, talking with the pupils involved, enlisting the support of professionals, and potentially involving parents.

SCOPE OF THE TECHNOLOGICAL CONTEXT

Another recommendation that emerged from the literature was the need to understand the broader technological context in order to assess the feasibility of technologies and consider how they might appropriately interface with other tools being used. For mobile learning it is critical to ensure the wireless network is robust, connectivity is possible through the firewall, mobile devices are available and all apps have been installed. Virtual worlds require reasonably substantial computing power and bandwidth to operate, so it is important to assess whether infrastructure is adequate and to source institutional support if required. When Web 2.0 technologies such as wikis and blogs are being utilized then it is important to consider how they will interface with other tools, for instance, either supplementing or replacing them. If a social networking system is to be used in conjunction with another course website then care needs to be taken to avoid duplication of material and activity, as well as to make clear to students where different contributions will take place. Similarly, it is important to consider how virtual worlds will be applied within a course or subject, for instance whether they will be the primary means of collaboration or a platform that is only used for conducting specific in-class activities and simulations. Furthermore, virtual worlds do not easily support document processing or exchange, so other platforms may need to be used if production and sharing of texts is required.

SELECT TECHNOLOGIES ACCORDING TO PEDAGOGICAL, TECHNOLOGICAL, CONTENT, AND CONTEXTUAL CONSIDERATIONS

Appropriate technology selection was a pervasive theme across the research literature. Selecting the right Web 2.0 technologies for the content that needs to be represented, the interactions that need to take place, and the pedagogies that need to be applied can impact on the quality of the student experience and the learning outcomes achieved. Cost, complexity, control, clarity, interoperability, and sustainability are seen as other factors worth considering. Virtual world platform selection may depend on the level of students being taught, the technology available, the functionality required for the intended activity, the costs of use and maintenance, and what is feasible within the institution. If social networking is being used it is seen as important to select tools within the system that are well suited to the tasks, with practical examples including using wall posts to support the development of writing skills and image galleries for architectural students to develop design portfolios.

Mobile devices vary according to their affordability, functionality, platform compatibility, among others, so educators need to ensure that students have access to devices that meet the minimum requirements for the task. Whether or not to use a Bring Your Own Device policy is another worthwhile consideration, as these have been found to positively impact upon the authenticity of device use, the amount of online conversations that take place, and the perceived quality of learning experiences. On the other hand, a BYOD policy could potentially limit access to learning for students who cannot source required devices. Selection of mobile learning apps is seen to depend on intended learning outcomes, for instance games-based apps for rote learning of facts, productivity apps for higher order thinking, and content creation apps for collaboration. The quality of apps also warrants consideration, in terms of their accuracy, relevance, instructions, feedback, scaffolding, navigation, adaptability, and so on.

So drawing together factors emerging from the Web 2.0, social networking, mobile learning and virtual world technologies we can see that technology selection involves a complex set of considerations, that in essence relate to the pedagogies being used, the content being represented, contextual and pragmatic issues, and how these are (or are not) satisfied by the technologies. At a higher level, deciding on which technology platform/s to use (for instance, Web 2.0, social networking, virtual worlds) is a fundamental and important consideration, though one that again depends on pedagogies, content, context, and how the features of the technology may satisfy learning requirements. Consequently an understanding of the affordances of the technologies is essential, as outlined in Chapter 4.

DESIGN FOR AUTHENTIC AND MEANINGFUL LEARNING

Designing for authentic and meaningful learning was strongly recommended across the literature, in accordance with propositions in Chapter 3. Authentic Web 2.0 tasks using wikis and e-portfolios that incorporate student choice and are tightly integrated into course work have been observed to promote student participation. In social networking environments authentic tasks that relate to student issues and leverage the interactive features of the platform are proposed to encourage greater intellectual engagement and contribution than more artificial and highly structured tasks. Mobile devices can promote authentic and meaningful learning through capture and annotation of situated data (images, audio and video) based on real world experiences, as well as organizing and sharing data on the Internet. More open ended and productive tasks on mobile devices have been correlated with higher levels of student performance and satisfaction than closed, consumption-oriented activities.

Virtual worlds are particularly useful for facilitating experiential and situated learning through simulations and role-play activities, so that students can transfer the skills they are practicing to real-life contexts. The 3-D emulation provided by virtual worlds means they can also help to develop spatial knowledge and skills better than 2-D environments, or in some cases even better than real world experiences. Virtual worlds also enable educators and students to transcend time and space to complete activities that would otherwise be impractical or dangerous to undertake, for instance visiting historic villages or modeling molecular reactions. Thus, Web 2.0, social networking, mobile and virtual world technologies offer educators a host of innovative ways to offer authentic and meaningful learning experiences so as improve engagement and learning outcomes.

INTEGRATE SUPPORTIVE SCAFFOLDING

No matter what technology is being used, there is a wide range of scaffolding that educators can provide to support learning. For instance, scaffolding for Web 2.0 tasks can take the form of reflective prompts, templates, and exemplars. These have all been shown to support completion of Web 2.0 tasks, though it should be noted that too much guidance has been observed to stifle divergent thinking and reduce student satisfaction. In virtual worlds, scaffolding may take the form of in-world bulletin boards with task instructions, permanent in-world learning resources, or even scripted avatars to demonstrate activities. The idea of scaffolding was covered in Chapter 3 with relation to socio-constructivist learning, but the general concept of supporting student learning through the provision of resources can be applied across pedagogies and technologies.

CONSTRUCT THE ENVIRONMENT ACCORDING TO INTENDED ACTIVITY AND PEDAGOGY

The virtual worlds literature reminds us of the importance of designing the environment according to intended activity and pedagogy. For instance, placement of paths can indicate task sequence, social spaces can be used to encourage discussion, the placement of the teacher within the space can indicate their role in the activity, team spaces can be used to facilitate group work, large circular seating arrangements can be used to signify whole-class conversations, and colored furniture can denote roles in activities. Navigational aids are particularly important in virtual worlds in order to enable expedient participation in learning tasks, so real world navigational metaphors should be employed and signage should be easy to find and use. While these findings are all drawn from the virtual worlds literature, they remind us of the general importance of designing the environment to signal and support intended activity and pedagogy.

CONSIDER COGNITIVE LOAD AND MULTIMEDIA LEARNING EFFECTS

Unsurprisingly, the multimedia learning effects outlined in Chapter 4 influence cognition and hence learning in technology-mediated environments. This of course has implications for how educators should design tasks and content. For instance, mobile content should ideally be simple and intuitive to use, provide contextually relevant scaffolding, and use multimedia in a way that avoids cognitive overload. When designing virtual world tasks educators should consider whether the task itself is suitable for the environment. For instance, in one study conducting group consensus forming tasks in virtual worlds imposed an additional cognitive load that resulted in less effective learning. Alternately, a high degree of fidelity and detail in virtual worlds can provide visual and procedural realism that makes a contribution to conceptual development and the student experience. Examples include learning about Mayan architecture, computer hardware, or film set setup. While these are specific instances and technologies, they showcase how multimedia learning effects and cognitive load are important to understand and consider when designing technology-enhanced learning.

PROVIDE STUDENTS WITH A CLEAR RATIONALE FOR USING TECHNOLOGY

Given that some students may be reluctant to use technology for learning and assuming that there are good pedagogical motivations for using technology, it can be useful to provide students with the rationale for using technology in order to increase their motivation and engagement. For instance, the rationale for using Web 2.0 technologies may be for students to learn from peers, cultivate a sense of community, and promote task relevance. Linking the use of the virtual worlds to course objectives, for instance via simulation of phenomena and experiential learning, is particularly important because students are more likely to be unfamiliar with the operation of the technology. While the need to provide a clear rationale for using technology primarily emerged from the Web 2.0 and virtual worlds literature, it is relevant to all learning technology contexts.

EXPLICITLY DEVELOP STUDENTS' DIGITAL LEARNING CAPABILITIES

Explicit development of students' digital learning capabilities is encouraged across the literature (in accordance with Chapter 1). Even though students are increasingly familiar with how to use technology in their personal lives, they often need guidance on how to use technologies such as Web 2.0 tools effectively for learning purposes. Educators may not only need to support the development of Web 2.0 technical skills, but also more generic learning capabilities such as communication and critical thinking. While students generally find mobile devices and applications intuitive to use, guidance and modeling from the teacher may be needed for students to successfully use the devices and apps to complete productive learning tasks. Because students may be unfamiliar with the operation of virtual worlds, teachers can choose to provide out-of-class access to spaces, set pre-class practice activities, model operational skills, and offer in-class time to explore the functionality of the virtual worlds. Strategies may also be applied to provide students using virtual worlds with ongoing learning support in the form of video tutorials, reference guides, or buddy systems. So while different technologies and activities may differ in complexity, student digital learning skills and application of appropriate supporting strategies is a perennial consideration.

UTILIZE GENERAL PEDAGOGICAL STRATEGIES AND PRINCIPLES

When using technology-enhanced learning, there are a variety of general pedagogical strategies that teachers can apply in order to optimize student participation, outcomes and experiences. For instance, with Web 2.0 tasks teachers can encourage contribution by providing early feedback, setting periodical deadlines, enabling anonymous contributions, discussing posts in classes, assessing contributions, or direct requests for student input. When teaching in virtual worlds, educators still need to perform general functions that they would in face-to-face environments such as providing information, responding to student problems, facilitating discussion, and finding workarounds if problems occur. Thus, it is important that educators consider how they may transfer general pedagogical strategies (for instance, those covered in Chapter 3) to their particular technology-enhanced learning context.

SUPPORT EFFECTIVE COMMUNICATION

Technologies provide educators with a range of ways to enhance and encourage communication. The discursive and interactive functions of social networking systems (posts, replies, chats, polls, 'likes') can be used to encourage lively discussions about course content, where students learn through debate and negotiation of meaning. Different communication modes of virtual worlds can be used to suit different purposes, such as private chat for communication between two people, public chat for broadcasting information to a group, audio for more effective for extensive dialogue and discussions, and avatar gestures to signal attention or sentiments. The lack of face-to-face communication cues in virtual worlds can make synchronous communication difficult, so it can be useful to apply communication management strategies such as appointing conversation leaders, formulating protocols for turn taking during class discussions, and regularly asking whether people would like to contribute. The spatial features of virtual worlds can also be exploited to enhance communication, for instance by having pairs of students move into designated spaces to hold discussions, using avatar positioning for students to indicate their preferences, or utilizing flight to unobtrusively monitor discussions. Hence, technology provides a host of interesting ways to facilitate communication, with the common thread being that teacher guidance may be needed in order for students to select channels and utilize them in the most appropriate ways.

APPLY STRATEGIES TO ENCOURAGE SUCCESSFUL COLLABORATION

The importance of designing for and supporting effective collaboration was a strong theme across the literature. Collaboration on Web 2.0 activities can be encouraged by designing tasks that employ reasonably sized teams, genuinely require students to work together to create joint products, and (for longer term initiatives) encourage identity and personal expression. Strategies to support run-time Web 2.0 group work include having students assume roles within the team, providing scripts and collaborative cues, using Really Simple Syndication (RSS) to help track peer changes, and setting up online discussion areas to supplement productive spaces. Although many students will be familiar with how to use social networking, some students may require specific guidance on how to effectively use features of social networks to facilitate group work processes, and may also benefit from provision of teamwork strategies such as suggesting roles for people.

Collaboration using mobile devices can be facilitated through sharing of information among students from any location, more social participation, and division of tasks between team members. Group work processes in virtual worlds can be supported by setting complex tasks that require students to actively engage with one another, nurturing underlying teamwork skills such as leadership and interpersonal skills, and again by designating roles. Thus across the various technological platforms collaboration seems to be supported by designing tasks that require collaboration, helping students understand how technology can be used to assist collaboration, and actively guiding students' general teamwork processes.

ENABLE OPPORTUNITIES FOR REFLECTIVE AND VICARIOUS LEARNING

Technology provides educators with several ways of encouraging reflective learning. Many Web 2.0 technologies enable asynchronous posts to be made that allow students to reflect on each other's work and their own work over time. Blogs and wikis can be used for students to learn vicariously from the posts of other students, which is often particularly useful for less able students. The reflection and self-regulation that Web 2.0 technologies enable has been shown to improve learning outcomes in some cases. Similarly, through the open and persistent (recorded) nature of communication in social networking environments students can reflect on their actions and the contributions of others, as well as engage in socially mediated metacognition through collaborative tasks that require explicit reflection and feedback. In summary, across technologies educators can exploit openness and sharing to enable reflective and vicarious learning instead of relying solely on individualistic educational approaches.

PROACTIVELY ENGAGE IN THE LEARNING PROCESS

A common theme across the literature was the positive contribution that teacher engagement could make. The active engagement of teachers in Web 2.0 learning environments has been shown to positively correlate with student attitudes, involvement, and quality of contributions. Teacher engagement in social networking environments, such as initiating posts and responding to students, has been shown to increase student collaboration, higher order thinking, student satisfaction, and performance on tasks. However, the nature of teacher engagement warrants consideration. The more self-regulated rather than institutionally controlled nature of social networking environments often encourages students to contribute, so teachers may choose to adopt a more egalitarian rather than authoritative role in order to promote more active student participation.

ADOPT HIGH-QUALITY ASSESSMENT AND FEEDBACK PRACTICES

Technology-enhanced learning environments provide a range of new opportunities to promote high-quality assessment and feedback practices. Web 2.0 tools enable teachers to review learner progress over time, track individual contributions to collaborative processes, and facilitate peer assessment. Teacher feedback on Web 2.0 contributions is not only valued by students but can improve the quality of posts over time. Providing students undertaking mobile learning activities with regular and rapid feedback has been shown to improve learning outcomes and attitudes. Defining what will be assessed (e.g., quality rather than number of posts), setting appropriately high expectations, and utilizing peer feedback are proposed as important in social networking environments.

Integrating peer feedback into wiki and e-portfolio tasks has been found to result in significantly better performance and student satisfaction than when peer feedback is absent, with qualitative feedback resulting in better improvements than solely using ratings. Proposed strategies to promote effective peer assessment in Web 2.0 environments include providing students with training on how to peer assess, setting up anonymous peer assessment, incentivizing diligent execution (for instance by attaching a mark to it), and constraining the amount of peer assessment to reasonable levels through restrictions on post sizes and number of peer tasks marked. Thus, within the literature there are a range of strategies for assessment and feedback that can be abstracted across technologies.

MONITOR AND MANAGE PLAGIARISM

On the flip side of the reflective and vicarious learning enabled through open access to peer contributions is the possibility of plagiarism. Because copy-paste behaviors are so familiar to students based on nonacademic aspects of their lives, the risk of plagiarism needs to be explicitly and proactively addressed during Web 2.0 tasks through the provision of clear guidance about what is (and is not) appropriate. Similarly, in social networking environments the risk of plagiarism is also high because of the simplicity with which information can be transferred from the Internet. Plagiarism was not raised as an important issue in either the mobile learning or virtual worlds literature, perhaps because of the more personalized and less text-based nature of mobile and virtual worlds tasks. However, the possibility of plagiarism is always an increased risk during any non-face-to-face assessment so clear guidance about appropriate behavior and vigilant monitoring are necessary no matter which technology is being used.

FOSTER POSITIVE LEARNING COMMUNITIES

The fact that technologies can be used to connect people no matter where they are located means they can be used to foster positive learning communities. More discursive and subjective use of Web 2.0 tools, for instance blogs and Twitter, can be used for students to offer one another social support and promote community building. Strategies for creating positive learning communities in social networking environments include ice-breaker tasks to promote class rapport, rewards for best responses, teacher uploads of support materials, and early moderation of negative comments. Community building may also be encouraged by creating a space for social contributions, though it can be important to provide clarity around what is considered to be appropriate communication. Social networking environments can also be utilized to expand out the learning community to include students from other continents, external experts, mentors, and professionals. Applying strategies to promote presence in virtual worlds is proposed to support the cultivation positive learning communities.

LEVERAGE PROFESSIONAL LEARNING OPPORTUNITIES AND SUPPORT

The value of professional support for educators is emphasized across the literature. Web 2.0 professional learning can help teachers to make the important shift from instructive to more student-centered and facilitative approaches, and lack of professional support has been shown to inhibit effective use. Similarly, the way that teachers configure social networking environments can have a substantial impact on student participation and interaction, so professional learning is recommended to support the development of teacher skills. Virtual worlds professional development is proposed as particularly important due to the complexity of teaching in virtual world environments. Professional learning that is pedagogically grounded, adequately contextualized, and purposeful has been found useful to support the development of mobile learning pedagogies and facilitate required attitudinal shifts.

Provision of time for educators to learn, plan, design and develop resources was also a pervasive theme. Institutional support can have a critical impact on design and implementation of technology-enhanced learning initiatives, by providing the funds, access, infrastructure, policies and support personnel needed for success. The Web 2.0, mobile learning and virtual worlds literature also emphasizes the value of professional learning communities as a source of support for educators. This community approach to sharing of great teaching ideas and resources is the exact intention of the Learning Design community (as explained in Chapter 6).

Reflections on Technology-Enhanced Learning Design Principles

Some of the learning design principles (recommendations) above were not evident in all four bodies of literature. For instance, the theme relating to constructing the environment to support activity and pedagogy emerged predominantly from the virtual worlds literature. However, what was particularly interesting was that even though the themes may have only emerged for one or two educational technologies, they generally held relevance for all four platforms. Accordingly, all recommendations that arose from the Web 2.0, social networking, mobile learning and virtual worlds literature have been merged into the design principles.

The technology-enhanced learning design principles, benefits and constraints that have arisen from the literature can be loosely organized into clusters, as shown in Table 11.3. It is important to note that the mappings into clusters are by no means perfect or direct. For instance, the 'selecting technology' recommendation is relevant to both the 'communication' and the 'content representation' cluster, and quite potentially many others. As well, the fact that technologies can be used to establish identity, presence, and co-presence not only supports community building but potentially other aspects of learning. However, the organization into clusters does serve to illustrate relationships between benefits, limitations, and design recommendations, so as to highlight how educators might leverage particular potentials and overcome certain issues through use of associated design strategies. The fact that each technology-enhanced learning design benefit and issue relates to at least one principle shows how technology-enhanced learning design is in many ways a process of leveraging potentials and overcoming constraints.

It is also important to note that neither design nor technology is present as a cluster in the table. Rather, all of these important educational constituents are achieved and addressed through design and through technology. As we move into an increasingly technological world, technology shouldn't be something that

Table 11.3.   Relationships between Technology-Enhanced Learning Design Principles, Benefits, and Issues.

Cluster	Benefits	Issues	Principles
Pedagogy	• Pedagogical flexibility	• Inappropriate design	• Establish clear pedagogical motivations for using technology • Design for authentic and meaningful learning • Provide students with a clear rationale for using technology • Utilize general pedagogical strategies and principles • Integrate supportive scaffolding • Construct the environment according to intended activity and pedagogy
Access	• Provide access	• Technical issues	• Scope the technological context
Communication	• Facilitate communication		• Support effective communication • Select technologies according to pedagogical, technological, content and contextual considerations
Content representation	• Content representation & sharing • Easy contribution	• Cognitive load issues	• Consider cognitive load and multimedia learning effects
Collaboration	• Enhance collaboration	• Collaboration problems	• Apply strategies to encourage successful collaboration
Motivation & engagement	• Enhance motivation & engagement	• Negative student dispositions • Undesirable student behavior (misuse and distraction)	• Proactively engage in the learning process

Table 11.3.   (*Continued*)

Cluster	Benefits	Issues	Principles
Vicarious learning & reflection	• Facilitate vicarious learning and reflection	• Plagiarism	• Enable opportunities for reflective and vicarious learning • Monitor and manage plagiarism
Digital learning capabilities	• Develop digital capabilities	• Inadequate student digital capabilities	• Explicitly develop students' digital learning capabilities
Assessment & feedback	• Technology can enhance assessment and feedback	• Assessment and feedback challenges	• Adopt high-quality assessment and feedback practices
Student-centred learning	• Active and student-centered learning		• Understand and cater to students
Learning communities	• Develop learning communities • Identity & presence		• Foster positive learning communities
Protecting students		• Safety, privacy, and equity	• Uphold student safety and privacy
Teacher support		• Underdeveloped teacher digital skills • Negative educator dispositions • Teacher support issues (time, professional learning, institutional issues)	• Leverage professional learning opportunities and support

educators have to enumerate. Ideally it should be something that is integrated into learning design as a natural consequence of pedagogical needs. Similarly, design is the holistic process that educators undertake in order to synergistically weave all of the constituents together, not a separated process. Consequently, technology and design are implicit in all of the clusters represented Table 11.3.

Final Reflections on Abstracting Technology-Enhanced Learning Design

Having made quite an extensive effort to generate an abstracted understanding of technology-enhanced learning design, it is perhaps reasonable to reflect not only upon the outcomes of the analysis but also the process. While there is a large body of general educational technology literature that proposes recommendations for technology-enhanced learning design, and other large corpuses of empirical research that put forward recommendations for design and implementation using specific technologies, this is the first comprehensive and systematic effort to integrate the two areas.

Perhaps unsurprisingly, the empirical findings from the research on Web 2.0, social networking, mobile learning, and virtual worlds essentially agreed with claims from the general literature covered in early chapters, with no major contradictions noted. Interestingly, there were practical themes that emerged from the empirical literature that were not strongly represented among general literature, for instance providing students with a clear rationale for using technology, and the important role of vicarious learning in technology-enhanced contexts. Similarly, there were themes from the general literature that were not prominent among the empirical research, such as the role of learning analytics and evaluation in supporting design. The reason for the latter difference may be because both learning analytics and evaluation are implicit in research studies, which in most cases analyze and evaluate evidence collected from students. Nevertheless, the different emphases of the two bodies of literature are a pertinent reminder of the increased power and insight that may be derived by drawing from both general literature and empirical research evidence.

What the process of performing a detailed analysis of the empirical literature does provide is concrete evidence and substantiation upon which to ground general claims and abstractions. There is often little point handing abstractions to people, for without the underlying linkages through to real world examples and applications, abstractions tend to be meaningless. The fundamental nature of abstraction is that detail is necessarily forgone. So, for instance, if you feel as though many of the details contained proceeding chapters aren't fully captured in Tables 11.1−11.3, that's because they aren't! The tables aim to support integration and interrelation of knowledge by providing a birds-eye view of technology-enhanced learning design. But we have already established that design is a wickedly complex pursuit that cannot simply be reduced to a handful of components. Any attempt to reduce design knowledge into a small number of elements or attributes will inevitably result in oversimplification.

The analytic process that we have conducted provides the ability to trace back to the research evidence and argumentation, so that evidence-based design knowledge can be constructed rather than transmitted. It is the process of thinking through educational design using Web 2.0, social networking, mobile devices and virtual worlds that enables the development of deep and nuanced understanding of technology-enhanced learning benefits, issues and design principles. Accomplished design involves utilizing contextually relevant knowledge and evidence contained in the previous chapters, rather than simply working from a handful of tables.

With any abstraction process there is a temptation to try to make everything fit into a neat and elegant model. Can we use TPACK to encapsulate all of the design principles? Can we separate out elements focused on design from those focused on implementation? Possibilities such as these were considered, however, in each case such organizations were overly simplistic and artificial so as to compromise realism. Accordingly, the benefits, issues and principles of technology-enhanced learning have been presented prima facie based on the thematic analyses and without manipulation. It is contended that the personal act of interpreting the benefits, limitations and principles, with all of their varying interdependencies, and understanding their origins, is where in-depth design insights will be derived.

So is that it? I hear you ask. We have certainly covered considerable ground and developed substantial knowledge relating to technology-enhanced learning design. So what's left? Yes, we have constructed a good deal of understanding that can be used to inform technology-enhanced learning design. But the acquisition of knowledge is different from putting it into practice. In the next and final chapter we reflect on the state of technology-enhanced learning, it's future directions, and how educators and researchers can best prepare to make a positive difference.

References

Conole, G., & Jones, C. (2010). Sharing practice, problems and solutions for institutional change. In P. Goodyear & S. Retalis (Eds.), *Technology-enhanced learning: Design patterns and pattern languages* (pp. 277–296). Rotterdam: Sense Publishers.

Goodyear, P., & Retalis, S. (2010). Learning, technology and design. In P. Goodyear & S. Retalis (Eds.), *Technology-enhanced learning: Design patterns and pattern languages* (pp. 1–28). Rotterdam: Sense Publishers.

Rose, D. H., Harbour, W. S., Johnston, C. S., Daley, S. G., & Abarbanell, L. (2006). Universal design for learning in postsecondary education – Reflections on principles and their application. *Journal of Postsecondary Education and Disability, 19*(2), 135–151.

Sylwester, R. (1995). *A celebration of neurons.* Alexandria: Association for Supervision and Curriculum Development.

Winters, N., Mor, Y., & Pratt, D. (2010). The distributed developmental network. In P. Goodyear & S. Retalis (Eds.), *Technology-enhanced learning: Design patterns and pattern languages* (pp. 233–254). Rotterdam: Sense Publishers.

12

Technology-Enhanced Learning — Conclusions and Future Directions

ABSTRACT

This chapter aims to establish a positive vision for the technology-enhanced learning design field. It commences by summarizing the current state of technology-enhanced learning research, as established by the previous analysis, in order to clarify the foundations upon which the field can build. The future of learning technology is considered, in the first instance, by extrapolating trends in information and communication technologies throughout history. This process showcases how the most impactful technologies are those that bring information closer to us, support sharing, and offer more visceral learning experiences. The nature of learning technology trends occurring in recent Horizon Reports, for instance, gesture-based computing, augmented reality, Massive Open Online Courses, and table computing, are analyzed and explained in terms of Roger's Diffusion of Innovation Theory and Gartner's Hype Cycle. This leads to identifying teachers as the critical lynch pin in order for society to derive greatest educational benefit from the exponential advances in technology. Consequently, support for educators is argued as essential. Into the future the learning technology field will only optimize its progress if educators and researchers work together to understand design issues and possibilities. Directions forward for educators and researchers are proposed, emphasizing a research-driven, pedagogically focused, creative, and collaborative approach to technology-enhanced learning design.

The Current State of Technology-Enhanced Learning Design

Through our explorations of the educational literature, what can we surmise about the current state of technology-enhanced learning design?

Firstly, in today's world, technology integration is an educational imperative. There are several key drivers for technology integration, including developing students' digital learning skills, curricula and policy documents, professional requirements for educators, promoting access to learning, catering to today's learners, and, most importantly, the desire to use technology to improve learning outcomes. However, educators need to adopt a critical approach to using technology in order to overcome naïve assumptions such as technological determinism and the idea that all younger students will automatically know how to use technology for learning purposes.

The Technology, Pedagogy And Content Knowledge (TPACK) Framework (Mishra & Koehler, 2006) has become a well-known way to conceptualize the different areas that educators need to consider when integrating technology into their lessons and courses. Several instruments for measuring the TPACK knowledge of educators have been developed, though concerns exist surrounding their ability to clearly distinguish the different knowledge components and the reliability of having teachers self-rate their abilities. While TPACK constitutes a general framework for supporting educator thinking, it makes no commitments about which sorts of pedagogies or technologies may be useful, what may be successful approaches to teaching within particular subject areas, or how to consider the context when creating technology-enhanced modules of work. Thus, TPACK provides a useful organizing and descriptive framework, but little guidance to support technology-enhanced learning design practices.

There are a variety of pedagogies that educators can choose to utilize when designing technology-enhanced learning, which can operate at a range of different levels. High-level pedagogical perspectives that encapsulate overarching beliefs about how learning occurs include behaviorism, cognitivism, constructivism, social constructivism, and connectivism. There are also several sorts of pedagogical approaches that can be applied in lessons or modules, such as collaborative learning, problem-based learning, inquiry-based learning, constructionist learning, design-based learning, and games-based learning. At a more instantaneous level there are numerous pedagogical strategies that teachers can apply, for instance, monitoring the alternative conceptions of students, providing scaffolding and encouraging metacognition, to name but a few. Ultimately, however, educators are advised to utilize pedagogies and technologies in ways that provide students with authentic and meaningful learning experiences.

Technology affordances and multimedia learning effects provide two generally applicable frameworks that can be used to help think through the selection and deployment of technologies for learning purposes. A focus on affordances draws the designer's attention to what tools can offer to learners in terms of action potentials. Multimedia learning effects such as the multimedia effect, the modality effect, the redundancy effect, the split attention effect, the signaling effect and the personalization effect all utilize what is known from cognitive science to inform the way words, sound, images, animations and so on are effectively combined. Although affordances and multimedia learning effects have historically been two quite separate areas, they can be mutually informing when making technology selection and deployment decisions.

Anderson and Krathwohl's (2001) Taxonomy of Learning Teaching and Assessing, with its knowledge types (factual, conceptual, procedural, metacognitive) and cognitive processes (remember, understand, apply, analyze, evaluate, create), provides a general way to conceptualize the representation of content across discipline areas. Technology can support representation of content by enabling access, retrieval, representation, organization, summarization, visualization, simulation, calculation, documentation, manipulation, programming, and sharing of information. Sharing of content among the educational community has been assisted through developments such as learning objects, open educational resources, creative commons licensing, and Massive Open Online Courses.

Teaching is best positioned as a design science, because it requires creative and scientific thinking in order to solve ill-structured problems. Design thinking capabilities are inherently challenging to develop, but are supported through sustained practice, reflection, exemplars, and expert guidance. Fundamentally, designing for learning involves understanding and catering to students, creating tasks that help students achieve learning outcomes, ensuring alignment between different aspects of the design, and promoting accessibility. The Learning Design field aims to support the representation and sharing of great teaching practice, and has attempted to promote representation and sharing through the development of technical standards, pattern descriptions, visualization approaches, visualization tools, pedagogical planner tools, and a learning activity management system (LAMS). While these learning design initiatives and educational models generally provide useful reference points, none have infiltrated deeply into teacher practice. The greatest success potentially lies in having educators develop a deep understanding of design issues, and adopting a reflective, collaborative, and design-focused mindset.

Contemporary technologies such as Web 2.0, social networking, mobile devices and virtual worlds subtend a variety of learning design possibilities for educators. For instance, wikis enable teams of students to collaboratively develop knowledge bases, and blogs allow students to create reflective e-portfolios through which they can solicit feedback from peers. Social networking can be used to facilitate community-building activities instead of, or in conjunction with, a learning management system. Mobile learning supports educational access and participation from any location, thus offering a range of opportunities for in-the-field data capture and sharing. With their ability to represent 3D environments, virtual worlds enable educators to provide students with access to simulations, modeling, and role-play experiences that may otherwise be too impractical or infeasible to utilize.

Abstracting findings and observations from across the research literature, it is apparent that contemporary technologies subtend a range of benefits to educators. The pedagogical flexibility availed by learning technology platforms can be used to provide access to learning, facilitate remote communication, enhance collaboration, promote identity and presence, represent and share content, support easy contribution, enhance motivation and engagement, facilitate vicarious learning and reflection, develop digital capabilities, promote active and student-centered learning, enable new forms of assessment and feedback, and foster learning communities. Yet, the literature also highlights a range of issues associated with the use of technology to promote learning, including technical problems, insufficient student and teacher digital capabilities, cognitive load issues, collaboration problems, negative student and teacher dispositions, assessment and feedback issues, plagiarism, undesirable student behavior, underdeveloped teacher digital skills, negative educator dispositions, inappropriate learning designs, lack of teacher support, as well as safety, privacy, and equity issues.

Distilling design recommendations from the Web 2.0, social networking, mobile learning, and virtual worlds research literature into themes suggests the following principles for technology-enhanced learning design:

(1) Establish clear pedagogical motivations for using technology
(2) Understand and cater to students
(3) Uphold student safety and privacy
(4) Scope the technological context
(5) Select technologies according to pedagogical, technological, content, and contextual considerations
(6) Design for authentic and meaningful learning
(7) Integrate supportive scaffolding
(8) Construct the environment according to intended activity and pedagogy
(9) Consider cognitive load and multimedia learning effects
(10) Provide students with a clear rationale for using technology
(11) Explicitly develop students' digital learning capabilities
(12) Utilize general pedagogical strategies and principles
(13) Support effective communication
(14) Apply strategies to encourage successful collaboration
(15) Enable opportunities for reflective and vicarious learning
(16) Proactively engage in the learning process
(17) Adopt high-quality assessment and feedback practices
(18) Monitor and manage plagiarism
(19) Foster positive learning communities
(20) Leverage professional learning opportunities and support.

The benefits, issues and design principles present in the technology-enhanced learning research literature can be organized into clusters of concerns, as illustrated in Figure 12.1.

Thus, we have been able to confidently establish the current state of technology-enhanced learning design, as it is represented in the research literature. But what of the future?

Figure 12.1.   Thirteen Clusters of Concerns Relating to Technology-Enhanced
Learning Design.

Technology-Enhanced Learning Futures

One central reason that we try to understand the past is so that we can prepare for the future. While not pretending that we can predict the future with any certainty, it can be helpful to analyze trends in order to understand the nature of technological and corresponding social change over time. Understanding the nature of technological change helps us to appraise where we will concentrate our forward planning efforts, and also respond appropriately to emerging technology developments. It takes courage to make predictions — it is much easier to dismiss predictive efforts as mere speculation that ignores the more important foundational principles of the field. However, failure to make predictions and anticipate the future can have potentially severe consequences, as the radical changes in the business models of the music and video industries most recently exemplify. More positively, in education, pre-empting change enables us best prepare and adapt in order to optimize learning for students.

As a starting point, let's take a look at some information and communication technology (ICT) advancements throughout history that have revolutionized society. Figure 12.2 contains a chronology of some ICT developments over the previous two millennia, along with a brief explanation of the essential nature of the innovation[6].

From Figure 12.2, we can deduce that revolutionary ICT innovations have been those that provide more immediate access to information, support dissemination of information, and offer richer media experiences. Accordingly, educators should be on the look out for future technological developments that bring information closer to us, support sharing, and offer more visceral learning experiences. Technologies with these characteristics (such as augmented and virtual reality) are the most likely candidates to create sustained change in our society.

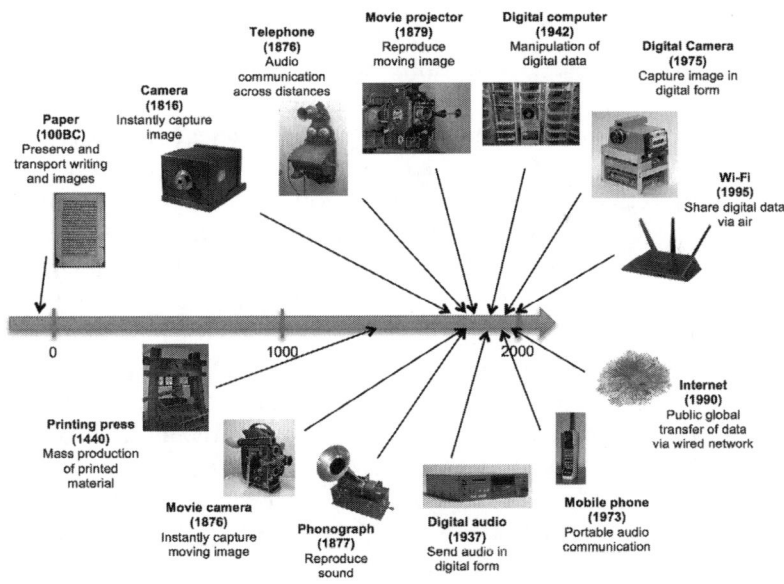

Figure 12.2.   Brief Chronology of ICT Developments in the Previous Two Millennia.

---

[6]Note that some dates and images are approximate due to evolutionary nature of inventions or the absence of accurate documentation.

Figure 12.2 also illustrates the rapid acceleration in technological developments over time, with the vast majority of advancements over the last two millennia being made in the last two centuries. This is in rough accordance with Moore's Law, which stipulates that computing power tends to increase exponentially over time (doubling each year). We should expect that into the future technological advancement will be multiplicative, not linear.

It is also helpful to examine the nature of technology predictions so that we can understand their likely accuracy and respond to them appropriately. The New Media Consortium (NMC) Horizon Reports (https://www.nmc.org/nmc-horizon) can be used to provide insight into the nature of more recent educational technological predictions. Each year, the Horizon Reports outline anticipated trends in educational technology usage in the short (<1 year), medium (2-3 years), and long-term (4-5) years, based on the perceptions of expert educators from around the world. A summary of the anticipated trends for K-12 and Higher Education from 2009 to 2016 are provided in Tables 12.1 and 12.2 respectively.

In the first instance, the most recent years of Tables 12.1 and 12.2 provide a useful indication of the educational technology trends that experts anticipate will be influential in the future (such as wearable technologies, robotics, artificial intelligence, as well as augmented and virtual reality). Thus, we may choose to preference these in our educational technology visioning and explorations.

Perhaps even more usefully, Tables 12.1 and 12.2 also illustrate the nature of educational technology trends and predictions. For example, we can see that some trends such as gesture-based computing and augmented reality have remained as medium and long-term educational technology predictions for several years but have not become a part of mainstream teaching practice. Other predictions such as cloud computing and mobile learning have remained as short-term trends for several years, rather than becoming an integrated and standard part of what teachers do in their classes. To this extent, Tables 12.1 and 12.2 illustrate that educational uses of technologies often take considerably longer to infiltrate into mainstream practice than anticipated.

The core reason that penetration of technology into mainstream educational practice can take longer than anticipated is because, while the performance of technology increases exponentially, the application of technology depends entirely on people. Roger's (2010) Diffusion of Innovations theory explains how people go through a process of knowledge raising, persuasion,

Table 12.1. Educational Technology Trends in K-12 Horizon Reports (2009–2016).

K-12	2009	2010	2011	2012	2013	2014	2015	2016
<1 year	• Collaborative environments • Online communication tools	• Cloud computing • Collaborative environments	• Cloud computing • Mobile devices	• Mobile devices & apps • Tablet computing	• Cloud computing • Mobile learning	• BYOD • Cloud computing	• BYOD • Maker spaces	• Maker spaces • Online learning
2-3 years	• Mobiles • Cloud computing	• Games-based learning • Mobiles	• Games-based learning • Open content	• Games-based learning • Personal learning environments	• Learning analytics • Open content	• Games & Gamification • Learning analytics	• 3D Printing • Adaptive learning technologies	• Robotics • Virtual reality
4-5 years	• Smart objects • The personal web	• Augmented reality • Flexible displays	• Learning analytics • Personal learning environments	• Augmented reality • Natural user interfaces	• 3D printing • Virtual & remote laboratories	• The Internet of Things • Wearable technology	• Digital badges • Wearable technology	• Artificial intelligence • Wearable technology

Table 12.2. Educational Technology Trends in Higher Education Horizon Reports (2009–2016).

H.E.	2009	2010	2011	2012	2013	2014	2015	2016
<1 year	• Mobiles • Cloud computing	• Mobile computing • Open content	• Electronic books • Mobiles	• Mobile apps • Tablet computing	• Massively Open Online Courses • Tablet computing	• Flipped classroom • Learning analytics	• Bring Your Own Device (BYOD) • Flipped classroom	• BYOD • Learning Analytics & Adaptive Learning
2-3 years	• Geo-everything • The personal web	• Electronic books • Simple augmented reality	• Augmented reality • Game-based learning	• Game-based learning • Learning analytics	• Games and gamification • Learning analytics	• 3D printing • Games and Gamification	• Makerspaces • Wearable technology	• Augmented and Virtual Reality • Makerspaces
4-5 years	• Semantic-aware applications • Smart objects	• Gesture-based computing • Visual data analysis	• Gesture-based computing • Learning analytics	• Gesture-based computing • Internet of Things	• 3D printing • Wearable technology	• Quantified self • Virtual assistants	• Adaptive learning technologies • The Internet of Things	• Affective computing • Robotics

decision making, implementation and confirmation in the adoption of new technologies. What's more, different people will go through these stages at different times, depending on their preparedness for and acceptance of change. Roger's (2010) theory proposes that only a small proportion of 'innovators' will initially lead the uptake of innovations, followed by some 'early adopters,' a sizeable proportion of 'early majority' and 'late majority,' and finally the 'laggards' in order for the innovation to reach full utilization (see Figure 12.3). In an education context, we can see that it is not simply the presence of a learning technology innovation that matters, but the preparedness and propensity of educators to use it.

Tables 12.1 and 12.2 also show how some trends, for instance tablet computing and Massive Open Online Courses (MOOCs), emerge without extended forewarning or prediction. Is there a predictable pattern of integration for trends such as these? Gartner's (2017) Hype Cycle provides a model for explaining how some technology innovations arise rapidly and eventually find their place within mainstream practice. The model proposes five phases of technology infiltration: (1) a technology trigger, (2) peak of inflated expectations, (3) trough of disillusionment, (4) slope of enlightenment, and (5) plateau of productivity (as illustrated in Figure 12.4). Essentially, Gartner's Hype Cycle illustrates how society often tends to overestimate and then

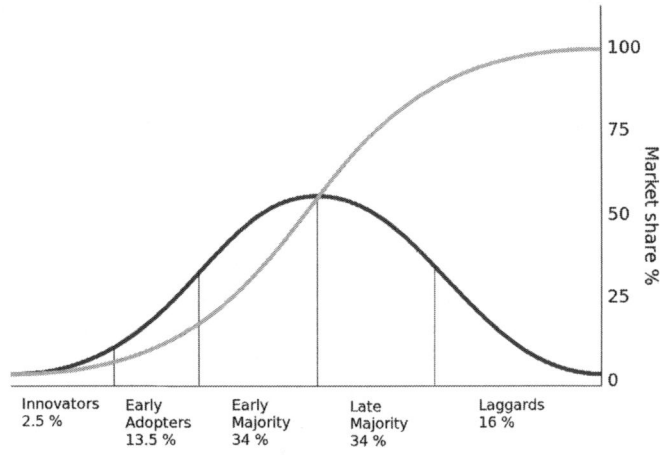

Figure 12.3.   Roger's (2010) Diffusion of Innovation. *Source*: Image courtesy of Jeremy Kemp, CC-BY-SA.

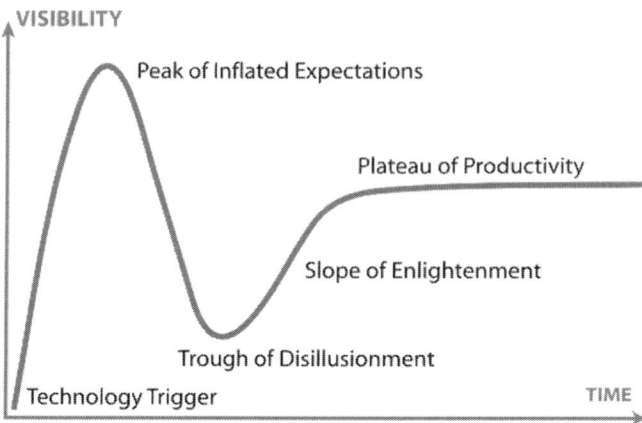

Figure 12.4. Gartner's Hype Cycle.

underestimate the utility of a disruptive technology, before it finds its place within our day-to-day practice.

In summary, we can see that while technology may increase exponentially in power, diffusion of educational technology innovation into teaching practices can be difficult to predict. This predictive uncertainly is because the diffusion of innovation relies on people, with their varying propensities and perceptions. However, it appears to be technologies that support sharing and also bring information closer to us in richer forms that tend to revolutionize society.

Consequently and as a thought experiment, what can we predict for the future of learning and technology? The possibilities are limited only by our imagination. Intelligent applications will increasingly use real-time learning analytics to personalize learning pathways and guide students (Mor, Craft, & Maina, 2015). Augmented reality will enable the integration of 'perfectly situated scaffolding' into the student learning experience (Bower, Howe, McCredie, Robinson, & Grover, 2014). Wearable technologies can be used to provide learners with a first-person point-of-view in order to enhance presence and engagement (Bower & Sturman, 2015). We can also imagine that real-time video capture and 3D-model construction will soon enable seamless 'blended reality' environments to be created, where people from remote locations can appear to be in the same space as one another to participate in shared and embodied learning experiences (Bower, Lee, & Dalgarno, 2017). However, as we have seen from Roger's (2010) Diffusion of Innovations theory, it is very difficult to know when these advancements will infiltrate into educational practice. This is because their application not only depends on the technologies being available, but also on the capacity and propensity of teachers to use them.

The Critical Role of Teachers

So what are the implications of increasingly powerful learning technologies for education and educators? Are coal-face teachers at risk of becoming obsolete as technologies become more intelligent and content becomes freely available? It is more critical now than ever before that educators and researchers consider how we can continue to help learners thrive in a world that is profoundly changing, within the context of increasingly rich technological tools and systems (Beetham et al., 2013).

At this point it is perhaps appropriate for us to revisit the aims of technology-enhanced learning, from the point of view of what we hope to achieve for students. Ultimately and ideally, educators and researchers should be striving to help individuals and society prosper in an uncertain future. As Goodyear and Retalis (2010a) observe:

> Good technology-enhanced learning design is characterized by a commitment to helping people create circumstances in which learning can be experienced as coherent with what is most deeply valued in the rest of life, as a source of pleasure, growth and transformation. (p. 18)

These are very difficult things for computers alone to achieve, because they depend on a deep and affective understanding of the learner. If we, as a society, are to engage students in authentic and meaningful learning experiences, it necessitates a shift whereby students are not merely learning from technology in isolation, but learning with technology in context. Moreover, it is hard to imagine that computers will have the same capacity as humans to inspire students and make emotive connections that impact on long-term motivation and life goals. Yes, we should anticipate an increasing role of technology and artificial intelligence in education. However, as Gartner's Hype cycle indicates, we shouldn't overestimate technology's role in education. We just need to understand that over time technology will increasingly have a place within and among educational practice and society.

What does become of crucial importance is that teachers help students to prepare for a future where technology plays an increasingly prominent role. From a purely vocational perspective, predicting and developing the capabilities required for the future can be challenging because of the rapid pace of technological and social change (OECD, 2016). But what we can say with some confidence is that more generic skills such as interdisciplinary and collaborative problem solving capabilities will become more and more important for students to possess (Beetham et al., 2013). Thus, modeling and guidance by teachers is critical.

And the critical role of the teacher was perhaps the most pervasive theme throughout all of the technology-enhanced learning literature. It is the teacher, through their pedagogical agency, that ultimately makes technology-enhanced learning happen, and determines the success or otherwise of the learning experience. The evidence in the proceeding chapters has demonstrated how the teacher can influence the quality of access, communication, content representation, collaboration, motivation and engagement, vicarious learning and reflection, digital capabilities development, assessment and feedback, student-centered learning, student protection and community development.

On top of all of these important design elements, teaching also involves performative aspects whereby teachers amplify learning through their very presence and engagement (Beetham & Sharpe, 2013). This was observed across the empirical research studies including for Web 2.0 (Churchill, 2009), social networking (Callaghan & Bower, 2012; Çoklar, 2012; Lampe, Wohn, Vitak, Ellison, & Wash, 2011; Shih, 2011), mobile learning (Alrasheedi & Capretz, 2015; Falloon & Khoo, 2014), and virtual worlds (Hämäläinen & Oksanen, 2012). Thus, rather than assuming that technology will replace teachers, we need to fully acknowledge the critical role of the teacher in technology-enhanced learning contexts, and provide them with as much support as possible so as to maximize their positive impact.

Supporting Educators

While teachers can seek out and choose to engage in professional learning opportunities, the one technology-enhanced learning design area of concern that falls somewhat outside the teacher's control is the support that they are offered. Professional learning and support was widely identified throughout the literature as critical in order for teachers to successfully design and implement technology-enhanced learning (Beckers, Dolmans, & van Merriënboer, 2016; Brady, Holcomb, & Smith, 2010; Cochrane, 2014; Crook & Harrison, 2008; Dalgarno, Lee, Carlson, Gregory, & Tynan, 2011; Lumkin, Cram, Eade, Buck, & Evans, 2011; Ng & Nicholas, 2013; Redecker, Ala-Mutka, Bacigalupo, Ferrari, & Punie, 2009). In fact, in one major international survey the majority of teachers reported *moderate* to *high* professional development needs in the use of technologies in the workplace (OECD, 2014).

If teachers are the key determinant of successful learning, and the primary external input that can impact on the quality of teacher practice is professional learning and support, institutions and governments are well advised to concentrate on providing extensive and ongoing professional learning opportunities and support for teachers. While cheaper hardware is likely to make provision of technology-enhanced learning simpler, it is the development of highly capable teachers — as the prerequisite for high-quality learning design and implementation — that should be of central focus (OECD, 2016).

It is also crucial to think about the sorts of professional learning and assistance that is offered to teachers so as support their technology-enhanced learning practices. Quite often, training workshops and in-situ assistance primarily focus on technical skills and developing educator familiarity with tools. However, to achieve genuine and lasting change in teacher practice it is essential that teachers rethink what they do (Biggs & Tang, 2011; Laurillard et al., 2013). Designing for learning requires much more than knowing about how technologies work. Design of technology-enhanced learning now and in the future means being able to see the creative potential in technologies, centering students in active learning experiences, providing cross cultural learning opportunities, offering flexible and blended access to learning, and designing for sustainability over time (Beetham et al., 2013). Being able to achieve these high level and integrative goals takes considerable skill, dedication and support.

One way that educators can satisfy many of their professional learning needs is to engage in communities of practice. Becoming a member of a professional community of practice, either within or outside the institution, is seen as crucial in order for teachers to source support and resources that help them effectively design and apply technology-enhanced learning approaches

(Burden, Hopkins, Male, Martin, & Trala, 2012; Cochrane, 2014; Crook & Harrison, 2008; Goodwin, 2012; Gregory et al., 2015; Pegrum, Oakley, & Faulkner, 2013; Redecker et al., 2009). Engaging in dialogue with other designers can also provide educators with valuable feedback about the pedagogical efficacy of their designs (Beetham et al., 2013). Accordingly, it is important that educators seek out, form, and proactively engage in professional learning communities. Ideally these professional learning communities will prioritize engagement with research.

A Research-Driven and Collaborative Approach to Technology-Enhanced Learning Design

If we are to optimize the support that is provided to educators then we also need to reflect upon the sort of research that the technology-enhanced learning field conducts and how it is conducted. Analysis of the Web 2.0, social networking, mobile learning and virtual worlds literature revealed some interesting trends with respect to the focus of research being undertaken. Broadly speaking, the focus of the research for each body of literature seemed to change over time, from:

(1) The hypothetical possibilities of the technology; to
(2) Case studies (for instance, reporting on the type of activity that transpired, student perceptions, teacher perceptions, and the extent to which learning occurred); to
(3) Studies comparing traditional approaches without the technology to approaches that use the technology; then eventually
(4) Studies that examine how different design features and implementation approaches impact on the student experience and the learning outcomes achieved.

Ultimately, it is the latter that is the most useful for educators, because it moves beyond wholesale consideration of a technology to derive an in-depth and evidence-based understanding of how they can positively impact upon learning through their technology-enhanced learning design practices. So, while appreciating the need for a natural evolution of research foci as new technology-enhanced learning possibilities emerge, the field would be well served by quite quickly shifting energy toward conducting studies that examine the relative impact of different designs.

There is also a need for more coordinated research across the learning technology field. In order to really start to understand technology-enhanced learning design, we cannot ever expect to find answers in a single study or even set of studies. Individual studies will always be bound by the specific context in which they were conducted, which is variable and can significantly influence results. We must look for trends across studies, while at the same time attempting to account for their transferability and generalizability. To a great extent, that has been the purpose of this book — to offer the background knowledge across a variety of studies that helps develop an abstracted understanding of technology-enhanced learning design. But we also need to engage in this process continually and collectively as a field, identifying empirical gaps in design knowledge, conducting targeted research that enables us to understand the implication of different approaches, and finding patterns across studies that enable us to progress as a design science.

In order to maximize the progress of the learning technology field, educators and researchers need to collaborate. To come at teaching from a design science perspective involves identifying challenges, envisioning new possibilities, testing learning environment interventions, and feeding back formative research findings into future cycles of innovation and design (Zhang, 2009). For this, the best outcomes can only be achieved by having researchers and practitioners working closely together (Holmberg, 2014). If educators and researchers combine their strengths they are better placed to identify the most pertinent problems and come to understand situated design issues.

Design-based research is proposed as a fruitful way for educators and researchers to work together, in order to address authentic design problems at stake (Holmberg, 2014). Design-based research is a more recent research methodology that focuses on the iterative design and testing of interventions in real educational contexts in order to develop design principles that can have practical impact on practice (Anderson & Shattuck, 2012). One positive aspect of design-based research is that it situates educational researchers and teachers as proactive agents for change in learning environments, as opposed to merely responding to new waves of technology (Zhang, 2009). Through design-based research educators and researchers working together can come to a better understanding of technology-enhanced learning design in their context, and also contribute to the knowledge base of the field in a way that enables design principles and patterns to emerge. Having educators and researchers work together to solve design problems is in direct accordance with a 'scholarship of teaching' approach (Kreber & Kanuka, 2013; Trigwell, Martin, Benjamin, & Prosser, 2000).

Further, the learning technology field would benefit from softening, or ideally even disintegrating, many of the role boundaries that separate educators and researchers. Drawing upon research evidence and collecting data to evaluate the efficacy of designs enables educators to more accurately refine their approaches over time. Having academics engage closely in coalface educational practices enables them to understand practical issues associated with teaching, so that they can conduct research that is both realistic and useful. Thus, in an ideal world, educators would consider themselves researchers and researchers would all be working in teaching contexts, mutually supporting one another to achieve the goal of enhanced student learning. In other words, ideally, research and practice would always be integrated.

Final Reflections and Directions Forward

This book began by proposing that the design of technology-enhanced learning was a tantalizing problem. And despite all of the research and analysis that we have covered, tantalizingly, it still remains in the large part unsolved. Yes, we have developed some principles for design, based upon findings and observations from the literature. But it is not possible to prescribe how the principles should be applied in each specific design context, nor how to creatively combine them. This book has not provided any absolute directions or answers — to do so in a design field would be an oversimplification and misleading.

However, we have distilled the essence of the research so as to inform research-driven (evidence-based) practice. Just as Schön (1987) has pointed out that we learn design by working with expert designers, the intention of this book has been to place the reader in touch with the work of researchers and designers from across the world in order to learn from their collective wisdom. The proposition is that a deep and nuanced understanding of technology-enhanced learning research enables us to formulate principles that we can apply as required during design processes, as opposed to following prescriptive models or naïve intuition. Understanding the nature of technology-enhanced learning design, rather than just specific applications, means that educators and researchers can more confidently transfer their design knowledge to changing technological and environmental contexts.

Some readers may have already realized that we can take this abstraction process one step further. When we are studying the effect of using learning technologies, what are we really studying? Actually, the fact that we are using technology is, from one perspective, inconsequential. Really, what we are studying is pedagogy, and technology is just the means via which we distribute knowledge between people and facilitate experience. As McKenney (2015) points out, technology merely constitutes a mode of delivery and interaction. And it is proposed that studying pedagogy through the lens of technology – for instance, the presentation of information, how to support collaboration, the impact of different scaffolding and approaches to task design – results in a deeper and more nuanced understanding of what it takes to teach, generally. Consequently, in order to develop fundamental and transferable learning design capabilities, educators and researchers are encouraged to view technology as a mediating tool, and study what is mediated rather than fixating on the tool itself.

And finally, a comment on the art of learning design. Throughout this book we have primarily focused on the science of learning design, through examination of the research literature. But the design of effective technology-enhanced learning is both an art and a science (Mor et al., 2015). And to the extent that learning design is an art, it requires significant creativity (Goodyear & Retalis, 2010b). Please do not mistakenly assume that this book has advocated a purely empiricist approach to design. Yes, research can inform as well as provoke our thinking, and as such should be incorporated into the design process. But we need to understand and accept that, although the research provides us with evidence that can be used to guide our design decisions, it is unlikely to ever capture the overwhelmingly positive educational impact of an elegant and captivating design idea that sparks a subject and students to life. It is the creative application of design knowledge that makes the critical difference.

So the best answer to how we should design technology-enhanced learning is as tantalizing as the question. The best answer to what it takes to design technology-enhanced learning is that it takes everything. Great design requires that people draw upon all of their experience and wisdom, take into account all of the contextual factors, consider the aims (which in reality are normally wickedly multifaceted), deeply understand their students, utilize all of their knowledge and skills, deploy all of their intuition, savvy and nous to creatively design effective solutions to the educational problems at hand.

Fortunately, this intense investment is also a source of great reward. In my experience over many years as a learning designer and teacher educator, it is apparent that there is something intrinsically fulfilling about the process of educational design. Almost everyone enjoys being creative, analytical, and socially purposeful. Consequently, for many people with an interest in or passion for education, the design of technology-enhanced learning holds natural appeal. More directly than a piece of art, a great learning design enables us to exercise our deep internal drive to be creative, in a way that can have a positive impact on someone's or many peoples' quality of life. A great learning design can provide learners with insights that make them more capable, satisfied and well-rounded human beings. Accordingly, people of all backgrounds and confidence levels are encouraged to engage wholeheartedly in technology-enhanced learning design processes, both reflectively and with peers.

While this book has covered intellectual knowledge associated with technology-enhanced learning design, critical tacit knowledge and embodied experience can only come through practice. As the ancient proverb goes, "the finger pointing at the moon is not the moon." There is a big difference between knowing the direction to travel and arriving at the destination. In order to bring the knowledge presented in this book to full fruition, it is crucial to practice design. And it is through practice, especially if collaborating, that another great phenomenon occurs. While our aim may be to design authentic and meaningful lessons for others, in my experience, it is actually us, as designers, that end up learning immense amounts, about pedagogy, technology and learning. And as we learn and feed that knowledge into our designs, it has a tremendous amplifying effect on the quality of the student experience and how much they learn, which highlights the importance, responsibility and privilege of being a teacher.

So in conclusion, please allow me to provide you with the following encouragements. Engage in technology-enhanced learning design and analysis with passion, creativity, wisdom and flair. Retain a focus on how what we do as educators and researchers can have a colossal positive effect on people's lives, and indeed society. Invest all of the knowledge you have acquired and continue to learn into your designs. Share your knowledge and designs with the educational community. By working scientifically and artistically using the design knowledge that we acquire and develop, together, we can make a big difference.

References

Alrasheedi, M., & Capretz, L. F. (2015). Determination of critical success factors affecting mobile learning: A meta-analysis approach. *TOJET: The Turkish Online Journal of Educational Technology, 14*(2).

Anderson, L., & Krathwohl, D. (2001). *A taxonomy for learning, teaching and assessing: A revision of Bloom's taxonomy of educational objectives.* New York, NY: Longman.

Anderson, T., & Shattuck, J. (2012). Design-based research: A decade of progress in education research? *Educational Researcher, 41*(1), 16–25.

Beckers, J., Dolmans, D., & van Merriënboer, J. (2016). e-Portfolios enhancing students' self-directed learning: A systematic review of influencing factors. *Australasian Journal of Educational Technology, 32*(2), 2.

Beetham, H., Conole, G., de Freitas, S., Ellaway, R. H., Jones, C., Masterman, L., … Traxler, J. (2013). Designing for learning in an uncertain future. *Rethinking pedagogy for a digital age – Designing for 21st century learning* (pp. 258–281). New York, NY: Routledge.

Beetham, H., & Sharpe, R. (2013). An introduction to rethinking pedagogy. In H. Beetham & R. Sharpe (Eds.), *Rethinking pedagogy for a digital age–Designing for 21st century learning* (pp. 1–15). New York, NY: Routledge.

Biggs, J., & Tang, C. (2011). *Teaching for quality learning at university* (3rd ed.). Maidenhead: McGraw-Hill.

Bower, M., Howe, C., McCredie, N., Robinson, A., & Grover, D. (2014). Augmented Reality in education – Cases, places and potentials. *Educational Media International, 51*(1), 1–15.

Bower, M., Lee, M. J. W., & Dalgarno, B. (2017). Collaborative learning across physical and virtual worlds: Factors supporting and constraining learners in a blended reality environment. *British Journal of Educational Technology, 48*(2), 407–430.

Bower, M., & Sturman, D. (2015). What are the educational affordances of wearable technologies? *Computers & Education, 88*, 343–353.

Brady, K. P., Holcomb, L. B., & Smith, B. V. (2010). The use of alternative social networking sites in higher educational settings: A case study of the e-learning benefits of Ning in education. *Journal of Interactive Online Learning, 9*(2), 151–170.

Burden, K., Hopkins, P., Male, T., Martin, S., & Trala, C. (2012). iPad Scotland evaluation. Retrieved from http://www.janhylen.se/wp-content/uploads/2013/01/Skottland.pdf

Callaghan, N., & Bower, M. (2012). Learning through social networking sites — The critical role of the teacher. *Educational Media International, 49*(1), 1−17.

Churchill, D. (2009). Educational applications of Web 2.0: Using blogs to support teaching and learning. *British Journal of Educational Technology, 40*(1), 179−183.

Cochrane, T. D. (2014). Critical success factors for transforming pedagogy with mobile Web 2.0. *British Journal of Educational Technology, 45*(1), 65−82.

Çoklar, A. N. (2012). Evaluations of students on Facebook as an educational environment. *Online Submission, 3*(2), 42−53.

Crook, C., & Harrison, C. (2008). *Web 2.0 technologies for learning at key stages 3 and 4: Summary report.*

Dalgarno, B., Lee, M. J. W., Carlson, L., Gregory, S., & Tynan, B. (2011). Institutional support for and barriers to the use of 3D immersive virtual worlds in higher education. Paper presented at the 28th Annual Conference of the Australasian Society for Computers in Learning in Tertiary Education: Changing Demands, Changing Directions.

Falloon, G., & Khoo, E. (2014). Exploring young students' talk in iPad-supported collaborative learning environments. *Computers & Education, 77,* 13−28.

Gartner. (2017). Gartner's hype cycle. Retrieved from http://www.gartner.com/technology/research/methodologies/hype-cycle.jsp. Accessed on February 1, 2017.

Goodwin, K. (2012). *Use of tablet technology in the classroom.* NSW Department of Education and Communities. Retrieved from http://clic.det.nsw.edu.au/clic/documents/iPad_Evaluation_Sydney_Region_exec_summary.pdf

Goodyear, P., & Retalis, S. (2010a). Learning, technology and design. In P. Goodyear & S. Retalis (Eds.), *Technology-enhanced learning: Design patterns and pattern languages* (pp. 1−28). Rotterdam: Sense Publishers.

Goodyear, P., & Retalis, S. (Eds.). (2010b). *Technology-enhanced learning: Design patterns and pattern languages.* Rotterdam: Sense Publishers.

Gregory, S., Scutter, S., Jacka, L., McDonald, M., Farley, H., & Newman, C. (2015). Barriers and enablers to the use of virtual worlds in higher education: An exploration of educator perceptions, attitudes and experiences. *Educational Technology & Society, 18*(1), 3−12.

Hämäläinen, R., & Oksanen, K. (2012). Challenge of supporting vocational learning: Empowering collaboration in a scripted 3D game — How does teachers' real-time orchestration make a difference? *Computers & Education, 59*(2), 281−293.

Holmberg, J. (2014). Studying the process of educational design — Revisiting Schön and making a case for reflective design-based research on teachers' "conversations with situations." *Technology, Pedagogy and Education, 23*(3), 293−310.

Kreber, C., & Kanuka, H. (2013). The scholarship of teaching and learning and the online classroom. *Canadian Journal of University Continuing Education, 32*(2).

Lampe, C., Wohn, D. Y., Vitak, J., Ellison, N. B., & Wash, R. (2011). Student use of Facebook for organizing collaborative classroom activities. *International Journal of Computer-Supported Collaborative Learning*, 6(3), 329–347.

Laurillard, D., Charlton, P., Craft, B., Dimakopoulos, D., Ljubojevic, D., Magoulas, G., ... Whittlestone, K. (2013). A constructionist learning environment for teachers to model learning designs. *Journal of Computer Assisted Learning*, 29(1), 15–30.

Lumkin, K., Cram, C., Eade, J., Buck, R., & Evans, D. (2011). *3D virtual worlds project report 2011*. Retrieved from http://www.macict.edu.au/projects/virtual-worlds-project/

McKenney, S. (2015). Toward relevant and usable TEL research. In M. Maina, B. Craft, & Y. Mor (Eds.), *The art & science of learning design* (pp. 65–74). Rotterdam: Sense Publishers.

Mishra, P., & Koehler, M. J. (2006). Technological pedagogical content knowledge: A framework for teacher knowledge. *Teachers College Record*, 108(6), 1017–1054.

Mor, Y., Craft, B., & Maina, M. (2015). Learning design – Definitions, current issues and grand challenges. In M. Maina, B. Craft, & Y. Mor (Eds.), *The art & science of learning design* (pp. ix–xxv). Rotterdam: Sense Publishers.

Ng, W., & Nicholas, H. (2013). A framework for sustainable mobile learning in schools. *British Journal of Educational Technology*, 44(5), 695–715.

OECD. (2014). TALIS 2013 results: An international perspective on teaching and learning. Retrieved from http://dx.doi.org/10.1787/9789264196261-en

OECD. (2016). Skills for a digital world. Retrieved from http://www.oecd-ilibrary.org/science-and-technology/skills-for-a-digital-world_5jlwz83z3wnw-en

Pegrum, M., Oakley, G., & Faulkner, R. (2013). Schools going mobile: A study of the adoption of mobile handheld technologies in Western Australian independent schools. *Australasian Journal of Educational Technology*, 29(1), 66–81.

Redecker, C., Ala-Mutka, K., Bacigalupo, M., Ferrari, A., & Punie, Y. (2009). Learning 2.0: The impact of Web 2.0 innovations on education and training in Europe. *Final report. European Commission-Joint Research Center-Institute for Porspective Technological Studies, Seville.*

Rogers, E. M. (2010). *Diffusion of innovations*. Simon and Schuster.

Schön, D. A. (1987). *Educating the reflective practitioner: Toward a new design for teaching and learning in the professions*. Josey Bass.

Shih, R.-C. (2011). Can Web 2.0 technology assist college students in learning English writing? Integrating Facebook and peer assessment with blended learning. *Australasian Journal of Educational Technology*, 27(5), 829–845.

Trigwell, K., Martin, E., Benjamin, J., & Prosser, M. (2000). Scholarship of teaching: A model. *Higher Education Research & Development*, 19(2), 155–168.

Zhang, J. (2009). Comments on Greenhow, Robelia, and Hughes: Toward a creative social web for learners and teachers. *Educational Researcher*, 38(4), 274–279.

ICT innovations timeline image attributions for Figure 12.2

Source:

- Paper image: By Moefuzz, CC BY-SA 4.0, https://commons. wikimedia.org/w/index.php?curid=50888029
- Printing press image: By Gun Powder Ma, CC BY-SA 3.0, https://commons.wikimedia.org/w/index.php?curid=8021365
- Camera image: By Liudmila & Nelson, Public Domain, https://commons.wikimedia.org/w/index.php?curid= 11099664
- Movie camera image:
- Public Domain, https://commons.wikimedia.org/w/index. php?curid=658432
- Telephone image: By Biswarup Ganguly, CC BY 3.0, https:// commons.wikimedia.org/w/index.php?curid=49000948
- Phonograph image: By Norman Bruderhofer, CC BY-SA 3.0, https://commons.wikimedia.org/w/index.php?curid=427395
- Movie projector image: By Marcin Wichary, CC BY 2.0, https://commons.wikimedia.org/wiki/File:Simplex_Model_E-7_Movie_Theater_Projector,_MoMI.jpg
- Digital audio image: By DRs Kulturarvsprojekt, CC BY-SA 2.0, https://upload.wikimedia.org/wikipedia/commons/4/4e/ Sony_digital_audio_recorder_PCM-7030_% 286498655653%29.jpg
- Digital computer image: By Parrot of Doom, CC BY-SA 3.0, https://upload.wikimedia.org/wikipedia/commons/2/21/ SSEM_Manchester_museum_close_up.jpg
- Digital Camera image: By Brett Jordan, CC BY, https://www. flickr.com/photos/x1brett/4928370431
- Mobile phone image: By Redrum0486, CC BY-SA 3.0, https://commons.wikimedia.org/w/index.php?curid=6421950
- Internet image: By Steve Jurvetson, CC BY 3.0 https://www. flickr.com/photos/jurvetson/916142
- Wifi image: Evan Amos, Public domain, https://commons. wikimedia.org/wiki/File:Netgear-Nighthawk-AC1900-WiFi-Router.jpg

Index